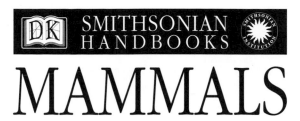

SMITHSONIAN HANDBOOKS

MAMMALS

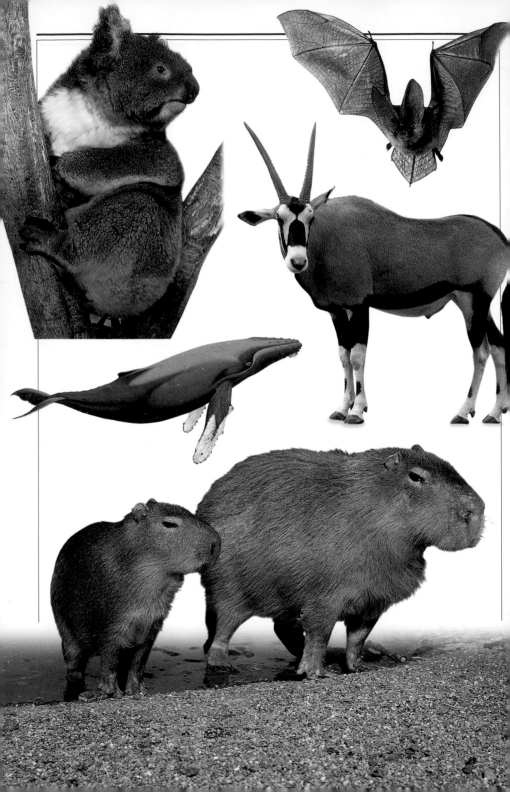

SMITHSONIAN HANDBOOKS

MAMMALS

Editorial Consultants
JULIET CLUTTON-BROCK
DON E. WILSON

LONDON, NEW YORK, MUNICH,
MELBOURNE, AND DELHI

DK DELHI
Senior Project Editor Sheema Mookherjee
Senior Art Editor Aparna Sharma
Editor Kajori Aikat
Designers Kavita Dutta, Sabyasachi Kundu
DTP Designers Pankaj Sharma, Balwant Singh
Managing Editor Ira Pande
Managing Art Editor Shuka Jain

DK LONDON
Project Editor David Summers
Project Art Editor Kirsten Cashman
DTP Designer Rajen Shah
Production Controller Elizabeth Dodd
Picture Researcher Cheryl Dubyk-Yates
Senior Editor Angeles Gavira
Senior Art Editor Ina Stradins
Category Publisher Jonathan Metcalf
Special Consultant and Writer Steve Parker
US Editors Gary Werner, Margaret Parrish

First US edition, 2002
2 4 6 8 10 9 7 5 3
Published in the United States by
DK Publishing, Inc.
375 Hudson St.
New York, New York 10014

Copyright © 2002
Dorling Kindersley Limited

A Penguin Company

Library of Congress Cataloguing-in-Publication Data

Mammals. p. cm. – (Dorling Kindersley handbooks)
ISBN 0-7894-8404-8 (alk. paper)
1.Mammals – Identification. I.DK Publishing, Inc.
II Series.

QL703 M3626 2002
599–dc21 2001047823
Reproduced by Colourscan, Singapore
Printed and bound by Kyodo Printing Co., Singapore

see our complete product line at

www.dk.com

CONTENTS

INTRODUCTION

Mammals are the most familiar group of vertebrates. They are also the most varied and adaptable, having found ways to survive in the broadest range of habitats, from the oceans to the poles. Within this variety, mammals share some fundamental characteristics: they are warm-blooded, give birth to live young, feed their young on milk produced in mammary glands, and all but a few have a covering of hair on their bodies.

L IFE ON EARTH has changed over millions of years through the process of evolution. This has produced a vast array of living things, including untold millions of animal species, from worms, scorpions, and flies to fish, frogs, reptiles, birds – and mammals. In such lists, the mammal group is usually put at the very top, as though natural processes have been aiming to produce them as an end-point. Mammals are certainly successful in terms of being widespread over a variety of habitats, and they are relatively large in body size and numbers. However, they should not be looked upon as an evolutionary peak. Other animal groups, such as birds in the air, insects on land, and fish and crustaceans in the sea, are equally successful in evolutionary terms, and they outnumber mammals both in terms of species as well as in the total count of individuals. But mammals do possess some unique and fascinating qualities.

◁ A LONG HISTORY
Fossil remains show that small, shrewlike mammals such as this Megazostrodon appeared on Earth over 200 million years ago. This was the time when early dinosaurs were also spreading across the land.

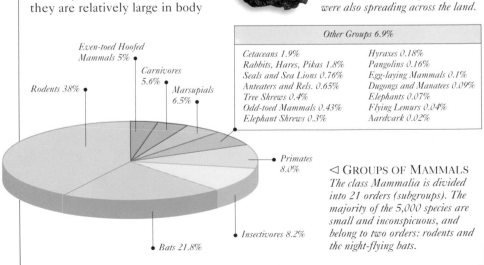

Other Groups 6.9%	
Cetaceans 1.9%	Hyraxes 0.18%
Rabbits, Hares, Pikas 1.8%	Pangolins 0.16%
Seals and Sea Lions 0.76%	Egg-laying Mammals 0.1%
Anteaters and Rels. 0.65%	Dugongs and Manatees 0.09%
Tree Shrews 0.4%	Elephants 0.07%
Odd-toed Mammals 0.43%	Flying Lemurs 0.04%
Elephant Shrews 0.3%	Aardvark 0.02%

Even-toed Hoofed Mammals 5%

Carnivores 5.6%

Rodents 38%

Marsupials 6.5%

Primates 8.0%

Insectivores 8.2%

Bats 21.8%

◁ GROUPS OF MAMMALS
The class Mammalia is divided into 21 orders (subgroups). The majority of the 5,000 species are small and inconspicuous, and belong to two orders: rodents and the night-flying bats.

SUCCESS STORY

Mammals have a complex body chemistry, which maintains a constant raised body temperature. This requires them to eat large amounts of food, in comparison to cold-blooded species such as reptiles and insects. However, it also allows them to remain active in cold conditions; mammals can survive high on mountains during winter, and in the far north and south near the poles. This means mammals are among the few animal groups to thrive in such harsh habitats. The mammal group also displays some of the most complicated behaviors in the animal kingdom. Most species can learn from experience, and the longest-lived, such as elephants, are able to accumulate and pass on invaluable skills and knowledge to their offspring. Some form complex societies with sophisticated methods of communication, in which individuals help each other to survive.

△ INTELLIGENT
Apes have the capacity for problem-solving and the use of tools. This chimpanzee has learned to use a stick to get a meal from a termite mound.

◁ ADAPTABLE
Mammals have colonized almost every habitat, from hyraxes in barren, rocky mountains (left), to whales that can swim huge distances through the sea.

▽ SOCIABLE
Because female mammals suckle their young, there is an extended period of family care. Many species carry social patterns into adulthood, forming groups such as prides, herds, troops, and schools.

HUMANS AND OTHER MAMMALS

People have a history of long and close associations with other mammals – we can identify with their warmth, furriness, alertness, facial expressions, active movements, and complex behavior. Throughout history, mammals have even been objects of worship, condemnation, or sacrifice. They have also long been domesticated for various uses, including companionship, provision of food, and as beasts of burden. This process of selective breeding for desirable qualities, such as temperament or strength, has often given rise to considerable change and variety – take for example the huge number of domestic dog breeds, few of which greatly resemble their ancestor, the wolf. This book focuses on the species that still inhabit the wild and live mostly independently of, though certainly not unaffected by, humans. They, more than ever, need our consideration and care.

△ WORKING MAMMALS
Buffalo, yak and other cattle, horses, asses, camels, llamas, and elephants are all part of a long list of powerful mammals used to pull, carry, and perform other physical tasks.

◁ WORSHIP
In ancient Egypt, the jackal was worshipped as the embodiment of the god Anubis. Today the cow, elephant, and monkey are still considered to be sacred in India. In some societies, species such as lions, tigers, and bears are held in mixed regard as god or devil.

◁ STUDY
The detailed study of mammalian biology is important in the search for ways to protect threatened species.

◁ CONSERVATION
Large mammals such as right whales have been hunted for centuries. Today, attention focuses on their conservation, but for some species it may already be too late.

HOW THIS BOOK WORKS

THIS BOOK COVERS the 21 different orders that make up the class Mammalia. Within each of these orders, individual species entries are arranged according to the family they belong to. The sample page below shows a typical entry, with information organized into text, bands, and symbols.

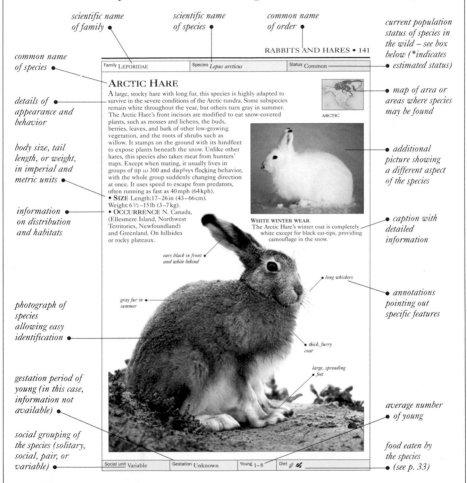

scientific name of family

scientific name of species

common name of order

current population status of species in the wild – see box below (*indicates estimated status)

common name of species

map of area or areas where species may be found

details of appearance and behavior

body size, tail length, or weight, in imperial and metric units

information on distribution and habitats

photograph of species allowing easy identification

gestation period of young (in this case, information not available)

social grouping of the species (solitary, social, pair, or variable)

additional picture showing a different aspect of the species

caption with detailed information

annotations pointing out specific features

average number of young

food eaten by the species (see p. 33)

RABBITS AND HARES • 141

Family LEPORIDAE   Species *Lepus arcticus*   Status Common

ARCTIC HARE

A large, stocky hare with long fur, this species is highly adapted to survive in the severe conditions of the Arctic tundra. Some subspecies remain white throughout the year, but others turn gray in summer. The Arctic Hare's front incisors are modified to eat snow-covered plants, such as mosses and lichens, the buds, berries, leaves, and bark of other low-growing vegetation, and the roots of shrubs such as willow. It stamps on the ground with its hindfeet to expose plants beneath the snow. Unlike other hares, this species also takes meat from hunters' traps. Except when mating, it usually lives in groups of up to 300 and displays flocking behavior, with the whole group suddenly changing direction at once. It uses speed to escape from predators, often running as fast as 40 mph (64 kph).
• **SIZE** Length: 17–26 in (43–66 cm). Weight: 6½–15 lb (3–7 kg).
• **OCCURRENCE** N. Canada, (Ellesmere Island, Northwest Territories, Newfoundland) and Greenland. On hillsides or rocky plateaux.

ARCTIC

WHITE WINTER WEAR
The Arctic Hare's winter coat is completely white except for black ear-tips, providing camouflage in the snow.

ears black in front and white behind

long whiskers

gray fur in summer

thick, furry coat

large, spreading feet

Social unit Variable   Gestation Unknown   Young 1–8   Diet

IN THIS BOOK, the population status of each species is mainly based on the IUCN Red List of Threatened Species (see p. 46), as follows: *Extinct in the wild* Exists in captivity only. *Critically endangered* Faces an extremely high risk of extinction. *Endangered* Faces a very high risk of extinction.

Vulnerable Faces a high risk of extinction. *Lower risk* Dependent on conservation not to qualify for any of the above categories. *Common* Found in relatively high densities over a wide range. *Locally common* Found in relatively high densities within a restricted area or areas.

WHAT IS A MAMMAL?

MAMMALS ARE THE most familiar kinds of animals in our daily lives. Most of our pets and domesticated animals are mammals. So are the creatures that people like to watch in wildlife parks, zoos, and nature reserves. As mammals, humans too have all the typical features of the group. In fact, our closest relatives belonging to the animal world – apes and monkeys – are mammals.

MAMMAL CHARACTERISTICS

Mammals have three main features that set them apart from other classes of animals, including other vertebrates (animals with an internal skeleton – fish and reptiles, as well as mammals). First, mammals are warm-blooded, or to be more accurate, they are endothermic and homeothermic. This means they generate heat within their body to keep themselves at a fairly high temperature, usually 95–104°F (35–40°C), and they maintain this temperature at a constant level despite variations in the surroundings. Second, mammals have hair or fur. Even mammals that seem to be hairless, such as whales and dolphins, have a few hairs here and there on their bodies. Third, female mammals feed their newborn offsprings on milk that is produced by glands in their body. These are known as mammary glands, and give the name Mammalia to the whole group.

relatively large
• head

• coat of thick fur

mamary
glands •

young
feeding •

△ MAMMALS AND MILK
A female mammal (as in the Mona Monkey shown here) feeds her newborn on milk from her mammary glands. These are specialized types of sweat glands in the skin, usually located on the female's chest or abdomen.

hair-covered •
body

external •
ears

• jaws with different
kinds of teeth

• keen eyes

• flexible neck

• five-toed feet

• four strong
limbs

◁THE MAMMALIAN BODY
A typical mammal such as the wolf has a large head with keen eyes, ears, and nose. The strong jaws are equipped with several kinds of teeth (see p.18). The long body, four limbs, and tail (see p.16) are mostly covered by hair. However, some mammal groups have evolved very different body shapes (see opposite).

THREE GROUPS OF MAMMALS

Mammals are often divided into three groups, depending on the way they reproduce. In the monotremes or egg-laying mammals, the female lays eggs that hatch into babies. In the marsupial or pouched mammals, the babies develop for a short time in the mother's uterus or womb. They are born at a very early stage of development – tiny, unable to see or hear, with hardly formed limbs, and no fur. The newborn babies then crawl to a pocketlike flap on the female's body, the marsupium, where they feed on the mother's milk and continue to develop. The third and largest group comprises the placental mammals (see p. 22). Here, the offspring develop to a more advanced stage in the uterus, where they receive nourishment from the placenta. Hence, the young of placental mammals are born in a more developed state than marsupial mammals.

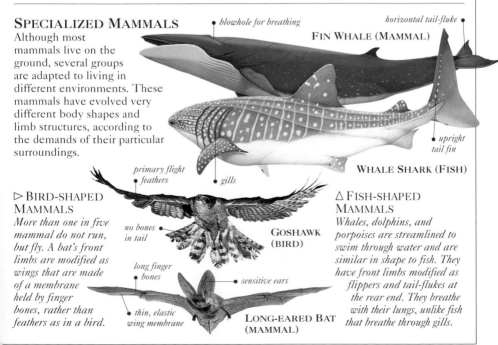

△ EGG-LAYING MAMMALS
The five species of monotremes are the four echidnas (seen here is the Short-beaked Echidna) and the Platypus.

◁ POUCHED MAMMALS
The 292 or so species of marsupials include kangaroos (such as the Western Grey Kangaroo shown here), wallabies, koalas, possums, bandicoots, and smaller kinds that resemble rats, mice, and shrews.

SPECIALIZED MAMMALS

Although most mammals live on the ground, several groups are adapted to living in different environments. These mammals have evolved very different body shapes and limb structures, according to the demands of their particular surroundings.

• *blowhole for breathing*

FIN WHALE (MAMMAL)

• *horizontal tail-fluke*

• *upright tail fin*

WHALE SHARK (FISH)

• *primary flight feathers*

• *gills*

▷ BIRD-SHAPED MAMMALS
More than one in five mammal do not run, but fly. A bat's front limbs are modified as wings that are made of a membrane held by finger bones, rather than feathers as in a bird.

• *no bones in tail*

GOSHAWK (BIRD)

• *long finger bones*

• *sensitive ears*

• *thin, elastic wing membrane*

LONG-EARED BAT (MAMMAL)

△ FISH-SHAPED MAMMALS
Whales, dolphins, and porpoises are streamlined to swim through water and are similar in shape to fish. They have front limbs modified as flippers and tail-flukes at the rear end. They breathe with their lungs, unlike fish that breathe through gills.

EVOLUTION

L IKE ALL LIVING things, mammals have evolved over long periods of time. The 4,475 or so mammal species alive today are only a small proportion of all the mammals that have lived on earth. Fossil evidence suggests that the first mammals appeared around the same time as the early dinosaurs, over 200 million years ago. However mammalian features such as feeding young on milk, were not preserved as fossils. Prehistoric mammals must be identified from their fossilized remains, particularly the teeth and skull (see opposite).

MAMMAL ANCESTORS

The ancestors of early mammals were small, active predators – a subgroup of mammal-like reptiles known as therapsids. Fossils suggest that some therapsids had developed fur, and were possibly endothermic (warm-blooded), on the way to becoming true mammals. These earliest mammals date from the Middle Triassic Period. They had new features in the skull (see panel, opposite), a lighter and more flexible skeleton, and erect limbs aligned under the body, rather than sprawling out by the sides, as in reptiles. By 200 million years ago, early mammals hunted in the undergrowth for small prey. For the next 135 million years, dinosaurs dominated the land. However, mammals persisted, although none was larger than a pet cat. They probably came out at night, when it was too cool for the great reptiles to be active.

△ EARLY MAMMAL
The remains of one of the earliest mammals, Megazostrodon, discovered in Lesotho, Africa, date from the Late Triassic Period. They indicate a creature 4¾in (12 cm) in length, outwardly resembling today's shrews or tree shrews.

MOERITHERIUM (50–35 MYA)   PHIOMIA (35 MYA)   GOMPHOTHERIUM (20 MYA)

TRIASSIC	JURASSIC	CRETACEOUS
Mammal-like reptiles common in this period. First mammals and first dinosaurs appear.	Dinosaurs dominate the land as giant plant-eaters and fierce meat-eaters. Mammals are small, nocturnal insect-eaters that probably laid eggs (monotremes).	Dinosaurs continue to diversify into many groups. Mammals continue as small nocturnal
YEARS AGO (MILLIONS) 205	142	

RAPID EVOLUTION

Dinosaurs died out 65 million years ago. Soon after, in the early Tertiary Period, mammals underwent great change. Even those that are highly evolved from their four-legged ancestors, appeared early in this period. Mammals now developed into hundreds of new kinds. Some of these disappeared, but others persisted and established the mammalian groups of today. By 50 million years ago, the first whales swam in the oceans and early bats flew in the air.

▽ EVOLVING FAMILIES

Some mammal groups were once much more common than today. Although the elephant group includes only three surviving species, it has a long and diverse history that has included over 160 species.

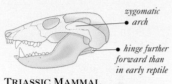

EARLY REPTILE

hinge at back of skull

uniform teeth

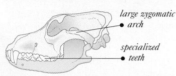

TRIASSIC MAMMAL

zygomatic arch

hinge further forward than in early reptile

MODERN MAMMAL

large zygomatic arch

specialized teeth

▢ DENTARY BONE

EVOLVING SKULL

The mammal's reptilian ancestors had teeth that were all much the same, and also several bones in the lower jaw. As mammals evolved, the lower jaw was reduced to one dentary bone, and the teeth became different shapes. The zygomatic arch developed to anchor stronger chewing muscles.

DEINOTHERIUM
(22–2 MYA)

ASIATIC ELEPHANT
(PRESENT)

▽ TIMELINE

Mammals survived with little change, as small predators, through most of the Mesozoic Era. At the start of the Cenozoic Era, with the dinosaurs gone, mammals (and birds) evolved rapidly and soon came to dominate the land.

TERTIARY		QUARTERNARY
predators. Marsupial and placental mammal groups probably appear.	Mammals undergo rapid evolution. By 40 million years ago, most present-day groups are established.	Series of Ice Ages greatly alter the habits of various mammals Appearance of modern humans coincides with disappearance of many large mammals – mammoths, giant elk, and others.
65	1.8	PRESENT

CENOZOIC ERA

DIVERSITY

Mammals are the most widespread and diverse of all animal groups. They live in more habitats, and in more regions of the world, than any other major group of animals. This is partly due to the mammalian feature of endothermy (warm-bloodedness), which allows mammals to stay active in the coldest places, such as polar seas.

EXTREME SIZE AND SHAPE

The size range of mammals is unsurpassed by all other animal groups. The largest mammal is the Blue Whale, which is not only the biggest creature alive today, but also one of the largest animals ever to have lived on earth. It is more than 70 million times heavier than the smallest mammals, such as the Hog-nosed Bat or Pygmy Shrew, which are smaller than a human thumb. Between these two extremes are mammals of almost every imaginable size and shape, including mice that are smaller than some insects, otters and dolphins that can outswim fish, fruit bats with wingspans greater than that of most birds, and massive buffaloes with horns longer than adult human arms.

◁ LARGEST MAMMAL
A well-fed female Blue Whale weighs over 150 tons (150 tonnes) and is up to 98 ft (30 m) long. This is about the same as the size of the largest dinosaurs, such as Argentinosaurus.

▷ REACHING HIGH
A Giraffe reaches leaves 20 ft (6 m) above ground. Everything about this mammal is elongated: its immense neck, drawn-out snout, and stiltlike legs. Even its tongue extends 18 in (45 cm) from its mouth.

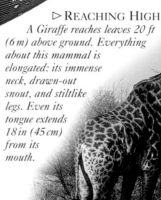

△ SMALLEST MAMMAL
The Hog-nosed or Bumblebee Bat is nearly as light as a feather – just around $1/16$ oz (2 g). It has a body that is $1^1/4$ in (30 mm) long, wings that are 6 in (15 cm) across, and is found in caves in south-west Thailand. White-toothed Pygmy Shrews are known to be almost as light.

MODES OF LIFE

Mammals live and travel in almost every habitat on earth. Different species are adapted to dwelling in all kinds of terrestrial habitats and to cope with a huge range of temperatures and terrains, from the icy tundra and cold mountain peaks, to tropical rainforest, coniferous and deciduous woodland, grassland and scrub, and even the most barren and arid deserts. Mammals are also found in the air, in both fresh- as well as saltwater, in the soil, and in underground caves. Despite the need to breathe air, some mammals, such as the sperm whales and beaked whales, regularly visit the depths of the sea.

△ ON LAND
The fastest terrestrial animal is the Cheetah, which can reach 63 mph (100 kph). The Pronghorn of North America is almost as rapid.

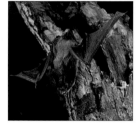

△ IN BRANCHES
Koalas, possums, and gliders, some lemurs and monkeys are arboreal – spending their lives in trees.

△ IN THE AIR
Although bats are the only true fliers among mammals, several others, such as flying lemurs, are expert gliders.

△ IN WATER
Mammals such as otters visit water often. Others such as seals stay in it for long periods. Whales, dolphins, and porpoises never leave their aquatic habitat.

SIMILAR BUT DIFFERENT

During millions of years of evolution, closely related mammals changed as they adapted to different environments. Tree-rats have large eyes and run nimbly through branches, but their close cousins the mole-rats are almost blind and burrow underground. Conversely, mammals that are only distant relatives have evolved to become very similar due to their common lifestyles and habitats.

▷ MARSUPIAL MOLE
This outwardly resembles the European Mole in almost every respect, except color, yet it belongs to an entirely different order: the marsupials.

△ EUROPEAN MOLE
Although this mole is an insectivore, it resembles the Marsupial Mole in size and appearance. It also has spadelike front claws, a stocky body, and tiny eyes and ears – adaptations for living underground.

ANATOMY

MOST MAMMALS HAVE an anatomical structure that includes a readily identifiable head and neck, a long body, four limbs which end in five digits (fingers or toes) each, and a tail. This basic structure was evident in the earliest mammals, 200 million years ago. However, over the years evolution has modified the design into a huge variety of sizes and shapes.

ENDOSKELETON

The bones of the skeleton are the body's internal supporting framework (endoskeleton). They are light, yet strong and stiff, and linked at flexible joints to permit movement. The same bones occur in similar positions in most mammals, although in the horse, the finger and toe bones have been lost.

▷ MOST
COMMON
*The ratlike shape
is most common
since two of every
five mammal
species is a
rodent.*

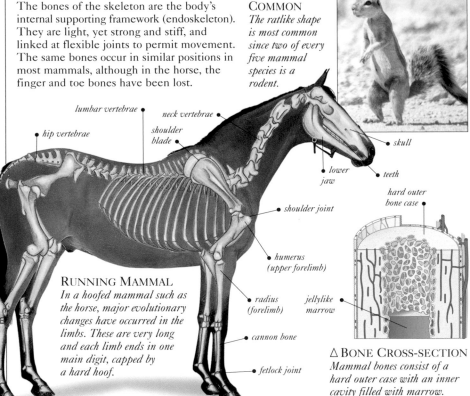

lumbar vertebrae •

• hip vertebrae

neck vertebrae •

shoulder
blade •

skull •

lower
jaw •

teeth •

hard outer
bone case •

• shoulder joint

• humerus
(upper forelimb)

RUNNING MAMMAL
*In a hoofed mammal such as
the horse, major evolutionary
changes have occurred in the
limbs. These are very long
and each limb ends in one
main digit, capped by
a hard hoof.*

• radius
(forelimb)

jellylike •
marrow

• cannon bone

• fetlock joint

△ BONE CROSS-SECTION
*Mammal bones consist of a
hard outer case with an inner
cavity filled with marrow.*

MAMMAL LIMBS

The outer shape of mammalian limbs, and the bones inside, vary greatly. They depend on how the mammal moves: legs on the ground, wings in air, or flippers in water, so its overall design is specialized. In many species, the limb has other tasks in addition to movement, such as catching prey or grooming fur.

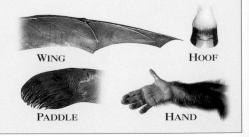

WING

HOOF

PADDLE

HAND

AQUATIC ADAPTATIONS

A cetacean such as a dolphin has one of the most highly evolved anatomies – its body shape and structure are very different from the original or primitive mammal design. As adaptations to pushing through water, the dolphin's head, neck, and body are streamlined and tapering, with hardly any hairs on the smooth skin.

• snout (beak)

△ BREATHING
A cetacean's nostrils, or blow hole, are high on its forehead. To breathe, it has to expose the top of its head above the water's surface.

• upper jaw (rostrum)

• flippers (pectoral fins)

• hairless skin

• rounded shape

• lower jaw (mandible)

• "finger" bones inside flippers

• slender ribs

• flexible spine

△ DOLPHIN SKELETON
The dolphin's skeleton is highly modified for swimming. Its forelimbs are paddles while its hind limbs are absent. The tail flukes used for swimming are stiffened muscle and other tissues, unsupported by bones.

• tail flukes

• backbone extends to tail stock

ADAPTATIONS FOR FLYING

A bat's hind limbs are similar in overall structure to the limbs of most other mammals. However, its forelimbs are highly evolved as wings. The upper arm bone is short and stout, and the forearm bones are longer. The main part of the wing membrane, or patagium, is held out by the extremely elongated digits or fingers. The membrane itself is a thin layer of muscles and elastic fibers sandwiched between two layers of skin. It is derived from the skin webs that are present between the fingers of most other mammals (including humans). The wings are flapped by powerful muscles in the shoulders and chest.

patagium •

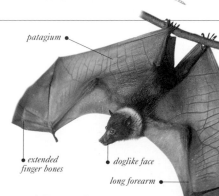

• extended finger bones

• doglike face

long forearm •

△ FRUIT BAT
The fruit bat's powerful wings enable it to fly long distances.

TEETH

Mammals are unique in having a lower jaw directly hinged to the skull, making the jaw a powerful tool. Unlike other vertebrates, mammals also have teeth that are varied in shape, for specialized tasks. This is known as heterodont dentition. There are four main tooth types. Incisors at the front have straight, sharp edges for biting and gnawing. Canines (eye teeth) are long and pointed to rip and tear. Premolars and molars (cheek teeth) are broad-topped for crushing, or sharp-edged for shearing. These teeth are developed differently in various species. Carnivores have long canines for stabbing and tearing animal prey. Grazers have very small or no canines, but their premolars and molars are massive and ridged for powerful chewing.

sharp cutting edge

broad, grinding surface

multicusped chewing surface

CARNIVORE CHEEK TOOTH

HERBIVORE CHEEK TOOTH

OMNIVORE CHEEK TOOTH

molars   *premolars*   *canine*   *incisors*

△ TOOTH TYPES

The mongoose is an omnivorous mammal with a very wide diet. Its generalized dentition includes all four types of teeth, numbering 40 in total.

cochlea turns vibrations into signals for brain

ossicles transmit vibrations to cochlea

ear drum picks up sound vibrations

ear canal

△ EAR

The bones that once linked the jaw to the skull (as in other vertebrates) have become specially adapted in mammals into a sophisticated hearing mechanism.

△ MEAT-EATERS

Several meat-eating mammals have specialized teeth called carnassials. On each side of these are the rearmost upper premolar and front lower molar. Carnassials have sharp edges and close like shears to slice gristle and crack bone.

◁ NONEATING TASKS

Mammals such as male hippopotamuses, cats, and dogs, expose their canines as a threat display to rivals. Several mammals also groom their fur with their teeth.

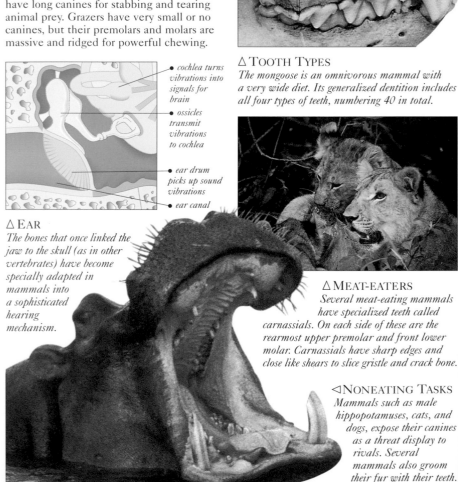

SKIN AND HAIR

Mammalian skin has several important functions. It encases and protects the body's delicate internal parts. It provides animals with the sense of touch. Sweat glands in it release watery sweat, which draws heat from the body as it evaporates, to keep it at a fairly constant temperature. Its sebaceous glands make natural oils or waxes to keep the skin supple and waterproof. Skin also produces hair or fur, which is unique to mammals. The skin of large herbivores, such as elephants, is more than 1¼ in (3 cm) thick, giving protection against predators such as lions and also against pests such as biting flies.

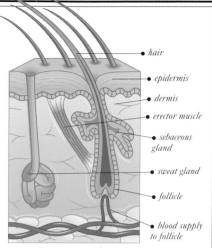

- hair
- epidermis
- dermis
- erector muscle
- sebaceous gland
- sweat gland
- follicle
- blood supply to follicle

△ SKIN CROSS-SECTION
A mammal's skin consists of two layers: the outer epidermis that is dead and tough, and the inner dermis that contains glands and touch sensors.

▷ WHISKERS
Whiskers (vibrissae) are hairs around the nose; the first part to contact the surroundings as the mammal moves along.

◁ SPINES
Mammals such as porcupines and hedgehogs have enlarged, stiff, sharp-tipped hairs known as spines, prickles, or quills, used mainly for protection.

TIGER   DOLPHIN   ARMADILLO

△ TYPES OF SKIN
The tiger's skin has stripes for camouflage in grass. The dolphin's skin is hairless to glide through water. The armadillo's skin grows horny external plates for protection.

TEMPERATURE CONTROL

Mammals are homeothermic (their body temperature remains at a fairly constant high level). They can regulate their temperature through behavior, such as wallowing in mud or resting in shade, constricting or widening blood vessels that carry heat to the skin, shivering, raising or lowering their metabolic rate, or sweating.

▷ PANTING
Mammals with thick coats do not cool down by sweating. They pant instead, to get rid of body heat in the warm breath, and by the evaporating saliva.

REPRODUCTION

MAMMALIAN REPRODUCTION is sexual. This means that an egg cell from a female joins with a sperm cell from a male, to produce a fertilized egg that grows into a new individual. Unlike some simpler living beings, mammals cannot reproduce asexually, where young are produced by just one parent (unless artificial cloning is used). Mammalian reproduction has many unique features, especially the growth of the young inside the specialized uterus or womb lined with the placenta from which the unborn fetus gets its nourishment.

COURTSHIP AND MATING

Courtship ensures that a female and male mammal of the same species come together to breed healthy, viable offspring. Courting may involve sound, scent, and sight. Calls, usually by males, attract potential partners from far away. Many female mammals produce scents that inform males that they are in breeding condition. Displays of body postures and movements enable each partner to assess the other's fitness as a suitable mate.

△ BREEDING COMPETITION
Some male mammals battle each other for the chance to mate with females. The biggest and strongest win: they are most likely to father the healthiest offspring.

◁ MATING
In mammals, fertilization is internal: the male sperm cells pass into the female's body, ready to fertilize her eggs.

▽ BREEDING SEASON
Most mammals, such as seals, gather to breed only at a certain time of the year. The young are raised during the most favorable season, usually spring or summer, when there is plenty of food available.

EGG-LAYING MAMMALS

Monotremes form a very small order that do not give birth to formed young, but instead lay eggs. The young develop within the eggs inside the mother's body. After the babies hatch, they feed on her milk as is the case with other mammals. The five species of monotremes are the Platypus and four kinds of echidnas. They are from S.E. Asia and Australia. In the echidna, the eggs, and later the young, are carried in the female's pouch.

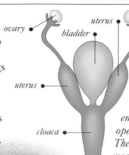

ovary • *uterus* • *bladder* • *fallopian tube* • *uterus* • *cloaca*

◁REPRODUCTIVE SYSTEM
The digestive, urinary, and reproductive tracts empty into one single opening called the cloaca. The word "Monotreme" means "one hole".

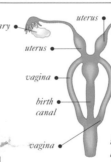

◁PLATYPUS
The mother Platypus makes her breeding nest inside a riverbank tunnel. She lays her eggs and then keeps them warm and protected for an incubation period of 10 days, until the babies hatch. She has no teats (nipples). Milk oozes from her mammary glands onto her belly, for the babies to lap.

MARSUPIALS

The name marsupial derives from the Latin term for "leathery pouch." In most of the 292 marsupials, the female has a pouch – the marsupium – on her abdomen. Her babies are born at a very early stage of development compared to the young of placental mammals (see p. 22). Then, they crawl into their mother's pouch, where they continue to develop, safe and protected.

ovary • *uterus* • *ovary* • *uterus* • *vagina* • *birth canal* • *vagina*

◁REPRODUCTIVE SYSTEM
A female marsupial has two vaginas, where the male's sperm enter to fertilize the eggs, and two uteri (wombs). The young is born through a central birth canal, which may form only temporarily.

▷JOURNEY'S END
A newborn marsupial (like this Tammar Wallaby) is naked and tiny, with flipperlike limb buds. Unable to see or hear, it uses smell to "swim" through its mother's fur, from the birth opening to the pouch.
It has undergone early growth during a one-month gestation in the womb. It now attaches itself to a teat in the pouch to feed on milk, growing for another six months, before venturing out.

▷JOEY
Older marsupial young (joeys) leave the pouch for short periods, returning to suckle and rest, or if threatened. The pouch can open forward (as in the kangaroo) or backward (as in the Koala).

PLACENTAL MAMMALS

All mammal species, except for monotremes and marsupials, are placental mammals. The placenta is a body part that develops inside the female's uterus (womb), alongside the unborn young. It is specialized to pass oxygen and nutrients from the mother's blood to the offspring, and to remove waste substances, allowing the unborn young to grow to an advanced stage in the uterus. The name "placental mammal", however, is not very accurate, as a rudimentary placenta also develops in the uterus of a marsupial mother.

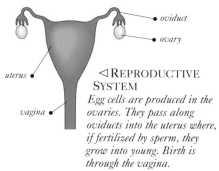

◁ REPRODUCTIVE SYSTEM

Egg cells are produced in the ovaries. They pass along oviducts into the uterus where, if fertilized by sperm, they grow into young. Birth is through the vagina.

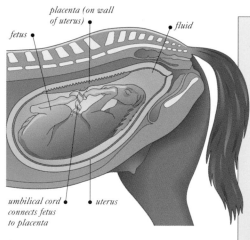

△ INSIDE THE UTERUS

The placenta is embedded in the inner lining of the uterus and is linked to the developing young (fetus) by blood vessels that form the umbilical cord. Fluid cushions the fetus from knocks and jolts. The placenta is expelled shortly after the baby.

▷ JUST BORN

Some newborn mammals are able to walk and run within minutes of birth. These are usually species born in the open and at risk from predators, such as Wildebeest. Babies born in a breeding nest are usually less well developed.

FIRST BREATHS

The baby in the womb receives oxygen from its mother's blood through the placenta and does not have to breathe. However, as it is born, the placenta detaches from the uterus and the baby immediately needs air. The births of mammals such as dolphins, porpoises, and whales (cetaceans), and Dugongs and manatees (sirenians), occur underwater. After birth, the baby must get to the surface quickly to breathe in air. Often, the mother or another adult gently pushes and supports the newborn on its journey to the surface of the water.

△ UNDERWATER BIRTH

Land mammals usually emerge head-first to make their passage through the birth canal easier. However, baby dolphins and other cetaceans emerge tail-first as their streamlined bodies slip smoothly through the birth canal.

PARENTAL CARE

A feature of mammal reproduction, which is uncommon among animals in general, is the long period of parental care. Offspring are fed on the mother's milk for weeks, or even months. They are also kept warm, safe, and protected. This is invariably by the mother, but in some species also by the father, and, in some social mammals, by other members of the group too. The longest time for parental care extends to ten years or more, especially in large mammals such as elephants, great apes, and humans.

◁ FAST BREEDERS

Small rodents such as mice are regular food for a range of predators. Rapid breeding is used as self-defence for the whole species. In one year, a pair of House Mice can produce more than 1,000 offspring of 2–3 generations, if all survive.

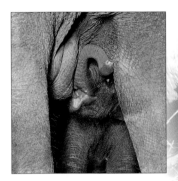

△ LACTATION

The time during which a mother mammal suckles (feeds) her offspring on her milk is known as the lactation period. It may vary from 10–14 days in some small rodents, to as much as three or four years in elephants.

△ FEW OFFSPRING

Larger mammals, such as this baboon, produce just one or two offspring. This allows the parents to put more time into caring for the young, leading to a better chance of survival.

GROWING UP

A consequence of increased parental care among mammals is that offspring enjoy a longer "childhood" or period of learning. They can observe their parents and group members, and try out activities such as hunting and testing out different food items in a trial-and-error fashion.

◁ PLAYING

Young mammals such as foxes may seem to have carefree fun through playing sessions. But the play has a serious purpose, as it helps to develop keen senses, quick reactions, strength, and agility. Such abilities will be needed in adulthood to catch food, ward off enemies, and compete with rivals at breeding time.

SOCIAL GROUPS

MAMMALS SHOW a whole range of social behaviours. Sociability tends to be more pronounced in plant-eating species than in meat-eaters. However, as part of the mammalian trait of adaptability, social groupings also vary with habitat, season, breeding and life cycle, and food availability. Most mammals live with others of their kind for a time, when young are being reared.

SOLITARY MAMMALS

Carnivorous mammals such as cats, some bears, mustelids (the weasel group), and viverrids (civets and mongooses) tend to be more solitary than group-dwelling. This is partly to reduce competition for food among hunters in one area. However, members of the dog family show the opposite trend and form well-organized packs.

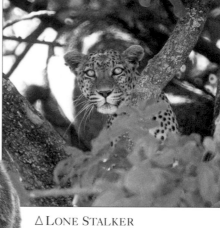

△ LONE STALKER
Cats are solitary, nocturnal stalkers. Two cats together are either a mating pair, or a mother with offspring. Lions are the only exception and form groups or prides.

◁ HOME TERRITORY
Bears, like other large carnivores, each set up a home range. But the ranges of male Brown Bears overlap those of females, so the sexes meet occasionally for mating.

FORMING PAIRS
Some mammals, especially primates, form male–female pairs the whole year round or even for several years. Certain gibbon species pair for life. This system saves the energy and risks of competing anew for partners at each breeding season. However, recent studies show that such partnerships are not always monogamous; one partner may mate outside the pair while the other partner is absent.

△ IN HARMONY
Some gibbons reinforce their pair bond by making duetlike calls, especially at dawn. The calls also warn other gibbons to avoid the pair's territory.

EXTENDED GROUPS

Several species of monkeys and foxes live in family groups consisting of the female, often her male partner, and their offspring. In some species such as lions, wolves, and gorillas, the group is extended by other close relatives and perhaps a further generation or two of offspring. Mature males may live alone and only associate with the group for mating. Many hoofed animals form large herds of one species, or even of mixed species such as zebras, gazelles, and antelopes–this provides safety in numbers.

△ RABBIT WARREN
Rabbits form stable groups of up to about 20 individuals, with approximately equal numbers of females and males. Senior-ranking females occupy the bigger and safer nesting chambers nearest the center of the warren.

◁ ELEPHANT HERD
The elephant herd is led by a matriarch, and usually contains related females and their offspring. As with many large herbivores, young males form bachelor groups, while older males are solitary.

▷ KILLER WHALE POD
The Killer Whale pod, of up to 30, is led by a senior female, with subordinate males and females, and their offspring. It may develop into a multi-generational unit. Mature males leave briefly to mate with females in other pods.

WORKING AS A COMMUNITY

The Naked Mole-rat of East Africa has a social system unique among mammals, and which is more akin to insect societies. It lives in a colony of up to 80, dominated by a "queen." Only she gives birth to young and suckles them. Other members, or "courtiers" of the colony care for the offspring. Workers dig tunnels and gather food, which they bring back to share in the colony's central chamber.

SENSES AND COMMUNICATION

MAMMALS NOT ONLY use their senses to find the way, locate food, and identify danger, but also to interact with others of their own kind. Their intricate array of communications, such as calling and scent-marking, is used for courtship, competition for dominance, and repelling intruders from a territory.

SENSES

Mammals have the five main senses of most animals: sight, hearing, smell, touch, and taste. Habitat influences which senses are best developed. Underground, some moles and mole-rats are virtually blind but extremely sensitive to touch and vibration. In thick forest, where sight is limited, monkeys use sounds to communicate. Zebras and antelopes on open plains tend to have acute sight.

large, sensitive ears

big front-facing eyes

prehensile tail

△ UNDERGROUND
The Star-nosed Mole lives underground and has little need of vision. The tentacles around its nose are extremely sensitive to touch and, combined with acute smell, allow it to feel and sniff for prey and a mate.

ECHOLOCATION

Cetaceans and bats use echolocation or sonar to navigate and find prey. The mammal makes sounds that bounce off nearby objects and return as echoes, which give information about the size, location, and distance of the object.

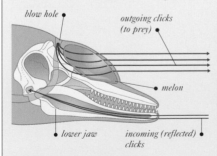

blow hole

outgoing clicks (to prey)

melon

lower jaw

incoming (reflected) clicks

△ NIGHT SENSES
The cycle of daily activity is another factor affecting sense development. The nocturnal Bushbaby, or Galago, which lives in the forests of Africa, has very large, front-facing eyes to pick up the slightest trace of light, as well as big ears to locate faint sounds in the darkness.

REFLECTED SOUND
Sounds from a dolphin's blowhole are focused by the melon on its forehead. Returning echoes pass through the lower jaw to the ear.

COMMUNICATION

Dawn in a tropical forest is filled with whoops, screeches, howls, and other calls, mainly from monkeys and other primates. These sounds are produced as a form of intraspecific (between members of the same species) communication and have several purposes: they may reinforce bonds between a male–female pair; they allow each member of a troop to know where the other members are; they tell members of a group which individual is dominant, or warn them of danger; they proclaim that a particular patch of forest is occupied as a territory and warn rivals of the same species to keep out. Such communications are found throughout the mammal group, and involve the senses of sight and smell as well as vision.

△ LOUD HOWLS
Howler monkeys of South America produce some of the loudest sounds in the entire animal kingdom. The male howler's dawn call, proclaiming the group's presence, can be heard more than 1¼ miles (2 km) away.

△ SCENT MARKING
Many mammals leave droppings or spray urine around their home range as a sign to others to keep out. Some rub scents from glands on to rocks or other surfaces for the same reason.

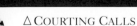

△ COURTING CALLS
The male humpback whale produces a series of varied moans, screams, clicks, and wails, partly as a courtship "song" to attract females. Each male's unique song lasts up to 30 minutes.

◁ MUTUAL GROOMING
Mammals groom their fur to get rid of dirt and tangles. However, they also groom others of their kind to strengthen bonds within a social group.

LOCOMOTION

A TYPICAL MAMMAL moves around by using its four limbs. This is known as quadrupedal locomotion. However, there are many variations, as well as exceptions, to this basic action. Some mammals are bipedal, such as the kangaroo and wallaby. Bats fly, moles tunnel, gibbons swing with their front limbs, gerbils hop, and seals swim using their rear limbs. Whales and dolphins do not use their limbs at all – their tail flukes contain no limb bones.

LIMB LENGTHS

The length of a mammal's limbs compared to the size of its body gives an indication of its speed. Long legs, as in horses and deer, generally mean faster locomotion. Insectivores such as moles and shrews shuffle slowly since their prey (worms and slugs) do not move rapidly. The short limbs and long bodies of mustelids, such as weasels, slow down surface speed but allow them to enter prey burrows.

▷ PLANTIGRADE

In this gait, the mammal walks on its heel (calcaneum), foot (metapodial), and toe (digit) bones. Bears, badgers, and humans have this type of posture.

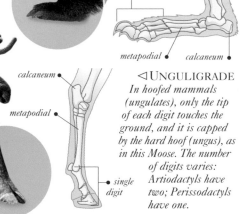

digits

metapodial • calcaneum •

◁ UNGULIGRADE

In hoofed mammals (ungulates), only the tip of each digit touches the ground, and it is capped by the hard hoof (ungus), as in this Moose. The number of digits varies: Artiodactyls have two; Perissodactyls have one.

calcaneum •

metapodial •

single digit •

▷ DIGITIGRADE

In this gait the weight is borne by four or five digits (no hoof). The central part of the foot (metapodial) does not touch the ground. In some cases the foot is very long, making the heel look like a backward-facing knee. Carnivores, such as cats and dogs, walk in this way.

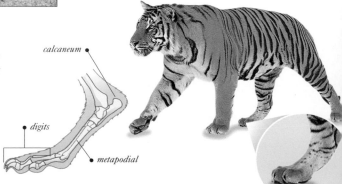

calcaneum •

digits •

metapodial •

HOPPING AND JUMPING

Two-footed hops and leaps are used by several types of marsupials, such as kangaroos and wallabies, and also rodents such as jerboas and springhares. The foot portion of the rear limb is relatively huge and provides a cushion for the animal to "bounce" along smoothly.

▽ ENERGY EFFICIENT

As a mammal using bipedal hops moves faster and faster, the gait becomes more energy-efficient than running. Energy is stored in the large tendons of the hind limbs, and the tail swings up and down for momentum.

THROUGH THE AIR

Mammals from various groups, such as squirrels and possums, can glide. But only bats are capable of truly sustained, controlled flight. However, they comprise more than one-fifth of all mammal species, making flight among mammals a relatively common feature. Some species of free-tailed bats can fly at more than 35 mph (55 kph).

▷ GLIDER
The Flying Lemur has the largest area of gliding membrane compared to body size of any mammal.

◁ FLIER
To save weight, a bat has a tiny rear body and hind limbs, compared to its head and chest.

BRACHIATION

The group of apes called gibbons moves by swinging hand-over-hand, suspended from branches. This specialized method of locomotion is known as brachiation. The fingers of the hands have evolved into hooks, and the thumb is not able to grasp as in other apes or humans.

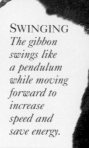

SWINGING
The gibbon swings like a pendulum while moving forward to increase speed and save energy.

IN WATER

Aquatic mammals have evolved fins and flippers to move through water (see p. 42). The whale flexes its backbone up and down by alternately contracting muscles along it to move the tail flukes.

◁ WHALE TAIL
The tapering flukes with rear-curved tips are designed to allow water to roll off efficiently, without swirls that would act as brakes.

FEEDING

MAMMALS, BEING warm-blooded, need far more food to burn for body heat than cold-blooded creatures of equivalent size. Almost anything that is organic, from flesh, to eggs, fungus, vegetation, fruits, nuts, bark, sap, honey, droppings, or blood, is food for a mammal of some kind.

MEAT EATERS

The major group of mammals known as the order Carnivora includes mostly animals that eat meat and little else. Families in it include the felids (cats), canids (dogs, foxes, and wolves), mustelids (stoats and otters), and viverrids (mongooses, linsangs, and genets). Exceptions are certain canids and ursids (bears) such as the Spectacled Bear and Giant Panda, which eat very little meat. All seals, sea lions, whales, and dolphins devour flesh, varying from krill to fish, as well as each other. On a smaller scale, the order Insectivora also contains prey-eating species, such as shrews and moles.

▷ CATCHING FISH
The mustelid family has a number of species that are chiefly fish-eaters. These include the aquatic otters and semi-aquatic minks, which have sharp teeth to grasp and tear up their slippery prey.

◁ FAST HUNTER
The Cheetah is a typical cat, hunting fast-moving prey such as hares and gazelles, which it knocks down by the sheer speed of its charge.

△ SCAVENGER
Jackals will eat any scraps left behind by other predators. However, they are also efficient hunters in their own right.

LIQUID DIET

A Vampire Bat consumes only blood, obtaining all the essential nutrients from it. It makes an incision with its teeth and laps the blood that oozes out, rather than sucking it out.

▷ BIG DRINKER
The Vampire Bat licks up half its own body weight in blood in 10 minutes.

△ BIG EATER
A Pygmy Shrew loses body heat fast since it has a large surface area for its size. Its energy needs are so great that it eats its own weight in food daily.

△ TINY PREY
The Aardvark is a specialized consumer of ants and termites. It licks up thousands of these prey daily and chews them with its peglike cheek teeth.

FILTER FEEDERS
The biggest mammals – the baleen whales – eat some of the smallest prey. The size discrepancy between consumer and consumed, and the passive nature of filter-feeding (the whale simply gulps in vast mouthfuls of water and combs out its food), makes it difficult to think of these mammals as predators or carnivores. A hungry Blue Whale is known to gulp down more than 4 tons (4 tonnes) of its exclusive diet – shrimplike krill – in the span of just one day.

comblike
baleen plates

△ GIANT SIEVE
Baleen is a cartilage-like substance that forms bristly filter plates, which hang from the whale's upper jaw. The Bowhead has the longest baleen plates at 13 ft (4 m).

OMNIVORES
Many mammals are omnivores, taking a huge range of foods, from vegetation, nuts and berries to eggs, flesh, insects, crops, and carrion. The largest mammalian omnivores are bears. In this family, only the Polar Bear eats almost nothing but meat; other species are much more adaptable. The American Black Bear's diet is almost nine-tenths vegetarian. However, like all other bears, it takes advantage of seasonal gluts, such as spawning salmon in early fall. Raccoons are another group of opportunistic feeders, which eat almost anything that comes their way. Certain mammals that are chiefly carnivorous, including wolves, dogs, and foxes, and a few cats, such as the Margay, can also turn to omnivory in times of need.

△ VEGETARIAN BEAR
Despite its bulk, sometimes up to 660 lb (300 kg), the American Black Bear climbs trees and bushes to pluck fruits and berries with its flexible lips.

HERBIVORES

Plant food generally has far less nutrients and energy than meat. It is also more difficult to break down in the digestive system. Herbivores spend much longer each day, eating huge quantities of food, compared to carnivores. One benefit over meat-eating mammals is that plants are incapable of movement and do not need to be hunted down. However, some plants have forms of self-defense, such as thorns and poison. Most herbivores have well-developed premolars and molars to thoroughly grind their meal.

△ BIGGEST EATERS
The largest land mammals, elephants, take in up to 330 lb (150 kg) of food daily. But due to poor digestion, almost half passes through virtually unchanged.

◁ GRAZERS AND BROWSERS
Grazers feed on grasses and low plants. They include gazelles and zebras. Browsers, such as deer, eat a wider range of vegetation from bushes and trees, as well.

△ NUTS AND SEEDS
Fall, in temperate regions, sees a surplus of nuts and berries. Rodents, such as chipmunks, hide food or bury it, to eat later.

DIGESTING VEGETATION

Hoofed herbivores are of two types. The hindgut fermenters (wild horses and zebras) chew their food and swallow it into the stomach. It then passes into the cecum, to be digested by a process known as fermentation. The foregut fermenters (or ruminants) comprise most other artiodactyls. The food they swallow is fermented in the first stomach chamber or rumen. It is then regurgitated for further chewing, and swallowed again into the rest of the digestive tract.

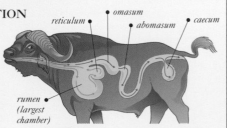

reticulum •   omasum •
   abomasum •   caecum •

rumen • (largest chamber)

△ RUMINANTS
Buffaloes chew food twice, once as it is gathered, and again after it has part-fermented in the rumen. This is known as chewing the cud.

DIET SYMBOLS

In this book, the wide variety of foods consumed by the different mammals is represented by symbols, which are explained as follows. Wherever relevant, or of particular interest, more details on the diet are given in the text for each species entry.

LARGE
MAMMALS
Usually herbivorous ungulates like deer, antelopes, zebras, cattle, sheep, and goats.

AQUATIC
MAMMALS
Seals, sea lions, Walrus, whales, dolphins, porpoises, and sea cows.

SMALL
MAMMALS
Up to about 12 in (30 cm), mostly herbivorous: mice, rats, voles, rabbits, and squirrels.

BIRDS
Both ground-dwelling birds (such as quail), as well as water birds (such as ducks); also chicks in nests.

REPTILES
Lizards and snakes, sometimes tortoises, turtles, crocodiles, or alligators.

AMPHIBIANS
Frogs, toads, salamanders, and newts, although many are poisonous.

CEPHALOPODS
Larger molluscs with long tentacles: squid, octopus, and cuttlefish.

FISH
Solitary or shoaling, fast or slow, surface or bottom dwelling fish.

KRILL
Shrimplike marine crustaceans, which form swarms of billions.

MOLLUSCS
Snails and slugs, sea-snails, and shellfish: clams, oysters, mussels, and abalones.

WORMS
Soft-bodied dwellers on land such as insect grubs or aquatic crustacean larvae.

ARTHROPODS
Joint-legged animals: insects, centipedes, spiders, crabs, and crayfish.

OTHER
INVERTEBRATES
Starfish, sea-cucumbers, and jellyfish.

EGGS
Mainly eggs of birds, often in nests, or of reptiles, which may be buried.

HONEY
Specialized product of bees; also similar substances from other insects.

VEGETATION
Above-ground plant material: leaves; also stems, flowers, and soft twigs.

GRASS
Leafy blades, but also nutritious creeping stems and roots.

FRUITS
Usually soft, fleshy fruits and berries, rather than hard fruits (see Nuts).

NUTS
Very hardcased fruits or seeds that are split open for the softer kernels within.

SEEDS
Seed matter of ripe flowers that are not too fleshy or too hardcased.

GRAIN
Starchy seeds of wild and domesticated grass (such as wheat or rice).

ROOTS
Includes other underground plants like bulbs, corms, and tubers.

FUNGI
Mushrooms, toadstools, bracket fungi, also yeasts and lichens.

BARK
The dead outer layer of a tree (often nibbled through to reach the sap beneath).

AQUATIC PLANTS
Freshwater and marine; aquatic herbivores such as Manatees consume both.

DESERT MAMMALS

DESERTS MAY BE hot or cold, windy or calm, rocky or sandy, high-altitude or low, but the one common factor is that they are always dry. Compared to other major animal groups, such as insects and reptiles, mammals need plenty of water. Mammals that have become adapted to desert life have undergone major changes in the way their bodies take in, handle, and release water.

GETTING WATER

Carnivores living in deserts gain enough moisture from freshly-killed prey, in the form of blood and body fluids, to satisfy their liquid intake. This transfers the challenge of obtaining water to obtaining food. Herbivores get water from plants, especially succulents. Smaller plant-eating mammals store seeds in burrows to retain their moisture, and lick dew from pebbles and stones. Small mammals may also block up the entrances to their tunnels, to retain moist, cool air within.

▽ EFFICIENT ORYX

Oryx have very efficient kidneys that excrete little urine, and they also produce very dry droppings.

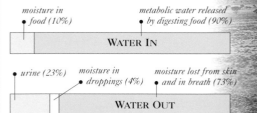

moisture in
• food (10%)

metabolic water released
• by digesting food (90%)

WATER IN

• urine (23%)

moisture in
• droppings (4%)

moisture lost from skin
• and in breath (73%)

WATER OUT

△ WATER BALANCE

The above diagram illustrates how a kangaroo rat survives arid desert conditions. It is entirely dependent on its food, for water. The water taken in has to balance that which is lost in order to prevent the animal from becoming dehydrated.

◁ FOOD AND WATER STORE

A camel's fatty hump is both stored food as well as on-board moisture, as the fat is broken down to yield energy, the breakdown producing metabolic water. A thirsty camel has been known to drink more than 13 gallons (50 liters) of water in a few minutes.

FINDING FOOD

Large desert herbivores can detect rain using their acute sense of smell and so move towards areas of future plant growth. Even smaller herbivores can travel long distances to temporary food surplus; the Lesser Egyptian Jerboa can cover 6 miles (10 km) in a single night. Some smaller herbivores even collect and store this bounty. The kangaroo rat may cache up to 11 lb (5 kg) of spare seeds in its burrow.

▷ ON WATCH

In open habitats, sight is the main sense for detecting danger. In a colony of meerkats, a few stand upright to scan over the ground for predators. They also peer up to spot birds of prey.

◁ STORING FOOD

The Fat-tailed Dunnart is a voracious hunter of insects and worms across Australia's desert and scrubby outback. It stores surplus food as body fat in the base of its tail.

COPING WITH THE HEAT

Large desert mammals such as Oryx, Dama Gazelles, Gerenuk, and camels, are active in the cooler dawn and dusk. By day they rest in any shade they find, near bushes or hillocks. They often move to new feeding grounds at night, when it is less hot and they are less visible to predators. Oryx may trek 19 miles (30 km) through the darkness, chewing the cud as they walk. They also allow their body temperature to rise by 9°F (5°C) above normal, before they start to lose water in cooling sweat.

▷ LOSING HEAT

In warm-blooded mammals, large body surfaces act as radiators to lose heat. The Fennec Fox of the Sahara Desert has huge ears that act as body coolers and also detect the faint scrabbles of small prey on the sand.

◁ NIGHT FORAGING

Small desert mammals like the Four-toed Jerboa usually hide away in their tunnels or burrows during daytime heat. They emerge at dusk to forage, using their large eyes, ears, and whiskers both to locate food and to stay alert for danger.

GRASSLAND MAMMALS

GRASSLAND TENDS TO form where the climate is too dry to support tree growth, but too moist for a desert. Life for mammals here is dominated by long dry periods interrupted by occasional rains, with the risk of wildfires during drought. The plant food variety is limited, with few grass species, and there is a lack of trees or landscape features to provide cover in such an open habitat.

HERDS

On the open plains, there are few places for large mammals to hide. One method of self-protection used by grassland herbivores is to gather in herds for "safety in numbers." While some herd members eat or rest, others are alert, leaving several eyes, ears, and noses ready to sense danger. If one member detects a predator, it can warn the others by calls and actions. In some cases herd members cooperate to drive off an enemy. The largest herds of mammals are found on the African savanna where zebras, antelopes, and gazelles gather in vast aggregations.

▽ MIGRATION
In the savanna, rainfall is patchy and some regions have fresh plant growth while others are dry. Large herbivores, such as wildebeest, migrate regularly in search of new pasture or water.

△ MIXED HERDS
Different mammal species form mixed herds to pool their resources. Giraffes can see far across the landscape, while zebras have an excellent sense of smell.

◁ HUNTING PACKS
Many grassland predators, such as hyenas, jackals, and lions, hunt in groups or packs. By doing so they can kill large prey such as a wildebeest, which provides food for several days.

SPEED AND MOVEMENT

There are few ravines, forests, or other features on the grassland to provide cover or to act as obstacles. Consequently, speed has become an important feature of large mammals found there. Evolution favors predators that are fast enough to run down victims, such as the Cheetah in Africa; and prey that are speedy enough to escape hunters, such as the Pronghorn in North America. These are the two fastest runners in the animal kingdom. However, chases tend to be short sprints since running is very energy-consuming. A Cheetah gives up after 20 seconds or so, as it runs out of breath and energy.

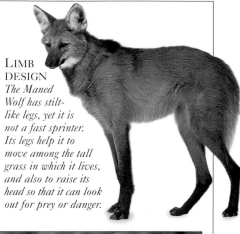

LIMB DESIGN

The Maned Wolf has stilt-like legs, yet it is not a fast sprinter. Its legs help it to move among the tall grass in which it lives, and also to raise its head so that it can look out for prey or danger.

△ SELECTION IN ACTION

In any herbivore herd, some animals are weaker than others. Hunters, such as lions, single out a victim that is easier to catch.

BURROWING

One way of creating hiding places in grassland is by digging. Many small mammals, especially rodents such as prairie dogs, voles, rats and mole-rats, find shelter from predators, extreme climatic conditions, and fire in this way. Often, the burrows have mounds around the entrances, to prevent flooding. The largest burrows, big enough to accommodate a human, are made by the Aardvark of Africa, a specialized ant- and termite-eater. In the Australian grasslands, wombats make shelters almost the same size as those of the Aardvark.

▷ LIVING UNDERGROUND

Each prairie dog family has a highly organized network of tunnels and chambers. Neighbouring burrows combine to form a minitownship.

FOREST MAMMALS

TREES ARE HOSTS to different species of mammals. They provide food, shelter, safety from ground predators, and nesting sites. Mammals, such as the woolly and spider monkeys, are wholly arboreal ("tree-dwelling") and hardly ever touch the ground. Others, such as martens and the ocelots, are "semi-arboreal", and equally at home on the ground or in trees.

MOVEMENT IN TREES
Many arboreal mammals move through the branches by jumps and leaps. Most acrobatic of all, are the Old World gibbons, with their hooklike hands, and the New World Monkeys, which grip with their hands and feet as well as the muscular prehensile tail. Squirrels have sharp claws to dig into bark, muscular paws, a long tail for balance, and large eyes to judge distances before leaping. Tree porcupines, raccoons, and anteaters tend to shuffle along slowly and securely.

▷ LEAPING
Primates tend to keep their bodies upright while jumping. Lemurs use their long, powerful rear legs for propulsion, the long tail for balance, and all four limbs to cushion the landing.

△ GLIDING
Mammals such as possums, gliders, flying lemurs, and flying squirrels parachute through the forest on flaps of skin, which stretch out between their limbs. They are actually gliders rather than true fliers.

LIVING ON THE GROUND
Forest trees provide abundant food in the form of leaves, blossoms, seeds, fruits, and nuts. Ground-based mammals, from mice and voles to wild pigs, tapirs, deer, and Okapi, take advantage of this rich supply. The decaying carpet of leaves and twigs also encourages a host of worms, slugs, insects, and other small creatures, which become prey for small mammal hunters such as elephant-shrews and solenodons.

◁ CAMOUFLAGE
Most forest mammals are shades of brown to blend in with their surroundings. Young deer and wild boar have dappled coats to merge with the undergrowth. Arboreal cats have spots or patches to blend in with the shadows among the branches.

LIFE IN TREES

The tree canopy in a tropical forest, where leaves, fruits, and flowers grow all year, holds most of the forest mammal's food. Consequently arboreal mammals are more likely to thrive here. In temperate forest, food resources are seasonal and the canopy is generally more open, allowing greater plant growth on the ground. Here it is often more profitable for mammals to venture down from the trees and forage for food on the forest floor.

△ NEST BUILDING

Small mammals use holes in tree trunks to build homes, like the squirrel's nest (drey).

△ SLOWEST MAMMAL

Among the slowest-moving mammals are sloths. They eat mainly leaves, hanging upside down from branches with their long, sharp, hooked claws. Sloths only come down from trees to defecate or to move to another tree as food runs out. On the ground, sloths are often at the mercy of predators since they are clumsy walkers.

△ FIVE LIMBS

Spider monkeys are named after their long, slim limbs. Their "fifth limb" is the prehensile tail, which can support the whole weight of the body.

▷ ROOSTING

Bats, the true forest fliers, roost during the day on branches or in tree holes. At night, they fly out in search of food.

POLAR AND MOUNTAIN MAMMALS

THE LAND AND SEAS near the Poles, and the tops of tall mountains are some of the harshest habitats. They are cold, with bitter winds and a covering of snow and ice. Food is scarce and hard to access. However, several mammals are adapted to survive in these conditions. They have little competition, except for birds, since temperatures are too low for reptiles and amphibians to survive.

KEEPING WARM

A high priority for mammals in cold climates is to retain body heat. This is done by thick fur, usually an outer coat of longer guard hairs that give protection and shrug off rain and snow, and a dense undercoat to keep in heat. Under the skin is a thick layer of fat that also acts as insulation. Parts projecting from the body such as the nose and ears are small, since they lose heat fastest and are at risk from frostbite. In the worst weather, most mammals simply rest in any sheltered place, curled up to minimize loss of warmth.

△ SHAGGY COATS
The Muskox's outer coat has very long hairs reaching one yard in length around the main body. The Yak of Central Asia has a similar thick overcoat of fur.

COVERED WITH FUR △
The Polar Bear is completely covered with fur, apart from its eyes and nose tip. Even the soles of its paws are furred, both to keep in heat and to obtain a grip on slippery ice.

◁ UNDER THE FROZEN OCEAN
Seals have an excellent memory for the location of breathing holes in the ice. They even re-cut a hole with their teeth when the ice is a few inches thick. Seals and sea lions spend hours hauled out of the water, grooming their fur coats with their teeth and flipper claws. This is vital for animals in cold places, since their fur is truly a survival blanket.

CHANGING COATS

Like many polar animals, the Arctic Fox molts its fur twice each year and grows two distinctive coats. Each provides camouflage as the surroundings change with the seasons. Stoats in the far north grow white coats in winter, when they are called Ermines, and molt these for brown fur in the summer. Further south, where snow and ice covers the ground much more briefly, the same species is brownish all year.

◁ SUMMER COAT
The Arctic Fox's summer coat is light gray or gray-brown in some individuals, and browner and darker in others. This blends in with rocks, earth, and shrubby plants.

▷ WINTER COAT
The winter coat is white and twice as thick as the summer coat. It gives camouflage for stalking in the snow.

ON THE HIGH SLOPES

Mammals living in the mountains have strong limbs and feet, which give good grip on slippery wet rocks or icy slopes. Like many ungulates of the peaks, the Mountain Goat has very large, wide hooves for a foothold on every kind of surface. In common with Chamois, Ibex, and other mountain-dwellers, these goats ascend to the high pastures in spring, to feed on summer vegetation. In the fall they return to the lower slopes and the shelter of bushes and trees.

MANAGING ALTITUDES

A particular problem facing mountain mammals is the thin air, which contains reduced amounts of oxygen. Many species have adapted to this problem by evolving blood with extra numbers of red cells.

▷ HIGH UP
Vicuñas are found in the Andean tundra at heights of almost 16,500 ft (5,000 m).

△ SURE FOOTEDNESS
Each hoof of the wild goat has a hard, sharp outer rim and a soft inner pad, providing excellent grip. Few predators can catch these herbivores as they escape to almost inaccessible vertical rocky cliffs and shelter on tiny, narrow ledges.

AQUATIC MAMMALS

MAMMALS FIRST EVOLVED on land as four-legged animals that walked and ran. Aquatic mammals changed greatly from the original mammalian design to meet the different demands of life in water, and they became the most modified of all mammal species. Some of these modifications in shape and movement are clearly visible, while others are less obvious.

MOVEMENT

Moving through water requires much more energy, as it is a "thicker" medium than air. The Cheetah can reach a speed of about 62 mph (100 kph), but the Killer Whale, weighing about 400 times as much, reaches only half this speed. Aquatic mammals have broad, flat surfaces to push through water. Dolphins, whales, Dugongs, and Manatees propel themselves with their tail flukes and use their flippers for steering. Semiaquatic species such as otters use their highly webbed feet.

◁PROPULSION
The Killer Whale can gain enough speed to leap clear of the water, despite its massive bulk of up to 10 tons (10 tonnes). This leap, followed by a huge splash as it crashes back in, is known as breaching. (See also p. 29).

△ BODY SHAPE
Water mammals such as the dolphin have smooth, streamlined bodies to slip through water easily. The dorsal fin stops the body from spiralling and the flippers are used for steering and maneuvering.

AGILITY△
Agile swimmers such as the Common Seal can catch fast-moving aquatic prey. Sea lions swim with front flippers, while seals use hind flippers.

TEMPERATURE CONTROL

Many aquatic mammals live in the Poles, where seas are cold year round and may freeze in winter. Here, maintaining body temperature is a vital function. This is helped by having smaller extremities, since these lose heat fastest. Mammals such as seals and sea lions have dense coats and hairs coated with water-repelling oils. Size is also a factor, since heat is lost through a mammal's body surface and bigger mammals lose heat more slowly. This is why most truly aquatic mammals are large, with the great whales largest of all.

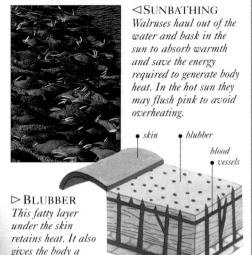

◁ SUNBATHING
Walruses haul out of the water and bask in the sun to absorb warmth and save the energy required to generate body heat. In the hot sun they may flush pink to avoid overheating.

skin • blubber
blood
vessels

▷ BLUBBER
This fatty layer under the skin retains heat. It also gives the body a smoother shape, and offers a degree of protection.

MARINE LIFESTYLE

The Sea Otter is a truly marine mammal. It has the thickest hair of any mammal, to protect it in water, and rarely comes ashore. It feeds while floating on its back and even sleeps afloat, secured in beds of seaweed.

▷ MARINE MEALS
The Sea Otter places a shellfish on its belly and smashes them open with a stone, to eat.

△ CHAMPION DIVER
The Sperm Whale probably makes the deepest and longest dives of any mammal, staying underwater for almost two hours and reaching depths of 1,000 ft (300 m). The rare beaked whales may make dives as lengthy and deep.

SURVIVING UNDERWATER

Aquatic mammals must come to the surface regularly to obtain fresh supplies of oxygen, since all mammals do so by breathing in air. Pinnipeds (seals and sea lions) and cetaceans (whales, porpoises, and dolphins) and are able to retain oxygen in their muscles. The oxygen is stored in a special protein, myoglobin, and can be released gradually during a dive. Some seals have ten times more myoglobin in their muscles, than land mammals.

WATCHING MAMMALS

MAMMALS ARE EASY to watch since they are all around us. Depending on where we live, we can see pet cats and dogs in homes, horses in fields, sheep and cows on farms, and squirrels and monkeys in woodlands. Studying these mammals can reveal many details of behavior. However, watching truly wild mammals in their natural habitats requires more planning and preparation.

ACCESSIBLE MAMMALS

Wild mammals are very alert for potential danger. Most people tend to move about noisily, so wild mammals usually hide before humans arrive on the scene. Many mammals are nocturnal and are able to see people clearly in light levels where humans can hardly see at all. Successful mammal-watching requires planning, preparation, and patience. Plan by finding out about the habits and behaviors of the target species (throughout the day and over the different seasons) from detailed field guides and similar sources. Prepare by surveying sites very observantly, for clues such as burrows, nests, footprints in mud or sand, tufts of fur on thorns, droppings, and signs of eating, such as empty nut shells, gnawed carcasses, claw scratches on tree trunks, trampled grass, or broken branches.

△ CLOSE TO HOME
A host of wild mammals, many active by night, live in gardens and parks. Suitable food may lure them out for study. An infra red lamp or flashlight helps human vision without frightening the animals.

◁ PARKS AND ZOOS
Wildlife parks, zoos, and nature reserves are places to observe mammal species. However, the behavior of captive animals differs from that of wild ones.

WATCHING GUIDELINES

Much of the advice for watching mammals safely is based on common sense. Avoid going out alone in case of accidents or other mishaps. Do not move about in a place during darkness, unless familiarized with it by daylight. Wear suitable warm, waterproof clothing; weather can change rapidly and nights can get very cold. Avoid steep slopes, slippery rocks, and banks near water. Carry equipment in a backpack, to leave both hands free for balance when clambering about. Never take chances where large and potentially dangerous species may be found.

IN THE WILD

Getting close to exciting, large mammals in the wild is a complex and potentially hazardous process. There is also a chance of experiencing frustratingly "empty" days. This type of mammal-watching is best undertaken as part of an organized group – there is a large choice of outings from luxury tours to survival-type treks. Guides and rangers know where different species are likely to be at a certain time of the day or season. They can give advice on routes and on using hides, where one can watch wildlife concealed, allowing the animals to behave more naturally.

△ UNDERWATER ACTION
Snorkeling and scuba-diving reveal an incredible undersea world where dolphins, seals, otters, and other aquatic mammals move with grace and agility.

△ ON SAFARI
Mammals become used to vehicles that act as mobile bases for humans. The viewers are kept safe and the animals relatively undisturbed.

EQUIPMENT

Modern, lightweight electronic equipment makes recording mammals – by photograph, video, film, or audio tape – much easier. However, traditional items such as a notebook and pencil, field guide, and binoculars are still essential.

◁ CAMERA
Telephoto (long) lenses get you close to the subject. Fast-exposure film catches rapid movement and copes with low light.

◁ BINOCULARS
Practice using the binoculars with one hand only. Keep them ready around your neck to view the subject at once.

◁ NOTEBOOK
Keep a notebook to make lists of species observed. A sketch is also better than trying to recall details later.

◁ CAMCORDER
The video camera should be ready for instant use. Prefocus on a likely spot and check light settings.

THREATENED MAMMALS

MAMMALS FACE MANY hazards in the modern world. The IUCN Red List (see below) names over 1,000 mammal species, almost one in four, as facing a threat, with 180 species being "critically endangered." The dangers vary for different mammals, but they are nearly all due to human activity.

ON THE BRINK

Many of the critically endangered mammals are relatively large species such as big cats, rhinoceroses, cetaceans, and bovids (cattle and relatives). Information regarding population numbers and breeding rates is easier to collect for these species, and the degree of threat can be assessed more accurately, compared to that of small species such as rodents. Total numbers of a species are important, but so are the populations of its subspecies, and especially how they are distributed. Small, isolated groups are at risk from epidemics, or from genetic problems due to inbreeding, as the total "gene pool" for the species shrinks.

△ CRITICALLY ENDANGERED
With a population of probably less than 100, the Javan Rhinoceros is on the verge of extinction, due chiefly to clearance of its lowland forest habitat.

△ ENDANGERED
Tigers number several thousand, as a result of conservation. Their situation, however, is still very serious.

△ SPECIFIC THREATS
The Pink River Dolphin faces specific threats such as water pollution by heavy-metal chemicals, and disruption of its echolocation.

THE RED LIST

The Red Lists of Threatened Species are published by the International Union for the Conservation of Nature and Natural Resources (IUCN). Drawn up every few years with the help of data gathered by more than 10,000 scientists from all over the world, the Lists are a global directory to the status of animals, plants, and other living things on our planet. The 2000 List places mammal species in one of eight categories such as lower risk, vulnerable, critically endangered, and so on, with "threatened" used as a general term underlying the entire list.

MAJOR THREAT

The largest overall threat to most mammals is habitat destruction. Expanding human population takes over land to raise crops and livestock, build houses and roads, and to extract natural resources. Forests are felled for the short-term gain of timber and farmed for a few years. They suffer soil erosion, and the displaced species, especially arboreal types such as monkeys and tree kangaroos, never return.

▷ MAN-MADE FIRES

The world's richest habitats are being burned down in tropical forests of the Amazon region, W. Africa, and S.E. Asia.

POLLUTION

Mammals and their habitats are polluted in a variety of ways, including chemical pollution of rivers and oil spills, and also suffer from the effects of climate change. Aquatic species eat polluted prey and suffer from low-grade poisoning known as bioamplification.

◁ OIL SPILL

A mammal's coat is its survival blanket. Polluting oils ruin the fur's protective properties. The mammal swallows the oil while grooming itself and suffers further harm.

HUNTING

Since the 1980s, an agreement between a majority of nations has banned the slaughter of many big whale species. However, a fast-growing threat is hunting wild animals for the trade in bushmeat. Protected species such as monkeys, gorillas, and dolphins are hunted for their flesh, which is often sold openly at markets.

△ POACHING

Hunting for skins and body parts is now banned for many species. But people are still tempted into poaching to make a living.

◁ WHALING

Species not included in the ban on whaling have now become threatened. Cetaceans breed slowly and may take decades to recover.

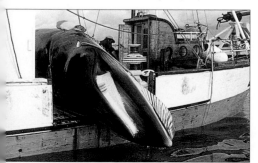

CONSERVATION

MANY MAMMALS suffer from general threats to wildlife, such as habitat destruction and pollution. Helping these species is part of the overall process of wildlife conservation. Some mammals face more specific problems and need more specialized conservation measures. (See also Introduced Species, p. 51).

HABITAT PROTECTION

Since habitat destruction is the biggest overall threat faced by wild animals (see p. 47), habitat conservation is the most effective way of protecting them. This is the rationale behind establishing national parks and nature reserves. Such preserved habitats provide every resource that a species needs to thrive. However, these areas need to be large enough for mammals such as big cats and ungulate herds to find enough food, establish territories, and reproduce without the problems of inbreeding.

△ REFORESTATION
If soil erosion has not been too severe, trees may be planted in an area which was once forest, as here in a reforestation project in Guatemala.

◁ PROTECTED PARKS
In a protected area, rangers patrol the borders for poachers, while the park animals are prevented from raiding surrounding crops or livestock.

STAR SPECIES

Some animals such as Giant Pandas, dolphins, and tamarins, naturally arouse attention and sympathy because they look cuddly and appealing. Others such as bears and big cats command respect and awe due to their power. The "star status" of these mammals is often used by wildlife organizations to grab headlines and photo opportunities. However, all threatened mammal species, including those that evoke shudders of horror in the lay person, such as obscure rats and bats, deserve to live securely in their natural habitats.

▷ SYMBOL OF CONSERVATION
The Giant Panda is the globally recognized symbol of the World Wide Fund for Nature (WWF) – a leading organization for nature conservation.

CAPTIVE BREEDING

Some mammals face such a severe plight that captive breeding is the last resort before extinction. Zoos and parks involved in breeding programmes swap individuals to maintain genetic diversity for a healthy population. They also prepare captive-bred individuals for life in the wild. Arabian Oryx and Golden Lion Tamarins are among many species that have benefitted.

▷ GOLDEN LION TAMARIN
The critically endangered Golden Lion Tamarin has been a target of conservation efforts since the 1960s. It has bred well in primate centers and has been re-introduced in S. E. Brazil since the mid-80s.

CONSERVATION MONITORING

How does one assess which mammals are in greatest danger, and which are the best ways to save them? An army of scientists, wildlife rangers, and conservation volunteers is constantly gathering data to reveal the best solutions. Detailed information on blood samples and stomach contents, to broad patterns such as migratory routes viewed by aerial survey, is analyzed.

△ SATELLITE TRACKING
Wide-ranging mammals such as this Beluga can be tracked around the world by a radio device attached to them. Its signals are received by a local receiver or a satellite.

△ DEHORNING
Conservationists sometimes cut off the rhinoceros's horn (which is insensitive to pain) to counter the threat of poaching.

▷ BACK HOME
Some mammals, especially primates such as baby Orangutans, are captured for the pet trade. When rescued, they need to be reintroduced to the ways of the forest, helped by trained staff at rehabilitation centers.

MAMMALS AND HUMANS

A TTITUDES TO MAMMALS around the world vary in different cultures, even toward the same species. A horse may be a thoroughbred race champion, a beast of burden, a lifelong friend, or a meaty meal. Many species have been domesticated or selectively bred over generations for human use.

DOMESTICATION

One of the chief features in domestication is reduced aggression and increased tameness or response to training. Perhaps the first domesticated species was the dog, bred from the Gray Wolf more than 10,000 years ago. Mammals utilized for their strength include horses, oxen, buffalo, and elephants. Pigs, sheep, and goats also have a long history of domestication. In recent times deer and antelopes have been farmed. There is also huge interest in "fancy" breeds such as rabbits and guinea pigs, while rats and mice are used for medical research.

△ CASH COWS
At least 180 breeds of cattle are selected to cope with varying climates around the world, and to produce milk and meat. The hides are tanned for leather, and the carcass rendered for other uses.

▽ USEFUL CATS
Cats were probably first kept by the Ancient Egyptians more than 5,000 years ago, to hunt mice. They have been worshipped, as well as burned at the stake as devils.

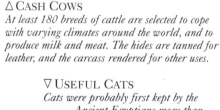

HORSE DOMESTICATION

The domestic horse (*Equus caballus*) may have originated more than 4,000 years ago in the Central Asian plains. Its ancestor possibly resembled Przewalski's Wild Horse. The mule is the offspring of a male donkey and female horse.

PRZEWALSKI'S WILD HORSE

MULE

THOROUGHBRED

FERAL MAMMALS

Feral species are those that have been domesticated, and have then "escaped" human control to live partly or wholly in the wild again. They include horses such as North American Mustang ponies and English New Forest ponies, various types of dogs, cats, and pigs, and also camels. Dromedaries (one-humped camels) were taken to Australia in the 1840s by explorers and have since established feral herds there.

◁FERAL DOGS

The Dingo may have been a type of domestic dog that has reverted to living wild again over the past few thousand years in Australia and S.E. Asia. It interbreeds readily with domestic dogs – in some parts of Australia half of all dingoes are interbred dingo-dogs.

INTRODUCED SPECIES

A major threat facing some mammals is posed by other mammal species introduced from other regions by humans. In Australia, a wealth of native marsupial mammals has suffered greatly from introduced species such as rabbits and Brown Rats. The newcomers compete with native species for food, prey on them, or carry diseases against which they have little natural resistance.

▽ GRAY SQUIRREL

The North American Gray Squirrel was brought to Europe around the 1870s. Larger and more aggressive than the native Red Squirrel, it quickly spread as the latter declined.

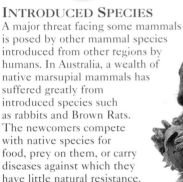

REINTRODUCED SPECIES

Captive breeding (see p. 49) can help to save a mammal species, which may then be reintroduced into its native area. However, once a species is lost, its habitat may be taken over by other species. The reintroduced individuals may then face unusually severe competition to re-establish a new population in that area.

◁PÈRE DAVID'S DEER

Père David's Deer, extinct in its native China, has existed only in captivity in English parks from about 1900. In the 1980s it was reintroduced to China.

CLASSIFICATION

THE ANIMAL KINGDOM is divided into groups called phyla. One major phylum is Chordata (animals that have a backbone), and mammals are grouped under this in a class called Mammalia. This class is further divided into 21 orders (listed below), each made up of one or more families, in turn made up of one or more genera (singular genus), which is a group of closely related species.

EGG-LAYING MAMMALS
ORDER Monotremata   FAMILIES 2   SPECIES 5

MARSUPIALS
ORDER Marsupialia   FAMILIES 22   SPECIES 292

INSECTIVORES
ORDER Insectivora   FAMILIES 6   SPECIES 365

BATS
ORDER Chiroptera   FAMILIES 18   SPECIES 977

ELEPHANT-SHREWS
ORDER Macroscelidea   FAMILIES 1   SPECIES 15

FLYING LEMURS
ORDER Dermoptera   FAMILIES 1   SPECIES 2

TREE SHREWS
ORDER Scandentia   FAMILIES 1   SPECIES 19

PRIMATES
ORDER Primates   FAMILIES 11   SPECIES 356

PROSIMIANS
SUBORDER Strepsirhini   FAMILIES 6   SPECIES 85

MONKEYS AND APES
SUBORDER Haplorhini

MONKEYS
FAMILIES 3   SPECIES 242

APES
FAMILIES 2   SPECIES 21

ANTEATERS AND RELATIVES
ORDER Xenarthra   FAMILIES 4   SPECIES 29

PANGOLINS
ORDER Pholidota   FAMILIES 1   SPECIES 7

RABBITS, HARES, AND PIKAS
ORDER Lagomorpha   FAMILIES 2   SPECIES 80

RODENTS
ORDER Rodentia   FAMILIES 30   SPECIES 1,702

CETACEANS

ORDER Cetacea   FAMILIES 13   SPECIES 83

BALEEN WHALES

SUBORDER Mysticeti   FAMILIES 4   SPECIES 12

TOOTHED WHALES

SUBORDER Odontoceti   FAMILIES 9   SPECIES 71

CARNIVORES

ORDER Carnivora   FAMILIES 7   SPECIES 249

DOGS AND RELATIVES

FAMILY Canidae   SPECIES 36

BEARS

FAMILY Ursidae   SPECIES 8

RACCOONS AND RELATIVES

FAMILY Procyonidae   SPECIES 20

MUSTELIDS

FAMILY Mustelidae   SPECIES 67

CIVETS AND RELATIVES

FAMILY Viverridae   SPECIES 76

HYENAS AND AARDWOLF

FAMILY Hyaenidae   SPECIES 4

CATS

FAMILY Felidae   SPECIES 38

SEALS AND SEA LIONS

ORDER Pinnipedia   FAMILIES 3   SPECIES 34

ELEPHANTS

ORDER Proboscidea   FAMILIES 1   SPECIES 3

HYRAXES

ORDER Hyracoidea   FAMILIES 1   SPECIES 8

AARDVARK

ORDER Tubulidentata FAMILIES 1   SPECIES 1

DUGONG AND MANATEES

ORDER Sirenia   FAMILIES 2   SPECIES 4

HOOFED MAMMALS

ODD-TOED HOOFED MAMMALS

ORDER Perissodactyla FAMILIES 3   SPECIES 19

HORSES AND RELATIVES

FAMILY Equidae   SPECIES 10

RHINOCEROSES

FAMILY Rhinocerotidae   SPECIES 5

TAPIRS

FAMILY Tapiridae   SPECIES 4

EVEN-TOED HOOFED MAMMALS

ORDER Artiodactyla FAMILIES 10 SPECIES 225

PIGS AND PECCARIES

FAMILY Suidae and Tayassuidae   SPECIES 17

HIPPOPOTAMUSES

FAMILY Hippopotamidae   SPECIES 2

CAMELS AND RELATIVES

FAMILY Camelidae   SPECIES 7

DEER, MUSK DEER, AND CHEVROTAINS

FAMILY Cervidae, Moschidae,   SPECIES 56
and Tragulidae

PRONGHORN

FAMILY Antilocapridae   SPECIES 1

GIRAFFE AND OKAPI

FAMILY Giraffidae   SPECIES 2

CATTLE AND RELATIVES

FAMILY Bovidae   SPECIES 140

EGG-LAYING MAMMALS

A LSO KNOWN as monotremes, the five species of egg-laying mammals are zoological curiosities of two distinct types. The single species of Platypus dwells in freshwater habitats in eastern Australia. It is a strange mix of ducklike beak, otter-shaped body, webbed feet, and flattened, beaver-like tail. It is also one of the very few poisonous mammals, with a venomous spur in the heel region of juveniles and adult males.

The four species of echidnas (spiny anteaters) are generalist consumers of ants, termites, worms, and grubs. Three long-beaked (long-nosed) species occur on the island of New Guinea. The Short-beaked (Short-nosed) Echidna is found there too, and also across most of Australia, in a variety of habitats.

True to their group name, all five species lay eggs. The female then feeds her hatched young on milk, like all mammals. Adult monotremes lack teeth and grind their food between plates or spines in the mouth.

Family TACHYGLOSSIDAE	Species *Tachyglossus aculeatus*	Status Lower risk

SHORT-BEAKED ECHIDNA

Also known as the Spiny Anteater, the Short-beaked Echidna is covered with long, thick spines, intermixed with short hairs. It has a small head, no external neck, and a protruding snout, with electro-receptors that help it to detect its insect prey. Its long tongue of around 6¾ in (17 cm) is covered with fine barbs for trapping insects. The Short-beaked Echidna is active during the day and night. It becomes torpid in extremely hot or cold weather, its body temperature falling to 39° F (4° C).
• **SIZE** Body length:12–18 in (30–45 cm). Tail: ⅜ in (1 cm).
• **OCCURRENCE** Australia, Tasmania, and New Guinea.
In all habitats, except tropical and montane rain forest.
• **REMARK** Although it belongs to the most primitive order of mammals, it is the most widespread mammal in Australia.

AUSTRALIA,
TASMANIA,
NEW GUINEA

long, thick spines with shorter hairs • in between

thin, protruding snout

short limbs •

Social unit Solitary	Gestation 23 days	Young 1	Diet 🐜 〜

Family TACHYGLOSSIDAE	Species *Zaglossus bartoni*	Status Endangered

LONG-BEAKED ECHIDNA

A long, downward-curving snout, which may exceed 8 in (20 cm) in length, with a tiny mouth at its tip, gives this species its name. The white tips of its defensive spines are only just visible through the sleek black coat of this slow-moving animal, which curls itself into a ball during times of danger. This echidna is active both during the day and at night. Probing the earth for worms with its bill, it impales them with hooked spines at the tip of its long tongue and then swallows them. The female digs a burrow for her egg, but carries and suckles the hatched young in her pouch.
• **SIZE** Body length: 23½–39 in (60–100 cm). Tail: None.
• **OCCURRENCE** New Guinea. In montane forest and alpine grassland.
• **REMARK** This is the largest monotreme, or egg-laying mammal.

barely visible spines

downward curving snout

NEW GUINEA

Social unit Solitary	Gestation Not known	Young 1	Diet 🐜 🐛

Family ORNITHORHYNCHIDAE	Species *Ornithorhynchus anatinus*	Status Vulnerable*

PLATYPUS

A beak for its mouth, webbed feet, a flattened, scaly tail, and reptilelike gait make the Platypus a unique mammal. It has a velvety, plum-coloured, waterproof coat, and its probing beak senses waterborne electrical signals sent out by its small aquatic prey, which includes insect larvae, trout eggs, freshwater shrimp, and horsehair worms. The Platypus is nocturnal, but may be active during the day in winter. It makes its home in a branched tunnel in the riverbank, with nesting chambers lined with vegetation.
• **SIZE** Body length:16–23½ in (40–60 cm). Tail: 3¼–6 in (8.5–15 cm).
• **OCCURRENCE** E. Australia and Tasmania. In waterways of lightly forested or montane habitats.

beak-like snout

AUSTRALIA, TASMANIA

partially webbed hind feet

mammary glands

fully webbed forefeet

Social unit Solitary	Gestation 1 month	Young 1	Diet 🐛 🦐

MARSUPIALS

NAMED AFTER the marsupium, or pouch, of the adult female, the 292 species of marsupials are distinguished from other mammals by their method of reproduction. The young are born at a very early stage of development, after a short time in the womb. They have rudimentary limbs, closed eyes, and no fur. They can do little except crawl to the pouch or belly region of the mother. Here, they attach firmly to the nipples and feed on her milk, as they continue development for weeks or months. Gradually, they leave the pouch for longer periods to feed and fend for themselves.

Most marsupials live in Australia, having evolved without competition from other mammals, to take up many lifestyles and habitats. The 22 families have diversified into large grazing kangaroos, smaller wallabies, tiny leaping rat-kangaroos, arboreal and gliding possums, bear-shaped wombats, tunneling moles, fierce shrew- and cat-like carnivores, and many other types. Certain marsupial species are also found in New Guinea, including the tree-kangaroos. Around eighty species, mainly small tree-dwellers, are found in South America. One, the Virginia Opossum, has spread to North America.

Family DIDELPHIDAE	Species *Didelphis virginiana*	Status Lower risk*

VIRGINIA OPOSSUM

The largest of the American marsupials, the Virginia Opossum has succeeded in expanding its range rapidly in North America. It has benefited from human habitation both in terms of shelter – it nests in piles of debris or in outbuildings – and of food, since it scavenges on scraps. This nocturnal omnivore has a wide-ranging diet that includes grubs and eggs, flowers, fruits, and carrion, and it sometimes raids poultry or damages garden plants. When threatened, it may feign death or "play possum," sometimes for several hours. Varying from grey to red, brown, and black, it has white-tipped guard hair and thick underfur.
• **SIZE** Body length: 13– 20 in (33–50 cm). Tail:10–12 ½ in (25–54 cm).
• **OCCURRENCE** W., C., and E. USA, Mexico, and Central America. In grassland, and tropical and temperate forest.

unkempt appearance •

N. & C. AMERICA

pale, gray-white face •

five long-clawed toes on each foot •

• *hairless, partly prehensile tail*

Social unit Solitary	Gestation 12–13 days	Young 5–13	Diet

Family DIDELPHIDAE	Species *Chironectes minimus*	Status Lower risk

WATER OPOSSUM

The only aquatic marsupial, this opossum has fine, dense, water-repellent fur, and long, webbed toes on its rear feet. Both the male and the female have a pouch with a muscular opening that can be closed tightly underwater. Also called the Yapok, this nocturnal animal feeds on fish, frogs, and other freshwater prey, which it grasps using its dextrous, clawless front paws. During the day it rests in a leaf-lined den near water.

N., C., &
S. AMERICA

• **SIZE** Body length:10–16 in (26–40 cm).
Tail:12–17 in (31–43 cm).
• **OCCURRENCE** S. Mexico to C. South America. In tropical and temperate forest.

black and gray
• *patches on back*

black-masked •
face

stout tail with whitish
• *tip*

Social unit Solitary	Gestation 2 weeks	Young 2–5	Diet

Family DIDELPHIDAE	Species *Marmosa murina*	Status Lower risk*

MURINE MOUSE OPOSSUM

Pale buff to gray on its upperparts, this species has short, velvety fur which is creamy white below. It has a black face mask, prominent eyes, and erect ears. Its strongly prehensile tail is much longer than its head and body, and the female uses it to carry leaves from one place to another. The Murine Mouse Opossum is found near forest streams and human habitation, and feeds at night on insects, spiders, lizards, birds' eggs and chicks, and some fruits. A fast, lithe climber, it uses an old bird's nest, tree hole, or tangle of twigs among tree branches in which to shelter during the day.

S. AMERICA

• **SIZE** Body length:4 1/4–5 3/4 in (11–14.5 cm).
Tail:4 3/4–5 1/4 in (13.5–21 cm).
• **OCCURRENCE** N. and C. South America. In tropical forest and rain forest.

strongly
• *prehensile tail*

buff to gray
• *upperparts*

large eyes •

fine, velvety
fur

Social unit Solitary	Gestation 13 days	Young 5–10	Diet

Family DASYURIDAE	·	Species *Ningaui ridei*	Status Lower risk*

INLAND NINGAUI

Also known as the Wongai Ningaui, this shrew-like marsupial has a sharply conical head with small eyes and ears, and a coat that is uniformly brown, with an orange tinge on the cheeks and belly. It is a fierce predator of invertebrates less than ⅜in (1 cm) in size, such as beetles, crickets, and spiders, and hunts at night among clumps of spinifex (hummock grass), using its sharp senses of smell and hearing. By day it rests in thick undergrowth or the discarded holes of lizards and rodents.

AUSTRALIA

tail as long as body

rough brown coat

• **SIZE** Body length: 2–3in (5–7.5cm). Tail: 2–2¾in (5–7cm).
• **OCCURRENCE** C. Australia. In spinifex desert, with or without woodland cover.
• **REMARK** This species was identified by zoologists as late as 1975.

sharp, thin snout

Social unit Solitary	Gestation 13–21 days	Young 5–7	Diet 🐜

Family DASYURIDAE		Species *Sminthopsis crassicaudata*	Status Lower risk*

FAT-TAILED DUNNART

This small mammal has fawn or brown upperparts and white underparts, large eyes, upright ears, and a sharp, pointed nose. Its tail serves as a store for fat and becomes carrot-shaped as food intake increases. Once its food reserves are used up, the Fat-tailed Dunnart goes into torpor, sometimes for as long as 12 hours. It hunts at night on bare soil, or in leaf litter, pouncing upon prey and killing it with a bite on the neck, or subduing larger prey with a "death shake." Solitary during the summer breeding season, it may huddle in small groups in winter.

AUSTRALIA

large, upright ears

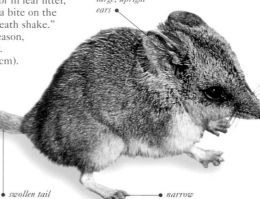

• **SIZE** Body length: 2¼ – 3½in (6–9cm). Tail:1½–2¾in (4–7cm).
• **OCCURRENCE** S. Australia, except the southwestern tip and eastern coast. In grassland, desert, farmland, and woodland.
• **REMARK** Since it prefers low, open vegetation, this is one native Australian mammal that has benefited from land clearing by European agricultural settlers.

swollen tail stores fat

narrow hindfeet

Social unit Solitary	Gestation 13 days	Young 8–10	Diet 🐜 🐛 🦗 🪳

Family DASYURIDAE	Species *Antechinomys laniger*	Status Vulnerable

KULTARR

The Kultarr moves with great speed and agility across woodland and semidesert scrub, leaping off its elongated hindfeet, but landing on its front feet. It is a small, fawn or brown marsupial with white underparts, very large eyes and ears, and a long, thin, tufted tail. Nocturnal by nature, it may dig shallow burrows or occupy crevices, or the dens of other animals. Like the Fat-tailed Dunnart (see opposite), it hunts by pouncing on its prey, giving a fatal bite on the neck.
• SIZE Body length: 2¾–4 in (7–10 cm). Tail: 4–6 in (10–15 cm).
• OCCURRENCE S. and C. Australia. In varied habitats from woodland and grassland, to desert.
• REMARK This is an elusive species: populations may appear in a spot and suddenly "disappear". The reason is unknown, but flooding of the animals' burrows during heavy rainfall may be a cause.

dark ring around eye •

AUSTRALIA

• *tufted tail*

Social unit Solitary	Gestation 12 days	Young 6–8	Diet 🌸 〰

Family DASYURIDAE	Species *Parantechinus apicalis*	Status Endangered

SOUTHERN DIBBLER

Rediscovered in 1967 after a gap of 80 years, this marsupial has a unique grizzled appearance, due to its white-flecked grayish brown fur. Clear white rings circle the eyes, and it has a white belly and a stout, hairy, tapering tail. This solitary forager hunts mainly invertebrates by day and night. However, its sharp canines also equip it to kill and eat small vertebrates, and it may sip nectar from *Banksia* flowers. Although mostly terrestrial, it can climb 6½–10 ft (2–3 m) up trees. It may dig its own burrow or occupy that of seabirds.
• SIZE Body length: 4–6½ in (10–16 cm). Tail: 3–4¾ in (7.5–12 cm).
• OCCURRENCE Southwestern tip of Australia, and Whitlock and Boullanger islands. In dense, coastal heath and shrubland, and *Banksia* forest.
• REMARK Among the island populations, in most years, all males die immediately after mating.

AUSTRALIA

white ring around eye •
stout, tapering, hairy tail •
pointed snout •

Social unit Solitary	Gestation 7 weeks	Young 8–10	Diet 🌸 🦎 🦴 🐀

Family DASYURIDAE	Species *Pseudantechinus macdonnellensis*	Status Lower risk*

FAT-TAILED PSEUDANTECHINUS

• *robust appearance*

reddish patches
• *behind ears*

Also known as the Red-eared Antechinus, this species has a carrot-shaped tail that swells with fat as a food store when it is wellfed. Grayish brown all over, it has red patches behind the ears, and a white-gray belly. The Fat-tailed Pseudantechinus is terrestrial and prefers rocky habitats with hummock grass and bushes. It is sometimes found in large termite mounds. Nocturnal by nature, it occasionally sunbathes in the morning near rocky shelters. It speedily pursues its prey and kills it with a bite on the neck, holding larger prey with its forepaws for an effective bite.

• **SIZE** Body length: 3¾–4¼ in (9.5–10.5 cm). Tail: 3–3¼ in (7.5–8.5 cm).

• OCCURRENCE W. and C. Australia. In rocky hills, grassland, and desert.

AUSTRALIA

Social unit Solitary	Gestation 45–55 days	Young 6	Diet 🐜 🦎

Family DASYURIDAE	Species *Dasycercus byrnei*	Status Vulnerable

KOWARI

A burrow-dwelling, nocturnal carnivore with a squirrel-like appearance, the Kowari is light fawn to gray on the back, lighter below, with a bushy black tail. Compact and powerfully built, it has a broad head with large eyes and erect ears. It expands its burrow after rain softens the hard, stony soil, and marks its home range with urine, feces, and chest gland scents.

• **SIZE** Body length: 5¼–7 in (13.5–18 cm). Tail: 4¼–5½ in (11–14 cm).

• OCCURRENCE C. Australia, especially "channel country" of Queensland and South Australia. In red clay desert.

broad, triangular
• *head*

fawn to gray
• *coat*

dense, bushy •
tail

AUSTRALIA

Social unit Solitary	Gestation 30–35 days	Young 6–7	Diet 🐜 🦎 🐍 🐁

Family DASYURIDAE	Species *Neophascogale lorentzii*	Status Lower risk*

SPECKLED DASYURE

Gray fur, sprinkled with long white hair, gives this species its name. It has short, powerful limbs with very long claws on all the digits, to enable it to excavate prey from soft soil, leaf litter, and rotting wood.

• **SIZE** Body length: 6½–9 in (17–22 cm). Tail: 6½–9 in (17–22 cm).

• **OCCURRENCE** New Guinea. In mixed, montane forest at high altitudes.

• **REMARK** This species is concentrated in pockets only; the reasons behind this uneven distribution are not known.

NEW GUINEA

long tail, tipped white

speckled gray and white fur

Social unit Solitary	Gestation Not known	Young 4	Diet 🐜

Family DASYURIDAE	Species *Dasyurus viverrinus*	Status Lower risk

EASTERN QUOLL

Sometimes called the Spotted Native Cat, this catlike marsupial is slim and agile, with a scattering of distinctive white spots on its brown or black body. It has a deep, narrow face, with large, erect ears. The tail is the same color as the body, but not spotted. The Eastern Quoll inhabits woody, shrubby, and grassy habitats, common in mixed agricultural areas. It hunts on the ground at night for large insects, small mammals, birds, and lizards, and also eats grasses, fruits, and carrion. The female is longer and 50 percent heavier than the male. She might bear as many as 20 young at a time, but since she has six teats in her pouch, only six offspring survive.

variable white spots on body

TASMANIA

long, erect ears

• **SIZE** Body length: 11–18 in (28–45 cm). Tail: 17–28 cm (6½–11 in).

• **OCCURRENCE** Tasmania. In forest, woodland, scrub, heath, and farmland.

• **REMARK** Previously found in S.E. Australia, the quoll was last sighted on the mainland near Sydney suburbs in the 1960s.

tail not spotted

Social unit Solitary	Gestation 3 weeks	Young 6	Diet 🐜🐀🐦🦎🌿🌱🐛

Family DASYURIDAE	Species *Sarcophilus linjarius*	Status Lower risk

TASMANIAN DEVIL

Found across Tasmania, particularly in the forests of the northeast, the "devil" has a compact black body like that of a small bear, with a white band on its chest and sometimes on its rump. This nocturnal hunter and scavenger feeds on animals of various sizes, and has sharp teeth and massive jaws for masticating the bones of its prey.

TASMANIA

• **SIZE** Body length: 20½–32 in (52–80 cm). Tail: 9–12 in (23–30 cm).
• **OCCURRENCE** Tasmania. In all major habitats, including urban areas.
• **REMARK** This is the largest marsupial carnivore.

sparsely haired, erect ears

powerful jaws

Social unit Solitary	Gestation 30–31 days	Young 4	Diet

Family MYRMECOBIIDAE	Species *Myrmecobius fasciatus*	Status Vulnerable

NUMBAT

darker fur on rump   *narrow head*

Now found only in the extreme southwest tip of Australia, the Numbat has orange-brown body fur with six or seven white transverse bars from behind the shoulder to its rump, which has darker fur. Its narrow head has a dark stripe running along each large eye. Also known as the Banded Anteater, it feeds almost exclusively on termites, using its strong claws to dig for them, and licking them up with its 4 in (10 cm) long tongue.
• **SIZE** Body length: 20–28 cm (8–11 in). Tail: 16–21 cm (6½–8½ in).
• **OCCURRENCE** W. Australia. In eucalypt forest and woodland.

• **REMARK** The Numbat has 52 teeth, more than any other land mammal.

AUSTRALIA

Social unit Solitary	Gestation 14 days	Young 4	Diet

Family PERAMELIDAE	Species *Perameles gunnii*	Status Critically endangered

EASTERN BARRED BANDICOOT

white bands on hindquarters •
• tall, erect ears

Virtually extinct in the wild in Western
Australia, this species is now found mainly
in Tasmania. It has rabbitlike ears and broad
whitish bands across its hindquarters. Resting
by day, it forages alone at night.

AUSTRALIA,
TASMANIA

• **SIZE** Body length:
10½–14 in (27–35 cm).
Tail: 2¾–4¼ in (7–11cm).
• **OCCURRENCE**
Australia and Tasmania. In
open grassland and wooded
urban areas.

Social unit Solitary	Gestation 12.5 days	Young 1–5	Diet

Family PERAMELIDAE	Species *Macrotis lagotis*	Status Vulnerable

BILBY

huge, slightly
furry ears •
• blue-grey fur

Also known as the Rabbit-eared Bandicoot,
this species has huge ears, long hind feet, and
a tricolored tail: gray, black, and white.
A powerful digger, it has an excellent sense of
hearing and of smell, and hunts only after dark.
• **SIZE** Body length:12–22 in (30–55 cm).
Tail: 6–11½ in (20–29 cm).

AUSTRALIA

• **OCCURRENCE** N.W.
Australia. In open grassland
and desert.
• **REMARK** The males are
more bulky than females and
may be twice as heavy.

Social unit Solitary	Gestation 13–16 days	Young 2	Diet

Family PERORYCTIDAE	Species *Echymipera kalubu*	Status Lower risk

KALIBU ECHYMIPERA

• stiff hairs on back

Extremely variable in color and size, this bandicoot
may be brown, copper, yellow, or black, with buff
underparts. It has a conical snout, hairless tail,
and spiny hairs. This nocturnal species is
mostly insectivorous, but also eats fruits.
• **SIZE** Length: 8–20 in (20–50 cm).
Tail: 2–5 in (5–12.5 cm).

• naked ears

NEW GUINEA

• **OCCURRENCE**
New Guinea. In
grassland and forest.

elongated, conical •
snout

Social unit Solitary	Gestation 14 days	Young 1–3	Diet

Family NOTORYCTIDAE	Species *Notoryctes typhlops*	Status Endangered

MARSUPIAL MOLE

This small, elusive mammal is well-adapted to its burrowing way of life. Probing with its horny nose, it scoops aside sand with its spade-like foreclaws and kicks it back with its hindfeet. It makes tunnels down to 2.5 m (8 ft) in the desert soil, or simply "swims" through loose sand, grubbing for something to eat. Its silky coat is off-white to cinnamon, stained a dark red in iron-rich areas, and its eyes are reduced to vestigial lenses. The female's pouch opens backwards, so as not to fill up with sand.
• SIZE Length: 12–18 cm (4¾–7 in). Weight: 40–70 g (1½–2½ oz).
• OCCURRENCE S.W. and S. Australia. In sandy desert.

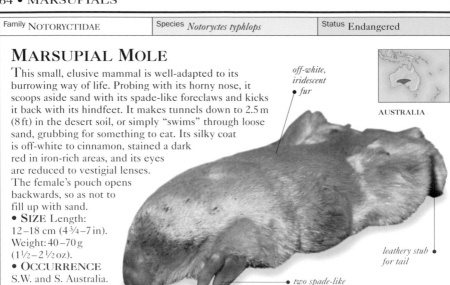

off-white, iridescent fur

AUSTRALIA

leathery stub for tail

two spade-like foreclaws

Social unit Solitary	Gestation Not known	Young 1–2	Diet 🐜 〰 🍄

Family VOMBATIDAE	Species *Vombatus ursinus*	Status Lower risk*

COMMON WOMBAT

Like a small bear in appearance, the Common Wombat is a prolific digger and makes a single-exit tunnel up to 200 m (655 ft) long. It emerges at night to graze on slopes above creeks and valleys, and in winter it may sunbathe at dawn and dusk. A powerful body, broad head, stocky limbs, and flattened claws equip it for burrowing.
• SIZE Length: 70–120 cm (28–47 in). Weight: 25–40 kg (55–88 lb).
• OCCURRENCE E. Australia and Tasmania. In forest, coastal scrub, and Australian alpine heathland.

lighter fur on back

AUSTRALIA

compact, robust frame

Social unit Solitary	Gestation 33 days	Young 1	Diet 🌱 🍃 🌾

Family PHASCOLARCTIDAE	Species *Phascolarctos cinereus*	Status Lower risk

KOALA

Living and feeding almost totally in eucalyptus trees, the Koala
occasionally descends to change perches or aid digestion by eating gravel.
It has a uniquely adapted liver that can break down the toxic substances
in eucalypt leaves – its only food. With a compact body and large head, it
has a woolly, greyish brown coat that is whitish on the neck and chest,
and mottled at the rump. Koalas bellow at each other during the mating
season, and dominant males mate more often than the
junior ones. The single young of this marsupial "bear"
is suckled in the pouch for six
months and then clings
to the mother's back
until it is a year old.
This species has
few natural
enemies, apart
from raptors, but
forest clearance poses
a man-made threat.
• SIZE Length:
65–82 cm (26–32 in).
Weight: 4–15 kg (8¾–33 lb).
• OCCURRENCE E. Australia.
In eucalypt forest and woodland
below 1,000 m (3,300 ft).
• REMARK The Koala feeds
for four hours each night, but is
inactive for the rest of the day.

AUSTRALIA

*large, round,
white-tufted
• ears*

smooth black muzzle •

soft, long fur •

SEDENTARY LIFESTYLE
The Koala wedges itself in the
fork of a tree and dozes for long
periods. The first two toes on its
forefeet are opposing, allowing a
pincer-like grip of thin branches.

*short, powerful •
limbs*

Social unit Solitary	Gestation 35 days	Young 1	Diet 🍃

| Family PHALANGERIDAE | Species *Phalanger orientalis* | Status Lower risk |

COMMON CUSCUS

The color of this animal varies from white to black across its range of many small islands. Generally, however, it has a dark stripe along its back, and the lower part of the female's tail is hairless and tipped white. Resembling a combination of a sloth and a monkey, this nocturnal species is a deliberate, but agile climber with strong, grasping digits. Its tail is prehensile with a rough underside.
• **SIZE** Body length:15–19 in (38–48 cm). Tail:11–17 in (28–43 cm).
• **OCCURRENCE** New Guinea, Solomon Islands, and surrounding smaller islands. In forest.

dark stripe along back
white-tipped tail in female

• **REMARK** The docile Cuscus is a popular pet among the local population.

NEW GUINEA,
SOLOMON
ISLANDS

pointed face with large eyes

| Social unit Solitary | Gestation 2–3 weeks | Young 1–2 | Diet |

| Family PHALANGERIDAE | Species *Trichosurus vulpecula* | Status Lower risk |

SILVER-GRAY BRUSH-TAIL POSSUM

A familiar animal found in many habitats, this possum is generally silver-gray, with shorter fur tinged coppery-red in the north of its range, and longer, dark gray to black fur in the south. It bounds and climbs with ease, foraging at night in trees, using its forepaws to manipulate food. A vocal animal, it hisses, chitters, grunts, and growls, and chatters its teeth when startled. The Brush-tail Possum nests in tree hollows, fallen logs, rock piles, holes in creek banks, or roofs. Both sexes maintain exclusive areas around their nest sites, although the male may live with the female for a short while during the mating season.
• **SIZE** Body length:14–23 in (35–58 cm). Tail:10–16 in (25–40 cm).
• **OCCURRENCE** Australia and Tasmania. In all habitats with tree cover, and suburban parks and gardens.
• **REMARK** Once found all over Australia, this possum now has a much reduced range.

erect, long, naked ears

sharp, curved claws

gripping digits

tail darker than body

AUSTRALIA,
TASMANIA

| Social unit Solitary | Gestation 16–18 days | Young 1 | Diet |

Family PETAURIDAE	Species *Gymnobelideus leadbeateri*	Status Endangered

LEADBEATER'S POSSUM

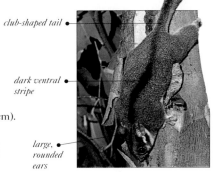

club-shaped tail •

Gray with a dark stripe along its back, the Leadbeater's Possum is a speedy and elusive nocturnal species that forages in trees for small insects, resin, sap, and nectar. Colonies of up to eight comprise a breeding pair and its offspring. The females defend the group's territory.

dark ventral • *stripe*

• **SIZE** Body length:6–7in (15–17cm). Tail: 6–8in (14.5–20cm).
• **OCCURRENCE** Australia (Victoria). In montane ash forest.
• **REMARK** It was rediscovered in 1961 after 52 years.

AUSTRALIA

large, rounded ears •

Social unit Social	Gestation 20 days	Young 1–2	Diet 🐜 ✹

Family PETAURIDAE	Species *Dactylopsila trivirgata*	Status Lower risk

STRIPED POSSUM

slender body •

Conspicuous, skunklike stripes, and a bushy, white-tipped tail are the chief features of this small nocturnal possum. Like the skunk (see pp. 256–257), it can also emit a foul odor from its anal glands. Slender-bodied and agile, it has long fingers and strong claws for gripping, and an elongated fourth digit that it uses to probe branches for insects, ants, and termites.

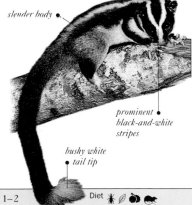

prominent • *black-and-white stripes*

• **SIZE** Body length: 9½–11in (24–28cm). Tail:12–15½in (31–39cm).
• **OCCURRENCE** New Guinea and N.E. Australia. In rain forest.

AUSTRALIA, NEW GUINEA

bushy white • *tail tip*

Social unit Variable	Gestation Not known	Young 1–2	Diet 🐜 ✏ 🐚 🐀

Family PETAURIDAE	Species *Petaurus norfolcensis*	Status Lower risk

SQUIRREL GLIDER

black stripe on head •

whitish • *belly*

A furry gliding membrane, extending from the fifth front toe to the back foot, and a bushy tail used as a rudder allow this squirrel to parachute over distances of 165ft (50m). Blue-grey to brown-gray on the back, and creamy white below, it has a dark stripe on its head, and erect, hairless ears. Highly active, agile, and speedy, it has strong, sharply clawed digits for climbing. The nocturnal Squirrel Glider lives in a leaf-lined nest in a tree hollow. It feeds on nectar and pollen, and strips bark with its incisors to eat resin and larvae.

long and • *pointed face*

• **SIZE** Body length:7–9in (18–23cm). Tail: 9–12in (22–30cm).
• **OCCURRENCE** Australia (N.E. Queensland to C. Victoria). In eucalypt and coastal forest.

AUSTRALIA

furry, prehensile • *tail*

Social unit Social	Gestation 20 days	Young 1–2	Diet 🐜 ✹

Family PSEUDOCHEIRIDAE	Species *Pseudocheirus peregrinus*	Status Lower risk

QUEENSLAND RINGTAIL

Adapted to lead a life in the trees, the Queensland Ringtail has sharp molars to chew its leafy diet, a large intestine that efficiently breaks down plant fiber, a strongly prehensile tail that is naked and rough on the last third of its underside, and forefeet with two opposing first digits to allow a strong grip of branches. Its coat is rufous, gray, or dark brown-gray, and its small ears have white patches behind them. Feeding at night on tender leaves, it savors eucalyptus, acacia, tea tree, and paperbark. In the north of its range it nests in a tree hole, while in the south it makes a squirrel-like drey or spherical nest of twigs, bark, and grass.

white patches behind ears

- **SIZE** Body length:12–14 in (30–35 cm). Tail:12–14 in (30–35 cm).
- **OCCURRENCE** E. Australia and Tasmania. In forest, thickets, coastal scrub, and suburban parks and gardens.
- **REMARK** The male helps care for the young by carrying them on its back, watching over them in the nest, and feeding them – a rare occurrence among marsupials.

AUSTRALIA, TASMANIA

first half of tail dark

white tail tip

Social unit Social	Gestation Up to 30 days	Young 1–3	Diet

Family PSEUDOCHEIRIDAE	Species *Petauroides volans*	Status Lower risk

GREATER GLIDER

charcoal-gray coat

This highly arboreal marsupial can glide over distances of 330 ft (100 m) by spreading out the furred gliding membrane between its elbows and rear feet. Trees used as a landing pad by this animal have regular scratch marks created by its sharp claws, which help it to grip bark. The large ears and eyes of this nocturnal species face the front, so that it can judge distances accurately in the dark, with the help of stereophonic hearing and stereoscopic vision. The Greater Glider occurs in two color forms: one is charcoal-black to gray, tinged with brown (seen here), while the other is pale gray or mottled cream. Male–female pairs share the same den in a tree hollow. The offspring stays in the mother's pouch for five months and then spends two more months in the den or riding on the mother's back. By ten months, the male offspring is driven out of the den by the father, while female young remain with the mother for another year.

gliding membrane

- **SIZE** Body length:14–19 in (35–48 cm). Tail:18–23½ in (45–60 cm).
- **OCCURRENCE** E. Australia. In forest dominated by eucalypt species.

AUSTRALIA

- **REMARK** This is the largest gliding marsupial.

enormous tail used for steering during glides

Social unit Pair	Gestation Not known	Young 1	Diet

Family TARSIPEDIDAE	Species *Tarsipes rostratus*	Status Lower risk

HONEY POSSUM

Living wholly on a diet of nectar and pollen, the Honey Possum is a tiny, nocturnal animal with a bristle-tipped tongue, a pointed snout, and long, prehensile tail. Its toes have padded tips and sharp claws to grip bark and glossy leaves.
• SIZE Body length: 2½–3½ in (6.5–9 cm). Tail: 2¾–4¼ in (7–10.5 cm).
• OCCURRENCE S.W. Australia. In sandy heathland and tropical woodland.
• REMARK This is one of the smallest possums.

AUSTRALIA

dark dorsal stripe

long, thin snout

Social unit Social	Gestation 21–28 days	Young 1–4	Diet ✳

Family ACROBATIDAE	Species *Distoechurus pennatus*	Status Lower risk

FEATHERTAIL POSSUM

Identified by its white face with four black stripes, and a quill-like, prehensile tail, this nocturnal possum darts across branches, gripping them with its sharp claws, trapping cicadas. It has a sixth pad on its hind feet, a feature shared only with the Pygmy Glider (see below).
• SIZE Body length: 4½–5½ in (10.5–13.5 cm). Tail: 5–6½ in (12.5–15.5 cm).
• OCCURRENCE New Guinea. In rain forest, lower mossy forest, and regenerating forest near villages.

NEW GUINEA

light brown to gray fur

slender, quill-like tail

black eye stripes

Social unit Social	Gestation Not known	Young 1–2	Diet 🦗 🌿 ✳

Family ACROBATIDAE	Species *Acrobates pygmaeus*	Status Lower risk

FEATHERTAIL GLIDER

Also called the Pygmy Glider, this tiny, nocturnal marsupial has a bristled tail that it uses as a rudder. Its gliding membrane extends between its front and rear limbs, and its toes have sharp claws to dig into bark with, and padded tips that allow it to grip smooth and shiny surfaces.
• SIZE Body length: 2¾–3 in (6.5–8 cm). Tail: 2¾–3 in (7–8 cm).
• OCCURRENCE E. Australia. In forest from sea level to 5,000 ft (1,400 m).
• REMARK This is the smallest gliding marsupial.

AUSTRALIA

long, bristled tail

forward-facing eyes

Social unit Social	Gestation Not known	Young 1–4	Diet 🦗 ✳

Family BURRAMYIDAE	Species *Cercartetus lepidus*	Status Lower risk*

LITTLE PYGMY POSSUM

This is the only pygmy possum with a gray underside; the upperparts are fawn or brown. It has a blunt face and large, erect ears, and can hang from its prehensile tail, which stores excess food as fat at its base. It feeds at night in low bushes or on the ground.

prominent, large,
• erect ears   *short, blunt face •*

- **SIZE** Body length: 2–2¾ in (5–6.5 cm). Tail: 2½–3 in (6–7.5 cm).
- **OCCURRENCE** S.E. Australia and Tasmania. In all wooded habitats, except rain forest.
- **REMARK** This is the smallest possum species.

AUSTRALIA, TASMANIA

Social unit Solitary	Gestation 30–51 days	Young 3–4	Diet

Family POTOROIDAE	Species *Hypsiprymnodon moschatus*	Status Lower risk

MUSKY RAT KANGAROO

Bounding along on all fours, this potoroid marsupial (see below) is medium chocolate-brown above and lighter below, with five-toed hind feet. Both sexes emit a musky odor during breeding.

slender head with   *long scaly •*
• large eyes   *tail*

- **SIZE** Body length: 6½–11 in (16–28 cm). Tail: 4¾–7 in (12–17 cm).
- **OCCURRENCE** N.E. Queensland. In dense rain forest.
- **REMARK** Unusually for a marsupial, it hoards excess food.

AUSTRALIA

Social unit Solitary	Gestation Not known	Young 2	Diet

Family POTOROIDAE	Species *Potorous longipes*	Status Endangered

LONG-FOOTED POTOROO

Resembling a combination of a rat and a kangaroo, this potoroo bounds on its back feet and scrabbles for food using its short forelimbs with strong claws. A nocturnal fungus-eater, it digs conical pits for food and helps disperse fungi spores.

brown-gray
dorsal fur •

- **SIZE** Body length: 15–16½ in (38–42 cm). Tail: 12–13 in (31–33 cm).
- **OCCURRENCE** S.E. Australia. In temperate rain forest.

long,
stout
tail

AUSTRALIA

Social unit Solitary	Gestation 38 days	Young 1	Diet

Family POTOROIDAE	Species *Bettongia penicillata*	Status Lower risk

BRUSH-TAILED BETTONG

A fungus-eater like the potoroos (see opposite), the Brush-tailed Bettong is pale to orange-gray above and pale gray below. Its long tail has a black crest on the upperside and is used for carrying nesting material. When disturbed, this bettong bounds at high speed with its head down, and tail held out straight, with the crest raised. A nocturnal forager, it scrapes up woodland soil to find fungi, and by day it shelters in a domed nest made of bark, leaves, and grass.
• **SIZE** Body length:12–15 in (30–38 cm). Tail:11½–14 in (29–36 cm).
• **OCCURRENCE** S.W. Australia. In open forest and woodland.

AUSTRALIA

pale gray to orange-gray coat

large black eyes

tail as long as body

Social unit Solitary	Gestation 21 days	Young 1	Diet 🌱 🐛 🪱 ⬤⬤

Family MACROPODIDAE	Species *Petrogale penicillata*	Status Vulnerable

BRUSH-TAILED ROCK WALLABY

Adapted for leaping and scrambling over rocky surfaces, the Brush-tailed Rock Wallaby can leap as high as 13 ft (4 m), and has specially padded, rough soles on its hind feet for excellent grip. Its coat is medium to dark brown on the back, grayer on the shoulders, and reddish on the flanks and rump; its feet and bushy tail tip are black or dark brown. Feeding by night, it rests in cool rock crevices in the day.
• **SIZE** Body length: 20–23½ in (50–60 cm). Tail: 20–28 in (50–70 cm).
• **OCCURRENCE** S.E. Australia. Introduced in New Zealand and Hawaii. In rocky forest.
• **REMARK** Once abundant, this species saw a rapid decline in the early twentieth century as it was killed for its fur and was also perceived as an agricultural pest. Many populations now comprise only 10–12 animals, indicating future declines.

pale stripes on cheeks

mid to dark brown fur

feet black or dark brown

AUSTRALIA

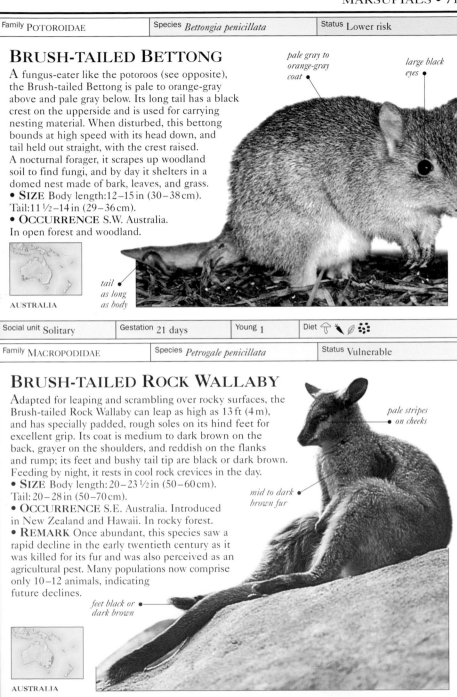

Social unit Social	Gestation 30–32 days	Young 1	Diet 🍃 🌱 🐚

Family MACROPODIDAE	Species *Lagorchestes conspicillatus*	Status Lower risk

SPECTACLED HARE-WALLABY

white guard hair •

Adapted to its arid habitat in various ways, this white-grizzled gray-brown wallaby uses the least amount of water of any mammal its size. It hardly drinks, does not sweat or pant unless the temperature is above 86°F (30°C), and produces concentrated urine. The orange eye-patches give it the name Spectacled Hare-wallaby. It nibbles grass or leaves at night, burrowing under large clumps of spinifex.

• **SIZE** Body length:16–19in (40–48cm). Tail:14½–20in (37–50cm).
• **OCCURRENCE** N. Australia. In tropical grassland, open forest, and woodland.

orange • *eye-patches*

AUSTRALIA

gray-brown coat •

Social unit Solitary	Gestation 29–31 days	Young 1	Diet 🍃 🌿

Family MACROPODIDAE	Species *Thylogale stigmatica*	Status Lower risk

RED-LEGGED PADEMELON

ears reddish brown *at base* •

With a compact body, slender head, and long, erect ears, the Red-legged Pademelon (a type of small wallaby) tends to be brown-gray in rain forest, but paler fawn in open woodland. Active both by day and night, it is usually solitary, but may gather in groups to feed. Often living on the forest edge, it depends on leaf cover for protection from predators, such as Dingoes, Tiger Quolls, and large pythons. When threatened, it gives a loud alarm thump with its hind feet and flees rapidly for shelter under dense cover.

compact body •

• **SIZE** Body length:15–23in (38–58cm). Tail:12–18½in (30–47cm).
• **OCCURRENCE** N. and E. Australia, and New Guinea. In rain forest, mixed savanna and woodland, and open forest.

AUSTRALIA, NEW GUINEA

thick tail •

Social unit Solitary	Gestation 20–30 days	Young 1	Diet 🌿 🍎 🍃 ⦂

| Family MACROPODIDAE | Species *Setonix brachyurus* | Status Vulnerable |

QUOKKA

reddish facial fur

This marsupial has a compact, rounded body and coarse brown fur tinged red around the face and neck. Very rare in mainland Australia, the Quokka survives on the Rottnest and Bald Islands off the southwest coast, where introduced predators such as foxes are absent. These wallabies are often harmed when tourists feed them inappropriate food.

dense brown coat

- **SIZE** Body length: 16–21½in (40–54cm). Tail:10–14in (25–35cm).
- **OCCURRENCE** S.W. Australia. In temperate forest.

AUSTRALIA

| Social unit Social | Gestation 27 days | Young 1 | Diet |

| Family MACROPODIDAE | Species *Wallabia bicolor* | Status Lower risk |

SWAMP WALLABY

blackish face

brown to black fur

Also referred to as the Stinker or Black Wallaby, this brown-black species has a much darker face, snout, and feet, and the blackish tail is often white-tipped. It has an unusual loping gait with its head held low and tail straight behind. It feeds at night on a wide-ranging diet of plant matter, including toxic plants such as hemlock. The Dingo and Red Fox are its enemies.

- **SIZE** Body length: 26–34in (66–85cm). Tail: 26–34in (65–86cm).
- **OCCURRENCE** E. Australia. In tropical and temperate forest.

dark tail

AUSTRALIA

| Social unit Solitary | Gestation 33–38 days | Young 1 | Diet |

| Family MACROPODIDAE | Species *Macropus robustus* | Status Lower risk |

HILL WALLAROO

lightly furred ears

shaggier fur than other kangaroos

This dark gray to reddish brown wallaby is found in a range of habitats, but prefers rocky outcrops, cliffs, and boulder piles. It shelters there by day, moving by late afternoon to forage on grasses and other kinds of leaves. Also called the Euro or Hill Kangaroo, it resembles other brown wallabies, but its posture, with shoulders, back, and elbows together, and wrists raised, is distinctive.

nostrils bare and black

- **SIZE** Body length: 2½–4½ft (0.8–1.4m). Tail: 23½–35in (60–90cm).
- **OCCURRENCE** Almost all of Australia. In grassland, desert, and tropical and temperate forest.

AUSTRALIA

| Social unit Solitary | Gestation 32–34 days | Young 1 | Diet |

Family MACROPODIDAE	Species *Macropus fuliginosus*	Status Lower risk

WESTERN GRAY KANGAROO

This species is one of the largest and most abundant of kangaroos, and has thick, coarse fur which varies from light gray-brown to chocolate brown, with a dark brown to black muzzle, and a paler chest and belly. Powerfully built, it has a strong and tapering tail. The Western Gray Kangaroo lives in stable groups of 2–15, whose members recognize one another through smell. The male kangaroo has an especially distinctive body odor and is about twice the size of the female. Aggressive during the mating season, males fight each other for females, also battling for food and resting sites. Antagonists lock arms and attempt to push each other over, and may also lean back on their tails to kick with their rear feet. This species grazes at night, usually feeding on grasses, it also browses on shrubs and low trees.

AUSTRALIA

*light gray-brown
to chocolate
brown body*

- **SIZE** Body length: 3–4½ ft (0.9–1.4 m). Tail: 30–39 in (75–100 cm).
- **OCCURRENCE** S. Australia.
In open forest, woodland, shrubland, wet and dry heathland, and grassy savanna.
- **REMARK** This species is culled since it is regarded as an agricultural pest. It is also hunted for its meat and skin.

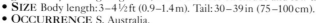

large ears

*finely haired, dark
brown to black muzzle*

Social unit Social	Gestation 30–31 days	Young 1	Diet 🌿

powerful tail

thick, coarse hair

powerfully built body

shorter forefeet

POWERFUL MOVER
This kangaroo lopes
rabbitlike when
moving slowly, using
all four limbs, with the tail as a
brace. However, it bounds swiftly
on its hind feet over longer distances,
and the male covers as much as
33 ft (10 m) in one leap.

CARRYING THE YOUNG
The young, or joey, of the
Western Gray Kangaroo
remains attached to the
teat in its mother's pouch
for 130–150 days. It leaves
the safety of the pouch
for short periods once it
is about 250 days old,
but returns quickly
when threatened by
predators – usually
dingoes or large
birds such as wedge-
tailed eagles.

joey in mother's pouch

long, tapering tail

Family MACROPODIDAE	Species *Macropus parma*	Status Lower risk

PARMA WALLABY

The smallest member of its genus, this red- or gray-brown wallaby
is characterized by a black stripe in the center of its back, and a white
stripe on each cheek. It has erect, rounded ears, shorter than those of
most wallabies, and a white throat and belly. The male is slightly
heavier than the female, with a broader chest and stronger forelimbs.
This solitary and reclusive animal remains camouflaged in dense
undergrowth by day and feeds at night, grazing and browsing on a wide
range of plants, under cover of vegetation or with its head held low to
the ground. Its existence is adversely affected by forest clearance and
the burning of forest floors.
• **SIZE** Body length:18–21 in (45–53 cm). Tail:16–21 ½ in (41–54 cm).
• **OCCURRENCE** E. New South Wales; introduced
to Kawan Island, New Zealand. In eucalyptus forest
and rain forest, with dense undergrowth.
• **REMARK** Believed to be extinct for about a
century, the Parma Wallaby was "rediscovered" on
Kawan Island, New Zealand, in
1965 and on the Australian
mainland in 1967.

AUSTRALIA

*erect, rounded •
ears*

*• white stripe
along cheeks*

*red or gray-brown
• fur on back*

RESTING ON ITS HAUNCHES
The Parma Wallaby seldom lies down and
usually rests by sitting with its tail
between its legs. When hopping, its body
is held horizontally close to the ground,
with forepaws folded against its chest.

*long, muscular
tail •*

Social unit Solitary	Gestation 34–35 days	Young 1	Diet

Family MACROPODIDAE	Species *Macropus rufus*	Status Common

RED KANGAROO

The largest living marsupial, the Red Kangaroo is found over much of Australia. Its population varies greatly from year to year. When rainfall is high, numbers may reach 12 million, falling to less than half this figure during drought. Females will not conceive if food is scarce due to lack of rain, and in prolonged drought, males do not produce sperm. Red Kangaroos live in groups of 2–10, with a single dominant male, although up to 1,500 kangaroos may gather at a water hole in dry conditions. A kangaroo warns its group members of danger by stamping its foot or thumping its tail. The group then flees, in short bursts of speed reaching 30 mph (50 kph). This kangaroo is nocturnal but it may sometimes forage in the early morning or late afternoon.
• **SIZE** Body length: 3¼–5¼ ft (1–1.6 m).
Tail: 30–47 in (75–120 cm).
• **OCCURRENCE** Australia. In savanna grassland, desert, and temperate forest.
• **REMARK** Regarded as a pest in Australia, the Red Kangaroo is hunted widely for its meat and skin.

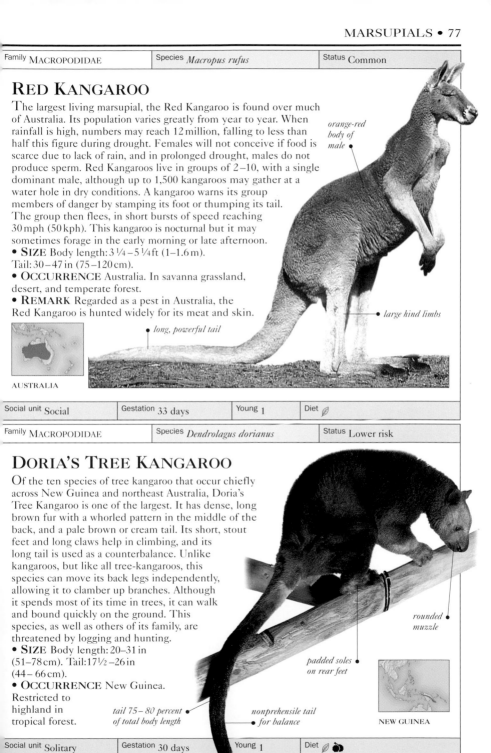

orange-red body of male

large hind limbs

long, powerful tail

AUSTRALIA

Social unit Social	Gestation 33 days	Young 1	Diet 🍃

Family MACROPODIDAE	Species *Dendrolagus dorianus*	Status Lower risk

DORIA'S TREE KANGAROO

Of the ten species of tree kangaroo that occur chiefly across New Guinea and northeast Australia, Doria's Tree Kangaroo is one of the largest. It has dense, long brown fur with a whorled pattern in the middle of the back, and a pale brown or cream tail. Its short, stout feet and long claws help in climbing, and its long tail is used as a counterbalance. Unlike kangaroos, but like all tree-kangaroos, this species can move its back legs independently, allowing it to clamber up branches. Although it spends most of its time in trees, it can walk and bound quickly on the ground. This species, as well as others of its family, are threatened by logging and hunting.
• **SIZE** Body length: 20–31 in (51–78 cm). Tail: 17½–26 in (44–66 cm).
• **OCCURRENCE** New Guinea. Restricted to highland in tropical forest.

rounded muzzle

padded soles on rear feet

tail 75–80 percent of total body length

nonprehensile tail for balance

NEW GUINEA

Social unit Solitary	Gestation 30 days	Young 1	Diet 🍃 🫐

INSECTIVORES

DESPITE THEIR NAME, insectivores do not restrict their diet to insects, but also eat other small prey such as worms, spiders, and slugs. Nor are they the only animals to eat insects – many other mammal species do too. There are 365 insectivores, in six families, and they have much in common. They are mostly small, nocturnal, and they retain anatomical features shown by their ancient ancestors, the early mammals. These include up to 48 simple teeth; a small brain compared to body size, with few surface folds; and in the male, testes that stay in the abdomen. An insectivore's eyes and ears are small, but the snout is elongated, flexible, and very sensitive. There are five clawed toes on each foot and, usually, a medium-length tail.

Insectivores follow three main lifestyles. Shrews, hedgehogs, moonrats (gymnures), tenrecs, and solenodons are terrestrial, busily foraging for small creatures at night and perhaps by day too. Moles and golden moles are burrowers, spending most of their lives tunnelling in search of soil insects, worms, and grubs. Web-footed tenrecs, water shrews, otter-shrews, and desmans are semi-aquatic and catch a variety of water creatures including fish and frogs.

Various types of hedgehogs, moonrats, shrew-moles, and especially shrews are widespread in many parts of the world. However, three insectivore families are more localized. These are solenodons on the Caribbean islands of Cuba and Hispaniola, tenrecs in Madagascar and equatorial Africa, and golden moles in Africa, south of the Sahara.

Family ERINACEIDAE	Species *Erinaceus europaeus*	Status Common

WESTERN EUROPEAN HEDGEHOG

Roaming urban parks, gardens, hedgerows, fields, and woods at night, the Western European Hedgehog snuffles, hoglike, for worms, insects, birds' eggs, and carrion. By day, it shelters in a nest of grass and leaves under a bush, log, or outbuilding, or in an old burrow. Its rotund body is covered with short, pointed spines, except for the head, undersides, and limbs. Uniformly gray-brown in color, it has small ears and a short tail. In defense, the Western European Hedgehog tucks its head and legs into its belly and curls itself into a spiny ball. It can also run or climb with surprising agility.
• **SIZE** Body length: 9 –10 ½ in (22 – 27 cm). Tail: None.
• **OCCURRENCE** W. Europe to C. Scandinavia, N. Russia, and Siberia.
• **REMARK** The spines appear on a newborn hedgehog within hours of its birth.

short spines on back

uniform gray-brown coat

EUROPE

Social unit Solitary	Gestation 31– 35 days	Young 4 – 6	Diet 🐜 ●

Family ERINACEIDAE	Species *Hemiechinus auritus*	Status Locally common

LONG-EARED HEDGEHOG

• *banded spines*

long ears •

This desert hedgehog has black, brown, yellow, or white bands on its spines, and coarse fur on its whitish face, limbs, and belly. Its long ears help radiate heat, and it can survive in dry habitats for long periods without food or water.
• **SIZE** Body length: 6–10½ in (15–27 cm).
Tail: ⅜–2 in (1–5 cm).
• **OCCURRENCE** Ukraine to Mongolia; Libya to Pakistan. In steppe and arid habitats.
• **REMARK** It may hibernate in summer if food is scarce.

AFRICA, ASIA

Social unit Solitary	Gestation 35–42 days	Young 1–6	Diet 🐛 ● 🐌 ⠿

Family ERINACEIDAE	Species *Echinosorex gymnura*	Status Lower risk*

MOONRAT

black, gray, and white
• *streaks on coat*

rough, coarse
• *outer fur*

Looking like a mix between a hedgehog and a small pig, the Moonrat has rough, spiky fur and a long scaly tail. A nocturnal hunter, it forages for prey and swims for fish and crustaceans. Its territory-marking scent smells of rotten onions.
• **SIZE** Body length: 10–18 in (26–46 cm).
Tail: 6½–12 in (16–30 cm).
• **OCCURRENCE** S.E. Asia. In lowland tropical forest, often near water.

ASIA

Social unit Solitary	Gestation 35–40 days	Young 2	Diet 🦐 🐛 🦗 🐟 🪱

Family SOLENODONTIDAE	Species *Solenodon paradoxus*	Status Endangered

HISPANIOLAN SOLENODON

Fast and agile, the Hispaniolan Solenodon scrabbles on the forest floor for prey, sniffing it out with its long, mobile snout and stunning it with a poisonous bite, which it also uses for defence. This shrewlike, nocturnal insectivore varies from black to reddish brown, and its feet, long tail, and ear tips are almost hairless.

reddish brown coat

CARIBBEAN

• **SIZE** Body length: 11–12½ in (28–32 cm).
Tail: 6½–10 in (17–26 cm).
• **OCCURRENCE** Dominican Republic as well as Haiti. In forest and shrubland.
• **REMARK** There are two species of solenodon: Hispaniolan and Cuban. Both are endangered.

almost hairless,
• *long tail*

Social unit Solitary	Gestation Not known	Young 1–3	Diet 🐛 🦂 🐌 🍃

Family TENRECIDAE	Species *Tenrec ecaudatus*	Status Common

TAILLESS TENREC

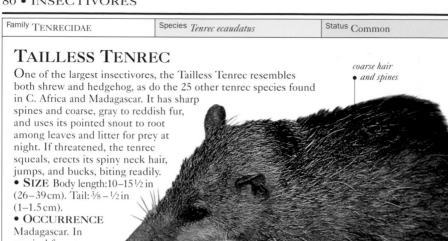

One of the largest insectivores, the Tailless Tenrec resembles
both shrew and hedgehog, as do the 25 other tenrec species found
in C. Africa and Madagascar. It has sharp
spines and coarse, gray to reddish fur,
and uses its pointed snout to root
among leaves and litter for prey at
night. If threatened, the tenrec
squeals, erects its spiny neck hair,
jumps, and bucks, biting readily.
• **SIZE** Body length:10–15½ in
(26–39 cm). Tail: ⅜–½ in
(1–1.5 cm).
• **OCCURRENCE**
Madagascar. In
tropical forest
and savanna.

*coarse hair
and spines*

*gray to reddish
fur*

*long,
mobile snout*

MADAGASCAR

Social unit Solitary	Gestation 50–60 days	Young 10–12	Diet

Family CHRYSOCHLORIDAE	Species *Eremitalpa granti*	Status Vulnerable

GRANT'S GOLDEN MOLE

With a small, compact body covered in soft, silky hair,
Grant's Golden Mole may vary from steel gray to buff or
almost white. Adapted to burrowing in various ways, this
mole has tiny, almost invisible eyes, a hard, naked nosepad, and three long, broad claws on each foot.
Hardly ever seen above ground, it pushes
through loose sand as if
swimming, making burrows in
deeper soil or near the surface in
compacted sand. Active during
the day and at night, it detects
the movement of its prey while
digging in the soil.
• **SIZE** Body length: 2¾–3¼ in
(7–8 cm). Tail: None.
• **OCCURRENCE** S.W. Africa.
In coastal sand dunes.
• **REMARK** A very specialized
species, this mole is particularly
vulnerable to habitat destruction
or isolation due to parts of its
range being separated by mining
and other industrial activities.

gray or buff coat

AFRICA

*blunt head for
burrowing*

Social unit Solitary	Gestation Not known	Young Not known	Diet

Family SORICIDAE	Species *Scutisorex somereni*	Status Unconfirmed

ARMOURED SHREW

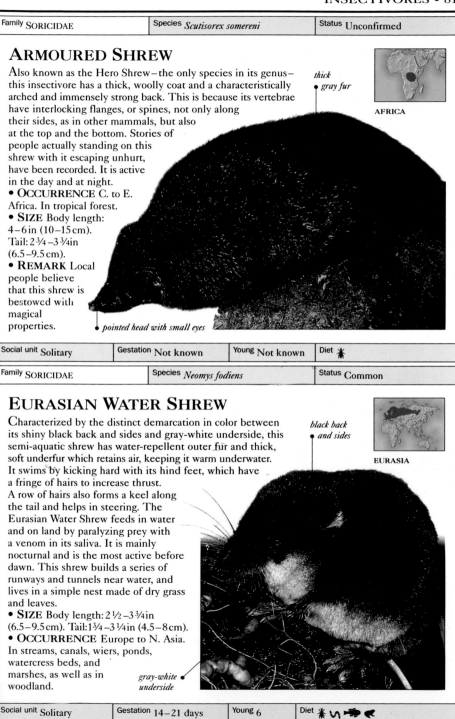

Also known as the Hero Shrew – the only species in its genus – this insectivore has a thick, woolly coat and a characteristically arched and immensely strong back. This is because its vertebrae have interlocking flanges, or spines, not only along their sides, as in other mammals, but also at the top and the bottom. Stories of people actually standing on this shrew with it escaping unhurt, have been recorded. It is active in the day and at night.

thick gray fur

AFRICA

• OCCURRENCE C. to E. Africa. In tropical forest.
• SIZE Body length: 4–6 in (10–15 cm). Tail: 2¾–3¾ in (6.5–9.5 cm).
• REMARK Local people believe that this shrew is bestowed with magical properties.

pointed head with small eyes

Social unit Solitary	Gestation Not known	Young Not known	Diet 🐛

Family SORICIDAE	Species *Neomys fodiens*	Status Common

EURASIAN WATER SHREW

Characterized by the distinct demarcation in color between its shiny black back and sides and gray-white underside, this semi-aquatic shrew has water-repellent outer fur and thick, soft underfur which retains air, keeping it warm underwater. It swims by kicking hard with its hind feet, which have a fringe of hairs to increase thrust. A row of hairs also forms a keel along the tail and helps in steering. The Eurasian Water Shrew feeds in water and on land by paralyzing prey with a venom in its saliva. It is mainly nocturnal and is the most active before dawn. This shrew builds a series of runways and tunnels near water, and lives in a simple nest made of dry grass and leaves.

black back and sides

EURASIA

• SIZE Body length: 2½–3¾ in (6.5–9.5 cm). Tail:1¾–3¼ in (4.5–8 cm).
• OCCURRENCE Europe to N. Asia. In streams, canals, wiers, ponds, watercress beds, and marshes, as well as in woodland.

gray-white underside

Social unit Solitary	Gestation 14–21 days	Young 6	Diet 🐛 🐌 🐟 🐚

Family SORICIDAE	Species *Blarina brevicauda*	Status Common

NORTHERN SHORT-TAILED SHREW

grayish black coat

This robust shrew has short, grayish black fur, tiny eyes, concealed ears, and a hairy tail. Mostly active at night, it uses its senses of smell and touch to hunt out its prey from the soil, and disables it with a toxic bite. Unusually for a shrew, it eats voles, mice, and vegetation.

• SIZE Body length: 4¾–5½ in (12–14 cm). Tail: 1¼ in (3 cm).

• OCCURRENCE S. Canada to N. and E. USA. In deciduous and coniferous forest, bogs, and grassland.

N. AMERICA

relatively stout snout

Social unit Variable	Gestation 17–22 days	Young 3–7	Diet

Family SORICIDAE	Species *Suncus etruscus*	Status Unconfirmed

WHITE-TOOTHED PYGMY SHREW

pointed snout

Living on a diet of small insects, this species hunts actively for a few hours, and then rests, throughout the day and night. It relies on its speed to surprise and attack prey that is slower and larger than itself and also scavenges on recently dead insects. This minute mammal is a typical example of a shrew with its pointed snout; it has large ears, and fur that is mainly grayish brown.

• SIZE Body length: 1½–2 in (4–5 cm). Tail: ¾–1¼ in (2–3 cm).

• OCCURRENCE S. Europe, S. and S.E. Asia, N., E., and W. Africa.

EUROPE, ASIA, AFRICA

grayish brown coat

Social unit Solitary	Gestation 27–28 days	Young 2–5	Diet

Family TALPIDAE	Species *Condylura cristata*	Status Locally common

STAR-NOSED MOLE

dense, soft black fur

An unmistakable star-shaped nose, with 22 radiating tentacles to sniff out its prey in water, gives this mole its name. It forages during the day and night and is an expert swimmer.

• SIZE Body length: 7–7½ in (18–19 cm). Tail: 2½–3 in (6–8 cm).

• OCCURRENCE E. Canada to N.E. USA. In marshes, and along streams and lakes.

N. AMERICA

starlike tentacles on nose

Social unit Variable	Gestation Not known	Young 2–7	Diet

Family TALPIDAE	Species *Talpa euoropaea*	Status Common

EUROPEAN MOLE

Living underground in a central chamber with radiating tunnels, the European Mole is virtually sightless. It has short, dense black fur that can lie in any direction as the mole moves fowards or backwards in a tunnel. Strong shoulder muscles and outward-facing front paws with spadelike claws help it to push out soil from its burrow, which appears on the surface as molehills. This mole is active during the day and night and detects prey by touch, smell, and hearing. When worms are plentiful it paralyses them with a bite for future use. However, if not eaten in time, the worms recover and escape. A good swimmer, the European Mole can vacate its burrow in low-lying areas during floods.
• **SIZE** Body length: 4½–6½ in (11–16 cm). Tail: ¾ in (2 cm).
• **OCCURRENCE** Europe, extending to N. Asia. Woodland and grassland, as well as farmland.

cylindrical body covered almost • *completely by fur*

EURASIA

bright pink nose •

outward-facing front paws •

Social unit Solitary	Gestation 4 weeks	Young 3–4	Diet 🐛 🐜

Family TALPIDAE	Species *Desmana moschata*	Status Vulnerable

RUSSIAN DESMAN

Although it belongs to the mole family, a desman resembles a water shrew with a dense, lustrous coat. Its tail is flattened for use as a paddle and rudder, and its rear feet are fully webbed, while the front feet are partially so. Using its long, sensitive nose, it probes for food by night in riverbed mud and stones. Unusually for an insectivore, the Russian Desman lives in groups, several sharing a bank burrow.
• **SIZE** Body length: 7–7½ in (18–21 cm). Tail: 6¾–7½ in (17–21 cm).
• **OCCURRENCE** E. Europe to C. Asia. In slow-moving rivers, lakes, ponds, canals, and marshes.
• **REMARK** After centuries of hunting for its fur, the Russian Desman is now legally protected. However, it is still threatened by the loss of freshwater habitat as its diet consists entirely of water creatures.

EURASIA

long, coarse guard • *hairs*

flexible snout •

flattened tail as long as body •

Social unit Social	Gestation Not known	Young 3–5	Diet 🐜 🐛 🐌 🐟 🦐

BATS

MORE THAN one-fifth of all mammals, almost 1,000 species, are bats. These are the only mammals capable of sustained flight. A bat's front limbs are wings consisting of a thin, extensible, leathery membrane, the patagium, held out by long, slim finger and arm bones.

Bats live mainly in tropical and temperate forests worldwide. Some species are found in more open habitats, and in recent times a few species have adapted to live in human habitations.

Most bats belong to the suborder Microchiroptera and fly at night, using a sound-radar system to catch small aerial insects. Certain species have specialized diets such as fish, snails, or blood. In temperate regions they survive winter's lack of food by hibernating.

The suborder Megachiroptera consists of the larger flying foxes and fruit bats. As their name suggests, they consume fruit and other plant material.

Family MEGADERMATIDAE	Species *Macroderma gigas*	Status Vulnerable

AUSTRALIAN FALSE VAMPIRE BAT

pale gray to light brown fur •

Also known as the Ghost Bat, this species derives its name from the misconception that it feeds on blood. Large ears, a forked tragus (ear projection), and prominent noseleaf, make this bat unmistakable. It has pale gray or light brown fur and pale cream to brown wings. It roosts in large numbers in rocky crevices, but is affected by increased mining activity.

• **SIZE** Body length: 4– 4¾ in (10–12 cm).

AUSTRALIA

Forearm: 3¾–4¼ in (9.5–11 cm).
• **OCCURRENCE** W. and N. Australia. In tropical rain forest, grassland, and rocky hillsides.

cream to brown wings •

prominent ears •

Social unit Social	Gestation 11–12 weeks	Young 1	Diet 🐀🐁🦎🦇🦗

Family EMBALLONURIDAE	Species *Taphozous mauritianus*	Status Common

MAURITIAN TOMB BAT

A medium-sized "sheath-tailed" bat, the Mauritian Tomb Bat is distinguished from other members of its genus by its grizzled brown-black coat with white wings and underparts. Watchful as it roosts by day on walls and tree trunks, it uses echolocation to detect flying prey. It also produces a range of vocalizations that are audible to humans.

• **SIZE** Body length: 2¾–3½ in (7.5– 9.5 cm).

AFRICA

Forearm: 2¼ in (6 cm).
• **OCCURRENCE** W., C., E., and S. Africa, Madagascar, and Mauritius. In forest, dry habitats, and urban settlements.

grizzled coat •

roosts on open tree trunks •

Social unit Social	Gestation 90 days	Young 1	Diet 🦗

Family EMBALLONURIDAE	Species *Rhynchonycteris naso*	Status Common

PROBOSCIS BAT

With its long, pointed nose that extends over its mouth, this species is also known as the Sharp-nosed Bat. Grizzled gray-brown to yellowish fur, with two faint, wavy, cream stripes from shoulder to rump, make this streamlined bat distinctive. A fairly typical, small, insectivorous bat, it does, however, show unique roosting behavior. Groups of 5–10 (rarely more than 40) roost by day in a line, nose-to-tail on a branch or wooden beam. Each line includes a single dominant male that defends the feeding area, which is often near a patch of water. A horizontal line of Proboscis Bats on a beam in a boathouse, or a branch hanging over water, is a common, but striking sight.

- **SIZE** Body length:1 ½–2 in (3.5–5 cm). Forearm:1 ½–1 ¾ in (3.5–4 cm).
- **OCCURRENCE** Mexico, Peru, Bolivia, Brazil, French Guiana, Surinam, Guyana, and Trinidad. In lowland tropical forest along waterways.

DISTINCTIVE LOOKS
The most outstanding feature of this bat is its proboscis-like nose. Its fur is grizzled, with protruding tufts on its forearms, and its head is small in proportion to its body.

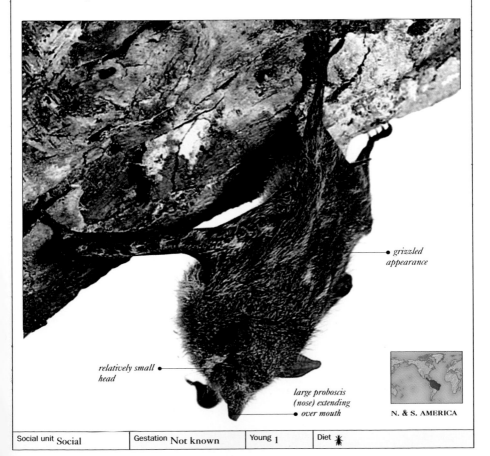

grizzled appearance

relatively small head

large proboscis (nose) extending over mouth

N. & S. AMERICA

Social unit Social	Gestation Not known	Young 1	Diet 🐜

Family PTEROPODIDAE	Species *Epomops franqueti*	Status Unconfirmed

FRANQUET'S EPAULETTED BAT

This species is a medium-sized fruit bat, the male of which is slightly heavier than the female, and has shoulder patches of long white hair resembling epaulettes. These may be drawn into the fur and hidden. Males make high-pitched whistling calls from their perches during the night to attract mates, and their collective din is a common sound in the African night. While males defend their calling perches from other males, these bats do not display territorial behaviour while feeding or roosting. The Franquet's Epauletted Bat may breed at any time of the year, females bearing two litters in areas where food – consisting chiefly of fruits such as figs, guavas, and bananas, as well as soft, young leaves – is plentiful. Usually found roosting in groups in the daytime, these bats prefer the foliage of trees and vines. Individuals rarely make physical contact, mothers alone taking care of their young until they are weaned. The pattern of palatal ridges on the roof of the mouth, specialized for drawing out fruit pulp and juices, distinguishes one species from another in this genus.

AFRICA

pale patch of hair at base of ear

• **SIZE** Body length: 4¼–6 in (11–15 cm). Forearm: 3¼–3½ in (8–9 cm).
• **OCCURRENCE** W. and C. Africa. In rain forest.

wide wingspan

thumb

brownish wing membrane

broad molars for crushing fruits to pulp

extremely long forearms

SPECIALIZED FEEDERS
Like other fruit bats, this bat uses its broad molars to crush fruits, rubbing its tongue against the palatal ridges of its mouth and sucking to draw out juices and pulp before spitting out the fruit fibers.

broad, rounded ears

Social unit Social	Gestation Not known	Young 1	Diet 🍃 🍂

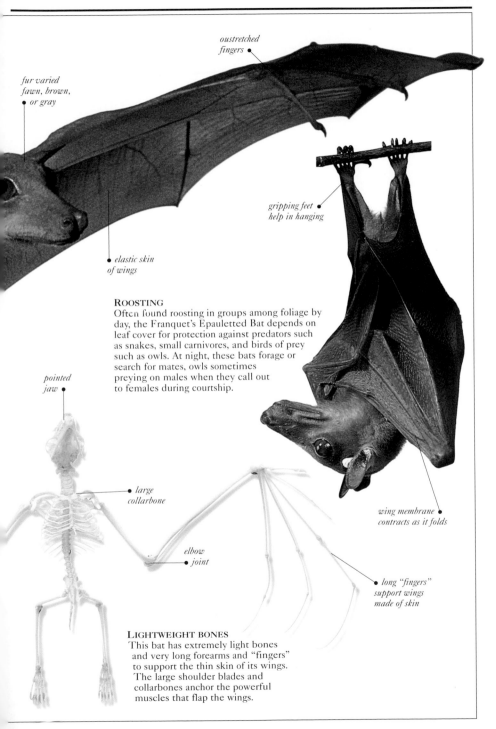

oustretched fingers

fur varied fawn, brown, or gray

gripping feet help in hanging

elastic skin of wings

ROOSTING
Often found roosting in groups among foliage by day, the Franquet's Epauletted Bat depends on leaf cover for protection against predators such as snakes, small carnivores, and birds of prey such as owls. At night, these bats forage or search for mates, owls sometimes preying on males when they call out to females during courtship.

pointed jaw

large collarbone

wing membrane contracts as it folds

elbow joint

long "fingers" support wings made of skin

LIGHTWEIGHT BONES
This bat has extremely light bones and very long forearms and "fingers" to support the thin skin of its wings. The large shoulder blades and collarbones anchor the powerful muscles that flap the wings.

Family PTEROPODIDAE	Species *Rousettus egyptiacus*	Status Common

EGYPTIAN ROUSETTE

Also known as the Egyptian Fruit Bat, this species may vary from dark brown to slate-gray on its upperparts, with lighter, smoky gray underparts. It is unusual among bats in having fur that extends about halfway along each forearm. Unlike most fruit bats, this species uses high-pitched echolocation clicks which allow it to find its way and roost in cool, dark caves.

AFRICA, ASIA

• **SIZE** Body length: 5½–6½ in (14–16 cm). Forearm: 3¼–4 in (8.5–10 cm).
• **OCCURRENCE** N., W., E., and S. Africa, W. Asia. In desert, tropical forest, and urban areas.

dark brown to gray body •
yellow or buff collar •

Social unit Social	Gestation 4 months	Young 1	Diet 🐝 🍃

Family RHINOPOMATIDAE	Species *Rhinopoma hardwickei*	Status Common

LESSER MOUSE-TAILED BAT

This bat is one of four *Rhinopoma* species, sometimes called Long-tailed Bats, all of which have long, thin, trailing, mouselike tails, that may be as long as the head and body. An inhabitant of arid, open areas, the Lesser Mouse-tailed Bat is able to withstand drier conditions than many other bats. When food is available in abundance, it may store fat for the long dry season, during which it remains inactive.

very long tail •

AFRICA, ASIA

• **SIZE** Body length: 2½–2¾ in (5.5–7 cm). Forearm: 1¾–2¼ in (4.5–6 cm).
• **OCCURRENCE** N. and E. Africa, W. to S. Asia. In desert and tropical forest – both covered and open areas.

leaflike structure on nose •

Social unit Social	Gestation 123 days	Young 1	Diet 🦟

Family NOCTILIONIDAE	Species *Noctilio leporinus*	Status Lower risk*

GREATER BULLDOG BAT

Velvety orange, brown, or gray fur with a distinctive pale stripe along its back characterize the Greater Bulldog Bat. By night, it hunts for fish, fiddler crabs, and other prey such as arthropods, snatching them from the ground or surface of water in rivers and estuaries, using its large, powerful, sharp-clawed hindfeet.

large nosepad •

drooping upper lip •

C. & S. AMERICA

• **SIZE** Body length: 3½–4 in (9–10 cm). Forearm: 3¼–3½ in (8–9 cm).
• **OCCURRENCE** Central America, N., E., and C. South America. In forest and near rivers.

enormous hindfeet •

Social unit Social	Gestation 60–70 days	Young 1	Diet 🐟 🦐 🦟

Family RHINOLOPHIDAE	Species *Rhinolophus hipposideros*	Status Vulnerable

LESSER HORSESHOE BAT

This bat has a head and body smaller than
a human thumb. Widespread in woods and scrub, it
faces the threat of habitat destruction – both its winter
hibernation sites, such as deep caverns, and summer
daytime roosts in tree holes, caves, chimneys, and
mine shafts, have been disturbed.
• **SIZE** Body length:1 ½ in (4 cm).
Forearm:1 ½ –1 ¾ in (3.5 – 4.5 cm).
• **OCCURRENCE** Europe,
N. Africa to W. Asia. In desert

EUROPE, AFRICA,
ASIA

and temperate forest,
in covered places.

horseshoe-shaped • noseleaf

broad wings • allow slow, hovering flight

Social unit Social	Gestation 2 months	Young 1	Diet 🦟

Family NATALIDAE	Species *Natalus stramineus*	Status Unconfirmed

MEXICAN FUNNEL-EARED BAT

Tiny and delicate, with rounded ears, soft, woolly fur, and a tail
joined by flight membranes to the legs, this is one of five species
of American Funnel-eared Bats, all found in the tropics. This
species may be distinguished by its rapid, almost butterfly-like
flight. Often encountered roosting by day in caves, which may
house hundreds of individuals hanging separately, it feeds by night
on small, flying insects.
• **SIZE** Body length:1 ½ –1 ¾ in
(4 – 4.5 cm). Forearm:1 ½ in (3.5 – 4 cm).
• **OCCURRENCE** W. USA to
N. South America. In tropical forest

N., C., & S.
AMERICA

and dry, semideciduous forest,
mostly deep within caves.

tail longer • than head and body

orange to yellowish • brown fur

Social unit Social	Gestation Not known	Young 1	Diet 🦟

Family MORMOOPIDAE	Species *Pteronotus davyi*	Status Common

DAVY'S NAKED-BACKED BAT

naked back •   large ears •

A common sight at night in urban areas, where it feeds
on moths, flies, and other flying insects attracted to street
lights, the Davy's Naked-backed Bat roosts by day in large
colonies in caves and mines, usually some distance away
from its main feeding areas. It is the smallest among
moustached bats (mormoopids), and its wings meet along
the center of its back, obscuring the fur beneath, and giving
it a "naked-backed" appearance.
• **SIZE** Body length:1 ½ –2 ½ in (4 – 5.5 cm).
Forearm:1 ½ –2 in (4 – 5 cm).
• **OCCURRENCE** Mexico
to N. and E. South America.

N. & S. AMERICA

In tropical forest.

brown or • orange fur

Social unit Social	Gestation Not known	Young 1	Diet 🦟

Family PHYLLOSTOMIDAE	Species *Anoura geoffroyi*	Status Common

GEOFFROY'S TAILLESS BAT

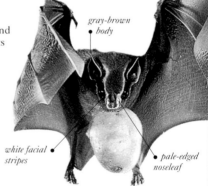

gray-brown fur

Also known by the alternative name, Geoffroy's Hairy-legged Bat, this bat's tail is reduced to a furred membrane. Its triangular, upright nose gives it a third name: Geoffroy's Long-nosed Bat. It hovers in front of night-blooming flowers, feeding on nectar and pollen with its long, brush-tipped tongue – playing an important role in pollinating several plant species. Large colonies of bats roost in caves and tunnels.
• **SIZE** Body length: 2¼–3in (6–7.5cm). Forearm: 1½–1¾in (4–4.5cm).
• **OCCURRENCE** Mexico, Caribbean, N. South America. In tropical and evergreen forest.

N., C., & S. AMERICA

extended lower jaw

Social unit Social	Gestation Not known	Young 1	Diet

Family PHYLLOSTOMIDAE	Species *Uroderma bilobatum*	Status Common

TENT-MAKING BAT

gray-brown body

A gray-brown species with white stripes on its face and back, this is one of about 15 species of leaf-nosed bats that roost in "tents" – shelters made by biting palm or banana leaves so that they fold over. About 2–50 individuals live in these tents, which protect them from sunlight, rain, and predators. This bat chews on fruits, sucking out their juices.
• **SIZE** Body length: 2¼–2½in (6–6.5cm). Forearm: 1½–1¾in (4–4.4cm).
• **OCCURRENCE** Mexico to C. South America. In deciduous and evergreen forest.

N., C., & S. AMERICA

white facial stripes

pale-edged noseleaf

Social unit Social	Gestation 4–5 months	Young 1	Diet

Family PHYLLOSTOMIDAE	Species *Vampyrum spectrum*	Status Lower risk

SPECTRAL BAT

dark brown or orangish back

A wingspan of 3¼ft (1m) makes this bat (also known as Linnaeus' False Vampire Bat), the largest in the Americas. It is not a blood sucker, but a powerful predator that hunts other bats, rodents such as mice and rats, and birds such as wrens, orioles, and parakeets. It grabs its prey directly in its mouth and kills it with a powerful bite. By day it roosts in groups of up to five, inside hollow trees. This species is at risk from habitat loss.
• **SIZE** Body length: 5¼–6in (13.5–15cm). Forearm: 4–4¼in (10–11cm).
• **OCCURRENCE** Mexico to N. South America, and Trinidad. In evergreen forest.

N., C., & S. AMERICA

protruding ears

Social unit Variable	Gestation Not known	Young 1	Diet

Family PHYLLOSTOMIDAE	Species *Desmodus rotundus*	Status Common

VAMPIRE BAT

The Vampire Bat is distinguished by its pointed, bladelike canines and upper incisors. From dusk, this strong flier searches for a warm-blooded victim – a bird, domestic animal, or even a human being. It bites away the fur or feathers without the victim noticing, and laps up to 1 fl oz (25 ml) of blood over 30 minutes.

N., C., &
S. AMERICA

• **SIZE** Body length:
2¾ – 3¾ in
(7–9.5 cm).
Forearm:
2¼ in (5.3 cm).
• **OCCURRENCE**
Mexico, Central and
South America.
In forest, woodland,
grassland, and cities.
• **REMARK** Among
the most social
of mammals,
it roosts
in groups
and often
shares blood by regurgitation.

*dark, greyish
brown fur*

*paler
underside*

strong forearms

long thumbs

Social unit Social	Gestation 7 months	Young 1	Diet Blood

Family PHYLLOSTOMIDAE	Species *Pipistrellus pipistrellus*	Status Common

COMMON PIPISTRELLE

The 70 or more species of pipistrelles are distinguished from each other by their size, color, and dental features. The Common Pipistrelle is the most widespread of these. Emerging from its roost in the early evening, it preys on small insects such as common flies, caddis flies, mayflies, and moths. By day, the Common Pipistrelle roosts in cracks, crevices, buildings, and bat boxes. It hibernates through the winter, like other bats from temperate regions. This bat communicates by an array of vocal signals, males calling out to females during courtship. Nursery colonies may contain 1,000 mothers, each recognizing and nursing her single young.

*dark,
leathery
wings*

EUROPE, AFRICA,
ASIA

• **SIZE** Body length:1½–2 in (3.5–4.5 cm).
Forearm:1¼–1½ in (2.8–3.5 cm).
• **OCCURRENCE** Europe to N. Africa,
W. and C. Asia. In temperate and coniferous
forest, parkland, riverbanks, suburban
gardens, and urban areas.
• **REMARK** Pipistrelle bats often emerge
from their roosts in enormous swarms to
keep from being ambushed by predators.

Social unit Social	Gestation 44 days	Young 1	Diet 🐜

Family VESPERTILIONIDAE	Species *Nyctalus noctula*	Status Lower risk*

COMMON NOCTULE BAT

This bat is one of the largest and the most widespread of the six noctule species. It has sleek, golden, aubern, or reddish fur, and short, broad ears. The female is slightly larger than the male. A powerful flier, the Common Noctule Bat dives steeply to catch large flying insects such as crickets and chafers, using echolocation to track them. It also forages on insects that are attracted to light or are found over garbage dumps. During the breeding season in late summer and early autumn, the male bat becomes territorial, calling out to females from tree hollows. In spring, the female may produce up to three young, whereas most small bats have only one offspring. In summer, the females form nursery colonies of over 100 individuals in trees and buildings. Later in the year, they gather in groups around the usually solitary males.

EUROPE, ASIA

- **SIZE** Body length: 2¾–3 in (7–8 cm). Forearm: 1¾–2¼ in (4.7–5.5 cm).
- **OCCURRENCE** Europe to W., E., and S. Asia. In temperate forest and urban areas.
- **REMARK** The Noctule Bat hibernates for part of the winter and then migrates up to 2,000 km (1,200 miles) to newer summer feeding grounds.

ROOSTING
By day, the Noctule Bat roosts in the hollows of trees, often competing with starlings for tree-holes, as well as in buildings, or among rocks. It emerges early in the evening from its roost and forages high above the ground or in the tree canopy.

short, sleek fur

wings folded during roosting

short, broad ears

powerful wings for flying

widely spaced eyes

greyish brown flight membrane

broad muzzle

reddish yellow or golden fur

large body

Social unit Social	Gestation 70–73 days	Young 1–3	Diet 🐜

| Family VESPERTILIONIDAE | Species *Plecotus auritus* | Status Lower risk* |

BROWN LONG-EARED BAT

The large ears, about three-quarters the length
of its head and body combined, distinguish this
bat. The ears help it detect prey, such as moths,
midges, mosquitoes, and flies, which it picks off the
vegetation in swooping flights. The Brown Long-eared
Bat roosts in buildings and trees, females and young
forming nursery colonies. In winter it
hibernates in caves, mines, and cellars.
• SIZE Body length:1½–2 in (4–5 cm).
Forearm: 9–11 in (23–28 cm).
• OCCURRENCE Europe to C. Asia.
EURASIA   In sheltered, lightly wooded areas.

huge ears

*small,
dark face*

*hair with
light tips*

| Social unit Social | Gestation Not known | Young 1 | Diet 🦗 |

| Family VESPERTILIONIDAE | Species *Myotis daubentonii* | Status Common |

DAUBENTON'S BAT

One of about 87 species in the
widespread genus *Myotis* – small brown,
mouse-eared bats – this bat flutters above
water to catch flying insects in its mouth,
curled wing pouch, hind legs, or tail membrane,
giving it another name, the Water Bat.
• SIZE Body length:1½–2½ in
(4–6 cm).
Forearm:1½ in
(4 cm).
• OCCURRENCE Europe
to N. and E. Asia. In temperate
EURASIA   forest, near lakes and rivers.

*gray flight
membrane*

tiny wingspan

*pale
underside*

*large hind feet
with splayed toes*

| Social unit Social | Gestation 53–55 days | Young 1 | Diet 🦗 🍎 🐚 |

| Family VESPERTILIONIDAE | Species *Mops condylurus* | Status Common |

ANGOLAN FREE-TAILED BAT

Common in a variety of habitats, this heavy
bat has a long, mouselike, "free" tail, not
enclosed by membranes. In the evening, it
emerges from its daytime roost in large, noisy
groups to protect itself from predators such as
owls, hawks, or snakes. Catching insects on
the wing, it drops the hard parts such as legs.
• SIZE Body length:
2¾–3 in (7–8.5 cm).
Forearm:1¾–2 in (4.5–5 cm).
• OCCURRENCE W., C.,
and E. Africa and Madagascar.
AFRICA   In desert and tropical forest.

*heavy, sturdy
body*

long ears

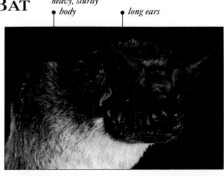

| Social unit Social | Gestation 80–90 days | Young 1 | Diet 🦗 |

ELEPHANT-SHREWS

FOUND ONLY IN Africa, the 15 species of elephant-shrews (order Macroscelidea) occupy a variety of habitats, from rocky hillsides to grassland and the forest floor. The group's common name is derived from the elongated, trunklike nose, which is extremely sensitive to touch and scent. Hearing and sight are also sharp.

Elephant-shrews bound around their territories by day, using their powerful back legs and long tails in the manner of a tiny kangaroo. They chase away intruders of their own kind, and follow well-maintained trails from their burrows to forage for small prey such as insects; some species also eat buds, berries, and other plant material.

Elephant-shrews resemble true shrews in appearance and habits, and have been classified as insectivores. However, certain aspects of their anatomy suggest that they may be more closely related to rabbits and hares (lagomorphs).

Family MACROSCELIDIDAE	Species *Rhynchocyon chrysopygus*	Status Endangered

GOLDEN-RUMPED ELEPHANT-SHREW

Distinctive and colorful in appearance, this elephant-shrew has a russet head and body, golden patches on its forehead and rump, and hairless, black legs, feet, and ears. When alarmed, it slaps its white-tipped tail on leaf litter as a warning and bounds away.
• **SIZE** Body length:10½–11½ in (27–29 cm). Weight:1¼ lb (525–550 g).

• **OCCURRENCE** Kenyan coast to the border of Somalia. In coastal, dry forest and scrub, including coral rag scrub.

AFRICA

distinctive golden rump patch

proboscis-like long beak

Social unit Solitary/Pair	Gestation 42 days	Young 1	Diet 🐜

Family MACROSCELIDIDAE	Species *Elephantulus rufescens*	Status Lower risk

RUFOUS ELEPHANT-SHREW

Gray or brown in color, with whitish underparts, this fleet-footed animal probes leaf litter with its long nose and licks up small invertebrates, especially termites, with its sticky tongue; it also feeds on fruits and other plant matter. It does not nest or burrow, but creates foraging trails, along which it flees from predators.
• **SIZE** Body length:4¾–5 in (12–12.5 cm). Weight:1¾–2⅛ oz (50–60 g).
• **OCCURRENCE** E. Africa. In arid woodland and grassland.
• **REMARK** This shrew is monogamous, each sex chasing away its rivals.

AFRICA

long, pointed snout

white-ringed eyes

white legs and feet

Social unit Solitary/Pair	Gestation 60 days	Young 1–2	Diet 🐜 🍃 🫐

FLYING LEMURS

ALSO KNOWN AS colugos, the two species of flying lemur make up the order Dermoptera. Both species live in the forests of Southeast Asia. Similar in size and form, they have unusual, ridged lower teeth to sieve sap and juices from fruits and other plant matter.

They are not lemurs, but they do have lemurlike faces, with large, front-facing eyes enabling them to judge distances precisely. They are not true fliers, but they are the most accomplished gliding mammals, able to swoop more than 330 ft (100 m) horizontally with minimal height loss, and swerve on the way with excellent aerial control. The extensive gliding membrane of tough skinlike tissue is known as the patagium.

Family CYNOCEPHALIDAE	Species *Cynocephalus variegatus*	Status Common

MALAYAN FLYING LEMUR

This arboreal species has a small head and ears, blunt snout, and large eyes. The fine, short coat is brownish gray with red or gray on the back, sometimes with lighter flecks to mimic lichen-covered branches of trees. Active at twilight and night, this flying lemur eats soft plant parts and scrapes up sap and nectar with its comblike incisors.
- **SIZE** Length:13–16 ½ in (33–42 cm). Front "wingspan": 26–30 in (65–75 cm).
- **OCCURRENCE** S.E. Asia. In forest, from coastal lowland to mountainous areas up to 3,300 ft (1,000 m).

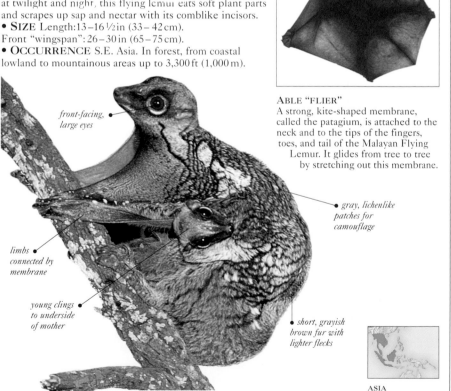

ABLE "FLIER"
A strong, kite-shaped membrane, called the patagium, is attached to the neck and to the tips of the fingers, toes, and tail of the Malayan Flying Lemur. It glides from tree to tree by stretching out this membrane.

front-facing, large eyes

gray, lichenlike patches for camouflage

limbs connected by membrane

young clings to underside of mother

short, grayish brown fur with lighter flecks

ASIA

Social unit Social	Gestation 60 days	Young 1	Diet 🌿 🍒 ❀

TREE SHREWS

NEITHER ENTIRELY arboreal, nor really shrews, tree shrews are squirrel-like inhabitants of tropical forests in South and Southeast Asia, belonging to the order Scandentia. Most are adept climbers, but a few of the 19 species hardly ever venture into trees.

Also called tupaids, from their family name, most tree shrews are long-bodied, agile, solitary, and diurnal. They forage for insects, worms, and occasionally fruits and berries. Their senses of sight, hearing, and smell are well-developed; however, unlike true shrews, they lack whiskers. The long, furred tail aids balancing, and the clawed fingers and toes grip well.

Previously, tree shrews were classified with insectivores, because of their diet of invertebrates, or with primates, due to common anatomical features such as a relatively large brain for the body size and, in the male, testes that descend into a bag or scrotum.

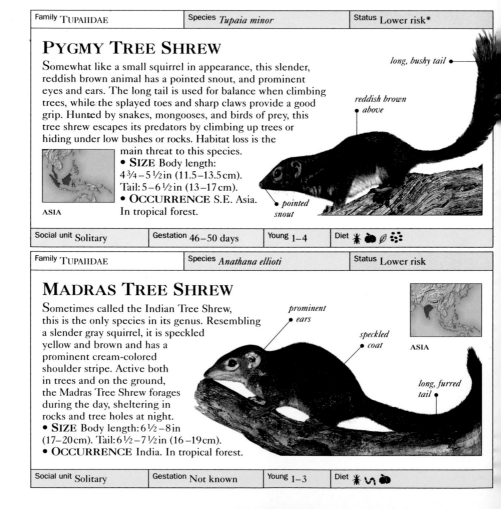

Family TUPAIIDAE	Species *Tupaia minor*	Status Lower risk*

PYGMY TREE SHREW

Somewhat like a small squirrel in appearance, this slender, reddish brown animal has a pointed snout, and prominent eyes and ears. The long tail is used for balance when climbing trees, while the splayed toes and sharp claws provide a good grip. Hunted by snakes, mongooses, and birds of prey, this tree shrew escapes its predators by climbing up trees or hiding under low bushes or rocks. Habitat loss is the main threat to this species.

long, bushy tail

reddish brown above

• **SIZE** Body length: 4¾–5½in (11.5–13.5cm). Tail: 5–6½in (13–17cm).
• **OCCURRENCE** S.E. Asia. In tropical forest.

pointed snout

ASIA

Social unit Solitary	Gestation 46–50 days	Young 1–4	Diet 🐜 🐛 🪱 ⋮⋮

Family TUPAIIDAE	Species *Anathana ellioti*	Status Lower risk

MADRAS TREE SHREW

Sometimes called the Indian Tree Shrew, this is the only species in its genus. Resembling a slender gray squirrel, it is speckled yellow and brown and has a prominent cream-colored shoulder stripe. Active both in trees and on the ground, the Madras Tree Shrew forages during the day, sheltering in rocks and tree holes at night.

prominent ears

speckled coat

ASIA

long, furred tail

• **SIZE** Body length: 6½–8in (17–20cm). Tail: 6½–7½in (16–19cm).
• **OCCURRENCE** India. In tropical forest.

Social unit Solitary	Gestation Not known	Young 1–3	Diet 🐜 🌿 🐛

PRIMATES
PROSIMIANS

B USHBABIES AND POTTOS in Africa, lemurs in Madagascar, and lorises in Asia, together forming the suborder Strepsirhini, are a step below monkeys and apes (simians) on the evolutionary ladder.

Most prosimians are arboreal, nocturnal, forest-dwellers, with large front-facing eyes, long limbs, and gripping digits equipped with nails rather than claws. Many have long, balancing tails, and communicate by calls, scents, and visual displays to attract mates or group members, or to repel intruders. Lemurs, in particular, are social, and several kinds form troops and are diurnal.

Numbering 77 species, prosimians are regarded as less specialized in form than simians. In this book, the tarsiers, from Southeast Asia, have been included in this group, although they appear to be in between prosimians and simians.

Family TARSIIDAE	Species *Tarsius bancanus*	Status Unconfirmed

WESTERN TARSIER

A nocturnal prosimian, the Western Tarsier is adapted to climbing and grasping the branches of trees. It has a small, compact body, slender fingers, and padded toes with sharp claws. These help it grip branches firmly. An opportunistic hunter that feeds chiefly on insects, it can rotate its head through 360 degrees, using its huge eyes and keen ears to detect prey or predators. It ambushes its victim by creeping up and leaping to seize it with its front paws. Its predators include nocturnal birds of prey, such as owls. This species usually sleeps on branches, rarely using nests for shelter. The young are carried by the mother at first but soon learn to cling to her fur.
• SIZE Body length: 4¾–6 in (12–15 cm). Tail: 7–9 in (18–23 cm).
• OCCURRENCE S.E. Asia. In primary and secondary tropical forest, and mangrove swamps.
• REMARK Habitat degradation has adversely affected the population of the little-known Western Tarsier.

round head
large eyes for spotting prey

ASIA

pale olive to reddish brown fur

Social unit Solitary	Gestation 180 days	Young 1	Diet

Family LORISIDAE	Species *Loris tardigradus*	Status Vulnerable

SLENDER LORIS

Like all of its family, this small, slender primate is nocturnal,
and has large, round eyes equipped with binocular and night
vision. It has a dark face mask with a pale central stripe, and
its soft, thick fur ranges from yellow-gray to dark brown above,
with silvery gray underparts. Mainly an insect-eater, this
species also feeds on soft shoots, buds, birds' eggs, and small
vertebrates. It moves cautiously from branch to branch until
it spots or smells its prey, then quickly snatches it with its
front paws. During the day it curls up to sleep in a secure
place such as a tree hole or dense leafy nest. When sleeping
on branches, it grips its perch firmly with its hands and feet,
each thumb or big toe opposing the other four digits.

• SIZE Body length:7–10 in (17– 26cm). Tail:Not present.
• OCCURRENCE S. India and Sri Lanka. In thick,
deciduous forest, as well as swampy, coastal forest.
• REMARK The Slender Loris's slow
movements and nocturnal habits help
it to escape the notice of predators,
but serious habitat degradation
is threatening its existence.

VICELIKE GRIP
The Slender Loris is able
to sleep on tree branches,
holding onto them with
firmly locked thumbs
and toes.

slender forelimbs

*rounded ears,
naked at edges*

*long toes
for grasping*

*large,
front-facing eyes*

*silver-gray
underparts*

ASIA

Social unit Solitary/Pair	Gestation 165–170 days	Young 1–2	Diet

Family LORISIDAE	Species *Nycticebus coucang*	Status Unconfirmed

SLOW LORIS

This species is named after its slow and deliberate movement, a characteristic that singles out lorises from all other primates, which are generally known for their leaps and bounds. The Slow Loris is pale gray-brown to red-brown, with a brown stripe from the top of the head to the middle of the back or base of the tail, and dark rings around its eyes and ears. It shares common features with the Slender Loris (see opposite), such as digits adapted for a strong grip, binocular vision, and an arboreal and nocturnal lifestyle.
• **SIZE** Body length:10–15 in (26–38 cm). Tail:⅜–¾ in (1–2 cm).
• **OCCURRENCE** S. Asia and S.E. Asia. In tropical forest, gardens, plantations, and bamboo groves

dense, soft brown fur   *dark rings around eyes*

• **REMARK** This loris continues to be hunted in some regions because its body parts are used to make traditional medicines.

ASIA

Social unit Variable	Gestation 190 days	Young 1–2	Diet

Family LORISIDAE	Species *Perodicticus potto*	Status Locally common

POTTO

A secretive and solitary nocturnal hunter, the Potto has very mobile limbs and can reach out at any angle to bridge gaps between branches, although it cannot jump. Its arms and legs are of similar length, with extremely powerful grasping hands and feet. It can remain immobile in trees for several hours to escape attention; if attacked, it lowers its head to batter its enemy with a spiny shield of bony protrusions on its neck. The Potto may be gray, brown, or red in color. Compared to a Thick-tailed Galago (see p.100), its eyes and ears are relatively small. This species feeds on fruits, leaves, sap, fungi, and small animals.
• **SIZE** Body length: 12–16 in (30–40 cm). Tail:1½–6 in (3.5–15 cm).
• **OCCURRENCE** W. and C. Africa. In tropical forest (especially the margins), lowland, and swamps.

AFRICA

small ears

prominent eyes

powerful hands

Social unit Variable	Gestation 194–205 days	Young 1–2	Diet

Family LORIDAE	Species *Arctocebus calabarensis*	Status Lower risk

CALABAR ANGWANTIBO

This primate is one of the two *Arctocebus* species (the other is the Golden Angwantibo found further south), and is golden brown on its upperparts but buff underneath. It has four equal-length limbs which it uses to climb slowly up branches. Its tiny second toe and the first toe, widely separated from the other three, provide a clamplike grip. Nocturnal by nature, the Calabar Angwantibo prefers newly grown secondary vegetation in treefall zones, clearings, and roadsides. It forages on insects, chiefly caterpillars, using sight and smell, rubbing hairy caterpillars to remove the irritating hairs. When threatened it rolls itself into a ball.
• **SIZE** Body length: 9–10 in (22–26 cm). Tail: ⅜ in (1 cm).
• **OCCURRENCE** W. Africa. In woodland.

orange to yellow upperparts

AFRICA

sensitive, moist nose

gripping toes

Social unit Social	Gestation 133 days	Young 1	Diet 🐜 🐌

Family GALAGONIDAE	Species *Galago crassicaudatus*	Status Locally common

GREATER GALAGO

The largest of all galagos, this species has huge eyes and ears to locate insects at night, catching them rapidly with its powerful hands. Its comblike teeth are used to scrape gum from trees. Also known as the Greater Bushbaby, it ranges from the size of a large squirrel to that of a pet cat, and varies from silver to gray, brown, or black. It tends to move on all fours and is unable to land on its hind limbs like some of the specialized, leaping galagos.
• **SIZE** Body length: 25–40 cm (10–16 in). Tail: 34–49 cm (13½–19½ in).
• **OCCURRENCE** C., E., and S. Africa. In tropical forest, woodland, and plantations.
• **REMARK** This animal's childlike wail gives its group the common name, Bushbaby.

huge ears

pale face mask

AFRICA

gripping feet with friction pads

long, bushy tail

Social unit Social	Gestation 126–135 days	Young 1–3	Diet 🐜 🐌 🐦

Family GALAGONIDAE	Species *Galago moholi*	Status Common

SOUTH AFRICAN GALAGO

prominent ears

diamond-shaped black eye-rings

Sometimes called the Lesser Bushbaby, this species makes kangaroo-like vertical leaps up branches to a height of 16 ft (5 m), using its hands and feet, regularly moistened with urine, to maintain its grip. It catches insects in midair by hand, or scrapes gum from trees with its comblike, lower front teeth. A solitary forager, the South African Galago sleeps huddled in groups during the day and may congregate again at night to groom and socialize. It is a shy animal, and is especially cautious before descending to the ground. Checking all directions, it may make several trial runs, calling out loudly when it spots a predator. Lithe and agile, it easily leaps out of trouble.

AFRICA

• **SIZE** Body length: 6–6½ in (15–17 cm). Tail: 4¾–10½ in (12–27 cm).
• **OCCURRENCE** E., C., and S. Africa. In acacia savanna and woodland.

large rear feet

furred tail

Social unit Variable	Gestation 121–124 days	Young 1–2	Diet 🦗

Family CHEIROGALEIDAE	Species *Cheirogaleus medius*	Status Lower risk

FAT-TAILED DWARF LEMUR

soft, woolly fur

With soft, woolly fur, buff or gray-red on its upperparts and whitish yellow underneath, the Fat-tailed Dwarf Lemur has prominent eyes, ringed with dark circles; and large ears that are mainly naked. It stores food as fat in its body and tail during the rains, to survive the 6–8 month dry season. At this time, it may become torpid in order to overcome food shortage, remaining huddled with others of its kind. When it revives, it becomes solitary again and clambers around trees and bushes at night, picking up and holding food in its forepaws while feeding. The Fat-tailed Dwarf Lemur usually eats fruits and other vegetation at the beginning of the year, while insects become a more important part of its diet as the year passes. By day, it rests in a nest made of leaves and twigs, in a tree hole or at the top of a tree.

prominent, naked ears

dark circles around eyes

whitish yellow underparts

• **SIZE** Body length: 7–10 in (17–26 cm). Tail: 7½–12 in (19–30 cm).
• **OCCURRENCE** W. and S. Madagascar. In primary and secondary dry forest.
• **REMARK** Like most lemurs, this species is threatened by the destruction of its forest habitat.

MADAGASCAR

"fat" tail to store food

Social unit Variable	Gestation 61–64 days	Young 1–4	Diet

Family LEMURIDAE	Species *Lemur catta*	Status Vulnerable

RING-TAILED LEMUR

Distinctively feline in its graceful appearance and movements,
the Ring-tailed Lemur has brownish gray to rosy brown
upperparts, with whitish gray underparts. It has distinctive dark,
triangular eye patches, a black nose, and a striking black-and-white
ringed tail that it uses to send visual signals. Unlike other lemurs,
this skilled climber is also often found on the ground, running
to take refuge in the forest canopy as soon as it is threatened.
It feeds on fruits, vegetation, bark, and sap at all levels of
the forest, using its hands to put food into its mouth. Very
sociable by nature, these lemurs are often found in groups
of 5–25 with a hierarchical core of adult females, who
dominate the males and defend their territory with loud
calls. Young females remain with their mothers and sisters,
whereas juvenile males move to other groups. The young
first clings to its mother's underside
and later rides on her back.
• **SIZE** Body length:15½–18 in
(39–46 cm). Tail: 22–24 in (56–62 cm).
• **OCCURRENCE** S. and S.W.
Madagascar. In dry forest and bush
of closed canopy deciduous forest,
adjoining rocky mountain outcrops,
and gallery forest along rivers.
• **REMARK** The main threat to
the Ring-tailed Lemur is from loss
of habitat through deforestation
and forest fires. It is also hunted
by humans for food and frequently
kept as a pet.

MADAGASCAR

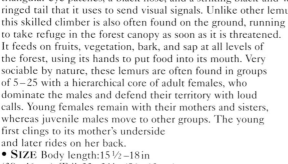

tail used for visual signaling

SCENT GLANDS
This lemur communicates by means
of scent secreted from glands in its
body. One of these glands is visible
here on the inside of the right arm.

black-and-white rings on tail

white face

catlike body posture

brownish gray to rosy brown upperparts

dark, triangular eye patch

Social unit Social	Gestation 134–138 days	Young 1	Diet 🐚 🍃 🌿

Family LEMURIDAE	Species *Lemur fulvus*	Status Lower risk*

BROWN LEMUR

Despite its name, this lemur is extremely variable in color and ranges from brown to yellow or gray, according to the subspecies. However, it usually has a dark face with lighter patches above the eyes and a thickly furred tail, carried archlike over its back when moving on the ground or along branches. Found in fluid groups, Brown Lemurs are highly adaptable to forest habitats and forage in trees and on the ground, feeding on fruits, vegetation, and sap. Each smears urine on itself for scent recognition. Home ranges overlap, but neighboring groups avoid contact.

MADAGASCAR

• **SIZE** Body length:15–20 in (38–50 cm). Tail:18–23 ½ in (46–60 cm).
• **OCCURRENCE** N. and W. Madagascar. In tropical forest.

thickly furred body

light patches above eyes

brown to yellow or gray coat

Social unit Social	Gestation 120 days	Young 1–2	Diet 🍎 🌿

Family LEMURIDAE	Species *Lemur macaco*	Status Lower risk*

BLACK LEMUR

All Black Lemurs have soft and relatively long fur, but only the male has the black coat after which the species is named. Females vary considerably in color from reddish brown to gray. The small head, with a pointed snout and large eyes, has a distinctive ruff around the neck and shoulders. Groups of 5–15 Black Lemurs, led by a single female, forage in trees, using their forelimbs to pick and tear food. Unlike most lemurs, this species is active for part of the night–human disturbance may be the cause of such behaviour. Experts recognize two subspecies of this poorly studied lemur: *Lemur macaco macaco* and *Lemur macaco flavifrons*.
• **SIZE** Body length:12–18 in (30–45 cm). Tail:16–23 ½ in (40–60 cm).
• **OCCURRENCE** N. Madagascar. In tropical, evergreen forest.
• **REMARK** The Black Lemur is under threat from a variety of activities including forest fires, land clearing for agriculture, as well as hunting by humans.

MADAGASCAR

black coat of the male

ruff around neck and ears

limbs adapted to climbing

long, furry tail

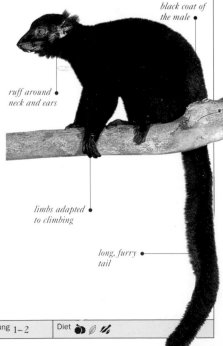

Social unit Social	Gestation 125 days	Young 1–2	Diet 🍎 🌿 🌾

Family LEMURIDAE	Species *Varecia variegata*	Status Endangered

RUFFED LEMUR

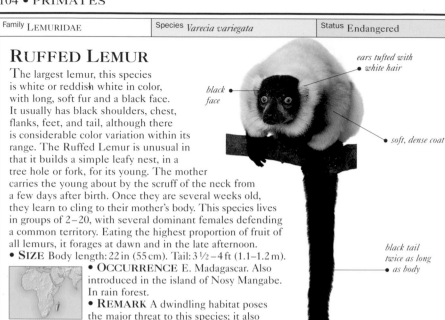

ears tufted with
● white hair

black ●
face

soft, dense coat

The largest lemur, this species
is white or reddish white in color,
with long, soft fur and a black face.
It usually has black shoulders, chest,
flanks, feet, and tail, although there
is considerable color variation within its
range. The Ruffed Lemur is unusual in
that it builds a simple leafy nest, in a
tree hole or fork, for its young. The mother
carries the young about by the scruff of the neck from
a few days after birth. Once they are several weeks old,
they learn to cling to their mother's body. This species lives
in groups of 2–20, with several dominant females defending
a common territory. Eating the highest proportion of fruit of
all lemurs, it forages at dawn and in the late afternoon.

black tail
twice as long
● as body

• SIZE Body length: 22 in (55 cm). Tail: 3 ½ – 4 ft (1.1–1.2 m).

• OCCURRENCE E. Madagascar. Also
introduced in the island of Nosy Mangabe.
In rain forest.

• REMARK A dwindling habitat poses
the major threat to this species; it also
continues to be hunted for food.

MADAGASCAR

Social unit Social	Gestation 90–102 days	Young 2–3	Diet 🌰 ⋮⋮ 🍃 ❀

Family LEMURIDAE	Species *Hapalemur griseus*	Status Unconfirmed

BAMBOO LEMUR

short muzzle ●

Gray all over, with a distinctive blunt
snout, this highly specialized lemur is
the only primate that is adapted to living among reeds
and rushes fringing lakes. Jumping from one reed stalk
to another, it clings to them, chewing on the bark and pith,
and plucking leaves, shoots, and buds to stuff into its mouth;
feeding in the early morning and late afternoon. Unlike
any others in its family, this species may be able to swim,
but this has not been confirmed as its habits have yet to be
properly studied. Groups of Bamboo Lemurs, led by one
dominant male, normally number 3–5, but may be as
large as 40. The single young is born around January
or February and is carried by the mother on her back.

• SIZE Body length: 16 in (40 cm). Tail: 16 in (40 cm).

• OCCURRENCE N. and E. Madagascar, around
Lake Alaotra. In reed beds and papyrus beds.

• REMARK Habitat loss and degradation is affecting
the existence of this extremely localized
species – already thought to be extinct
in parts of its range. Burning reed beds
along the lakeshore to
make way for agriculture
is a particular problem.

tail equal to ●
body length

MADAGASCAR

Social unit Social	Gestation Not known	Young 1	Diet 🍃

| Family LEMURIDAE | Species *Lepilemur mustelinus* | Status Lower risk |

WEASEL SPORTIVE LEMUR

This nocturnal prosimian has long, soft, brown fur, a gray head, and dark tail-tip. It has prominent naked ears, and large eyes for good night vision. As with other leaping primates, both eyes face forward and so provide stereoscopic vision, allowing this lemur to judge distances precisely. Adapted to life in the trees, the Weasel Sportive Lemur leaps from one branch to another, feeding on fruits and leaves, and is rarely seen on the ground. It has grasping feet, but its tail lacks the ability to grip.
• **SIZE** Body length:12–14 in (30–35 cm). Tail:10–14 in (25–35 cm).
• **OCCURRENCE** N.E. Madagascar. In rain forest.
• **REMARK** The habits of this species are poorly studied, and like all lemurs, its population is threatened by habitat loss, especially due to slash-and-burn cultivation.

forward-facing eyes

MADAGASCAR

grasping limbs

gray-brown fur

| Social unit Social | Gestation Not known | Young Not known | Diet |

| Family INDRIIDAE | Species *Propithecus verreauxi* | Status Critically endangered* |

VERREAUX'S SIFAKA

Generally white all over, Verreaux's Sifaka has brown-black areas on its face, crown, and the undersides of its limbs. Its hind legs and tail are extremely long, and its palms and soles are black. While walking on the ground it uses two legs, awkwardly hopping sideways, with its arms held aloft. In desert areas, it moves among the cactuslike vegetation without injuring itself, using high, springing leaps. When resting, one sifaka crouches behind another, in a line. Verreaux's Sifaka lives in varying social groups, calling out to dispute territorial boundaries between two groups. The name "Sifaka" is derived from the sound of its call.
• **SIZE** Body length:17–18 in (43–45 cm). Tail: 22–23 ½ in (56–60 cm).
• **OCCURRENCE** S. and W. Madagascar. In evergreen, gallery, and dry, deciduous forest, as well as spiny desert vegetation.
• **REMARK** Rapid habitat degradation is severely threatening this animal.

brown or black crown

black palms

MADAGASCAR

| Social unit Social | Gestation 150–162 days | Young 1 | Diet |

Family INDRIIDAE	Species *Indri indri*	Status Endangered

INDRI

The largest member of the lemur group, the Indri has a coat that is predominantly black with variable white patches on the back of the head, neck, and limbs; the ears have conspicuous black tufts. It has long hind limbs for taking enormous leaps, and virtually no tail. A vertical clinger and leaper, it remains inactive for long periods in the day, even though it is diurnal. Male–female pairs live with their offspring, with the male defending its territory, and the female having first access to food. Once common in Madagascar, this species is threatened by the loss of its rain forest habitat. Known locally as the Babakoto or "little father", its English name was actually derived from the local exclamation "indri indri", meaning "there it is", when first shown to explorers.

tufted • black ears

clings vertically •

very long • hindlimbs

• **SIZE** Body length: 23 ½ in (60 cm).
Tail: 2 in (5 cm).
• **OCCURRENCE** E. Madagascar. At all levels of montane rain forest.
• **REMARK** The Indri is the only species in its genus.

MADAGASCAR

Social unit Pair	Gestation 172 days	Young 1	Diet 🌿 🫐

Family DAUBENTONIIDAE	Species *Daubentonia madagascariensis*	Status Endangered

AYE-AYE

Also dubbed the "primate woodpecker," the Aye-aye listens intently for woodboring grubs inside trees, exposes them by gnawing the bark with its enormous front teeth, and finally picks them out with its long middle finger to eat. It has a coarse black coat with a mantle of white guard hairs. Shy and reclusive, it hides in its nest, made of sticks, during the day and emerges at night to feed.

shaggy • coat

huge ears with acute hearing •

• **SIZE** Body length: 16 in (40 cm).
Tail: 16 in (40 cm).
• **OCCURRENCE** N.W. and E. Madagascar. In forest, spiny desert, and plantations.
• **REMARK** Thought to be extinct, it was rediscovered in 1957.

MADAGASCAR   *elongated middle finger •*

Social unit Variable	Gestation 120–150 days	Young 1	Diet 🐛 🫐 🌰 ⚙ 🍄

PRIMATES
MONKEYS

T HE 242 species of monkeys, along with the apes, make up the primate suborder Haplorhini. Two monkey families are found in South and Central America: the small, soft-haired marmosets and tamarins in the family Callitrichidae; and the sakis, uakaris, and titis, which together with the spider, woolly, and howler monkeys are known as the New World Monkeys and belong to the family Cebidae.

A third family, from Africa and Asia, is the Cercopithecidae, or the Old World monkeys: guenons, colobus, mangabeys, macaques, baboons, and langurs. Typical monkeys are forest dwellers, with five grasping digits on each of the four flexible limbs, a long tail, and a large brain for the body size, giving considerable intelligence. Most species live in large social groups and eat a mixed diet of plants and small creatures.

Family CEBIDAE	Species *Lagothrix lagotricha*	Status Vulnerable

HUMBOLDT'S WOOLLY MONKEY

Woolly monkeys are characterized by their thick, closely curled fur, which is a darker shade on the head, hands, feet, and tail tip. The Humboldt's Woolly Monkey is gray with black flecks, and is stout and pot-bellied, with powerful shoulders, hips, and tail for swinging on branches. It has a large forehead and braincase and is known to be highly intelligent. These monkeys live in mixed troops, which may break up into subgroups for foraging, with a hierarchy based on age.
• **SIZE** Body length: 20–26 in (50–65 cm). Tail: 22–30 in (55–77 cm).
• **OCCURRENCE** Brazil, Peru, and Bolivia. In primary forest, especially flooded forest.
• **REMARK** Forest fragmentation has adversely affected this monkey, which needs large tracts of uninterrupted forest to thrive.

tail tip bare on underside

heavy shoulders

large forehead

blackish grey underside

grasping fingers

GENTLE NATURED
This monkey displays little aggression, and allows members of another troop to encroach on its territory.

S. AMERICA

Social unit Social	Gestation 233 days	Young 1	Diet

Family CEBIDAE	Species *Ateles geoffroyi*	Status Vulnerable

C. AMERICAN SPIDER MONKEY

Sometimes called Geoffroy's or Black-handed Spider Monkey, this species is distinguished by its black head, hands, and feet, and the "cowl" which surrounds its face. Like other spider monkeys, it uses its thumbless hands as hooks to help it swing through trees, or to pull branches towards its mouth in order to eat fruits, leaves, and flowers. The prehensile tail is often used as a fifth limb.

prehensile tail

• **SIZE** Body length: 20–25 in (50–63 cm). Tail: 25–33 in (63–84 cm).
• **OCCURRENCE** S. Mexico and Central America. In tropical forest and mangrove swamps.

black hands

N. & C. AMERICA

Social unit Social	Gestation 226–232 days	Young 1	Diet

Family CEBIDAE	Species *Ateles chamek*	Status Lower risk

CHAMEK SPIDER MONKEY

black face

This monkey has long black fur and black facial skin. A sociable species, it lives in troops, each with a large territory occupying 370–570 acres (150–230 hectares). The troop splits into variable subgroups to forage, greeting other groups with whoops and wails. Females use a quarter to a third of the troop's territory, leaving when mature to join other groups. The young of dominant females survive better into adulthood.

long, black fur

• **SIZE** Body length: 16–20½ in (40–52 cm). Tail: 32–35 in (80–88 cm).
• **OCCURRENCE** Peru, Brazil, and Bolivia, in the upper Amazon tributaries. In tropical forest.

S. AMERICA

Social unit Social	Gestation 225 days	Young 1	Diet

Family CEBIDAE	Species *Brachyteles arachnoides*	Status Critically endangered

MURIQUI

One of the largest monkeys in the Americas, the Muriqui or Wooly Spider Monkey has dense fawn fur and a black face. It is a slow forager, feeding on fruits, seeds, and leaves by pulling off branches with its hands.

thumbless hands

• **SIZE** Body length: 22–24 in (55–61 cm). Tail: 26–33 in (67–84 cm).

fawn body

• **OCCURRENCE** S.E. Brazil. In Atlantic tropical forest.
• **REMARK** Only a few hundred of the Southern (*Brachyteles arachnoides)* and Northern (*B. hypoxanthus*) Muriqui survive today.

S. AMERICA

Social unit Variable	Gestation 210–255 days	Young 1	Diet

| Family CEBIDAE | Species *Alouatta pigra* | Status Vulnerable |

MEXICAN BLACK HOWLER MONKEY

Also known as the Guatemalan Black Howler Monkey, this species is uniformly black, except for the male's white scrotal sac. Found in territories sometimes up to 25 hectares (62 acres) in area, each group of around seven members comprises females, juveniles, and a single adult male, which may be twice as heavy as the female. The Mexican Black Howler Monkey calls loudly at dusk and dawn to establish the troop's territory. It feeds on fruits, flowers, and leaves, subsisting on a single species of tree during poor seasons. It pulls branches to its mouth and bites off fruits, after sniffing to see if they are ripe.

uniform
• *black fur*

N. & C. AMERICA

• **SIZE** Body length: 20½–25 in (52–64 cm). Tail: 23–27 in (59–69 cm).
• **OCCURRENCE** Mexico and Central America. In tropical forest.
• **REMARK** This species was formerly thought to be a subspecies of the Mantled Howler (*Alouatta palliata*) of Central America. The two species overlap without interbreeding in Tabasco.

| Social unit Social | Gestation 190 days | Young 1 | Diet |

| Family CEBIDAE | Species *Alouatta seniculus* | Status Lower risk |

RED HOWLER MONKEY

One of the nine howler species, this monkey's loud calls carry more than 1½ miles (2.5 km) to inform others in the area of its territorial presence. It is usually found in small groups of an adult male, females, and young. When a new male supersedes the existing male, he may kill any offspring, so that the females mate with him and raise his young. Howlers lead a sluggish lifestyle due to a low–nutrient diet.

reddish gold "saddle" on
• *back*

S. AMERICA

• **SIZE** Body length: 20–25 in (51–63 cm). Tail: 22–27 in (55–68 cm).
• **OCCURRENCE** Colombia, Venezuela, Brazil, and Peru. In rain forest, mangrove swamps, and savanna woodland.

• *deep jowls*

reddish fur •

| Social unit Social | Gestation 191 days | Young 1 | Diet |

Family PITHECIIDAE	Species *Pithecia pithecia*	Status Lower risk

WHITE-FACED SAKI

No other New World monkey has such a striking difference between the sexes as the White-Faced Saki. The male is black with a white or pale gold face, and a black nose. The female is gray-brown with long white tips to her hair, and has a blackish face with a white stripe on either side of the nose. The fur on both is lank, falling to the sides from midback and nape to form a cowl on the crown. Both have a bushy tail.
• SIZE Body length:13½–14 in (34–35 cm). Tail:13½–17½ in (34–44 cm).
• OCCURRENCE North of the Amazon. In tropical forest: gallery, palm, and savanna.
• REMARK One of the five species of true sakis, it is closely related to the Bearded Saki and uakaris (see below).

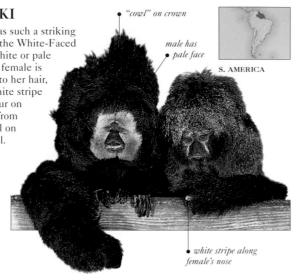

"cowl" on crown

male has pale face

S. AMERICA

white stripe along female's nose

Social unit Social	Gestation 170 days	Young 1	Diet 🐝 ⋮ 🐛 🦫 🐦 🍃

Family PITHECIIDAE	Species *Cacajao calvus*	Status Endangered

RED UAKARI

A bright red, skull-like, hairless face, and in adults a bald crown, characterize Red Uakaris. They are classified into subspecies according to color, such as white, golden, and red. The Red Uakari has shaggy red hair over its thin body. When this monkey is excited, it wags its short tail. Found in groups of up to 100, it inhabits the black-water forests of Brazil: part-flooded forest along small rivers, lakes, and swamps.
• SIZE Body length: 15–22½ in (38–57 cm). Tail: 5½–7½ in (14–18.5 cm).
• OCCURRENCE Brazil. In black-water forest.
• REMARK The Red Uakari is the only short-tailed monkey found in the Americas.

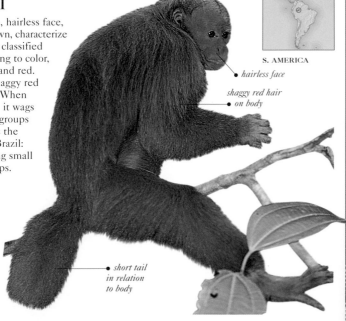

S. AMERICA

hairless face

shaggy red hair on body

short tail in relation to body

Social unit Social	Gestation Not known	Young 1	Diet ⋮ 🐝 🐛 🌿

Family PITHECIIDAE	Species *Callicebus moloch*	Status Lower risk

DUSKY TITI

The 20 or more titi species typically have thick, soft fur, a stocky body, short limbs, and ears almost hidden beneath fur. The Dusky Titi has a speckled brown back, while its underparts are orange. Its drab coloration and slow movements provide effective camouflage in the lower level of trees where it is found. The male and female form a monogamous pair, grooming frequently and defending a home range that extends over 15–30 acres (6–12 hectares). Just before dawn, they entwine tails and "sing" a duet to maintain their family and pair-bonds, and to declare their territory. The young stay with the pair for up to three years, and the male carries the infant and shares food with it for around a year.

dark face

orange sideburns

orange underparts

• **SIZE** Body length:10½–17in (27–43cm). Tail:14–22in (35–55cm).

• **OCCURRENCE** Brazil. In swamps and flooded tropical forest, notably forest edges.
• **REMARK** The Dusky Titi belongs to a group of 6–8 titi species that are found in the southern Amazonian forest.

S. AMERICA

long, bushy tail

Social unit Pair	Gestation 155 days	Young 1	Diet 🐛 🖊 🐜

Family AOTIDAE	Species *Aotus lemurinus*	Status Vulnerable

LEMURINE NIGHT MONKEY

Genetic studies show that there are probably ten species of night monkeys, rather than one as previously believed. Also called Douroucouli, or owl monkeys, from their hooting calls in the darkness, they clamber cautiously through the branches at night, searching for food. The Gray-bellied Lemurine Night Monkey (shown here) is yellow or gray beneath, while the monkeys found further south have red bellies. However, all night monkeys are speckled gray above, with white cheeks and chin, large white spots above the eyes, and three stripes from the crown to the face.

speckled fur on back

C. & S. AMERICA

• **SIZE** Body length: 12–16½in (30–42cm). Tail:11½–17½in (29–44cm).

dark, bushy tail-tip

grasping feet

• **OCCURRENCE** Ecuador and Colombia (west of the Andes) to Panama. In tropical forest.
• **REMARK** Night monkeys are the only nocturnal monkeys and are equipped with night vision.

black stripe extending to nose

Social unit Social	Gestation 120 days	Young 1	Diet 🐛 🐜 🖊

Family CEBIDAE	Species *Cebus apella*	Status Lower risk

BROWN CAPUCHIN

This New World monkey is found foraging with other species of monkeys, both to exploit their ability to find food and for protection from predators. It uses tools such as sticks and stones to crack hard nuts or to flush prey out of tree trunks. Also called the Tufted Capuchin for the short, upright crown hairs that form "horns" above its ears, this monkey is unusual in using the reverse-mount to mate. It has the widest range of all the monkeys found in the Americas.

pale ring around face

brown coat

• **SIZE** Body length:13–17 in (33–42 cm).
Tail:16–19 ½ in (41–49 cm).
• **OCCURRENCE** N., C., and E. South America. In tropical forest.
• **REMARK** The Golden-bellied Capuchin (*Cebus xanthosternos*), a closely related species, is critically endangered.

tail fully covered with fur

S. AMERICA

Social unit Social	Gestation 5 months	Young 1	Diet 🥜 ⦙⦙ 🌾 🦎 🦋

Family CEBIDAE	Species *Saimiri boliviensis*	Status Lower risk*

BOLIVIAN SQUIRREL MONKEY

white, tufted ears

This monkey has speckled orange and black fur, turning orange at the limbs and underside, and a white face and black muzzle. During courtship, the male becomes "fatted" around the shoulders and several males compete to win the largest number of females. Moving in groups of 40–200, Squirrel Monkeys, of which there are five species, form the largest and most active troops of all the monkeys found in South America. Extremely vocal, they disturb insects to feed on them, or follow other monkeys, catching insects in their wake.

speckled orange and black upperparts

• **SIZE** Body length:10 ½–12 ½ in (27–32 cm).
Tail:15–16 ½ in (38–42 cm).
• **OCCURRENCE** C. South America. In primary and secondary tropical forest, and swamp forest.
• **REMARK** The different species of squirrel monkeys are known as the "Gothic" or "Roman" types, depending on the shape of their arched white eyebrows. The Bolivian Squirrel Monkey belongs to the "Roman arch" group.

orange limbs

black, bushy tail-tip

slim tail

S. AMERICA

Social unit Social	Gestation 170 days	Young 1	Diet 🐜 🥜 ⦙⦙

Family CALLITRICHIDAE	Species *Callimico goeldii*	Status Vulnerable

GOELDI'S MONKEY

black "cape" •   *long, black • body hair*

Larger than most marmosets and tamarins, Goeldi's Monkey has long black fur and a "cape" of longer hair around its head and neck. Using its incisors, it makes gashes in trees and feeds on sap and gum. It also eats fruits, insects, and small vertebrates. Moving in stable, close-knit groups of up to ten, these monkeys are usually found in dense vegetation.
• SIZE Body length: 9 in (22–23 cm).
    Tail: 10–12½ in (26–32 cm).
    • OCCURRENCE N.W. South America. In tropical forest and bamboo groves.
    • REMARK Unlike other marmosets this species has wisdom teeth.

S. AMERICA

Social unit Social	Gestation 154 days	Young 1	Diet 🐛 ✹

Family CALLITRICHIDAE	Species *Leontopithecus rosalia*	Status Critically endangered

GOLDEN LION TAMARIN

red-gold • mane

Weighing twice as much as most marmosets and tamarins, the Golden Lion Tamarin has a mane of long, silky, red-gold fur and a grey face. The slender, long-clawed hands are used to hold fruits while eating and to probe into tree-holes and bark for grubs. Usually found in groups of 4–11 individuals, these monkeys differ from other marmosets in that the sexual activity of subordinate monkeys is not suppressed by the dominant pair. However, it is only the dominant pair that produces the young. The juvenile monkeys of the group often assist in rearing new infants.
• SIZE Body length: 8–10 in (20–25 cm). Tail: 12½–14½ in (32–37 cm).
• OCCURRENCE E. South America. In Atlantic tropical forest.
• REMARK Deeply affected by deforestation, this species has been the focus of conservation efforts since the 1960s. Having bred well in captivity, it has been reintroduced in the wild in S.E. Brazil. Its situation, however, is still precarious.

narrow • fingers

gray face •

• tail longer than body

S. AMERICA

Social unit Social/Pair	Gestation 129 days	Young 2	Diet 🐛 ✲

Family CALLITRICHIDAE	Species *Saguinus imperator*	Status Vulnerable

EMPEROR TAMARIN

Known for its flamboyant white
moustache, the Emperor Tamarin has
speckled gray- or red-brown fur, a
black head, and a fiery red-orange tail
that is white underneath. It is a small monkey often
forming a mixed group with a related species, such
as the Saddleback Tamarin (*Saguinus fuscicollis*). Each
species responds to the other's alarm calls. Feasting
on fruits in the wet season, the Emperor Tamarin
feeds on nectar and sap in the dry season, and on
insects, particularly crickets, year round. It pulls a
plant to its mouth and scans it for insects before
pouncing on them. Its two offspring are carried by
the father, except when being suckled by the mother.
• **SIZE** Body length: 9–10 in (23–26 cm).
Tail: 15½–16½ in (39–42 cm).
• **OCCURRENCE** W. South America. In tropical forest
as well as mountain areas.

• **REMARK** Marmosets and tamarins
form a distinct group of about 35 American
primate species. They differ biologically
from other New World monkeys, with
claws instead of nails, and bear two offspring
rather than a single young.

black face
curly, white moustache
speckled fur on body
claws on digits
tail reddish orange above and white underneath
tail longer than body

S. AMERICA

Social unit Social	Gestation 140–145 days	Young 2	Diet

Family CALLITRICHIDAE	Species *Callithrix pygmaea*	Status Lower risk*

PYGMY MARMOSET

Found only in the wetlands and tropical
forests of the Upper Amazon Basin, this
tiny monkey can fit into a human palm.
Its fur is speckled tawny with a long
cape of hair on the head that hangs over
its ears, while its face has a patch of bare skin in
a distinctive three-lobed shape. A specialized
gum-eater, the Pygmy Marmoset differs from
other marmosets in the way it feeds: it gouges
out ten or more holes in bark each day and scent
marks them, returning to these and older holes at intervals
to scrape up the sticky, oozing fluid with its long lower
incisors. Each group of 5–10 monkeys has one breeding pair,
with "helpers" to care for the young. However, the father
takes care of the offspring for the first few weeks.
• **SIZE** Body length: 4¾– 6 in (12–15 cm).
Tail: 7–9 in (17–23 cm).
• **OCCURRENCE** Upper Amazon Basin.
In tropical forest and wetland.
• **REMARK** The Pygmy Marmoset is the
smallest monkey in the world.

"cape" on head
bare skin on face
speckled fur
clawed fingers and toes
indistinct rings on tail

S. AMERICA

Social unit Social/Pair	Gestation 137–140 days	Young 2	Diet Sap

Family CALLITRICHIDAE	Species *Callithrix argentata*	Status Lower risk*

SILVERY MARMOSET

pink skin on face •

huge ears with concave edges •

One of 10–15 similar species found in the Amazon basin, the Silvery Marmoset has pale silvery-gray fur on its back, creamy white underparts, and a black tail. Its face and ears have pink skin but the huge ears have concave outer edges. Like other marmosets, each troop has one breeding pair, with helpers (usually siblings) who help bring up the young.
• **SIZE** Body length: 8–9 in (20–23 cm). Tail: 12–13½ in (30–34 cm).
• **OCCURRENCE** South of the Amazon basin. In tropical, especially inundated, forest.
• **REMARK** There is a great taxonomic diversity among the Amazonian marmosets, their distributions separated by the major and minor Amazon tributaries.

S. AMERICA

creamy white underparts •

Social unit Social	Gestation 140 days	Young 2	Diet 🌿 🫐 🐛

Family CERCOPITHECIDAE	Species *Papio papio*	Status Lower risk

GUINEA BABOON

The male of this species is larger than the female, with a black face and a mane that almost reaches its dark red rump. The Guinea Baboon usually forages in groups of about 40, but troops of up to 200 are not uncommon. Some males may have "harems" within the group whom they herd with a neck bite. However, females may sometimes try to mate surreptitiously with males from another group. The infant first clings to the mother's belly and is transferred to her back after a few weeks. The Guinea Baboon has a wide diet that varies from tough roots to juicy grubs and eggs, and sometimes farm crops. It plucks fruits with one hand, vigorously digs the earth with its hands for roots, and rips its food with its hands and teeth.
• **SIZE** Body length: 27 in (69 cm). Tail: 22 in (56 cm).
• **OCCURRENCE** W. Africa. In woodland savanna, gallery forest, and scrub.
• **REMARK** The smallest baboon species in the world, it is also the least known and has the smallest range of all baboons.

doglike snout • AFRICA

long, reddish chestnut mane •

dark red rump •

spadelike hands used to dig •

Social unit Social	Gestation 184 days	Young 1	Diet 🫐 ⋮⋮ 🥬 🐛 🐀 ●

Family CERCOPITHECIDAE	Species *Papio anubis*	Status Lower risk

OLIVE BABOON

Typically powerful and doglike, the Olive Baboon is speckled olive-green with a black face and rump. Both sexes have a gray ruff around the cheeks, although the male may be twice as large as the female. With plenty of stamina, this baboon runs fast on its long legs. It eats vegetation, insects, lizards, and even prey as large as gazelle fawns and lambs. Clad in their dark, "baby" fur, the young are tolerated in the troop; as they take on adult coloration, females move to the bottom of the social hierarchy, while males are driven away and must battle their way into a new troop.
• SIZE Body length: 20–34 in (60–86 cm).
Tail: 16–23 in (41–58 cm).
• OCCURRENCE W. and E. Africa. In tree savanna and thornbush, up to the forest edge.
• REMARK This is one of the largest baboons in Africa.

thick gray ruff around face

young darker in color

muscular limbs

AFRICA

Social unit Social	Gestation 180 days	Young 1	Diet

Family CERCOPITHECIDAE	Species *Mandrillus sphinx*	Status Vulnerable

MANDRILL

A scarlet nose, with bright blue flanges on either side, a yellow beard, and a mauve-blue rump make the male Mandrill an outstanding primate. The female's coloration is more subdued and she is about a third the size of the male. A forest-floor dweller, the Mandrill spends the day in troops, looking for fruits, seeds, eggs, and insects and small animals. Groups as large as 250 may split into smaller units, with a single male having a harem of 20 females.
• SIZE Body length: 25–32 in (63–81 cm). Tail: 2¾–3½ in (7–9 cm).
• OCCURRENCE W. C. Africa. In primary and secondary rain forest.
• REMARK The largest Old World monkey, the Mandrill is hunted for its meat.

speckled olive-gray fur

tail stump

yellow beard on male

all limbs of equal length

mauve and blue rump in male

AFRICA

Social unit Social	Gestation 152–182 days	Young 1	Diet

Family CERCOPITHECIDAE	Species *Theropithecus gelada*	Status Lower risk

GELADA BABOON

The most outstanding feature of the Gelada Baboon, a close
cousin of the baboons, is the bare pink patch on its chest. It
has brown fur, and adult males have a furry mane on the
head and shoulders. Sitting on its buttock pads, the
Gelada Baboon shuffles over grassland, rapidly
plucking grass blades and seeds and stuffing them
into its mouth with its dextrous hands. It lives in
huge troops, made up of smaller units consisting
of a male and his harem of inter-related females.
In time the male is driven away by a younger
contender, who kills his predecessor's offspring.
• SIZE Body length: 28–29 in (70–74 cm).
Tail: 18–20 in (46–50 cm).
• OCCURRENCE Ethiopia. In montane
plateaux and grassland.
• REMARK The only non-human primate in
its habitat, the Gelada Baboon
is threatened by the rapid
expansion of human activity
such as agriculture.

long face with snub nose

pink chest

nimble hands

medium-sized tail

AFRICA

Social unit Social	Gestation 150–180 days	Young 1	Diet 🌾

Family CERCOPITHECIDAE	Species *Erythrocebus patas*	Status Lower risk*

PATAS MONKEY

A white moustache and beard contrast with the darker face and body
of the Patas Monkey. A black border marks its brows and cheeks,
and its small ears are slightly tufted.
Slim-bodied and long-legged, with
short fingers and toes, it is a superb
runner. It lives in troops of up
to ten members, each having
a single male who stays on
the margins and acts as a
decoy for predators, while
females and young take
cover. At the height
of the dry season the
Patas Monkey turns
sluggish due to the
shortage of food and water.
• SIZE Body length: 23½–35 in (60–88 cm).
Tail: 17–28 in (43–72 cm).
• OCCURRENCE W. to
E. Africa. In arid grassland.
• REMARK The Patas
is the fastest running
monkey species.

black border around face

reddish brown on upperside

long, slim tail

slender body

short toes and fingers

AFRICA

Social unit Social	Gestation 167 days	Young 1	Diet 🐌 ✲ 🌾 🐛 🦎 ●

Family CERCOPITHECIDAE	Species *Cercocebus torquatus*	Status Critically endangered

RED-CAPPED MANGABEY

pink-gray face • • cheek pouches

This monkey has a sooty body and a pink-gray face, with a long muzzle, deep pits below its cheeks, known as "fossae,"and pale or white eyelids. It stuffs its cheek pouches with nuts, to bring out later in its hand and crack with its powerful teeth and jaws. Mainly terrestrial, the Red-capped Mangabey forms large troops of up to 90 monkeys, consisting of males, females, and young. There is a hierarchy among males, but subordinate males are allowed to mate, sometimes more often than the seniors. Troops occupy overlapping home ranges, foraging for food usually along rivers.
• **SIZE** Body length: 20–23 ½ in (50–60 cm). Tail: 23 ½–30 in (60–75 cm).

• **OCCURRENCE** W. Africa. In rain forest.
• **REMARK** Six species of *Cercocebus* ("white eyelid" mangabeys) are found across C. Africa.

AFRICA

sooty fur •

Social unit Social	Gestation 167 days	Young 1	Diet 🍃 ⦚ 🌰 🥬

Family CERCOPITHECIDAE	Species *Cercopithecus neglectus*	Status Lower risk*

DE BRAZZA'S MONKEY

One of the most terrestrial of the 20 or so members of its family, De Brazza's Monkey has speckled gray fur with a black crown, and a white-bordered orange strip on its forehead. Its upper lip and chin are covered with bluish white fur. A thin white stripe runs across its thigh, and its tail and limbs are darker. The male monkey is considerably larger than the female and has a bright blue scrotum. This species eats mainly seeds and fruits, and plucks and holds its food with one hand. Widespread, yet inconspicuous over its large range, it marks its territory with saliva and scent, and communicates by deep booming calls. Although territorial in nature, it tries to avoid, rather than confront, intruders.
• **SIZE** Body length: 20–23 in (50–59 cm). Tail: 23–31 in (59–78 cm).
• **OCCURRENCE** C. to E. Africa. In rain forest, swamps, and submontane forest.
• **REMARK** This is the only monogamous monkey in its family.

speckled • gray fur

AFRICA

long, furred tail

• black feet

Social unit Pair	Gestation 168 days	Young 1	Diet 🌰 ⦚

Family CERCOPITHECIDAE	Species *Macaca nigra*	Status Endangered

CELEBES CRESTED MACAQUE

hairy crest along crown

Also known as the Celebes Black Ape, this monkey is completely black in color, and has a very short tail. It has a crest that runs from its forehead to the back of its crown, which rises when the animal is aroused, and high, bony ridges on either side of its nose. This inconspicuous forest-dweller forms large, mixed-sex troops of more than 100. Gentle by nature, males display little aggression toward each other.

bony ridges on either side of nose

uniformly black body

• SIZE Body length: 20 ½ – 22 ½ in (52 – 57 cm). Tail: 1 ¼ in (2.5 cm).
• OCCURRENCE S.E. Asia (Sulawesi, formerly Celebes). In lowland rain forest, including some secondary forest.

ASIA

• REMARK The Celebes Crested Macaque is one of the six or seven macaque species that inhabit this region, each with its own particular range.

Social unit Social	Gestation 174 – 196 days	Young 1	Diet 🐛 🌿 🐝 🌾

Family CERCOPITHECIDAE	Species *Macaca fascicularis*	Status Lower risk

LONG-TAILED MACAQUE

A gray-white moustache on a pink face, and often a small, pointed crest on the crown, distinguish this macaque, probably the most common primate in Southeast Asia after humans. A good climber and swimmer, it also spends time on the ground, often around human habitations, especially temples in Bali, where it is revered. The Long-tailed Macaque moves around in noisy, quarrelsome groups that may sometimes number up to 100. However, the hierarchy is less defined than among other macaques. When threatened, it flees through trees or drops into the water and swims away.

gray-brown or red-brown upperparts

ASIA

• SIZE Body length: 14 ½ – 23 in (37 – 63 cm). Tail: 14 – 28 in (36 – 72 cm).
• OCCURRENCE S.E. Asia. In forest and mangrove swamps, along rivers, coasts, and offshore islands.
• REMARK The Long-tailed Macaque is sometimes trapped for the biomedical research trade.

light gray or whitish underside

Social unit Social	Gestation 160 – 170 days	Young 1	Diet 🐝 🌰 🐚 ⁙

Family CERCOPITHECIDAE	Species *Colobus guereza*	Status Lower risk*

GUEREZA

With a white border to its face and white "cloak" down its flank and rump, this monkey is also known as the Black-and-white Colobus. Its exceptionally long tail is also tipped white. The newborn monkey is fully white and later takes on the black-and-white coloration. A single male monkey leads a group of four or five females and young, defending his territory with roars and spectacular jumping displays. Although diurnal, it is known to wake up and roar at night. This thumbless monkey pulls branches toward its mouth and bites off leaves and fruits.It has a monotonous diet, over 70 percent of which may consist of a single tree species. Like other leaf monkeys, it has a complex, three-part stomach, which houses gut microbes that help break down cellulose, enabling it to gain optimum nutrition from its leafy diet.

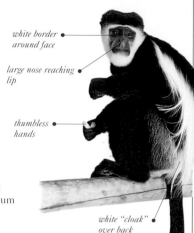

white border around face

large nose reaching lip

thumbless hands

white "cloak" over back

long black tail, tipped white

AFRICA

• **SIZE** Body length: 20 ½–22 ½ in (52–57 cm).Tail: 21–33 in (53–83 cm).
• **OCCURRENCE** S. Cameroon, east to Ethiopia, Kenya, and N. Tanzania. In light forest.

Social unit Social	Gestation 170 days	Young 1	Diet 🍃 🍒

Family CERCOPITHECIDAE	Species *Semnopithecus entellus*	Status Lower risk

HANUMAN LANGUR

A striking black face set in a hairy head, black extremities, and a gray to brown or golden-fawn body, characterize this monkey, which is identified with the demigod Hanuman and revered by Hindus. It has long limbs, and a long tail, held up in a curl. The social units of the Hanuman Langur are flexible, from peaceful troops with a number of males to those with only one male that are invaded by bachelors. Communication is made through whoops. An adaptable species, troops of Hanuman Langurs live near villages, feeding on leftovers and "offerings" from local people.

black, hairless face

black extremities

• **SIZE** Body length: 20–31 in (51–78 cm). Tail: 27–40 in (69–102 cm).
• **OCCURRENCE** Pakistan, India, Bhutan, Nepal, and Sri Lanka. All habitats, except rainforest.
• **REMARK** There are several species of langurs in the Indian subcontinent, ranging from the dark brown, white-headed Himalayan Langur to the small, pale fawn southern species of Sri Lanka that is half its size.

long limbs

ASIA

Social unit Social	Gestation 200 days	Young 1	Diet 🍃 🍒

Family CERCOPITHECIDAE	Species *Nasalis larvatus*	Status Endangered

PROBOSCIS MONKEY

Living in very restricted habitats bordering water, this large, arboreal monkey is known for its long and pendulous nose (more so in males). It is brick-red above, with paler orange flanks, throat, and cheeks, and is whitish on the underside. The Proboscis Monkey has a complex stomach to break down cellulose (see Eastern Black-and-White Colobus, opposite). Troops of 6–10 monkeys swim expertly across creeks and streams, and forage among trees. They are led by a single dominant male, which bares its teeth and uses loud nasal honks and penile erection to ward away invaders.

- **SIZE** Body length: 29–30 in (73–76 cm). Tail: 26 in (66 cm).
- **OCCURRENCE** Borneo. In lowland rain forest, mangrove swamps, and along rivers and coastlines.
- **REMARK** This rare and localized monkey is difficult to keep in captivity.

pendulous nose

whitish undersides

partially webbed feet

ASIA

Social unit Social	Gestation 166 days	Young 1	Diet

Family CERCOPITHECIDAE	Species *Rhinopithecus roxellana*	Status Vulnerable

GOLDEN SNUB-NOSED MONKEY

This monkey endures winter temperatures of 23°F (-5°C). Its long fur and bushy tail provide insulation as it moves in trees or on the ground on its strong, stout limbs. Heavily built, it has a pale blue, triangular face, with an upturned nose, and prominent jaws. Large troops of several hundred monkeys split into small bands of one male and several females, to forage and breed. Males are up to twice the size of the females, with black hair on the back. This monkey is preyed upon by eagles and, perhaps, leopards. It is also threatened by deforestation and hunting for its pelt.

- **SIZE** Body length: 21½–28 in (54–71 cm). Tail: 20½–30 in (52–76 cm).
- **OCCURRENCE** W. China. In montane forest.
- **REMARK** One of the four species of mountain monkeys, three found in China and one in Vietnam, the Golden Snub-nosed Monkey is the only species that is not critically endangered.

fiery red to golden fur

pale blue, triangular face

short digits on stout, powerful limbs

ASIA

Social unit Social	Gestation 195 days	Young 1	Diet

PRIMATES
APES

T HE 21 SPECIES of apes, comprising two families, make up the primate suborder, Haplorhini, along with monkeys.

Apes resemble Old World monkeys in many respects, being forest-dwellers with a flat face, forward-pointing eyes, flexible limbs, and grasping hands and feet. However, they are larger than monkeys, with a more upright posture, and have no tail.

The lesser apes, or gibbons, swing through Southeast Asian forests. The great apes are our closest relatives, and the most intelligent of animals. They include the Gorilla, Chimpanzee, and Pygmy Chimpanzee (Bonobo) of Africa, and Orangutan of Southeast Asia.

Gibbons form monogamous pairs, adult male Orangutans tend to be solitary while the African apes live in highly social groups.

Family HYLOBATIDAE	Species *Hylobates lar*	Status Endangered

WHITE-HANDED GIBBON

This gibbon has black skin with a white fur fringe around its face, and on its hands and feet. The rest of its body may vary from cream to red, brown, or almost black. The feet, like the palms of the hands, have bare, leathery soles providing effective grip. The big toe can grasp in opposition to the other toes, enabling this ape to walk upright along branches. The gibbon's arm-to-arm swinging movement from one tree to another, known as brachiation, saves energy by maintaining momentum, using the body as a pendulum. Active shortly after dawn, the male and the female "duet" to reinforce their pair-bond: the female begins with long, loud hoots that rise to a crescendo, and the male responds to these with simpler, quivering hoots.
• **SIZE** Length:16½–23 in (42–59 cm). Weight:10–17 lb (4.5–7.5 kg).
• **OCCURRENCE** S. China, Burma, Laos, Thailand, Malaysia, and N. Sumatra. In dry deciduous and moist evergreen rain forest, from lowlands to mountains.
• **REMARK** This gibbon is hunted in China.

arms longer than legs

young clinging to mother's chest

ASIA

Social unit Pair	Gestation 7–8 months	Young 1	Diet 🍑 🌿 🐛

Family HYLOBATIDAE	Species *Hylobates syndactylus*	Status Lower risk

SIAMANG

The largest of all gibbons, the robust, muscular Siamang stands at a height of 5 ft (1.5 m). Both sexes have uniform, black, shaggy fur; the male is slightly larger than the female, with a tuft of hair on his genital region, which at first glance may be mistaken for a tail. This species lives in very close-knit family groups consisting of the female (who is dominant), male, and one or two young. They rarely stray more than 100 ft (30 m) from each other, and are usually found less than 33 ft (10 m) apart. The family occupies a home range of about 116 acres (47 hectares), but defends only 60 percent of this territory, using powerful calls. The Siamang has dark gray, elastic skin on its throat, which inflates to the size of a grapefruit and amplifies its calls–the loudest among gibbons.
- **SIZE** Length: 35 in (90 cm). Weight: 22–33 lb (10–15 kg).
- **OCCURRENCE** Central part of the Malay Peninsula and Sumatra. In both primary and secondary rain forest.
- **REMARK** The Siamang can inhabit montane forest at higher altitudes than most other gibbons, because of its ability to retain body heat.

ASIA

arm span up to 5 ft (1.5 m)

fingers provide good grip

thumb opposes other digits

very long fingers

elastic, dark gray skin on throat

uniform black body

long arm bones

large rib cage

webbed second and third toes

shorter thighbones

LONG ARMS
The exceptionally long arms of the Siamang enable it to swing from tree to tree using its hands. Sometimes it walks on its feet with arms held aloft or sideways.

Social unit Social/Pair	Gestation 6½–7½ months	Young 1	Diet

Family PONGIDAE	Species *Pongo pygmaeus*	Status Endangered

BORNEAN ORANGUTAN

With arms that are twice the length of its body, and feet that can grasp branches like hands, the Bornean Orangutan is the largest arboreal animal. It has extremely flexible limbs, with wrist, hip, and shoulder joints allowing a wider range of movement than any other great ape. The Bornean Orangutan spends its life in the forest canopy; the male is more likely to descend to the ground, and even then, only rarely. He is bigger than the female with a long beard, large throat pouch, and long neck and arm hair which hangs like a cape. The female gives birth to a tiny infant once every seven or eight years (the longest interbirth interval of any animal), in a nest atop a tree, and the male–female pair remain together until the young is about eight years old. The male defends his home range by emitting long calls, and if necessary by fighting. Genetic research has led to two different species of orangutan being recognized: the Bornean Orangutan and the Sumatran Orangutan (*Pongo abelii*).
• SIZE Height: 3½–4½ ft (1.1–1.4 m). Weight: 88–175 lb (40–80 kg).
• OCCURRENCE Borneo. In primary rain forest.
• REMARK Although protected by law, young orangutans are still illegally captured and sold as pets. Rehabilitation projects have a good success rate, but some animals find it difficult to readjust to their natural habitat, which is also under threat.

ASIA

very long arms compared to body

capelike arm hair in male

coat varies from orange-red to gray-brown

slow, cautious movement on the ground

digits grip like thumb and fingers

FIST-WALKING
On the rare occasion when an Orangutan leaves the trees, it walks on the soles of its feet and clenched fists (not solely the knuckles). The arms of this ape are so long that it can almost stand upright, yet still touch the ground with its hands.

Social unit Variable	Gestation 8½ months	Young 1	Diet 🍌 ⌀ ✺ 🍂 ● 🐜 🐛

food manipulated between fingers and thumb •

EATING WITH HANDS
Orangutans use their fingers and teeth to prepare their food, stripping plants and scraping off the peel of fruits to expose the juicy flesh within. Their diet also includes honey, small animals such as lizards, termites, nestling birds, and eggs.

high forehead and • large brain

MEMORY AND EXPERIENCE
The orangutan appears to build up a four-dimensional "mental map" of its forest area. It knows where fruit trees are located, and which ones are likely to be fruiting for the time of year.

Family HOMINIDAE	Species *Pan troglodytes*	Status Critically endangered

CHIMPANZEE

AFRICA

One of the apes that most resemble humans, the Chimpanzee is highly expressive, often using its flexible, protrusible lips to make grimacelike "smiles" that actually indicate fear. It has arms that are much longer than its legs, and it walks on its knuckles and flat feet, with the big thumblike toe of the foot opposing the other toes and providing a good grip while climbing. Chimpanzees live in groups of 15–120, and parties of adult males are known to attack and kill intruding males. Although chiefly herbivorous, Chimpanzees may cooperate to kill and eat animal prey such as monkeys, small antelopes, and birds. The Chimpanzee not only uses tools but has also learned to make them. It uses stripped branches to scoop out termites from their nests and then licks them up.

- **SIZE** Length: 23–35 in (63–90 cm). Weight: 66–130 lb (30–60 kg).
- **OCCURRENCE** W. to C. Africa. In montane, primary, and secondary rain forest to woodland savanna.
- **REMARK** One of the world's most endangered animals, the Chimpanzee is close to humans in intelligence, emotions, and learning skills.

BUILDING A HOME
The mother chimpanzee builds a new nest in a tree for her young almost every night, by bending over and intertwining many branches to make a firm, leafy platform, away from predators.

facial skin darkens with age

flexible shoulders

sparse black hair over most of body

arms longer than legs

knuckles used for walking

big toe opposes other toes

Social unit Social	Gestation 8 months	Young 1	Diet

Family HOMINIDAE	Species *Pan paniscus*	Status Endangered

PYGMY CHIMPANZEE

Only slightly smaller than the Chimpanzee (see opposite), but with a slimmer body and relatively longer and more slender limbs, the Pygmy Chimpanzee or Bonobo was named a separate species in 1929. Its skin is mostly black, even on the juvenile's face, and its most obvious distinguishing mark is the neat, central parting of the hair on its crown. Sometimes found in troops of up to 80, the Pygmy Chimpanzee usually associates in smaller groups as it forages and grooms. Sexual relations are common between males, females, and young at various levels, and may be used to ease tensions within the group. Female chimpanzees, who are usually dominant, leave their family unit on reaching maturity, although the males tend to stay on.
• **SIZE** Length: 28–33 in (70–83 cm). Weight: Up to 86 lb (39 kg).
• **OCCURRENCE** C. Africa. In tropical forest and at the southern limit of their range, in savanna.
• **REMARK** Seriously threatened by hunting, the Pygmy Chimpanzee may soon become the first great ape to be extinct in the wild.

AFRICA

LONGTERM BONDING
The female suckles her young for three years. She then continues to protect, groom, and share a nest with it for another year or two.

central parting on crown

black skin

slim body

long, slender limbs

Social unit Social	Gestation 8 months	Young 1	Diet

Family HOMINIDAE	Species *Gorilla beringei*	Status Critically endangered

EASTERN GORILLA

The largest living primates, gorillas are classified as the Western Gorilla (*Gorilla gorilla*) and the Eastern Gorilla (*Gorilla beringei*). The latter includes both the Eastern Lowland Gorilla (*G. beringei graueri*), as well as one or more subspecies of mountain gorillas (*G. beringei beringei*). The Eastern Gorilla is distinguished by its dark, shaggy coat, extremely long arms, and chestnut brown eyes; the mountain subspecies having longer fur to retain body warmth at higher altitudes. The mature male Eastern Gorilla has a saddle of white fur on his back and is often referred to as the silverback. These gorillas are found in groups, each of which roam a home range of 1,000–2,000 acres (400–800 hectares). Apart from a core area, the ranges may overlap with territories of neighbouring groups. The dominant silverback male fathers most or all of the young in the group. He gains the attention of receptive females in various ways, including mock feeding, thumping plants, hooting loudly, chest-beating, or jump kicking. When threatened by intruders, the male begins to hoot. He then stands upright, beats his chest with cupped hands, and throws vegetation. If all else fails, he charges forward with a huge roar, and knocks down the aggressor with a massive hand-swipe.

• SIZE Height: 4 ¼–6 ¼ ft (1.3–1.9 m).
Weight: 150–460 lb (68–210 kg).
• OCCURRENCE C. and E. Africa. In montane rain forest, bamboo forest, swampy glades, and Afro-Alpine zone.
• REMARK The largest living primate, some Eastern Gorillas attract tourist income and receive protection. However, other populations are at continued risk from poaching.

AFRICA

PICKY EATER
Gorillas select their food carefully and then prepare each mouthful before they eat it. Their diet includes leaves, shoots, and stems, especially bamboo, as well as wild celery, nettles, thistles, fruits, roots, soft bark, and fungi.

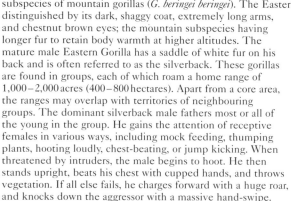

long, shaggy
• black coat

• hairy ridge
over brow

Social unit Social	Gestation 8 ½ months	Young 1	Diet

NESTING

Eastern Gorillas sleep in a new nest every evening. Adult males usually rest on the ground, while females sleep with their current offspring either on the ground or in forks of trees. An expectant female may build several nests within a few paces of each other, until she feels comfortable and gives birth. The infant is never left behind in the nest and accompanies the mother wherever she goes by clinging on to her fur.

bony crest on top of skull

exceptionally long forelimbs

young riding on mother's shoulders

SLOTHS, ANTEATERS, ARMADILLOS

F ORMERLY PART OF the order Xenarthra (or Edentata), these 29 species, are now classified into two separate orders: Cingulata (armadillos), and Pilosa (anteaters and sloths).

Found in a variety of habitats from S. USA to South America, members of these orders have unique strengthening joints called xenarthrales, in the lower spine. They also have a relatively small brain for the body size.

Apart from these features, however, the three groups are markedly different. Armadillos have protective armour, burrow extensively, and eat small animals as well as occasional plant material. Anteaters have a tubular snout and a long tongue for licking up ants and termites. Sloths, among the most arboreal of all mammals, have long fur and a small, rounded head, and eat mainly leaves and fruits.

Family BRADYPODIDAE	Species *Choloepus didactylus*	Status Unconfirmed

SOUTHERN TWO-TOED SLOTH

Characterized by its slender limbs and slow movements, this sloth has two hooked claws on its front feet and three on its rear feet. Its coarse, grey-brown fur may be tinged with green algae, which helps in camouflage as it hangs upside down from forest branches. Active at night, it moves so slowly through the canopy that its presence can barely be detected. It hardly ever descends to the ground – perhaps once a week to defecate – and at such times becomes vulnerable to predators such as Jaguars, Ocelots, and large eagles. Occasionally, it is hunted by humans.
• **SIZE** Length:18–34 in (46–86 cm). Weight:8¾–19 lb (4–8.5 kg).
• **OCCURRENCE** E. Venezuela, Guianas south to Ecuador, Peru, and the Amazon Basin of Brazil. In mature, disturbed, and secondary forest.
• **REMARK** The body temperature of this sloth is thought to be the lowest of any mammal.

S. AMERICA

long forelimbs with two hooked claws

three hooked claws on hindfeet

gray-brown, coarse fur

Social unit Solitary	Gestation 11 months	Young 1	Diet 🌿🐾

Family BRADYPODIDAE	Species *Bradypus torquatus*	Status Endangered

MANED THREE-TOED SLOTH

small head, eyes, and ears

darker mane

Active both during the day and night, this sloth blends remarkably well with its forest habitat, its grayish brown coat tinged green with algae and infested with ticks, beetles, and moths. The long, coarse outer hairs form a mane around its head and shoulders. Like the Southern Two-toed Sloth (see opposite), it only rarely descends to the ground, dragging itself along on its strong front legs. Its metabolic rate and temperature are very low. While its main defence is to stay unnoticed, it will lash out with its claws when confronted.
• SIZE Length:18–20in (45–50cm). Weight:7¾–8¾lb (3.5–4kg).
• OCCURRENCE Brazil(Bahia, Espirito Santo, and Rio de Janeiro). In coastal tropical forest.

fur hangs downwards

S. AMERICA

• REMARK In some areas, conservationists are trying to capture and relocate these sloths before tree felling takes place.

very small tail

Social unit Solitary	Gestation 5–6 months	Young 1	Diet 🥬

Family MYRMECOPHAGIDAE	Species *Tamandua tetradactyla*	Status Vulnerable*

SOUTHERN TAMANDUA

S. AMERICA

Sometimes called the Lesser Anteater, this species is pale yellow, with a black "vest" around its middle, a small pointed head, and a sparsely haired prehensile tail. Arboreal as well as terrestrial, it uses its long claws and powerful limbs to break up rotting logs and insect nests. It is active for eight-hour stretches, even at night.
• SIZE Length: 21–35in (53–88cm). Weight:7¾–19lb (3.5–8.5kg).
• OCCURRENCE S. Venezuela to N. Argentina and Uruguay. In diverse habitats, from rainforest to gallery forest, savanna, and plantations.

black patch on middle

long tail

downward-pointing muzzle

Social unit Solitary	Gestation 4–5 months	Young 1	Diet 🐜

Family MYRMECOPHAGIDAE	Species *Myrmecophaga tridactyla*	Status Vulnerable

GIANT ANTEATER

This species has a long, tubular snout widening to its small face, with tiny eyes and ears, massive forelegs, smaller rear legs, and a huge, bushy brown tail. Ambling along on its knuckles, it rips open ant hills and termite nests with its large front claws, lapping up its prey with its sticky, spine-covered tongue, which may be up to 2 ft (60 cm) long. The Giant Anteater defends itself from Pumas and Jaguars by rearing up, roaring, and slashing with its claws. Habitat destruction and hunting by humans for meat have threatened this species.

C. & S. AMERICA

• **SIZE** Length: 3¼–6½ ft (1–2 m).
Weight: 49–80 lb (22–39 kg).
• **OCCURRENCE**
Central to South America.
In grassland
and forest.

huge, bushy
brown tail

young riding on
mother's back

pale stripe
along sides

Social unit Solitary	Gestation 190 days	Young 1	Diet 🐜

Family MYRMECOPHAGIDAE	Species *Cyclopes didactylus*	Status Unconfirmed

SILKY ANTEATER

As the name suggests, this anteater has long, dense, silky fur that is usually smoky gray with a silvery sheen, often with a brown stripe running from shoulder to rump. Adapted to life in trees, the Silky Anteater grasps branches with its feet and hooklike claws, and long, thickly furred tail. This opportunistic feeder breaks open hollow stems inhabited by tree ants and licks them out with its long, sticky tongue. Hanging onto branches, it rests curled up in thick foliage or lianas; it is not known to build a nest. The male's territory appears to include those of several females.

underside of
tail-tip bare

large claws
on front feet

long
limbs

thickly
furred tail

• **SIZE** Length: 6½–8½ in
(16–21 cm). Weight: 5–10 oz (150–275 g).
• **OCCURRENCE** Mexico, and Central to
N. South America. In moist, lowland rain forest.
• **REMARK** The Silky Anteater rarely comes
to the ground and is especially vulnerable
to habitat loss by deforestation.

small,
pointed head

N., C., &
S. AMERICA

Social unit Solitary	Gestation Not known	Young 1–2	Diet 🐜

Family DASYPODIDAE	Species *Chaetophractus villosus*	Status Unconfirmed

LARGE HAIRY ARMADILLO

A creature of arid habitats, this species has coarse hair protruding from its thick armor, which comprises 18 or so bony, skin-covered bands. About seven or eight bands are movable, allowing the armadillo to roll into a ball to protect its vulnerable furry underside. A largely solitary species, it growls when threatened and defends itself by running away or digging burrows with its sharp claws. In summer, the Large Hairy Armadillo is chiefly nocturnal, feeding on a range of small prey, from insects and rodents to reptiles and carrion. In winter, it is more active during the day and feeds on a greater quantity of plant material. The Large Hairy Armadillo is hunted by humans throughout its range.
• **SIZE** Length: 9–16 in (22–40 cm). Weight: 2½–6½ lb (1–3 kg).
• **OCCURRENCE** S. South America. In sandy, semidesert areas.

S. AMERICA

large, pointed ears •

blunt head with pointed snout •

coarse hair •

Social unit Solitary	Gestation 60–75 days	Young 1–2	Diet 🐜 🦎 🐀 🐍 🍃

Family DASYPODIDAE	Species *Priodontes maximus*	Status Endangered

GIANT ARMADILLO

The largest of all armadillos, this species has 11–13 slightly movable, hinged plates over its body, and three or four plates over its neck. The long, tapering tail is also armored. This armadillo is dark brown, except for a pale, yellow-white head, tail, and band along the lower edges of its bony plates. The unusually large third front claw is used to rip through the earth for small prey such as termites, ants, worms, and snakes. The front claws are also used to dig a burrow in which it shelters by day. This armadillo is not social or territorial, and moves onto a new feeding area every 2–3 weeks.
• **SIZE** Length: 30–39 in (75–100 cm). Weight: 66 lb (30 kg).
• **OCCURRENCE** N. and C. South America. In a range of habitats, from grassland to tropical rain forest.
• **REMARK** This armadillo is the only species in its genus.

prominent upright ears •

S. AMERICA

hard, heavy armor •

Social unit Solitary	Gestation 4 months	Young 1–2	Diet 🐜 🐍 🦎

Family DASYPODIDAE	Species *Dasypus novemcinctus*	Status Locally common

NINE-BANDED ARMADILLO

Characterized by 8–10 flexible bands across its carapace, this most commonly seen armadillo digs an extensive burrow system, like others in its family. It produces multiple young of the same sex from a single fertilized egg.

8–10 flexible bands around middle

gray to yellow carapace

N., C., & S. AMERICA

• **SIZE** Length:14– 22½in (35 – 57 cm).Weight: 5½ –14 lb (2.5 – 6.5 kg).
• **OCCURRENCE** Mexico, and Central and South America. In grassland and forest.

Social unit Solitary	Gestation 8–9 months	Young 4	Diet 🐜 🦗 🐛 🐌 🍃

Family DASYPODIDAE	Species *Zaedyus pichiy*	Status Common

PICHI

When in danger, this small armadillo, the only species in its genus, grips the ground with its sharp-clawed feet, and relies on its bony shell for protection; or it wedges itself into a burrow, its armor facing outward. It digs a tunnel for shelter.
• **SIZE** Length:10–13½in (26– 34 cm). Weight: 2¼ – 4½ lb (1–2 kg).

rounded, low body

short, pointed head and ears

S. AMERICA

• **OCCURRENCE** Argentina and Chile, to Magellan's Strait. In grassland.

long, naked tail

Social unit Solitary	Gestation 60 days	Young 1–3	Diet 🐜 🦗

Family DASYPODIDAE	Species *Cabassous centralis*	Status Unconfirmed

NORTHERN NAKED-TAILED ARMADILLO

Found in a wide range of habitats, this large-eared armadillo has a specially enlarged middle claw on each forefoot for digging. This slow-moving species tears open ant and termite nests with its claws and licks up the insects with its long, sticky tongue, like an anteater. When threatened, it burrows into the ground, leaving its armor exposed.

broad head with blunt nose

C. & S. AMERICA

• **SIZE** Length: 12–16 in (30–40 cm). Weight: 4½–7¾ lb (2–3.5 kg).
• **OCCURRENCE** C. and N. South America. In grassland and forest.

narrow tail

Social unit Solitary	Gestation Not known	Young 1	Diet 🐜

PANGOLINS

I N BOTH LIFESTYLE and anatomy, pangolins resemble armadillos, anteaters, and sloths. However, they are unrelated and are classed in a separate order known as Philodata. The similarities between them are due to the fact that, in the course of evolution, they have all adapted in a similar way to their environment.

There are seven pangolin species, and they are all found in Africa and South Asia. Some are tree-dwelling, while others stay on the ground. None have any teeth. They gather their food, mainly ants and termites, with their extremely long, flexible tongue; food is swallowed whole and ground up in their stomach.

The most noticeable features of pangolins are their sharp-edged scales, made of horn, which cover most of the outward-facing parts of the body, and the tapering head and tail. The scales offer protection and camouflage. They are tilted by muscles at their base in the skin and are replaced periodically.

Family MANIDAE	Species *Manis pentadactyla*	Status Lower risk

CHINESE PANGOLIN

This agile animal lives in trees as well as on the ground. With powerful forelegs and a muscular, prehensile tail, it is an expert burrower and climber. In times of danger, it rolls itself into a ball, its body protected by its covering of scales. It uses its long tongue to scoop out ants and termites from their nests.
• **SIZE** Length: 21½–32in (54–80cm).
Weight: 4½–15lb (2–7kg).
• **OCCURRENCE** E. to S.E. Asia. In grassland and forest.

brown to yellow scales

heavy lids protect eyes

sharp claws on forelegs

ASIA

Social unit Solitary	Gestation 140 days	Young 1–2	Diet 🐜

Family MANIDAE	Species *Manis temminckii*	Status Lower risk

GRAND PANGOLIN

The streamlined body of this pangolin is covered with brown or yellow-brown overlapping scales, making it resemble the Chinese Pangolin (see above), although it is smaller in size. It uses its large claws to rip open ant and termite nests, both in trees and on the ground, for food.
• **SIZE** Length: 20–23½in (50–60cm).
Weight: 33–40lb (15–18kg).
• **OCCURRENCE**
E. to S. Africa.
In grassland,
tropical and
temperate
forest.

overlapping scales

AFRICA

small head

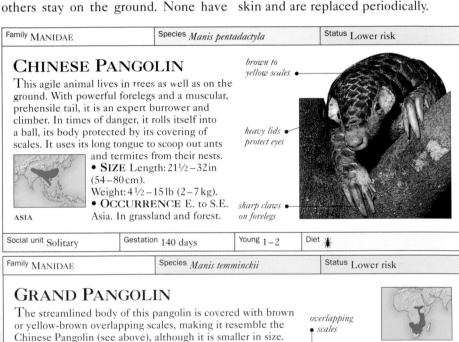

Social unit Solitary	Gestation 120 days	Young 1–2	Diet 🐜

RABBITS, HARES, AND PIKAS

T HE ORDER LAGOMORPHA, aptly meaning "leaping shape" includes rabbits, hares, and pikas. As targets for many predators, lagomorphs breed fast to maintain numbers, and detect danger with their extremely keen senses. Long ears catch slight sounds, and eyes high on the sides of the head give all-round vision. The powerful legs, especially the elongated hind pair, allow rapid escape. As gnawing mammals, lagomorphs are sometimes mistakenly thought to be rodents. Important differences include a second set of incisors in the upper jaw, lighter skull structure, slitlike nostrils, and a small, rounded, "bob" tail.

The more mouselike pikas, however, have rounded ears, four limbs of equal length, and no visible tail.

The 80 lagomorph species occur mainly in open habitats, from tundra to desert, and on all continents.

Family OCHOTONIDAE	Species *Ochotona princeps*	Status Vulnerable

AMERICAN PIKA

The egg-shaped, short-legged body of this pika, with no external tail, is typical of all its family. With a soft, dense coat, its back is grayish to cinnamon-brown, often richly tinged tawny or ochre, while its sides are a lighter buff. The soles of its feet are densely furred. It is usually found near a talus – an area of piled up, broken rocks surrounded by alpine meadows. Each talus is occupied by a solitary pika, which defends its territory with a short whistle. A patchwork of alternate male and female territories, of equal size, is formed across the area. The same short whistle, when used repeatedly, serves as a warning against predators, while the male emits a long, songlike call during courtship. The American Pika does not hibernate. Instead it makes a "hay pile" of grasses, herbs, and other plants near its burrow during late summer, as a winter store, often selecting plants that contain the most protein.

N. AMERICA

• SIZE Length: 6½–9 in (16–22 cm).
Weight: 4–6 oz (121–176 g).
• OCCURRENCE S.W. Canada and W. USA. In mountainous regions – mostly alpine meadows.

large, round ears with hair on both surfaces

small eyes

grayish to cinnamon-brown upperparts

buff underparts

Social unit Solitary	Gestation 30 days	Young 3	Diet 🌿

Family OCHOTONIDAE	Species *Ochotona curzoniae*	Status Common

BLACK-LIPPED PIKA

With sandy-brown upperparts and a yellow-white underside, the Black-lipped Pika or Plateau Pika has a distinctive black nose and lips. Extremely sociable, it lives in extended families occupying a single burrow system. Though this pika rarely lives beyond a year, in certain areas it is found in high density and thus viewed as a pest.
• **SIZE** Length: 5½ – 7½ in (14–18.5 cm). Weight: 4–6 oz (124–171 g).
• **OCCURRENCE** Himalayas, Nepal, Tibet, and W. China. On high altitude grassland.
• **REMARK** This pika is a key species in maintaining the biodiversity of the Tibetan Plateau.

dark ears with white margins

blackish nose

ASIA

sandy brown coat

Social unit Social	Gestation 21 days	Young 2–8	Diet 🌿

Family LEPORIDAE	Species *Pentalagus furnessi*	Status Endangered

AMAMI RABBIT

A uniform black coat, small eyes and ears, and a pointed snout characterize this rare species, found only on two islands of Japan. Nocturnal and herbivorous, the Amami Rabbit, also known as the Ryukyu Rabbit, feeds on plants such as pampas grass leaves, sweet potato runners, bamboo sprouts, and bark. It uses its long-nailed paws to dig nest-holes, and communicates by making clicking sounds. Little is known about the social and breeding habits of this rabbit.
• **SIZE** Length: 16½ – 20 in (42 – 51 cm). Weight: 4½ –11 lb (2 – 5 kg).
•**OCCURRENCE** Only on Amami and Tokuno islands of Japan. In tropical forest.
•**REMARK** Habitat destruction and predation are serious threats to this endangered species.

distinctive black fur

JAPAN

small ears

Social unit Variable	Gestation Unknown	Young 2–3	Diet 🌱

Family LEPORIDAE	Species *Sylvilagus aquaticus*	Status Locally common

SWAMP RABBIT

Highly territorial by nature, this able swimmer lives in wetlands and is always associated with water. It goes into water readily, especially when alarmed, and feeds on sedges, rushes, and aquatic plants. Active both day and night, it builds a nest on the ground made of weeds, lined with fur. This rabbit has a rusty brown or blackish coat with a white vent.
• SIZE Length:18–22in (45–55cm). Weight:3¼–5½lb (1.5–2.5kg).
• OCCURRENCE S.E. USA. In swamps, marshes, and forest.

N. AMERICA

cinnamon ring around eyes
short, sleek coat

Social unit Social	Gestation 37 days	Young 1–6	Diet

Family LEPORIDAE	Species *Sylvilagus floridanus*	Status Common

EASTERN COTTONTAIL

This rabbit is the most widely distributed species in its genus, occupying diverse habitats. It has long and dense fur, usually brown or gray, with a rusty nape, and a cottony white tail tipped reddish brown. The Eastern Cottontail feeds from late morning to evening, on lush green vegetation in summer, and bark and twigs in winter.
• SIZE Length:15–19½in (38–49cm). Weight:2¼–3¼lb (1–1.5kg).
• OCCURRENCE S.E. Canada to Mexico, Central America, N. South America, and Europe. In grassland, desert, and forest.

N., C., & S. AMERICA

long ears
brown to gray back
white feet

Social unit Social	Gestation 26–30 days	Young 3–7	Diet

Family LEPORIDAE	Species *Brachylagus idahoensis*	Status Lower risk

PYGMY RABBIT

The smallest of all North American rabbits, the Pygmy Rabbit is the only leporid species in the region that digs extensive burrow systems, with four or five widely spaced entrances. Feeding on big sagebrush and other related species, this rabbit is found in areas where these are easily available. It mostly forages at dawn and dusk, but in winter, could be active at any time of the day. This rabbit's coat is gray in winter and brown in summer, with the nape, chest, legs, and tail a cinnamon-buff.
• SIZE Length:9–11½in (22–29cm). Weight:13–16oz (350–450g).
• OCCURRENCE Great Basin Desert, USA. In areas of dense big sagebrush.
• REMARK This is the world's smallest rabbit.

N. AMERICA

short ears with fur on inner edge
long, silky coat

Social unit Solitary	Gestation 26–28 days	Young 4–8	Diet

Family LEPORIDAE	Species *Oryctolagus cuniculus*	Status Common

EUROPEAN RABBIT

The ancestor of all breeds of domestic rabbit, this species has been introduced in many countries throughout the world. It has a coat of black to light brown, with a dark collar, and a buff-colored nape. Buffish white underneath, it has long, black-tipped ears, long hindlegs, and extremely furry feet. Nocturnal in habit, the European Rabbit is the most social species of the order, with a strict hierarchy of dominance. It digs elaborate underground tunnels or warrens, with large breeding burrows, mothers of lower "rank" digging small burrows outside the main warren. Males are known to protect juveniles, irrespective of paternity, from females, who may attack and even kill any strange young.

EUROPE, AFRICA, AUSTRALIA, S. AMERICA

• **SIZE** Length:13½–20 in (34–50 cm). Weight: 2¼–5½ lb (1–2.5 kg).
• **OCCURRENCE** Native only to S.W. Europe and probably N.W. Africa. Introduced in South America, Australia, and New Zealand and other parts of Europe. In grassland.
• **REMARK** Responsible for widespread habitat destruction, the rapidly multiplying European Rabbit has created a virtual wildlife management disaster wherever it has been introduced.

CUDDLY PETS
In the Middle Ages, French monks who reared wild rabbits for food began cross-breeding those with different features. Now popular pets, domestic rabbits come in different sizes, ear shapes, fur types, and color patterns. The rabbit shown above is the Bicolored French Lop.

long ears tipped black

buff between shoulders

black-brown coat

furry feet

Social unit Social	Gestation 28–33 days	Young 3–12	Diet

Family LEPORIDAE	Species *Romerolagus diazi*	Status Endangered

VOLCANO RABBIT

Endemic to the volcanic region surrounding Mexico City, this rabbit is found in pine forests that have a dense undergrowth of bunch grasses, known as "zacaton." Found in groups of up to five, it is especially active in the early morning and evening. Unusual for its small, round ears, this species also has a small tail that is not visible externally. Its short, dense fur is yellow-black on the back and sides. The tip and base of the guard hairs on the underside are black.
• **SIZE** Length: 9–12½ in (23–32 cm). Weight: 13–21 oz (375–600 g).
• **OCCURRENCE** Around Mexico City. On forested, volcanic slopes with zacaton grasses.
• **REMARK** Threats to this species include habitat loss, hunting, and the seasonal burning of the zacaton.

N. AMERICA

• small, rounded ears
short, dense fur •

Social unit Social	Gestation 38–40 days	Young 2	Diet 🌱

Family LEPORIDAE	Species *Lepus europaeus*	Status Common

EUROPEAN HARE

This long-legged, large-eared hare has a prominent tail that is black on top and white below, and a distinctive, triangular black patch on the back of each ear-tip. Uniform in appearance, it is tawny or rusty on the chest and sides and darker on the back. This solitary hare spends the day hiding in a form – a shallow depression made in open fields or under cover of long grass or shrubs. During courtship it often displays what is called "mad March Hare behavior," akin to a boxing bout, with unreceptive females chasing away interested males.
• **SIZE** Length: 19–28 in (48–70 cm). Weight: 5½–15 lb (2.5–7 kg).
• **OCCURRENCE** Europe and Asia. Introduced in E. Canada, N.E. USA, South America, S.E. Australia, and New Zealand. In open country, farmland, steppe, and woodland.
• **REMARK** Although the European Hare has been introduced to many countries, there is a general concern over the decline of its numbers in Europe.

EURASIA

black triangle • on ear tips
long, curly hair on back •
• long legs
• conspicuous two-tone tail
• large hind feet

Social unit Solitary	Gestation 42 days	Young 1–10	Diet 🌿 🌱 🌾

Family LEPORIDAE	Species *Lepus arcticus*	Status Common

ARCTIC HARE

A large, stocky hare with long fur, this species is highly adapted to survive in the severe conditions of the Arctic tundra. Some subspecies remain white throughout the year, but others turn gray in summer. The Arctic Hare's front incisors are modified to eat snow-covered plants, such as mosses and lichens, the buds, berries, leaves, and bark of other low-growing vegetation, and the roots of shrubs such as willow. It stamps on the ground with its hindfeet to expose plants beneath the snow. Unlike other hares, this species also takes meat from hunters' traps. Except when mating, it usually lives in groups of up to 300 and displays flocking behavior, with the whole group suddenly changing direction at once. It uses speed to escape from predators, often running as fast as 40 mph (64 kph).
• SIZE Length:17–26 in (43–66 cm). Weight: 6 ½ –15 lb (3–7 kg).
• OCCURRENCE N. Canada, (Ellesmere Island, Northwest Territories, Newfoundland) and Greenland. On hillsides or rocky plateaux.

ARCTIC

WHITE WINTER WEAR
The Arctic Hare's winter coat is completely white except for black ear-tips, providing camouflage in the snow.

ears black in front and white behind

long whiskers

gray fur in summer

thick, furry coat

large, spreading feet

Social unit Variable	Gestation Unknown	Young 1–8	Diet

Family LEPORIDAE	Species *Lepus timidus*	Status Locally common

MOUNTAIN HARE

black ear-tips •

Also known as the Blue Hare, the Mountain Hare is smaller than the Brown Hare (see p.140) and has long, black-tipped ears and large, furry feet. Molting in late fall and spring, its winter coat is completely white, while in summer it turns brown. A browser of woody plants such as heather, gorse, and juniper, it prefers grasses when available and digs up the snow in winter to expose its food.

long ears •

brown summer •
coat

• SIZE Length:16 ½–24 ½ in (43–61 cm). Weight: 4 ½–7 ¾ lb (2–3.5 kg).
• OCCURRENCE Arctic region of Europe and Asia. In coniferous forest, tundra, and mountains.
• REMARK It is also grouped

EURASIA

with the Arctic Hare, expanding its range across Canada and USA.

Social unit Solitary	Gestation 50 days	Young 1–3	Diet

Family LEPORIDAE	Species *Lepus californicus*	Status Common

BLACK-TAILED JACKRABBIT

Enormous, black-tipped ears, up to 6 in (15 cm) long, help this hare to release excess body heat in hot, arid habitats, and to detect the faintest sounds of predators. It has a grayish brown to sandy coat, long legs, and a black tail with a black line extending to the rump. Found in different vegetation, such as sagebrush, creosote bush, mesquite, snakeweed, and juniper, it prefers succulent grasses and herbs, but can survive nibbling on woody twigs during drought or winter. When threatened, it "freezes" or lies still with its head pressed to the ground, or it runs very fast on a jagged course. It builds a shallow "form" or nest under a bush, and primarily stays within its home range, rather than defending a larger territory. The Black-tailed Jackrabbit displays complex courtship behavior, including long chases, pair jumping, and fights between male and female.

• *large ears*
tipped black

• *black rump*

• SIZE Length:18 ½–25 in (47–63 cm). Weight: 3 ¼–7 ¾ lb (1.5–3.5 kg).
• OCCURRENCE W. USA and N. Mexico. In arid grassland and desert.
• REMARK One of the speediest lagomorphs, it can run up to 35 mph (56 kph).

N. AMERICA

long, powerful feet •

Social unit Solitary	Gestation 41–47 days	Young 1–6	Diet

RODENTS

MORE THAN TWO out of every five mammal species are rodents. Typified by mice and rats, they are found on every continent, except Antarctica, and in almost every habitat.

Despite a variety of lifestyles, from treetop squirrels, to semiaquatic beavers and Capybaras, lemmings that live under snow in winter, leaping jerboas, and burrowing mole rats, most rodents share common features. They are relatively small animals that have compact bodies, move on four limbs, and have clawed feet, a long tail, and powerful teeth and jaws specialized for gnawing. In particular,

the four incisor teeth are long, deep-rooted, and grow continually. Rodents are equipped with acute senses of smell and hearing which, aided by numerous long and sensitive whiskers, make them extremely aware of their surroundings.

A few species, such as the Woodchuck, are solitary. However, most rodents are social, and some – like the lemmings, rats, mice, and prairie dogs – form enormous, loose-knit communities. Many small rodents breed very fast – some voles produce more than ten litters yearly. This counteracts predation and persecution by humans.

Family APLODONTIDAE	Species *Aplodontia rufa*	Status Lower risk

MOUNTAIN BEAVER

Known locally as the Sewellel, the Mountain Beaver has a long-haired coat that is black to red-brown above and yellow-brown below. It has a white spot below each ear and a flattened head. Its tail is short compared to those of beavers. This nocturnal rodent digs elaborate nests and tunnels under tree logs, with the entrances leading directly to a source of food such as bark, twigs, shoots, and succulents. Unlikely to travel far in its search for food, it carries back supplies to its nest, where they are consumed or stored.
A good climber of trees, the Mountain Beaver can reach heights up to 22 ft (7 m) and is known to destroy large numbers of young trees such as fir and spruce by gnawing. Although it is found in mountainous areas, it prefers lower elevations. It is preyed upon by skunks, weasels, foxes, coyotes, raccoons, and eagle owls.
• **SIZE** Body length: 12–18 in (30–46 cm). Tail: ¾–1 ½ in (2–4 cm).
• **OCCURRENCE** S.W. British Columbia (Canada) to C. California. In mountains and along coastlines.
• **REMARK** This beaver has benefited from tree felling since it builds its home under felled logs.

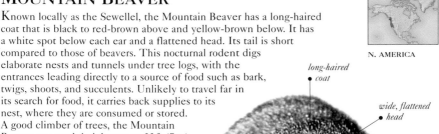

N. AMERICA

long-haired coat

wide, flattened head

Social unit Solitary	Gestation 28–30 days	Young 2–6	Diet

Family SCIURIDAE	Species *Marmota monax*	Status Common

WOODCHUCK

small ears

white area around nose

powerful build

Also called the Groundhog, this species is one of the largest and strongest squirrels. It has a stout body, short legs, a bushy tail, and brown fur that is grizzled or white-tipped. This able climber and swimmer feeds mainly in the afternoon, sometimes in groups, and eats grasses, clover, seeds, fruits, and small animals such as snails and grasshoppers. It often shows aggression to its own kind, especially when defending its burrow, and in the mating season when males fight for dominance. Defensive behavior includes back arching, jumping, stiffening the tail, and teeth chattering. In the fall, the Woodchuck digs a deeper burrow for its hibernation.
• **SIZE** Body length:12½–20½ in (32–52 cm).
Tail:3–4½ in (7.5–11.5 cm).

N. AMERICA

• **OCCURRENCE** Canada, Alaska, and E. USA. In woodland and fields.
• **REMARK** February 2 is known as Groundhog Day in North America, when this animal supposedly peers out to assess the weather.

Social unit Variable	Gestation 31–32 days	Young 1–8	Diet

Family SCIURIDAE	Species *Marmota flaviventris*	Status Locally common

YELLOW-BELLIED MARMOT

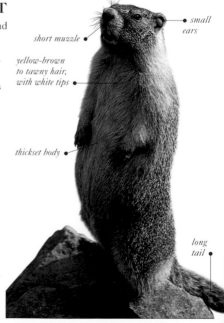

small ears

short muzzle

yellow-brown to tawny hair, with white tips

thickset body

long tail

This marmot has a thickset body with a short, broad head and strong claws. Its ears are small and covered with fur, and it has soft, woolly underfur on the back and flanks. In many, the coarse outer guard hair varies from yellow-brown to tawny, frosted with paler tips, although some individuals may be black. Adapted to a wide range of habitats, the Yellow-bellied Marmot has an extensive diet of grasses, flowers, herbs, and seeds. It feeds mainly in the morning and late afternoon, then grooms and suns itself with other members of its colony, which usually consists of one male and several females. Preyed upon by Coyotes, Bobcats, hawks, owls, and eagles, it takes cover in its burrow when threatened. In the fall, this rodent goes into a long hibernation in its burrow and may stay there for up to eight months.
• **SIZE** Length:13 ½–20 in (34–50 cm).
Tail:5–9 in (13–22 cm).

N. AMERICA

• **OCCURRENCE** W. Canada and W. USA. In varied habitats from the alpine zone, woodland, and forest clearings, to semidesert.

Social unit Social	Gestation 30 days	Young 3–8	Diet

Family SCIURIDAE	Species *Cynomys ludovicianus*	Status Lower risk

BLACK-TAILED PRAIRIE DOG

reddish brown
• upperparts

Also known as the Plains Prairie Dog, this squirrel is one of the five species of prairie dogs that derive their common name from their grassy habitat and characteristic doglike bark or "yip." It has brown or reddish brown fur, tipped white in summer and black in winter, and its whiskers and tail-tip are black. During territorial disputes, these squirrels aggressively flare their tails and bark, in what are known as "jump-yip displays." They feed on wheat grass, buffalo grass, globemallow, and rabbitbrush in summer, and thistles, cacti, and roots in winter.
• **SIZE** Body length:11–12 in (28–30 cm).
Tail: 2¾–4½ in (7–11.5 cm).
• **OCCURRENCE** Great Plains of North America. In grassland.
• **REMARK** The Black-tailed Prairie Dog causes massive destruction to crops and has been the subject of verysuccessful extermination campaigns in some regions.

small •
eyes

N. AMERICA

Social unit Social	Gestation 33–38 days	Young 1–8	Diet 🌿 🪲

Family SCIURIDAE	Species *Xerus inauris*	Status Locally common*

SOUTH AFRICAN GROUND SQUIRREL

Like the other ground squirrels, this African species has large, strong claws, enabling it to dig the extensive system of tunnels in which it lives. The fur on its back and head is brownish pink, and it has a white flank stripe, white face, feet, and belly, and black bands near the base and tip of its white tail. An opportunistic feeder, its diet ranges from seeds, bulbs, and fleshy roots to insects and birds' eggs. This squirrel lives in colonies of 6–10, occasionally as many as 30. It waits until well after sunrise before it emerges from its burrow, although on cold or overcast days it remains underground.
• **SIZE** Body length:8–12 in (20–30 cm).
Tail:7–10 in (18–26 cm).
• **OCCURRENCE** S. Angola, Zimbabwe, Botswana, South Africa, Namibia. In open country.

AFRICA

broad head
• with prominent eyes

• whitish line
above and
below eyes

Social unit Social	Gestation 42–49 days	Young 1–3	Diet 🌿 ⋯ 🪲 ●

Family SCIURIDAE	Species *Tamias striatus*	Status Locally common

EASTERN CHIPMUNK

This rodent is greyish or reddish brown all over with a central dark brown stripe running down its back, which is bordered on either side by grayish or reddish brown hairs followed by stripes of dark brown or yellow-orange leading to a white belly. Light and dark facial stripes border its eyes. Its bushy tail is dark on the upperside with a light gray border, and its rump is yellowish or reddish brown. However, the overall color and patterns on the coat vary from one region to another. Although sedentary by nature, the Eastern Chipmunk looks for food over a wide range of areas. Foraging activity peaks around mid-morning and mid-afternoon, with males more active in the morning and females more so in the afternoon. This solitary animal occupies a single burrow system and chases away trespassers from its core home territory, although a number of individuals may share a larger range. Both sexes make loud "chip" and "cuk" sounds that act as alarm calls to fellow chipmunks and other small animals living nearby. They are preyed upon by snakes, hawks, foxes, bobcats, and weasels. Chipmunks hibernate from fall to early spring, but they may come out of their burrows to feed on fine winter days.

N. AMERICA

small, rounded ears with pale borders

• **SIZE** Body length: 6–6½ in (15.5–16.5 cm). Tail: 2¾–4 in (7–10 cm).
• **OCCURRENCE** Canada (Lake Manitoba to Nova Scotia), south to Louisiana, Alabama, Georgia, and N. Florida. In deciduous woodland and bushy areas with abundant rock crevices.
• **REMARK** Female chipmunks become intolerant of their young soon after birth, prompting the offspring to set up their own homes when only two weeks old.

dark stripes with pale borders along back

Social unit Solitary	Gestation 31–32 days	Young 4–5	Diet ⣿ ◗

LONG AND SLIM
The chipmunk stretches its body to move through its burrow system, the tunnels of which are extremely narrow, to keep out larger predators such as weasels. Each burrow system may be 33 ft (10 m) long.

eyes bordered by light and dark stripes

well-haired tail, dark on upperside

large black eyes

forepaws used to hold food

grayish to reddish brown fur

creamish white belly

hind feet longer and broader than forefeet

OPPORTUNISTIC FEEDER
The Eastern Chipmunk is familiar in the wild to humans as a bold visitor to picnic sites. Although it can climb well, this chipmunk forages mainly on the ground for seeds, acorns, and nuts, which it manipulates with its forepaws. Its stuffs food into its cheek pouches and hoards in its burrow to eat later.

Family SCIURIDAE	Species *Spermophilus columbianus*	Status Locally common

COLUMBIAN GROUND SQUIRREL

Found in the mountain meadows of British Columbia, Canada, the Columbian Ground Squirrel is mainly brownish pink in color, with a tawny face and nose, pale gray patches on the sides of the neck, and a tail that is black above and gray below. Its fur is short and dense, and the underfur is darker in color. Adult squirrels "kiss" each other on meeting, or tilt their heads to sniff the scent glands near the mouth. Feeding on flowers, seeds, bulbs, and fruits, this species customarily takes a few steps, pauses to eat, and takes a few steps again. It also catches insects midflight and occasionally becomes cannibalistic. Adult males have overlapping territories, while females have exclusive ones.

tawny face and nose

brownish pink fur on back

dark brown underfur

N. AMERICA

- **SIZE** Body length:10 –11½ in (25–29 cm).Tail: 8–11.5 cm (3¼–4½ in).
- **OCCURRENCE** W. Canada to N.W. USA. In alpine and subalpine meadows.

Social unit Social	Gestation 24 days	Young 2 – 5	Diet

Family SCIURIDAE	Species *Sciurus vulgaris*	Status Lower risk

EURASIAN RED SQUIRREL

EURASIA

Not uniformly red, this squirrel varies from gray to red, brown, and black on its back, and is white below. In winter its coat may turn bright or dark grayish brown. The bushy tail is the same length as the body, while the ears are tufted, more so in winter. Adept at climbing and leaping, the Red Squirrel feeds on the ground or on branches, eating pine seeds, beechnuts, acorns, mushrooms, shoots, fruits, and bark, manipulating food with its forepaws. The drey (nest) is a ball of twigs in a branch fork or tree hole. The female makes a larger breeding nest, lined with soft material, for her young.

upright, tufted ears

red to gray, brown, or black pelt

long, bushy tail

- **SIZE** Body length: 8–10 in (20–25 cm). Tail: 6–8 in (15–20 cm).
- **OCCURRENCE** W. Europe to E. Asia. In forest, parks, and gardens up to the tree line.
- **REMARK** This species is threatened by deforestation and competition with the introduced Gray Squirrel.

Social unit Solitary	Gestation 38 days	Young 2 – 5	Diet

Family SCIURIDAE	Species *Sciurus carolinensis*	Status Common

EASTERN GRAY SQUIRREL

A native of North America that has now been introduced in parts of Europe, the Eastern Gray Squirrel is gray on the back and white to gray or pinkish brown on its underparts. Its face, back, and forelegs are tinged brown, and its tail is white or pale gray. Unlike the Red Squirrel (see opposite), its ears are not tufted. This medium-sized tree squirrel is an opportunistic feeder and "scatter-hoards" its food, carrying it in its mouth and burying it more than ¾ in (2 cm) below the soil surface. It displays a strong homing tendency, although males are known to travel long distances. A social animal, it warns other squirrels of danger through different sounds, and chatters its teeth when confronted.
• **SIZE** Body length: 9–11 in (23–28 cm). Tail: 6–10 in (15–25 cm).
• **OCCURRENCE** S. and S.E. Canada to C. and E. USA. Introduced to the UK and Italy. In temperate forest, especially where winter food is plentiful.
• **REMARK** This introduced species has largely replaced the Red Squirrel in the UK.

TREETOP HOME
The Eastern Gray Squirrel makes a "drey," or nest, out of twigs in the branches of trees, and lines it with grass or bark. Although it becomes inactive in winter, it may emerge from its nest to forage.

face tinged with brown

ears not tufted

dark to pale gray back

food held in forepaws

long, bushy tail

whitish underparts

N. AMERICA, EUROPE

Social unit Variable	Gestation 44 days	Young 1–5	Diet 🌱 🍂 🌰 ⚬ 🍄

Family SCIURIDAE	Species *Ratufa indica*	Status Vulnerable

INDIAN GIANT SQUIRREL

typical bent feeding posture

The huge, bushy tail of this large squirrel is longer than its head and body combined. Usually black above, its limbs and head are red-brown, while its underside is white. Its hands and feet are broad, and the claws are strong and well developed. Always alert, this squirrel makes giant leaps of 20 ft (6 m) from branch to branch in search of food. It builds a typical squirrel-type drey (nest) for resting and breeding. When alarmed, it flattens itself against a branch or hides behind a thick trunk.

short, round ears

• SIZE Body length: 14 –16 in (35–40 cm). Tail:14 –23 in (35–60 cm).

• OCCURRENCE Peninsular India. In deciduous and moist evergreen forest.

red-brown head

• REMARK Unlike other squirrels, this squirrel does not feed upright, but leans forwards on its hindlegs, using its tail for balance.

ASIA

uses hands to manipulate food

Social unit Solitary/Pair	Gestation 28 days	Young Not known	Diet 🐚 ❤ 🥬 🐜 ●

Family SCIURIDAE	Species *Heliosciurus gambianus*	Status Lower risk*

GAMBIAN SUN SQUIRREL

Speckled olive-brown in appearance, the Gambian Sun Squirrel has hairs banded in yellow, brown, and gray along its coat. There are 14 black bands on its tail and a white ring around each eye. When alarmed, this typical ground-and-tree squirrel climbs a tree away from the source of danger. It lines its nest, in a tree-hole, with fresh leaves each night.

AFRICA

• SIZE Body length:6 –8½ in (15.5–21cm). Tail:6 –12 in (15.5–31cm).

• OCCURRENCE Senegal to Sudan, south to Angola and N. Zambia. In woodland savanna and secondary forest.

white rings around eyes

rounded ears

• REMARK The sun squirrel gets its name from its habit of basking in the sun.

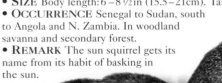

Social unit Solitary/Pair	Gestation Not known	Young 1–5	Diet ⁙ ❤ 🐚 🐜 ●

Family SCIURIDAE	Species *Callosciurus prevostii*	Status Lower risk*

PREVOST'S SQUIRREL

A striking and largely uniform color pattern characterizes this arboreal squirrel. Black on its upperparts and chestnut-red below, it has a gleaming white band running between these two colors from the nose to the thigh. Large, protruding eyes equip it with sharp vision. Prevost's Squirrel lives alone or in small family groups, communicating with birdlike calls and tail displays.

ASIA

white band along side from thigh to nose

protruding eyes

• **SIZE** Body length: 5–11 in (13–28 cm). Tail: 3¼–10 in (8–26 cm).
• **OCCURRENCE** S.E. Asia. In lowland and montane forest, farms, and gardens.
• **REMARK** It is one of the most brilliantly colored mammals.

black tail

chestnut limbs

Social unit Variable	Gestation 46–48 days	Young 2–3	Diet ![icons]

Family SCIURIDAE	Species *Petaurista elegans*	Status Common

GIANT FLYING SQUIRREL

A glider rather than a flier, this squirrel stretches out a thin, furred membrane between its front and rear limbs to travel over distances of more than 1,310 ft (400 m), from tree to tree. Usually gliding to avoid danger, it covers three times the distance that it loses in height, using its forelegs to navigate. The Giant Flying Squirrel has a tawny to reddish brown coat that is densely furred, with lighter underparts, and a black-tipped tail. An agile climber, it nests in tree-holes and forks of branches, emerging at night in search of food.

ASIA

thick fur

• **SIZE** Body length: 12–18 in (30–45 cm). Tail: 12½–24 in (32–61 cm).
• **OCCURRENCE** E. Afghanistan, N. India, W. China, and S.E. Asia. In coniferous forest.

black rings around eyes

membrane between limbs

black tail-tip

tawny to reddish brown coat

tough edge along membrane

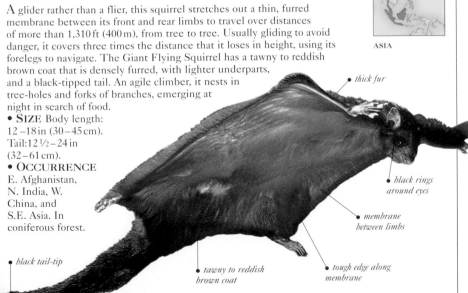

Social unit Pair	Gestation Not known	Young 1–3	Diet ![icons]

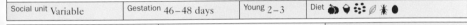

Family GEOMYIDAE	Species *Thomomys bottae*	Status Common

BOTTA'S POCKET GOPHER

This solitary, burrowing rodent has grayish brown upperparts and brownish orange underparts, with dark hair bases. It has external fur-lined storage pouches on its cheeks. Its flat skull, small ears closed by flaps, strong shoulders and forelegs, and rapidly growing, middle three claws, equip it to dig in loose and wet soil. Extremely territorial, this animal mostly stays underground, creating extensive subterranean burrow systems, in which it rests during the hot, dry summer months. Botta's Pocket Gopher communicates using a wide variety of sounds, ranging from scolding shrieks to soft mumbling and squeaking.
• SIZE Body length: 4½ –12 in (11.5–30 cm). Tail: 1½–3¾ in (4–9.5 cm).
• OCCURRENCE W. USA to N. Mexico. In desert to open forest.

N. AMERICA

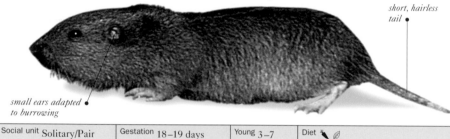

short, hairless tail

small ears adapted to burrowing

Social unit Solitary/Pair	Gestation 18–19 days	Young 3–7	Diet

Family HETEROMYIDAE	Species *Dipodomys merriami*	Status Common

MERRIAM'S KANGAROO RAT

A small rodent with a white stripe from its flank to the base of its tail, and distinctive white spots above its eyes and behind its ears, this nocturnal rodent moves with great speed over sandy desert soil. It hops like a kangaroo on its large hindfeet and uses its long, slender tail for balance. This rat digs, burrows, and searches for food, especially cockle- and sand-burrs in winter, and prickly pear and other cactus seeds in summer. It is often found grooming itself by taking rapid and energetic dust-baths. Hardy and industrious, it also moves on snow-covered ground in winter.
• SIZE Body length: 3¼– 5½ in (8–14 cm).
Tail: 5½–6½ in (14–16 cm).
• OCCURRENCE S.W. USA to N. Mexico. In desert.

N. AMERICA

white spots above eyes and behind ears

long tail

Social unit Social	Gestation Not known	Young 1–5	Diet

Family PEDETIDAE	Species *Pedetes capensis*	Status Vulnerable

SPRINGHARE

The only member in its family, the Springhare or Springhaas has a bushy, black-tipped tail and long, upright ears. It leaps across arid or semiarid country on its powerful hindlegs, easily covering 6½–9¾ft (2–3 m) per bound. This nocturnal rodent feeds on seeds, bulbs, and stems, as well as small creatures such as locusts and beetles. While eating, it bends forwards, loping rabbitlike on *short fore feet* all four limbs, and while resting on its haunches, it tucks its head between its rear legs and wraps its tail around its body. Always alert, it has acute senses of sight, hearing, and smell. Occasionally found in pairs, this animal makes several extensive burrows to use on different days.
• **SIZE** Body length:10½–16 in (27–40 cm). Tail:12–18½ in (30–47 cm).
• **OCCURRENCE** C. and E. Africa to S. Africa. In arid or semiarid country with scanty vegetation or light woodland.
• **REMARK** The Springhare is prized for its meat by African bushmen.

AFRICA

pinkish brown to gray coat

powerful tail tipped black

Social unit Solitary/Pair	Gestation 2 months	Young 1	Diet

Family CASTORIDAE	Species *Castor fiber*	Status Lower risk

EURASIAN BEAVER

An adept builder of dams, burrows, lodges, and canals, the Eurasian Beaver is similar to its American cousin (see pp.154–155) in habits, lifestyle, and appearance, but may be more heavily built. As with the American Beaver, it has oil glands at the base of its tail, which produce a lubricating secretion that it spreads through its fur while grooming, to waterproof it. Webbed hind feet and a rudderlike tail enable this nocturnal swimmer to maneuver in water, and it can remain submerged for almost 20 minutes. In areas which have many natural waterways, it does not build a lodge, but digs *small eyes* tunnels in the riverbank.
• **SIZE** Body length: 33–39 in (83–100 cm). Tail:12–15 in (30–38 cm).
• **OCCURRENCE** Europe and W. Siberia. Isolated populations in China and Mongolia. In lakes and rivers.

EURASIA

broad, scaly tail

Social unit Social	Gestation 105–107 days	Young 1–5	Diet

Family CASTORIDAE	Species *Castor canadensis*	Status Locally common

AMERICAN BEAVER

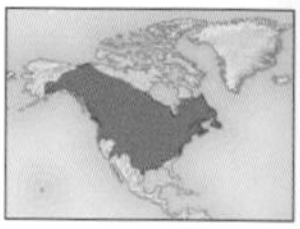

N. AMERICA

This mammal is adapted to aquatic life in various ways: its eyes have
a nictitating membrane (a transparent third eyelid) that enables it to
see underwater, its ears and nose shut with valvelike flaps, and the
lips close behind the incisors, allowing it to nibble with its mouth
shut. Webbed feet facilitate swimming, as does its long, flattened tail,
which it also flaps on the water surface as an alarm signal. The American
Beaver's long, coarse, reddish brown guard hair and dense gray
underfur retain body heat underwater and its long whiskers help it to
feel its way in the dark. It grasps its food with its front paws and
gnaws it with its teeth. Hissing, grunting, and tooth-sharpening may
sometimes accompany the competition for food. Usually living in
colonies of 4–8 related individuals, American Beavers are found
grooming each other, touching noses, wrestling, or dancing.
Members of a colony rest together in the lodge at daytime,
with females being more sedentary than males.

*yellowish to
reddish brown
• coat*

• **SIZE** Length: 29–35 in (74–88 cm).
Weight: 24–57 lb (11–26 kg).
• **OCCURRENCE** North America – except the
southwestern desert, peninsular Florida, and
Arctic tundra. In streams, ponds, and lakes.

*ears placed •
high on head*

blunt snout •

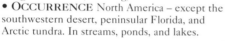
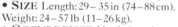

Social unit Social	Gestation 107 days	Young 3–4	Diet

ECOLOGICAL BIND
The American Beaver's extensive tree-felling and dam-building activity often lays waste wide tracts of land and water, considerably altering the local ecology. However, an alternative viewpoint is that beaver dams reduce floods, helping to preserve the habitat.

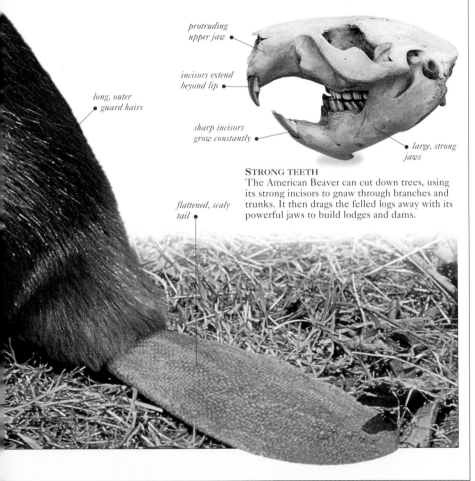

protruding upper jaw

incisors extend beyond lip

long, outer guard hairs

sharp incisors grow constantly

large, strong jaws

STRONG TEETH
The American Beaver can cut down trees, using its strong incisors to gnaw through branches and trunks. It then drags the felled logs away with its powerful jaws to build lodges and dams.

flattened, scaly tail

Family MURIDAE	Species *Reithrodontomys raviventris*	Status Vulnerable

SALT MARSH HARVEST MOUSE

Similar to the House Mouse in size and appearance
(see p.167), the Salt Marsh Harvest Mouse has more
hair on its slender and scaly tail. It is pinkish brown
to brownish gray on the upperparts and grayish
white underneath, and has large ears and
grooved upper incisors. An expert climber,
this nocturnal mouse builds sturdy summer
nests in tufts of grass or shrubs, but also
burrows in tunnel systems of other rodents
in winter. During this season, this mouse
uses the runways of these rodents to feed on
seeds, from the ground or from grass stems,
as well as on green shoots and insects.
• SIZE Body length: 2¾–3 in (7–7.5 cm).
Tail:1¾–4½ in (4.5–11.5 cm).
• OCCURRENCE USA
(San Fransisco Bay area of
California) and N. Mexico.
In grassland.

large ears •   N. AMERICA

pink-brown to •
gray-brown back

Social unit Solitary	Gestation 21–24 days	Young 1–7	Diet

Family MURIDAE	Species *Peromyscus leucopus*	Status Common

WHITE-FOOTED MOUSE

This species is characterized by large eyes, prominent ears,
white feet and underparts, a brown back, and a long, sparsely
haired tail. Active at night, it lives in pairs in a small den,
which it may dig, or which may be an abandoned nest, or a
hollow under a stone, log, or thicket. This den also houses the
breeding nest and the store of food, generally seeds
and insects, which is lightly covered with soil.
• SIZE Body length: 3½–4¼ in
(9–10.5 cm). Tail: 2¼–4 in
(6–10 cm).
• OCCURRENCE S.E.
Canada, C. and E. USA, and
N. Mexico. In thickets,
deciduous forest,
and grassland.

long, thinly
haired tail •

• white underparts

prominent
ears •

long whiskers •

N. AMERICA

Social unit Pair	Gestation 22–23 days	Young 1–6	Diet

Family MURIDAE	Species *Nyctomys sumichrasti*	Status Locally common

VESPER RAT

Adapted well to its arboreal existence, this species is found in colonies of nests made of twigs, leaves, and creepers. Its long, thumblike big toes help it grip branches efficiently, and it rarely climbs down to the ground. This brightly colored rat has tawny or pinkish brown upperparts, with darker hair along the center of its back. A dark ring encircles each eye, extending to the whiskers, and its ears are finely furred. Its tail is scaly with longer and heavier hairs on the tip. This nocturnal rat feeds mainly on fruits such as wild figs and avocados.
• SIZE Body length: 4¼–5 in (11–13 cm). Tail: 3¼–6 in (8.5–15.5 cm).
• OCCURRENCE Mexico and Central America, to C. Panama. In tropical forest.

tawny or brownish upperparts

dark ring around eyes

N. & C. AMERICA

white undersides

Social unit Social	Gestation Not known	Young 2–4	Diet 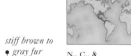

Family MURIDAE	Species *Sigmodon hispidus*	Status Lower risk

HISPID COTTON RAT

There are ten cotton rat species in the Americas, some quite rare, and some so plentiful that they are considered to be pests in the harvest season. The Hispid Cotton Rat, often viewed as a menace, has stiff brown-gray fur on the back and a greyish white coat underneath. It feeds on plants, insects, and crops. A good swimmer, it also catches crayfish, crabs, and frogs, as well as climbs up reeds into birds' nests, to eat eggs and chicks. Active during the day and night, this cotton rat lives in a sheltered depression in the ground, or in a burrow up to 30 in (75 cm) deep. It digs shallow pits as it feeds, and creates a network of well-worn foraging runways to its source of food.
• SIZE Body length: 5–8 in (13–20 cm). Tail: 3¼–6½ in (8–16.5 cm).
• OCCURRENCE S. USA, Central America, and N. South America. In forest, desert, mountain, and grassland.
• REMARK This species may cause damage to sweet potato and sugar cane crops.

stiff brown to gray fur

N., C., & S. AMERICA

Social unit Solitary	Gestation 27 days	Young 12	Diet

Family MURIDAE	Species *Mesocricetus auratus*	Status Endangered

GOLDEN HAMSTER

Familiar around the world as a pet, the Golden Hamster is restricted in
the wild to a small area from E. Europe to W. Asia. A small, robust rodent
with a very short tail, it has a blunt muzzle but a broad face, with small
eyes and prominent ears. Its soft, wooly coat is deep orange on the back,
a lighter shade on the face, cheeks, and flanks, and gray-white

ASIA

underneath. The forehead may have a black patch between, and in front
of, the eyes, while a black stripe may mark each cheek and the nape of
the neck. The Golden Hamster is active at night, dawn, and dusk.
Solitary by nature, it is known to be aggressive toward other hamsters.
It prefers cultivated grain fields and excavates a burrow down to 6½ft
(2m), rarely coming up except to feed. Its varied diet includes seeds,
nuts, and insects such as ants, flies, cockroaches, bugs, and wasps.
It stuffs its large cheek pouches with food, to eat later.
• SIZE Body length: 5–5¼ in (13–13.5 cm).
Tail: ½ in (1.5 cm).
• OCCURRENCE A few, scattered sites in W. Asia.
In grassland.
• REMARK The Golden Hamster is known to
hibernate in captivity.

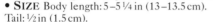

golden orange
• fur on back

CAREFUL GROOMING
The Golden Hamster cleans its coat,
and that of its young, of dirt, old
fur, tangles, and pests, such as
fleas, by using both its front
teeth and foreclaws.

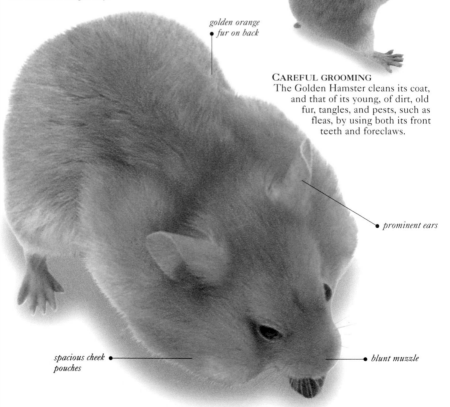

• prominent ears

spacious cheek •
pouches

• blunt muzzle

Social unit Solitary	Gestation 16–19 days	Young 6–10	Diet

Family MURIDAE	Species *Phodopus roborovskii*	Status Locally common

DESERT HAMSTER

Also called the Dwarf Hamster, this short-tailed, large-eared rodent is pale brown on its upperparts, with pure white underparts. Its rear feet are short and broad, with dense fur on the underside to protect them when jumping across hot, loose desert sand. The Desert Hamster digs a separate nesting burrow in firm, moist sand and lines it with hair shed by camels and sheep. Like other hamsters, it stuffs its cheeks with food, usually millet and grass seed, to take back into its burrow for storage. It also eats insects such as beetles, locusts, and earwigs.

prominent ears

pale brown upperparts

• **SIZE** Body length: 2¼–4 in (5.5–10 cm). Tail: 2¾–4¼ in (7–11 cm).
• **OCCURRENCE** Russia (Tuva), E. Kazakhstan, Mongolia, and neighbouring parts of China. In desert.
• **REMARK** Scrupulously clean, the Desert Hamster performs an elaborate daily grooming ritual.

ASIA

broad hindfeet

Social unit Solitary	Gestation 20–22 days	Young 3–9	Diet 🐛 🦗

Family MURIDAE	Species *Cricetus cricetus*	Status Lower risk*

BLACK-BELLIED HAMSTER

The largest hamster, this species has distinctively thick fur, which is red-brown on the back, mainly black on the underside, with white patches on the nose, cheeks, throat, flanks, and paws. It has large cheek pouches, which it inflates while swimming for extra buoyancy, or when alarmed. The Black-bellied Hamster feeds at dawn and dusk. In autumn, it hoards food in its burrow and then hibernates until spring, waking every 5–7 hours to feed. The burrow size varies with the age of the animal, and there are several oblique entrances and compartments for nesting, storage, and excretion.

EURASIA

white patches on parts of body

red-brown fur

• **SIZE** Body length: 8–13½ in (20–34 cm). Tail: 1½–2¼ in (4–6 cm).
• **OCCURRENCE** E. Europe to C. Asia. In steppe and farmland, and along riverbanks.
• **REMARK** The darker underside is very unusual in a mammal.

broad feet with long claws

Social unit Solitary	Gestation 18–20 days	Young 4–12	Diet 🐛 🍂 🦗 🌾

Family MURIDAE	Species *Meriones unguiculatus*	Status Locally common

MONGOLIAN JIRD

This rodent, familiar as a pet, is among the 13 species of gerbils found in the Middle East and Asia. Its coat has pale brown hair, tipped with black, giving it a speckled appearance, while its underparts are gray or white. Protruding black eyes dominate its short, broad head, and its long tail averages around 90 percent of its head and body length. Moving on all four feet, it leaps expertly on its long hindlegs and pounds its rear feet in staccato fashion during courtship. The Mongolian Jird makes elaborate underground burrows in the dry sand or clay soil of the steppe, and is often found sitting upright in front of the entrance. It shares the burrow with its mate and up to 12 young, which are weaned 20–30 days after birth. Active by day and night, summer and winter, it eats mainly seeds of buckwheat, millet, grasses, and sedges, storing excess food in the burrow.

ASIA

brown fur tipped • with black

• **SIZE** Body length:10–12.5 cm (4–5 in).
Tail: 9.5 –11 cm (3¾ –4 ¼ in).
• **OCCURRENCE** Mongolia, S.W. Russia, and N. China. In steppe and plains.
• **REMARK** Compared with other rodents, the Mongolian Jird has a recent history of being kept as a pet, since the 1960s. Its appealing looks and adaptable nature make it a popular choice.

tail almost as long as body •

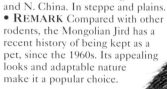

Social unit Social	Gestation 19–21 days	Young 1–12	Diet ⁙

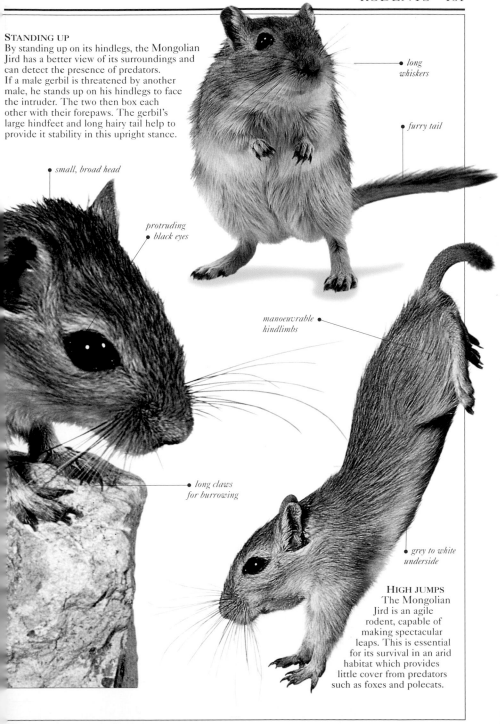

STANDING UP
By standing up on its hindlegs, the Mongolian Jird has a better view of its surroundings and can detect the presence of predators. If a male gerbil is threatened by another male, he stands up on his hindlegs to face the intruder. The two then box each other with their forepaws. The gerbil's large hindfeet and long hairy tail help to provide it stability in this upright stance.

• long
whiskers

• furry tail

• small, broad head

protruding
• black eyes

manoeuvrable •
hindlimbs

• long claws
for burrowing

• grey to white
underside

HIGH JUMPS
The Mongolian Jird is an agile rodent, capable of making spectacular leaps. This is essential for its survival in an arid habitat which provides little cover from predators such as foxes and polecats.

Family MURIDAE	Species *Pachyuromys duprasi*	Status Locally common

FAT-TAILED GERBIL

Found in the Sahara Desert, the Fat-tailed Gerbil has a long, fluffy coat, that is pale cinnamon on the back and sides, with blackish tips on the back hair. It has white underparts and feet, partly haired soles, long *large ears* • hindfeet, and a distinctive club-shaped tail. Large, sensitive ears enable it to receive long-range, low-frequency sounds across the desert sand. This docile burrower becomes active at dusk and emerges from its burrow to search for insects such as crickets, and for leaves, seeds, and other plant material.
• **SIZE** Body length: 3¾–5 in (9.5–13 cm). Tail: 2¼–6½ in (5.5–16.5 cm).
• **OCCURRENCE** Sahara Desert. In sparsely vegetated, semi-desert of sand and gravel.
• **REMARK** The Fat-tailed Gerbil has a store of body fat in its tail, which is used for nourishment and water when food is scarce.

black-tipped back hair •

AFRICA

club-shaped • *tail*

Social unit Variable	Gestation Not known	Young 1–6	Diet 🌱 ⦂⦂ 🦗

Family MURIDAE	Species *Hypogeomys antimena*	Status Endangered

MALAGASY GIANT RAT

Rotund and rabbitlike, this large rat has long ears and hindfeet, and hops rather than runs. The hair on its upperparts is coarse, dense, and gray to reddish brown, with a darker V-shaped patch over its nose. The limbs and belly are white, the tail is muscular and covered with stiff, short hairs. Locally known as the Votsotsa, the Malagasy Giant Rat digs burrow systems, with up to six entrances, in the sandy soil. It eats mainly fallen fruits and bark at night, manipulating the food with its forefeet in an upright position.
• **SIZE** Body length: 12–14 in (30–35 cm). Tail: 8½–10 in (21–25 cm).
• **OCCURRENCE** W. Madagascar. In coastal forest.
• **REMARK** This rat is threatened by the introduced Black Rat and by habitat loss.

MADAGASCAR

coarse, • *dense fur*

rabbitlike ears •

• *short, stiff hairs on tail*   *large claws* •

blunt nose •

Social unit Social	Gestation Not known	Young 1–2	Diet 🌰 ⌇ ⦂⦂

Family MURIDAE	Species *Tachyoryctes macrocephalus*	Status Lower risk*

BIG-HEADED MOLE RAT

Mole-like in habit, this rat spends a great deal of time in its burrow, which often exceeds 165 ft (50 m) in length. Like a typical burrower, it has a blunt, rounded head, small eyes and ears, a robust body, thick fur, and short limbs. This rat gnaws and digs with its large, protruding, orangish yellow incisors.
• **SIZE** Body length: Up to 12 in (31 cm).
Tail: 3 ½ – 4 in (9–10 cm).
• **OCCURRENCE** Ethiopia.
In wet highland, grassland, moorland, and cultivated areas.

stiff hairs on face
short limbs

AFRICA

Social unit Variable	Gestation Not known	Young Not known	Diet

Family MURIDAE	Species *Clethrionomys glareolus*	Status Common

BANK VOLE

Active mostly at dawn and night, this vole nests in burrows, thickets, and tree stumps. Varying geographically in size and weight, it is reddish to yellowish brown, with gray flanks and hindquarters.
• **SIZE** Body length: 2¾ – 5¼ in (7–13.5 cm).
Tail: 1 ½ – 2 ½ in (3.5–6.5 cm).
• **OCCURRENCE** W. Europe to N. Asia.
In temperate and coniferous forest, and wooded banks of rivers.

reddish or yellowish brown coat
large black eyes

EURASIA
tail half of body size

Social unit Social	Gestation 18 days	Young 2–8	Diet

Family MURIDAE	Species *Microtus arvalis*	Status Common

COMMON VOLE

Among the most common rodents in grassy and farmland habitats, this stocky vole has short, sandy to gray-brown fur on the back and gray fur underneath. The Common Vole feeds mainly on plants in summer and bark in winter, digging underground tunnels for larders and nests, and is active during the day as well as the night.
• **SIZE** Body length: 3 ½ – 4¾ in (9–12 cm). Tail: 1¼ – 1¾ in (3–4.5 cm).
• **OCCURRENCE** Europe, Ukraine, and Russia. In cultivated land and meadows.

small eyes
short, grayish brown fur

EURASIA

Social unit Social	Gestation 16–24 days	Young 2–12	Diet

Family MURIDAE	Species *Arvicola terrestris*	Status Locally common

EUROPEAN WATER VOLE

This burrowing rodent displays much variation in color and size. Its thick coat can be gray, black, or brown on the upperparts, and dark gray to white underneath; those voles that inhabit woods and meadows are half the size of those found near lakes, rivers, and marshes. The tail is generally rounded and about half the length of the body. This adept swimmer and diver is most active at dusk and dawn, feeding on plants, tree roots, rhizomes, bulbs, and tubers. Its main enemies are eagles, owls, wild and domestic cats, and the introduced predator, the American Mink (see p. 250). Water pollution and loss of habitat are also posing a growing threat to this species.

gray, brown, or black
• *upperparts*

EURASIA

thick furry
• *coat*

• **SIZE** Body length: 4¾–9 in (12–23 cm). Tail: 2¾–4 in (7–11 cm).
• **OCCURRENCE** Europe, Russia, and Iran. In lakes, rivers, streams, marshes, meadows, and woods.

Social unit Solitary/Pair	Gestation 21–22 days	Young 2–10	Diet 🌿🔨

Family MURIDAE	Species *Ondatra zibethicus*	Status Common

MUSKRAT

The largest species of burrowing vole, the Muskrat is adapted to swimming – its large back feet have small webs between the toes and are edged by stiff bristles or a "swimming fringe," and its long, furless tail is flattened and can be used as a rudder. Its nostrils and ears are covered by flaps during dives, which may last 20 minutes. The Muskrat lives in groups of up to ten, digging tunnels in banks or building beaverlike lodges with mud and reeds. The female builds her nest in a dry tunnel chamber or lodge platform. This species derives its name from the musky secretions from glands around its genital area.

long, coarse
guard hairs •

N. AMERICA, EURASIA

• **SIZE** Body length: 10–14 in (25–35 cm). Tail: 8–10 in (20–25 cm).
• **OCCURRENCE** North America, W. Europe, and Asia. Along banks of rivers, streams, and ponds.
• **REMARK** The Muskrat is valued commercially for its pelt.

relatively •
large hindlegs

Social unit Social	Gestation 25–30 days	Young 1–3	Diet 🌾🌿🍃🐚

Family MURIDAE	Species *Lemmus sibericus*	Status Common

BROWN LEMMING

black stripe on back ●

This chiefly nocturnal animal lives in large colonies and breeds prolifically. In the fall it migrates to low tundra areas and lakeshores, where it digs tunnels under peaty mounds or nests in vegetation. As the snows melt in spring, it again ascends to drier areas. With a diet of moss, herbs, and soft twigs, it feeds along worn trails, even under the snow in winter.

• **SIZE** Body length: 4 ¾ – 6 in (12–15 cm). Tail: ⅜ –½ in (1–1.5 cm).

• **OCCURRENCE** Alaska to Canada, N.E. Europe to N. Asia. In the tundra.

N. AMERICA, EURASIA

● *well-rounded shape*

Social unit Colony	Gestation 18 days	Young 4–13	Diet 🌿 🍄 ●

Family MURIDAE	Species *Lagurus lagurus*	Status Lower risk

STEPPE LEMMING

black stripe ● along back

Small and thickset, this nocturnal rodent is fully covered with long and waterproof fur to protect it from the harsh climate of the steppes. It digs burrows around 3 ft (1 m) deep in which to live, allowing it to survive the cold without hibernating, and it may also dig shallow temporary burrows for defense. The Steppe Lemming is light or cinnamon-gray in color, with continuously growing molar teeth that enable it to chew abrasive grasses in large quantities.

• **SIZE** Body length: 3 ¼ – 4 ¾ in (8 –12 cm). Tail: ⅓ –¾ in (0.7–2 cm).

• **OCCURRENCE** E. Europe to E. Asia. In steppe and semidesert areas.

EURASIA

Social unit Variable	Gestation 20 days	Young 8–12	Diet 🌿 🌾

Family MURIDAE	Species *Lemniscomys striatus*	Status Common

STRIPED GRASS MOUSE

This mouse is light buff or reddish orange, with paler forms found in W. Africa and darker ones in E. Africa. Foraging at dawn and dusk, it lives in holes with runways radiating toward its feeding grounds. It sheds the skin of its tail or feigns death when attacked.

• **SIZE** Body length: 4 –5 ½ in (10–14 cm). Tail: 4–6 in (10–15.5 cm).

• **OCCURRENCE** W., E., and S. Africa. In moist, grassy habitats.

stripes from ● neck to tail

● *thin, long tail*

● *rusty white sides*

AFRICA

Social unit Solitary	Gestation 28 days	Young 4–5	Diet 🌿 🐜

Family MURIDAE	Species *Apodemus flavicollis*	Status Common

YELLOW-NECKED FIELD MOUSE

Named for the yellow patch on its throat, this long-tailed rodent has a brown back and yellowish white underparts. Large, prominent eyes and ears are adaptations to its nocturnal habits, and large hindfeet allow it to leap across long distances. The Yellow-necked Field Mouse climbs up to 20 ft (6 m) in trees to forage and establish feeding places in crevices and birds' nests. It is aggressive toward its own kind and similar species such as the Wood Mouse (see below). The Yellow-necked Field Mouse communicates using shrill, high-pitched chirps and squeaks.

EURASIA

• *brownish back*

• *tail longer than body*

• *hind feet longer than forefeet*

• **SIZE** Body length: 3¼–5 in (8.5–13 cm). Tail: 3½–5¼ in (9–13.5 cm).
• **OCCURRENCE** Europe to the Urals, and Armenia. In temperate and coniferous forest (prefers deciduous woodland); at higher altitudes in the southern part of its range.

Social unit Solitary	Gestation 21–23 days	Young 3–8	Diet

Family MURIDAE	Species *Apodemus sylvaticus*	Status Common

LONG-TAILED FIELD MOUSE

Similar to but smaller than the Yellow-necked Field Mouse (see above), the Long-tailed Field Mouse has a yellow or orange-brown chest patch, a reddish to greyish brown coat, an ocher stripe between its forefeet, and whitish grey underparts. An adept runner and climber, this species digs burrows or inhabits tree holes, taking food to a safe place before eating it.
• **SIZE** Body length: 3–4¼ in (8–11 cm). Tail: 2¾–4¼ in (7–11 cm).
• **OCCURRENCE** Europe (including Iceland), C. Asia, and N. Africa. In farmland, riverbanks, moors, plantations, woodland, and urban areas.

EURASIA, AFRICA

tail shorter than body •

grayish to reddish • *brown coat*

Social unit Solitary	Gestation 23 days	Young 3–9	Diet

Family MURIDAE	Species *Mus musculus*	Status Common

HOUSE MOUSE

One of the most widely distributed mammals, the House Mouse thrives in human habitations, feeding on a wide range of food at night, dawn, and dusk. A small, slim rodent, it has small eyes, a pointed nose, and large ears. Its upperparts are grayish black to reddish brown, with shorter hair on the rump than on the back, and its underparts are white. The House Mouse lives in a family group of one dominant male and several females, and marks its territory with scent and urine. The female mouse is larger and stronger than the male.

WORLDWIDE

- **SIZE** Body length: 2¾–4¼ in (7–10.5 cm). Tail: 2–4 in (5–10 cm).
- **OCCURRENCE** Worldwide, except polar regions. In houses and other manmade structures – avoids woodland and arid areas.
  - **REMARK** This species has been widely bred as a pet and for scientific research.

nest made of any soft material

PROLIFIC BREEDERS
The young of the House Mouse are born hairless, with eyes and ears shut. The average litter size is 3–8, with around 10 litters in a favorable year.

pointed nose

grayish black to reddish brown upperparts

FEEDING IN A GROUP
The House Mouse is known to feed on a variety of food ranging from shoots to seeds, such as corn, oats, barley, and millet, and other human foodstuff.

hairless tail

shorter hair on rump

Social unit Social	Gestation 18–24 days	Young 3–8	Diet

Family MURIDAE	Species *Micromys minutus*	Status Lower risk

EURASIAN HARVEST MOUSE

Small and elegant, the Eurasian Harvest Mouse
is yellowish or reddish brown on its upperparts,
and white below. A good climber, its hindlegs are
longer than its forelegs and it has a long, hairless,
prehensile tail. It feeds on seeds, farmed cereals,
berries, and spiders, as well as insects by day and
night. This mouse builds a spherical nest of
shredded grass in a thicket or grassy clump,
20–51 in (50–130 cm) above ground level, usually
using an old bird's nest as a base. If food becomes
scarce, it is known to feed on its own young.
• **SIZE** Body length: 2–3 in (5–8 cm).
Tail: 1 ¾–3 in (4.5–7.5 cm).

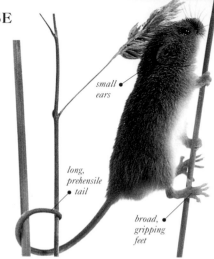

small ears

long, prehensile tail

broad, gripping feet

• **OCCURRENCE** Europe
to Japan. In fields, gardens,
wetland, grassland, and fringes
of humid tropical forest.
• **REMARK** The only Eurasian
rodent that has a prehensile tail.

EURASIA

Social unit Solitary	Gestation 21 days	Young 2–6	Diet

Family MURIDAE	Species *Acomys minous*	Status Vulnerable

CRETE SPINY MOUSE

Found only on the island of Crete, in Europe, where it was probably
carried by ships from Africa, this nocturnal mouse has inflexible
spines on its back and tail, and may be yellow, red, brown, or dark
grey. It readily sheds its tail to escape capture. Gregarious by nature,
it builds only a rudimentary nest, and other females assist the
mother at birth, helping with cleaning and biting the cord.

CRETE

• **SIZE** Body length: 3½–4¾ in (9–12 cm).
Tail: 3½–4¾ in (9–12 cm).
• **OCCURRENCE** Crete.
In arid areas.
• **REMARK** This
rodent has a long
gestation period
(5–6 weeks); the young
are born remarkably
well developed.

coarse spines on back

large, erect ears

tail covered with spines

narrow, protruding snout

Social unit Variable	Gestation 35–42 days	Young 1–5	Diet

Family MURIDAE	Species *Notomys alexis*	Status Common

SPINIFEX HOPPING MOUSE

Locally called the Dargawarra, this mouse lives in desert habitat covered by bushy, spiky grass known as spinifex. Obtaining all its moisture from its food, it does not need to drink water. However, it avoids dehydration in many ways: it produces highly concentrated urine, lives in deep underground burrows during the day, sleeps in groups (raising humidity levels), and feeds only at night. Sociable by nature, groups of ten mice including males, females, and young, share a common nest.

AUSTRALIA

large ears

sandy to ashy brown coat

long tail

long, narrow hindfeet

• **SIZE** Body length: 3½–7in (9–18cm). Tail: 5–9in (12.5–23cm).
• **OCCURRENCE** W. and C. Australia. In sand dunes, grassland, heath, and wood.
• **REMARK** The most widespread of all hopping mice, it is found across Australia's vast, sandy soil cover.

Social unit Social	Gestation 32–34 days	Young 1–9	Diet 🥜 🐛 ⋮⋮

Family MURIDAE	Species *Cricetomys gambianus*	Status Common

GAMBIAN RAT

This large, nocturnal rat eats a variety of moist or fleshy food, from termites to avocados, and peanuts to corn. It stores it in its huge cheek pouches, and also carries it back to its burrow. This is extensive, comprising several different chambers for food, resting, breeding, and defecation, with male and female rats occupying separate tunnels. The Gambian Rat has a bristly buff-brown coat, fading to white on the throat, flanks, and underside, with dark brown rings around its eyes, and a brown, thinly haired tail which is often tipped white. Its well-developed hindlegs make it a good jumper.

large ears

dark brown eye rings

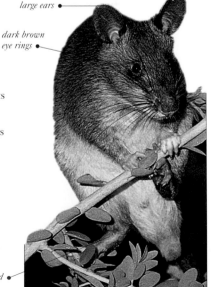

• **SIZE** Body length:14–16in (35–40cm). Tail:14½–18in (37–45cm).
• **OCCURRENCE** W., C., E., and S. Africa. From savanna to evergreen forest.

AFRICA

• **REMARK** This rat is reared both for its meat and as a pet. The skin is used for tobacco pouches in the Ruwenzori mountains.

well-developed hindlegs

Social unit Variable	Gestation 32–42 days	Young 2–4	Diet ⋮⋮ 🐛 🐜 ◉

Family MURIDAE	Species *Rattus norvegicus*	Status Common

BROWN RAT

Also known as the Common or Norway Rat, the Brown Rat has
established its presence all over the world largely due to its sharp senses,
great agility, and varied and opportunistic diet. Varying from brown to
gray-brown or black in color, it has comparatively small eyes and ears
and a long, sparsely haired tail. A good swimmer, diver, and climber,
it can roam a range of 1.8 miles (3 km) in a single night, hunting out food
with its keen sense of smell. Originally a herbivore, this nocturnal or
dusk-and-dawn feeder eats mainly seeds, fruits, vegetables, and leaves,
but also preys on fish, snails, and water insects. Packs of
up to 200 rats, dominated by the larger males,
are known to hunt creatures as big as rabbits,
poultry, and other large birds. Male rats
defend their territory, using scent to mark it
and to identify other members of the pack.
The female makes a nest of grass, leaves,
paper, rags, or any other material, and breeds
frequently.
• **SIZE** Body length: 8–11 in
(20–28 cm). Tail: 7–9 in (17–23 cm).
• **OCCURRENCE** Worldwide, except at
the poles—more common in colder countries.
In riverbanks, fields, and human habitations,
including sewage systems.

WORLDWIDE

WATER WORLD
The Brown Rat is an excellent swimmer and diver,
frequenting riverbanks and sewage networks. It
swims with its tail held out for balance. Hunting for
fish, crayfish, snails, and aquatic insects, it crunches
these up with its sharp teeth.

BRED FOR RESEARCH
This species is the ancestor
of rats bred for scientific
research and as pets, which
may be black-and-white
or white.

robust body •   *gray-brown to brown coat* •   *short nose* •

• *hairless tail*

Social unit Social	Gestation 22–24 days	Young 6–9	Diet

Family MURIDAE	Species *Rattus rattus*	Status Common

HOUSE RAT

In early Roman times, this rat was spread around the world from Asia, in cargo ships, also giving it the name Ship Rat. Slim-bodied and black, it has whitish pink feet and a gray to white belly. Its tail is unusually long. It is active at night, dawn and dusk, and prefers feeding on plant matter, but also eats insects, feces, garbage, and carrion. This rat roams in packs of 20–60, and may confront larger animals such as dogs. The female makes a nest of grass or any other material, often in a roof cavity.
• **SIZE** Body length:6¼–9½in (16–24cm). Tail:7–10in (18–26cm).
• **OCCURRENCE** Worldwide – common in Mediterranean countries. In human settlements, ports, and farms.
• **REMARK** This rat is notorious for carrying the fleas that spread plague.

WORLDWIDE

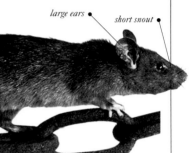

large ears
short snout

tail longer than body

Social unit Variable	Gestation 20–24 days	Young 4–10	Diet

Family MURIDAE	Species *Hydromys chrysogaster*	Status Locally common

GOLDEN-BELLIED WATER RAT

Australia's heaviest native rodent, this rabbit-sized water rat has broad hindfeet and webbed toes to survive in its permanently aquatic habitat. Brown to gray on its upperparts, and brown to golden yellow or cream underneath, it has abundant whiskers on its long, blunt muzzle, and a thick, white-tipped tail. Active at dusk and dawn, it is a powerful predator of shellfish (prying them open with its incisors), water snails, fish, frogs, turtles, birds, mice, and even bats.
• **SIZE** Body length:11½–15½in (29–39cm). Tail:9–13in (23–33cm).
• **OCCURRENCE** New Guinea, Australia, and Tasmania. In lakes, rivers, and along coastlines; it requires permanent water and prefers inhabited areas.
• **REMARK** It is a protected species in Australia.

AUSTRALASIA

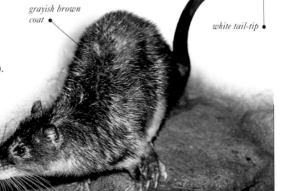

grayish brown coat

white tail-tip

abundant whiskers on long, blunt snout

Social unit Solitary	Gestation 35 days	Young 1–7	Diet

Family GLIRIDAE	Species *Glis glis*	Status Lower risk

EDIBLE DORMOUSE

Resembling a squirrel with its bushy tail and semiupright stance, the Edible or Fat Dormouse is brown to silver-gray, with white underparts and black eye-patches. It inhabits woods and outbuildings, nesting in tree-holes and roof crevices. In autumn it accumulates fat reserves in its body to prepare for its hibernation in a large, deep nest. Like other dormice, it communicates by squeaks and twitters, and lives in loose social groups with no hierarchy; however, the female remains solitary during pregnancy.

EURASIA

bushy, squirrellike tail

- **SIZE** Body length: 5–8 in (13–20 cm). Tail: 4–7 in (10–18 cm).
- **OCCURRENCE** S. and C. Europe, Asia Minor, Caucasus, and N.W. Iran. In deciduous and mixed forest.
- **REMARK** It was bred for food in ancient Rome, hence its name.

dark eye-patches

Social unit Social	Gestation 30–32 days	Young 2–11	Diet 🍃 ⋮ 🐁 ◗ 🐛 🐜 ●

Family GLIRIDAE	Species *Muscardinus avellanarius*	Status Lower risk

HAZEL DORMOUSE

Also known as the Common Dormouse, this species is as small as a House Mouse and has a yellow- or red-brown coat with white underparts, and a yellowish rump. The skin of its tail can detach if seized by a predator. An excellent climber and jumper, this specialized seasonal feeder eats flowers, grubs, and birds' eggs in spring; seeds and fruits in summer; and nuts in autumn.

short ears

EUROPE

densely furred tail

flesh-colored nose

- **SIZE** Body length: 6.5–8.5 cm (2½–3¼ in). Tail: 5.5–8 cm (2¼–3¼ in).
- **OCCURRENCE** From Mediterranean (excluding Iberian Peninsula) to S. Sweden, east to Russia.
- **REMARK** It hibernates deeply like all dormice, "dor" meaning "to sleep."

Social unit Solitary	Gestation 22–24 days	Young 2–7	Diet ⋮ 🍃 🐜 🐁 ●

Family DIPODIDAE	Species *Allactaga tetradactyla*	Status Endangered

FOUR-TOED JERBOA

A vestigial fourth toe on each hindfoot gives this species its name. In other respects it is like a typical jerboa, with tall, rabbitlike ears and long, hopping hindfeet. Its coat is speckled black and orange, with gray sides, an orange rump, and white underparts. Its long tail, used for balancing, has a black band near the feathery white tip. An avid burrower, this nocturnal animal shelters in tunnels from the heat of the midday sun.
• SIZE Body length: 4 –4¾ in (10–12 cm). Tail: 6–7 in (15.5–18 cm).
• OCCURRENCE N. Africa. In salt marshes and along coasts, and in clay desert, near barley fields.
• REMARK The existence of this species is threatened by desert reclamation.

AFRICA

rabbitlike ears

black band before white tail-tip

gray flanks

Social unit Solitary	Gestation 25–42 days	Young 2–6	Diet 🌱 🥬 ⋮⋮

Family DIPODIDAE	Species *Jaculus jaculus*	Status Common

LESSER EGYPTIAN JERBOA

Adapted for hopping at high speed on sandy soil, this jerboa has long hind feet, each with three toes on a pad of hairs, and a long tail that it uses for balance. Its fur is brownish orange on the back, grayish orange along the sides, and white on the underparts. Digging burrows with many emergency exits, it plugs these holes to keep out the heat and predators. It travels long distances at night, and takes sand baths to keep its coat clean.
• SIZE Body length: 4– 4¾ in (10–12 cm). Tail: 6½ –8 in (16–20 cm).
• OCCURRENCE N. Africa to W. Asia. In hills of loose sand, desert, and gravel plains.

AFRICA, ASIA

long, thin hindlegs

black band near white tail-tip

Social unit Solitary	Gestation Not known	Young 4–10	Diet ⋮⋮ 🌱 🔪 🍂

Family HYSTRICIDAE	Species *Hystrix africaeaustralis*	Status Common

CAPE PORCUPINE

The largest rodent in southern Africa, this stout-bodied porcupine has a dark brown to black coat with thick, cylindrical spines (quills) that are interspersed with ordinary hair. The white-tipped, brown-and-white banded quills are denser toward the back. Despite popular belief, the Cape (or Crested) Porcupine cannot shoot out its quills. Instead, it raises them when annoyed or threatened, and charges backward at the enemy. The quills detach easily and pierce the enemy's flesh, causing much pain. This porcupine uses grunts, piping calls, or quill rattles to communicate. The male helps to take care of the young.

AFRICA

- **SIZE** Body length: 25 – 32 in (63 – 80 cm). Tail: 4 ½ – 5 in (10.5 – 13 cm).
- **OCCURRENCE** C. to S. Africa. In a variety of habitats – especially rocky, hilly country with scrub cover.
- **REMARK** Cape Porcupines effectively defend themselves from larger animals such as lions, leopards, and hyenas, but are hunted by humans in large numbers because of the damage they cause to crops, and for their meat.

BURROWS FOR HOMES
An excellent burrower, the Cape Porcupine lives singly, in pairs, or in small groups, resting in caves or crevices with narrow openings during the day. It forages at night, aided by its keen sense of smell, and travels up to 9 miles (15 km) in search of food.

white-tipped quills •

• blackish coat

long, stout whiskers •

short legs • covered with bristles

white • neck patch

Social unit Variable	Gestation 6 – 8 weeks	Young 1 – 4	Diet

Family ERETHIZONTIDAE	Species *Erethizon dorsatum*	Status Common

NORTH AMERICAN PORCUPINE

More vocal than other porcupines, especially during its mating season in early winter, this North American species moans, grunts, sniffs, snorts, squeaks, sobs, hoots, and chatters. Its quills are yellowish white with black or brown tips and form a distinctive crest, which may be up to 3 in (8 cm) long, on the head. Short and stocky, it has small limbs and its heavy feet have naked soles with claws designed to aid gripping. Active at night, the North American Porcupine climbs trees extensively, feeding on soft bark and conifer needles in winter. In summer it eats roots, stems, leaves, seeds, flowers, and water plants. Its vision is mediocre, but its senses of smell and hearing are excellent. Mostly solitary, several individuals may share a den in winter, or shelter together in trees.

yellowish spines and brown fur on body •

• crest of long quills

• **SIZE** Body length: 26–32 in (65–80 cm). Tail: 6–12 in (15–30 cm).
• **OCCURRENCE** Canada, USA, and N. Mexico. In temperate forest and tundra – mainly riverbanks.

N. AMERICA

Social unit Solitary	Gestation 205–217 days	Young 1	Diet 🌿 ❧ ⁙ 🌱 🌾

Family ERETHIZONTIDAE	Species *Coendou prehensilis*	Status Locally common

BRAZILIAN PORCUPINE

This large, muscular porcupine is almost entirely arboreal and uses its flesh-colored prehensile tail and naked-soled feet with long, curved claws to climb slowly up branches. Much of its body is covered with yellow and white, black-tipped spines, but its flanks are naked. The Brazilian Porcupine shelters in thick foliage, in cavities in tree trunks, or in the ground, during the day. At dusk, it forages for leaves, fruits, bark, young shoots, and small reptiles, traveling over several hundred metres at night to a new tree. It communicates through a variety of sounds, isolated animals using a moaning call to contact each other.

large, heavy • body

yellow and • white spines

• **SIZE** Body length: 20 ½ in (52 cm). Tail: 20 ½ in (52 cm).
• **OCCURRENCE** N. and E. South America. In tropical forest.
• **REMARK** Its tail is as long as its body.

S. AMERICA

naked-soled feet •

Social unit Solitary	Gestation 195–210 days	Young 1	Diet 🌿 🐌 🍃 🐀

Family CAVIIDAE	Species *Cavia aperea*	Status Common

BRAZILIAN GUINEA PIG

The smallest of all cavylike rodents, the Brazilian
Guinea Pig or Cavy, is the ancestor of the domestic
guinea pig (*Cavia porcellus*). The five Guinea Pig
species all have a large head with a blunt snout, a
tailless body, and short legs, with four toes on the
forefeet and five on the hindfeet.
Although usually dark grayish brown,
some animals may be almost black.
Guinea Pigs are nocturnal and live in
grassland, sharing communal feeding
runways, but inhabit separate nests.
• **SIZE** Body length: 8–12 in
(20–30 cm). Tail: None.
• **OCCURRENCE** N.W. to
E. South America. In dry savanna,
brushland, and mountains.
• **REMARK** Newborn Brazilian
Guinea Pigs feed on solid food and
walk almost immediately after birth.

long, coarse coat   *stocky body*

S. AMERICA

Social unit Social	Gestation 60 days	Young 1–4	Diet

Family CAVIIDAE	Species *Dolichotis patagonum*	Status Lower risk

PATAGONIAN MARA

Also known as the Patagonian Cavy, this unusually large
and long-legged rodent resembles a deer in appearance. Its
behavior, too, varies from rodentlike tendencies when young
and when raising its young, to that of hoofed animals in the
adult stage. The Patagonian Mara has brownish orange
upperparts, a white collarlike neck patch, and a whitish fringe
on its short tail. Its long muzzle has dark bristles, and it has
large eyes and ears. Adult Patagonian Maras can run, jump,
and dig expertly. Male and female
pairs graze together on grass and
low shrubs, and may be found
in groups when raising young.
The female digs a large
burrow for the offspring.
• **SIZE** Length:
17–31 in
(43–78 cm).
Tail: 1 in (2.5 cm).
• **OCCURRENCE**
C. and S. Argentina.
In pampas grassland.
• **REMARK** Unusually
among rodents, male and
female maras
are known to
pair for life.

S. AMERICA

long ears

brownish orange upperparts

lighter underparts

short tail

thin, long legs

Social unit Pair	Gestation 70–80 days	Young 1–3	Diet

Family HYDROCHAERIDAE	Species *Hydrochaeris hydrochaeris*	Status Common

CAPYBARA

This species is the world's largest rodent and an excellent swimmer and diver, with eyes, nostrils, and ears set on the top of its head, and partially webbed toes. The young are born fully furred, and run, swim, and dive within hours of birth. Mixed groups including male–female pairs, and larger herds dominated by a single male, defend their home territory, moving on to find fresh grazing. Capybaras feed at dusk and dawn, sometimes raiding crops, and wallow during the midday heat.
• **SIZE** Length: 3½–4¼ ft (1.1–1.3 m). Tail: Vestigial.
• **OCCURRENCE** N. and
E. South America.
In lowland habitats
near water: forested
riverbanks,
wetland,
as well as
mangrove
swamps.

S. AMERICA

dark to light
brown hair, tinged
with yellow

small, rounded
ears

hooflike
claws

Social unit Variable	Gestation 150 days	Young 1–8	Diet

Family DASYPROCTIDAE	Species *Dasyprocta azarae*	Status Vulnerable

AZARA'S AGOUTI

Large and robust-bodied, this rodent is speckled
light to medium brown, and may sometimes
have a yellowish underside. Its short legs
are distinctive as the forefeet have five
toes, and the hindfeet have three. Azara's
Agouti has prominent eyes, nostrils, and
lips. It barks when alarmed, erecting
its rump hairs to appear larger.
• **SIZE** Length: 20 in (50 cm).
Tail: 1 in (2.5 cm).
• **OCCURRENCE** C. and S. Brazil,
E. Paraguay, and N.E.
Argentina. In tropical
forest, riverbanks, and
mangrove swamps.
• **REMARK** It is often
hunted for meat.

S. AMERICA

big, beady eyes

light to medium
brown body

large
lips

Social unit Variable	Gestation 120 days	Young 1–2	Diet

Family AGOUTIDAE	Species *Agouti paca*	Status Common

PACA

square head •

One of the largest living rodents, this expert swimmer rests in its shelter during the day and emerges to eat at night. Brown, red, or light gray on its upperparts, with four lines of pale dots along each side, it has a white or buff underside and a tiny tail. This species is sometimes hunted for meat and sport.

N. & S. AMERICA

• **SIZE** Body length: 23 ½ – 32 in (60 – 80 cm). Tail: ½ – 1 ½ in (1.5 – 3.5 cm).
• **OCCURRENCE** S. Mexico to E. South America. In tropical forest, preferably areas near water.

Social unit Solitary	Gestation 114–119 days	Young 1	Diet 🐟 🌿

Family CAPROMYIDAE	Species *Capromys pilorides*	Status Endangered

DESMAREST'S HUTIA

• blunt snout

• strongly built hind half

This volelike, nocturnal rodent has a large head, blunt nose, stocky body, and short limbs. Its strong, tapering tail and sharp, curved claws allow it to grip branches when foraging in trees for food.
• **SIZE** Body length: 22 – 23 ½ in (55 – 60 cm). Tail: 6 – 10 in (15 – 26 cm).

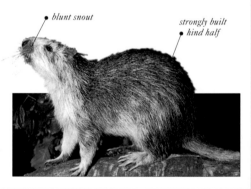

CARRIBEAN

• **OCCURRENCE** Cuban Archipelago. In tropical forest.
• **REMARK** Most species of hutia are severely threatened or extinct.

Social unit Solitary/Pair	Gestation 120–126 days	Young 1–4	Diet 🌿 🍂 🐟 🌾

Family CHINCHILLIDAE	Species *Lagostomus maximus*	Status Endangered*

PLAINS VISCACHA

black-and-white striped face •

grayish brown • upperparts

The largest member of the chinchilla family, this rodent has a large, thick head and strong legs. Found in noisy colonies of 20–50, this night-feeder damages pastures by digging tunnel systems, piling up the entrances with sticks, stones, and bones.
• **SIZE** Body length: 18 ½ – 26 in (47 – 66 cm). Tail: 6 – 8 in (15 – 20 cm).

S. AMERICA

• **OCCURRENCE** S. South America. In pampas and brushland.

Social unit Social	Gestation 153 days	Young 1–4	Diet 🌾 🍀 🌾

Family CHINCHILLIDAE	Species *Chinchilla lanigera*	Status Vulnerable

CHINCHILLA

Prized for its soft, silky fur, which protects it from the bitter mountain cold, this severely threatened species has been hunted and farmed for many years. It is now protected, but hunting continues illegally. Its coat is silvery gray-blue above and cream or yellowish on the underside, with long gray and black hair on the upper surface of the tail. In the wild, the Chinchilla forms colonies of 100 or more in rocky places, often taking shelter in caves and crevices. Active at night, it eats most plant material, especially grass and leaves, which are rich in fiber, holding its food in its front paws as it nibbles. It frequently sits up on its hind feet and looks around, to keep watch on its surroundings. If threatened, it rears up on its hind legs and spits hard at the enemy. During the winter breeding season, females become aggressive toward each other.
• **SIZE** Body length: 8–15 in (22–38 cm).
Tail: 3–6 in (7.5–15 cm).
• **OCCURRENCE** W. Chile. In the Andes mountains.

S. AMERICA

MINIATURE PET
Two pet Chinchillas take a dust bath (above), a ritual also conducted in the wild. The appealing looks and friendly nature of this small rodent make it a popular pet.

rounded ears

large, round eyes

thickly furred tail

long whiskers

long hind legs for jumping

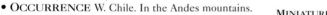

Social unit Social	Gestation 111 days	Young 2–4	Diet 🌿 🌱

Family MYOCASTORIDAE	Species *Myocastor coypus*	Status Common

NUTRIA

Resembling a beaver with a rat's tail, this nocturnal rodent has high-set eyes, nostrils, and ears, adapted to its aquatic habits. Its lips close behind the incisors, allowing it to gnaw even under water, and it has a long, rounded tail and webbed hind feet. This fast swimmer eats mainly water plants, as well as alfalfa, rice, rye grass, and the seedlings of bald cypress, holding and manipulating its food with its forepaws. Highly gregarious, it lives in family groups in bankside tunnels and marks its home range with secretions from its oral and anal glands. It builds platform nests in riverbanks, and the males defend the nest area after the litter is born.

• **SIZE** Body length:18½–23 in (47–58 cm). Tail:13½–16 in (34–41 cm).
• **OCCURRENCE** Chile, Argentina, Uruguay, S. Brazil, Paraguay, and Bolivia. Near lakes and rivers.
• **REMARK** Originally from South America, the Nutria has been introduced in North America and Europe, where it is farmed for its dense brown fur. There are now wild populations in several of these countries due to escaped farm animals having set up colonies.

S. AMERICA

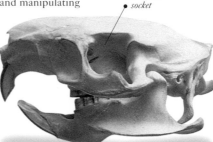

high-set eye
• socket

BEAVERLIKE PROFILE
The Nutria's skull resembles that of the beaver in many ways. The head is flat and heavily set, with a prominent upper jaw and sharp incisors protruding beyond the lips.

arched
• hindquarters

large head •

tapering
• muzzle

strong
claws on
• forefeet

• long,
rounded tail

Social unit Social	Gestation 127–139 days	Young 1–12	Diet 〰 ⍦ ⠸

| Family OCTODONTIDAE | Species *Octodon degus* | Status Locally common |

DEGU

This mountain-dwelling rodent looks like a large, stout mouse and has yellow-brown fur on its back and creamish fur underneath. Usually, it also has a yellow ring around its neck, and yellow furry "lids" above and below the eyes. Found in colonies in elaborate underground burrow systems, the Degu piles up sticks, stones, and animal dung around the entrances. It feeds on a wide variety of vegetation, and is known to eat cattle droppings in the dry season.
• **SIZE** Body length: 10–12 in (25–31 cm).
Tail: 3–5 in (7.5–13 cm).
• **OCCURRENCE** W. Chile.
In the Andes mountains.
• **REMARK** The tail
breaks off easily if
grabbed by a predator.

S. AMERICA

yellow-brown
• upperparts

yellow "lids"
• around eyes

tufted tail with
• black tip

pale gray •
to white feet

| Social unit Variable | Gestation 90 days | Young 4–6 | Diet |

| Family BATHYERGIDAE | Species *Heterocephalus glaber* | Status Locally common |

NAKED MOLE RAT

With hairless, loose pinkish gray skin and vestigial ears and minute eyes, this unusual looking, nocturnal rodent has a unique social system. It lives in colonies of 70–80, with a dominant female "queen" that breeds and is tended by several nonworkers, while the workers form head-to-tail digging chains in food-gathering galleries that radiate up to 130 ft (40 m) from the central chamber.
• **SIZE** Body length: 3¼–3½ in (8–9 cm). Tail: 1¼–1¾ in (3–4.5 cm).
• **OCCURRENCE** E. Africa. In arid land with a stable temperature.
• **REMARK** This rat lives underground and only surfaces to travel to another colony.

AFRICA

very sparse hairs over
• pinkish gray body

long, rounded
tail •

• long incisors   *• thick, clawed toes*

| Social unit Social | Gestation 66–74 days | Young 1–12 | Diet |

CETACEANS
TOOTHED WHALES AND DOLPHINS

T OOTHED WHALES and dolphins make up almost nine-tenths of all cetaceans. They include 71 species of porpoises, river dolphins, dolphins, white whales, and sperm whales.

In addition to the streamlined whale shape, with fins, flippers, and flukes, all members have teeth, in contrast to the baleen whales (see p. 204–205). However, in some species of beaked whales (Ziphiidae), the teeth hardly erupt out of the gums. The nostrils form a single blowhole, usually on the top of the head.

Many toothed whales have elongated jaws forming a "beak" at the front of the mouth and a bulging forehead known as the the "melon." The melon gathers and directs sound waves, which toothed whales use to locate prey and to navigate. The several species of social whales also use these sound waves to communicate.

Family PHOCOENIDAE	Species *Phocoena phocoena*	Status Vulnerable

HARBOR PORPOISE

A small and stocky animal, this porpoise has a rounded head with no beak, and small, spade-shaped teeth. The flippers are black and a dark stripe extends from them to the lower jaw. The front edge of its dorsal fin sometimes has a row of small, rounded lumps called tubercles (see right). The Harbor Porpoise usually forages alone for food on the seabed, seeking out areas of strong tidal currents to make prey capture easier. At times, however, it is found in hundreds where there is a concentration of prey. Shy of humans, it very rarely approaches boats. The female porpoise is larger than its male counterpart. The status of the Harbor Porpoise is considered to be vulnerable although it is found in large groups throughout its wide range. The threat is not so much from its natural predators, such as the Killer Whale and Great White Shark, but more so from human activity. The highest mortalities of porpoises are from entrapment in underwater fishing nets.

PACIFIC, ATLANTIC

round bumps (tubercles) along edge of • *dorsal fin*

• SIZE Length: 4½ – 6½ ft (1.4 m – 2 m). Weight: 110–200 lb (50–90 kg).
• OCCURRENCE N. Pacific and N. Atlantic. In open oceans and along coastlines.
• REMARK Despite its small size, this species sometimes dives to depths of over 655 ft (200 m).

triangular • *dorsal fin*

• *black back*

flukes dark above and • *below*

cream belly •

• *black pectoral flippers*

Social unit Variable	Gestation 10–11 months	Young 1	Diet

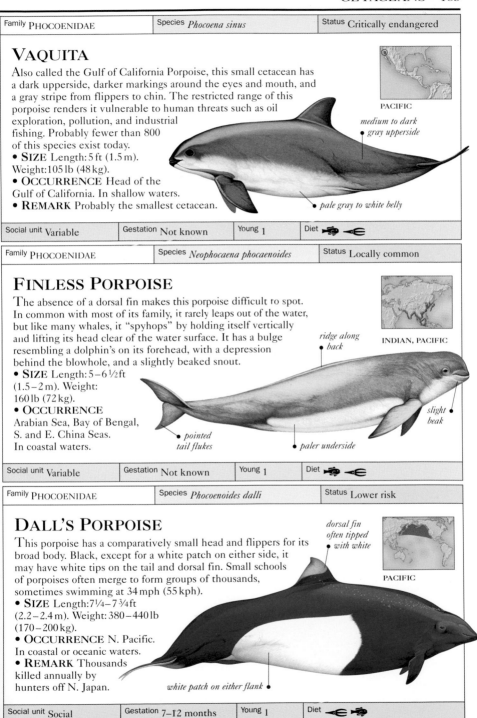

| Family PHOCOENIDAE | Species *Phocoena sinus* | Status Critically endangered |

VAQUITA

Also called the Gulf of California Porpoise, this small cetacean has
a dark upperside, darker markings around the eyes and mouth, and
a gray stripe from flippers to chin. The restricted range of this
porpoise renders it vulnerable to human threats such as oil
exploration, pollution, and industrial
fishing. Probably fewer than 800
of this species exist today.
• **SIZE** Length: 5 ft (1.5 m).
Weight: 105 lb (48 kg).
• **OCCURRENCE** Head of the
Gulf of California. In shallow waters.
• **REMARK** Probably the smallest cetacean.

PACIFIC

medium to dark
• *gray upperside*

• *pale gray to white belly*

| Social unit Variable | Gestation Not known | Young 1 | Diet |

| Family PHOCOENIDAE | Species *Neophocaena phocaenoides* | Status Locally common |

FINLESS PORPOISE

The absence of a dorsal fin makes this porpoise difficult to spot.
In common with most of its family, it rarely leaps out of the water,
but like many whales, it "spyhops" by holding itself vertically
and lifting its head clear of the water surface. It has a bulge
resembling a dolphin's on its forehead, with a depression
behind the blowhole, and a slightly beaked snout.
• **SIZE** Length: 5–6½ ft
(1.5–2 m). Weight:
160 lb (72 kg).
• **OCCURRENCE**
Arabian Sea, Bay of Bengal,
S. and E. China Seas.
In coastal waters.

ridge along
• *back*   INDIAN, PACIFIC

slight •
beak

• *pointed*
tail flukes   • *paler underside*

| Social unit Variable | Gestation Not known | Young 1 | Diet |

| Family PHOCOENIDAE | Species *Phocoenoides dalli* | Status Lower risk |

DALL'S PORPOISE

This porpoise has a comparatively small head and flippers for its
broad body. Black, except for a white patch on either side, it
may have white tips on the tail and dorsal fin. Small schools
of porpoises often merge to form groups of thousands,
sometimes swimming at 34 mph (55 kph).
• **SIZE** Length: 7¼–7¾ ft
(2.2–2.4 m). Weight: 380–440 lb
(170–200 kg).
• **OCCURRENCE** N. Pacific.
In coastal or oceanic waters.
• **REMARK** Thousands
killed annually by
hunters off N. Japan.

dorsal fin
often tipped
• *with white*

PACIFIC

white patch on either flank •

| Social unit Social | Gestation 7–12 months | Young 1 | Diet |

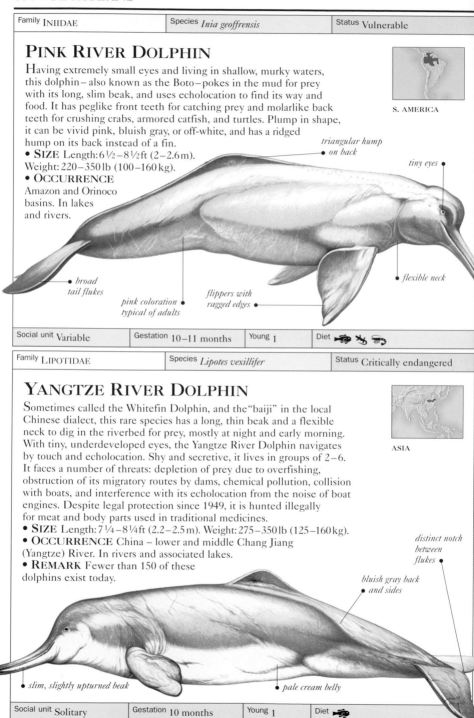

| Family INIIDAE | Species *Inia geoffrensis* | Status Vulnerable |

PINK RIVER DOLPHIN

Having extremely small eyes and living in shallow, murky waters, this dolphin – also known as the Boto – pokes in the mud for prey with its long, slim beak, and uses echolocation to find its way and food. It has peglike front teeth for catching prey and molarlike back teeth for crushing crabs, armored catfish, and turtles. Plump in shape, it can be vivid pink, bluish gray, or off-white, and has a ridged hump on its back instead of a fin.
- **SIZE** Length: 6½–8½ft (2–2.6m). Weight: 220–350lb (100–160kg).
- **OCCURRENCE** Amazon and Orinoco basins. In lakes and rivers.

S. AMERICA

triangular hump on back

tiny eyes

broad tail flukes

pink coloration typical of adults

flippers with ragged edges

flexible neck

| Social unit Variable | Gestation 10–11 months | Young 1 | Diet |

| Family LIPOTIDAE | Species *Lipotes vexillifer* | Status Critically endangered |

YANGTZE RIVER DOLPHIN

Sometimes called the Whitefin Dolphin, and the "baiji" in the local Chinese dialect, this rare species has a long, thin beak and a flexible neck to dig in the riverbed for prey, mostly at night and early morning. With tiny, underdeveloped eyes, the Yangtze River Dolphin navigates by touch and echolocation. Shy and secretive, it lives in groups of 2–6. It faces a number of threats: depletion of prey due to overfishing, obstruction of its migratory routes by dams, chemical pollution, collision with boats, and interference with its echolocation from the noise of boat engines. Despite legal protection since 1949, it is hunted illegally for meat and body parts used in traditional medicines.
- **SIZE** Length: 7¼–8¼ft (2.2–2.5m). Weight: 275–350lb (125–160kg).
- **OCCURRENCE** China – lower and middle Chang Jiang (Yangtze) River. In rivers and associated lakes.
- **REMARK** Fewer than 150 of these dolphins exist today.

ASIA

distinct notch between flukes

bluish gray back and sides

slim, slightly upturned beak

pale cream belly

| Social unit Solitary | Gestation 10 months | Young 1 | Diet |

Family PLATANISTIDAE	Species *Platanista gangetica*	Status Endangered

GANGES RIVER DOLPHIN

This rare, freshwater dolphin has distinctively broad flippers and a long, thin beak with protruding front teeth that interlock to make a cage for prey. A flexible neck allows it to turn its head at right angles to grub for food and scan the area with echolocating pulses. Although they appear to be identical, the dolphins living in the Indus River and those living in the Ganges–Brahmaputra system are considered to be different subspecies. Both types live in small groups of 4–6, occasionally as many as 30 or more.
• SIZE Length:7–8¼ft (2.1–2.5m). Weight:185lb (85kg).
• OCCURRENCE Pakistan and India, throughout the river systems of the Indus, Ganga, and Brahmaputra. In freshwater rivers.
• REMARK This is the only cetacean without a crystalline eye lens, making it blind.

ASIA

large, wide tail flukes

triangular ridge on back

upward curving mouth

paddle-shaped, ragged flippers

pinkish belly

Social unit Variable	Gestation 8–12 months	Young 1	Diet

Family DELPHINIDAE	Species *Lagenorhynchus obscurus*	Status Locally common

DUSKY DOLPHIN

Small and compact in shape, this dolphin has a complex and variable color pattern. However, it is mainly dark gray to blue-black on its upperside, and pale gray or white below, with a tapering gray stripe separating these two areas. Another forked pale patch embellishes each flank. There are three subspecies: *L. obscurus fitzroyi* found off South America, *L. obscurus obscurus* found off S. Africa, and an unnamed species found off New Zealand. The Dusky Dolphin, active day and night, feeds on small, schooling, open-water fish and squid, taking its prey from the surface as well as the depths.
• SIZE Length:5½–7ft (1.7–2.1m). Weight:155–185lb (70–85kg).
• OCCURRENCE W. and S. South America, S. Africa, and New Zealand. In coastal and continental shelf waters.

S. AMERICA, AFRICA, NEW ZEALAND

pale gray stripe between black back and white belly

gradually tapering head

tall, curved dorsal fin

forked pale patch on flank

black lips

Social unit Variable	Gestation 13 months	Young 1	Diet

| Family DELPHINIDAE | Species *Lagenorhynchus obliquidens* | Status Common |

PACIFIC WHITE-SIDED DOLPHIN

Although similar to the Dusky Dolphin (see p.185), this species has a continuous rather than forked pale side stripe. The forehead slopes gently from blowhole to beak. Known for aerial displays, this gregarious dolphin is frequently seen with other cetaceans. It feeds at dusk, night, and dawn.
• **SIZE** Length:7–8¼ft (2.1–2.5m). Weight:165–200lb (75–90kg).
• **OCCURRENCE** N. Pacific Ocean. On the continental shelf and in deep ocean.

tall, hooked dorsal fin

PACIFIC

dark edges on flippers

stripe from tail to above eye

pale belly

| Social unit Social | Gestation 10–12 months | Young 1 | Diet |

| Family DELPHINIDAE | Species *Lagenorhynchus albirostris* | Status Common |

WHITE-BEAKED DOLPHIN

This large, stocky dolphin is an acrobatic swimmer and readily bow-rides with boats. Its stubby beak meets the bulging melon of the forehead at a distinct angle. The black dorsal fin, tail flukes, flippers, and lower flanks contrast with the pale belly, beak, and side stripe. Once hunted for its meat and oil, this dolphin is still at risk from entanglement in fishing nets.
• **SIZE** Length:9¼ft (2.8m). Weight:770lb (350kg).
• **OCCURRENCE** E. Canada, N.E. USA, Greenland, and N. Europe. Along coastlines and in oceans.

tall, curved black fin

ATLANTIC

white underside

well-defined pale beak

| Social unit Social | Gestation Not known | Young 1 | Diet |

| Family DELPHINIDAE | Species *Grampus griseus* | Status Common |

RISSO'S DOLPHIN

Readily identified by its large size and beakless head, Risso's Dolphin is gray with a tall, sickle-shaped, dorsal fin. Sometimes nocturnal, it may join large schools of other dolphins and pilot whales. It faces threats such as asphyxiation in fishing nets and choking on plastic refuse.
• **SIZE** Length:12½ft (3.8m). Weight:880lb (400kg).
• **OCCURRENCE** Worldwide. In deep, temperate and tropical waters.

large, sickle-shaped dorsal fin

WORLDWIDE

scarred pale patches on body

long, hooked flippers

blunt, beakless head

| Social unit Social | Gestation 13–14 months | Young 1 | Diet |

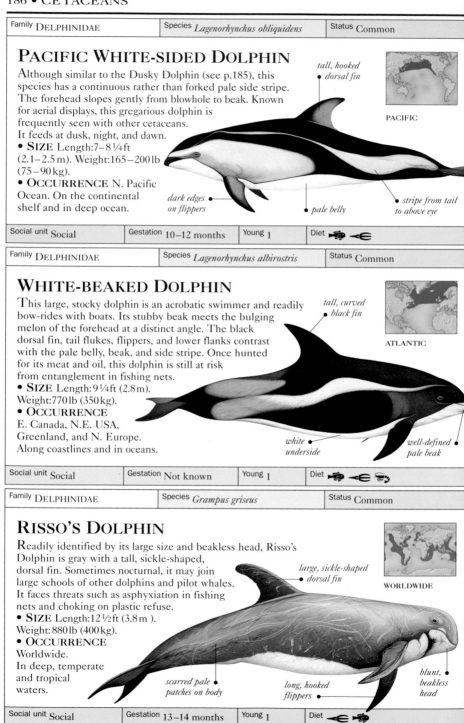

Family DELPHINIDAE	Species *Stenella longirostris*	Status Lower risk

SPINNER DOLPHIN

Probably no other cetacean displays such wide variations in appearance within the species, as this dolphin. There are three subspecies, as well as a dwarf version found in the Gulf of Thailand. Its body is slender, and its beak long and thin. The male can be identified by its post-anal hump. This highly social animal hunts at night. It swims in schools of tens to thousands, often alongside other dolphins and whales, and shoals of tuna. Its characteristic spinning leaps are probably used, along with various clicks, whistles, and screams, to communicate with others.
• **SIZE** Length: 4¼–6½ft (1.3–2m). Weight: 99–165 lb (45–75 kg).
• **OCCURRENCE** Worldwide. In tropical oceans.
• **REMARK** Spinner Dolphins are used by fishermen to help locate tuna shoals. Millions have been killed as a result of industrial fishing in the E. Pacific.

WORLDWIDE

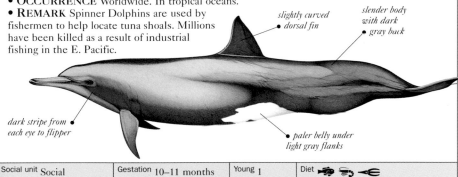

slightly curved dorsal fin

slender body with dark gray back

dark stripe from each eye to flipper

paler belly under light gray flanks

Social unit Social	Gestation 10–11 months	Young 1	Diet

Family DELPHINIDAE	Species *Stenella frontalis*	Status Locally Common

ATLANTIC SPOTTED DOLPHIN

This dolphin may be distinguished from the Pantropical Spotted Dolphin (see p.188) by its stouter body and beak, and a light band extending from the shoulder to the dorsal fin. However, like its pantropical relative, it is born without spots: these make their first appearance on the belly and then extend to the back with age. At night, it feeds on fish and squid that come up from deeper waters. During the day the Atlantic Spotted Dolphin feeds on midwater fish, and may even burrow for prey in the sandy bottom.
• **SIZE** Length: 5½–7½ft (1.7–2.3m). Weight: 310 lb (140 kg).
• **OCCURRENCE** Atlantic Ocean. In open waters and along coastlines.
• **REMARK** This dolphin is still hunted for meat and bait in the Caribbean Sea.

ATLANTIC

gray back up to dorsal fin

spotting varies with habitat

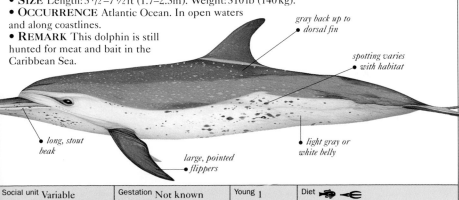

long, stout beak

large, pointed flippers

light gray or white belly

Social unit Variable	Gestation Not known	Young 1	Diet

Family DELPHINIDAE	Species *Stenella coeruleoalba*	Status Lower risk

STRIPED DOLPHIN

The basic blue-gray color of this dolphin's body is overlain by a
complex pattern of black and white stripes along its back and flanks.
A highly social cetacean, usually found in schools of 10–500, the Striped
Dolphin is well known for a wide variety of acrobatic leaps and spins
while racing across the ocean, and is often spotted riding pressure waves
in front of migrating great whales or ships. Sometimes it gathers in the
thousands, leaping high and whistling to keep in contact.
• **SIZE** Length: 6–8¼ ft (1.8–2.5 m). Weight: 240–360 lb (110–165 kg).
• **OCCURRENCE** Worldwide. In tropical and temperate waters.
• **REMARK** Although relatively common,
its numbers have declined in recent years.
In the early 1990s, the Mediterranean
population was devastated by
a viral disease.

WORLDWIDE

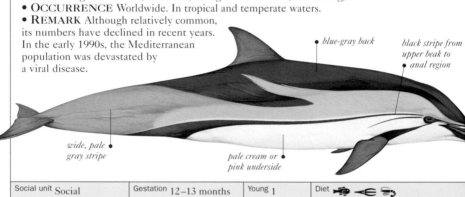

blue-gray back

*black stripe from
upper beak to
anal region*

*wide, pale
gray stripe*

*pale cream or
pink underside*

Social unit Social	Gestation 12–13 months	Young 1	Diet 

Family DELPHINIDAE	Species *Stenella attenuata*	Status Lower risk

PANTROPICAL SPOTTED DOLPHIN

One of the most common cetaceans, this streamlined dolphin is similar
to the Atlantic Spotted Dolphin (see p.187), but more slender. It has a
dark gray "cape" that runs from its forehead to the dorsal fin, while the
belly and lower flanks are pale gray. In adults, these are covered with
spots, which vary with habitat and increase with age. Adults may also
develop white lips. Large schools of thousands, often segregated into
mothers with their young, juveniles, and other groups, associate with
other cetaceans, especially Spinner Dolphins, and with shoals of tuna.
• **SIZE** Length: 5¼–8½ ft (1.6–2.6 m). Weight: Up to 260 lb (120 kg).
• **OCCURRENCE** Worldwide. In tropical and temperate waters.
• **REMARK** Like the Spinner Dolphin (see p.187), this
species is trapped as a bicatch in industrial
tuna fishing operations and
many are killed or
injured as a result.

WORLDWIDE

*slender, streamlined
body*

*oval, dark gray
"cape"*

*white lips on
adults*

*spotting on body
increases with age*

*pale
underside*

Social unit Social	Gestation 11–12 months	Young 1	Diet

Family DELPHINIDAE	Species *Tursiops truncatus*	Status Common

BOTTLENOSE DOLPHIN

A common "performer" at marine life centers, this is the largest of
the beaked dolphins. It shows enormous geographic variation in size
and color. In warmer waters it averages 6½ft (2 m) in length, and has
relatively large flippers, dorsal fin, and flukes, while in colder open
oceans it may be twice this size, but with proportionately smaller
extremities. Typically, it has a dark gray or black back and a cream
belly. Another possible species of Bottlenose Dolphin, *Tursiops aduncus*,
has been identified in the Indian and W. Pacific oceans.
• **SIZE** Length: 6¼–13 ft (1.9 – 4 m).
Weight: 1,100 lb (500 kg).
• **OCCURRENCE** Worldwide.
In temperate and tropical seas.
• **REMARK** This dolphin can be
swum with or stroked by
humans.

WORLDWIDE

short and
robust beak

large, hooked
dorsal fin

large tail
flukes

long, pointed
flippers

Social unit Variable	Gestation 12 months	Young 1	Diet

Family DELPHINIDAE	Species *Delphinus delphis*	Status Common

SHORT-BEAKED SADDLEBACK DOLPHIN

A distinctive yellow and gray blaze, shaped like an hourglass, runs along
the flank from the face to the tail of this dolphin. Dark stripes run from
its chin to its flippers and from the beak to the eyes. A fast swimmer, it
makes a variety of sounds – clicks, squeaks, and croaks – that can often
be heard from boats as it bow-rides. A second species of Saddleback
Dolphin (*Delphinus capensis*) is found in inshore waters. Both species,
however, hunt shoaling fish and squid to a depth of 985 ft (300 m).
• **SIZE** Length: 7½–8½ ft (2.3–2.6 m). Weight: 175 lb (80 kg).
• **OCCURRENCE** Worldwide. In deep tropical
and temperate waters.
• **REMARK** The Short-beaked
Saddleback Dolphin is
hunted in many parts
of the world.

WORLDWIDE

dark brown back

yellow or buff blaze
from mouth to below
the dorsal fin

pale gray blaze

white underside

long, narrow beak
with crease on melon

Social unit Social	Gestation 10–11 months	Young 1	Diet

Family DELPHINIDAE	Species *Orcaella brevirostris*	Status Locally common

IRRAWADDY DOLPHIN

A rounded, blunt head, ridged lips, bulging forehead, and creased neck characterize this river dolphin, which is capable of a variety of facial expressions due to a complex muscle structure. It is found in schools of 15 or less, in silt-laden estuaries, but some swim almost 930 miles (1,500 km) upstream, along the waterways of the Irrawaddy and Mekong.
• **SIZE** Length:7–9¼ft (2.1–2.8 m). Weight: 200–330 lb (90–150 kg).
• **OCCURRENCE** S.E. Asia and N. Australia. In brackish or freshwater.
• **REMARK** They may sometimes herd fish into fishermen's nets and receive rewards.

ASIA, AUSTRALIA

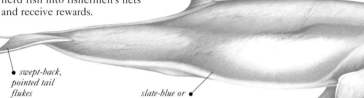

rounded head

swept-back, pointed tail flukes

slate-blue or gray body

creases on neck

Social unit Variable	Gestation 14 months	Young 1	Diet

Family DELPHINIDAE	Species *Lissodelphis borealis*	Status Common

NORTHERN RIGHT-WHALE DOLPHIN

Slim and slender, with small flippers and tail flukes, this dolphin's streamlined shape makes it a fast swimmer. It completely lacks a dorsal fin or dorsal ridge, and is named after the Northern Right-whale (see pp. 206–207), which also shares the same feature. This dolphin is almost fully black, except for a white strip below. This is much narrower than that of its cousin, the Southern Right-whale Dolphin (*Lissodelphis peronii*), which is found only in the Southern Hemisphere. Sociable in nature, these cetaceans form schools of 100–200, which merge into gatherings of thousands. Swimming in bouncing movements, they make a graceful sight, often leaping high and riding along with ships. Some dolphins are hunted in Japanese seas, while many are caught in squid driftnets off Japan, Taiwan, and Korea.
• **SIZE** Length: Up to 9¾ft (3 m). Weight: Up to 250 lb (115 kg).
• **OCCURRENCE** N. Pacific. In deep waters.
• **REMARK** This is the only dolphin without a dorsal fin.

PACIFIC

streamlined, slim body

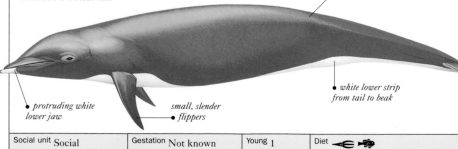

protruding white lower jaw

small, slender flippers

white lower strip from tail to beak

Social unit Social	Gestation Not known	Young 1	Diet

Family DELPHINIDAE	Species *Cephalorhynchus commersonii*	Status Locally common

COMMERSON'S DOLPHIN

Resembling the Killer Whale (see pp.194–195) in coloration, this dolphin has a smoothly sloping forehead, and rounded fins and tail flukes. It is white, except for black patches on its forehead, flippers, and belly, and between the dorsal fin and tail. The newborn calf is gray and becomes black and white with age. This expert swimmer and leaper forms schools of up to ten, occasionally expanding to 100. Those dolphins found around South America are 10–12 in (25–30 cm) shorter than those inhabiting the Indian Ocean.

S. AMERICA, INDIAN OCEAN

• **SIZE** Length: 4½–5½ ft (1.4–1.7 m). Weight: Up to 190 lb (86 kg).
• **OCCURRENCE** S. South America, Falkland Islands, and S. Indian Ocean. In shallow, muddy, coastal waters.

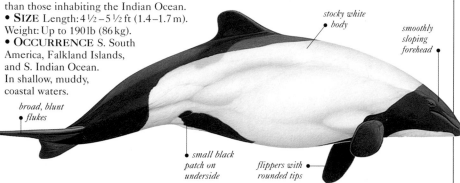

stocky white body

smoothly sloping forehead

broad, blunt flukes

small black patch on underside

flippers with rounded tips

Social unit Social	Gestation 11–12 months	Young 1	Diet 🦑 🐟 🦐

Family DELPHINIDAE	Species *Cephalorhynchus hectori*	Status Endangered

HECTOR'S DOLPHIN

Similar to a porpoise in outline, this small dolphin has a distinctively rounded dorsal fin and complex body pattern of black, white, and gray. Hector's Dolphin has a wide snout, and no beak or melonlike bulge on the forehead. Active and sociable, it swims in small groups of five or less, maintaining high levels of interaction through chasing, flipper-slapping, and touching. As an inshore species, it faces an increased risk from pollution and being trapped and killed in fishing nets.

NEW ZEALAND

• **SIZE** Length: 4–5 ft (1.2–1.5 m). Weight: Up to 125 lb (57 kg).
• **OCCURRENCE** New Zealand. In shallow, coastal waters.
• **REMARK** This is one of the rarest marine dolphins.

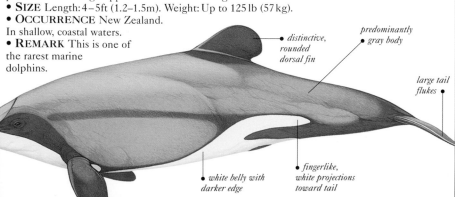

distinctive, rounded dorsal fin

predominantly gray body

large tail flukes

white belly with darker edge

fingerlike, white projections toward tail

Social unit Social	Gestation Not known	Young 1	Diet 🐟 🦐 🦑

Family DELPHINIDAE	Species *Globicephala macrorhynchus*	Status Lower risk

SHORT-FINNED PILOT WHALE

Distinctive in looks, this toothed whale is uniformly slate-gray or black, with an anchor-shaped pale patch on the throat and chest, and white streaks behind the dorsal fin and eyes. However, at sea it is almost impossible to distinguish it from its close cousin, the Long-finned Pilot Whale (*Globicephala melas*), the only difference being its shorter flippers. The Short-finned Pilot Whale appears to prefer warmer waters, and there is little overlap in the range of the two species. Male whales attain twice the weight of females and live 15 years longer. Scarring on their bodies suggests battles over females. Pilot Whales are highly sociable, forming schools of 10–100. They feed mainly on deep-water squid and octopus at night, often diving below 1,600 ft (500 m), and remaining underwater for more than 15 minutes.

slender body becomes more robust with age

tail with sharply pointed tips

- **SIZE** Length:16–23 ft (5–7m). Weight:1–2 tons (1–1.8 tonnes).
- **OCCURRENCE** Worldwide. In tropical and warm temperate waters.
- **REMARK** This whale is hunted by being driven into shallow waters.

off-white belly patch

Social unit Social	Gestation 14½–15 months	Young 1	Diet ⊰€ 🐙

Family DELPHINIDAE	Species *Pseudorca crassidens*	Status Locally common

FALSE KILLER WHALE

One of the largest dolphins, this uniformly black or slate-gray cetacean has a lighter blaze from its flippers to its belly, a centrally placed, tall, and hooked dorsal fin, and pectoral fins with an elbowlike bend. This slim-bodied whale swims extremely fast for its size and is a formidable hunter. It is equipped with 8–11 pairs of large, conical teeth and catches large, oceanic fish such as Salmon, Tuna, and Barracuda, as well as squid and smaller dolphins. Usually found in schools of 10–20, and rarely even up to 300, it makes various echolocating and communicating sounds, such as clicks and whistles. Known for spectacular leaps, it skillfully surfs breakers and bow waves.

slender head, tapers to round beak

- **SIZE** Length:16–20 ft (5–6m). Weight:1–1⅜ tons (1.3–1.4 tonnes).
- **OCCURRENCE** Worldwide. In deep and offshore, temperate or tropical waters – occasionally along coasts of oceanic islands, especially Japan and Hawaii.
- **REMARK** This whale is extremely susceptible to stranding on the shore, sometimes in large groups of up to 800–1,000.

angled flippers

Social unit Social	Gestation 11–16 months	Young 1	Diet ⊰€ 🐙 🐟

TAIL FLUKES
The tail flukes of the Short-finned Pilot Whale have concave trailing edges and a distinct notch in the middle. Often, they may be lifted above the surface before a long dive.

low, rounded dorsal fin

bulbous head

slate gray or black body

slender, curved flipper, close to the head

WORLDWIDE

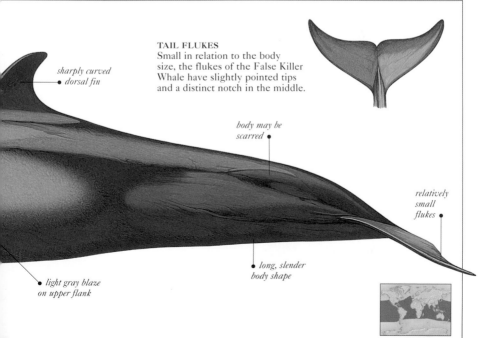

TAIL FLUKES
Small in relation to the body size, the flukes of the False Killer Whale have slightly pointed tips and a distinct notch in the middle.

sharply curved dorsal fin

body may be scarred

relatively small flukes

light gray blaze on upper flank

long, slender body shape

WORLDWIDE

Family DELPHINIDAE	Species *Orcinus orca*	Status Lower risk

KILLER WHALE

The most widely recognized species among toothed whales and dolphins, the Killer Whale is named for its extraordinary and diverse hunting techniques. The food it eats is equally diverse, ranging from herring to Great White Sharks, marine mammals such as small whales and seals, turtles, and seabirds. Its powerful and stocky body is ideally suited to hunting, its broad tail flukes propel it at high speeds, and the tall dorsal fin and paddlelike flippers provide stability. The distinctive black-and-white markings provide effective camouflage underwater, seen from above and below. Highly social in nature, the Killer Whale lives in long-lasting matriarchal pods or family groups. Male and female calves stay with the mother for life. As the young begin to reproduce, their offspring build up a multigeneration family around the matriarch. The average pod size is 30, but pods often merge to form "superpods" of 150. The pods travel in tight formation, with the females and calves in the center and the males around the fringes, or spread across distances of up to ¾ mile (1 km). Communication between whales is by highly distinctive cries and screams, which also act as social signals to reinforce group identity. The Killer Whale displays a variety of surface movements including spyhopping (rising slowly vertically, until its head is above the water), tail- and flipper-slapping, and breaching.

WORLDWIDE

dorsal fin forms isosceles triangle

conspicuous white eyepatches

white chin

• **SIZE** Length: Up to 30 ft (9 m). Weight: Up to 10 tons (10 tonnes).
• **OCCURRENCE** Worldwide. From estuaries to open oceans and icefields; common along coastlines and areas rich in marine life.
• **REMARK** Despite its name, the Killer Whale is approachable, rarely harming humans.

paddle-shaped flippers

flippers may be one-fifth body length

Social unit Social	Gestation 12–17 months	Young 1	Diet

ACE HUNTER
The Killer Whale is an ingenious hunter, working in coordinated groups to capture a wide variety of prey. It herds schools of fish together before attacking them from different angles. It tips over ice floes, dropping seals and penguins into the water to capture them, and intentionally beaches itself to pounce on unsuspecting seals.

robust, heavy body

predominantly jet black body

SPYHOPPING
The Killer Whale rises slowly out of the water, raising its head and most of its flippers above the surface, before sinking out of sight.

tail flukes black on upperside

sharply demarcated black-and-white areas

finger-shaped patch on belly

triangular fins may be seen above water

POD COORDINATION
Pods may travel closely together or spread apart, surfacing and diving in one coordinated movement.

TAIL FLUKES
The Killer Whale's wide tail flukes work as a propeller when it swims at high speed. They have a distinct notch in the middle and are white below.

Family MONODONTIDAE	Species *Delphinapterus leucas*	Status Vulnerable

BELUGA

The only all-white cetacean, the Beluga has a long, muscular body, no beak, an extremely flexible neck, and a fibrous dorsal ridge. The absence of a dorsal fin and its white skin are adaptations to life around and under floating ice. Tinged dark gray at birth, the skin gradually fades to become pure white. In an apparently unique departure from other cetaceans, the Beluga may molt in summer, when the skin may acquire a yellowish tinge. Well-known for emitting a wide variety of sounds, including squeaks, whistles, mews, clicks, and belches, the Beluga was nicknamed "sea canary" by whalers. It keeps to the upper edges of the Arctic icefields and has been radio-tracked diving to over 990 ft (300 m), to find prey.

ARCTIC

fibrous ridge along back

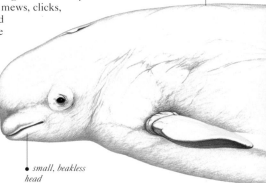

• **SIZE** Length:13–18 ft (4–5.5 m). Weight:1–1½ tons (1–1.5 tonnes).
• **OCCURRENCE** Circumpolar in the Northern Hemisphere. In temperate to Arctic waters.
• **REMARK** Severely depleted by whaling operations, the Beluga population is now threatened by chemical pollution.

small, beakless head

Social unit Social	Gestation 14 months	Young 1	Diet 🐟 ◀🦐 🦑

Family MONODONTIDAE	Species *Monodon monoceros*	Status Locally common

NARWHAL

With the most northerly range of any mammal, the Narwhal rarely strays south of 60° North. The most famous feature of the male is its tusk, which is actually a modified upper left tooth that grows in a clockwise spiral through its upper lip. The tusk is used as a weapon, but also to break open breathing holes in ice floes or for grubbing in the seabed. The mouth itself is toothless and the bulbous melon has no beak. The Narwhal's stocky body has no dorsal fin, and its small pectoral fins are upturned at the tip in adults. The C-shaped tail flukes of the adult are shaped like a fan, composed of two, joined semicircles (see right). Calves are born uniformly gray, but the adults have pale gray skin speckled black.

ARCTIC

Like the Belugas, with which they are often found, Narwhals form big schools segregated by age and sex, and use a wide variety of sounds, either for communicating with each other and warning against predators, or for locating their prey.
• **SIZE** Length:13–15 ft (4–4.5 m). Weight:¾–1⅝ tons (0.8–1.6 tonnes).
• **OCCURRENCE** Circumpolar. In oceans and along coastlines.
• **REMARK** The Narwhal is hunted for meat, oil, skin, and tusks.

small flippers

Social unit Social	Gestation 14–15 months	Young 1	Diet 🐟 ◀🦐 🦑

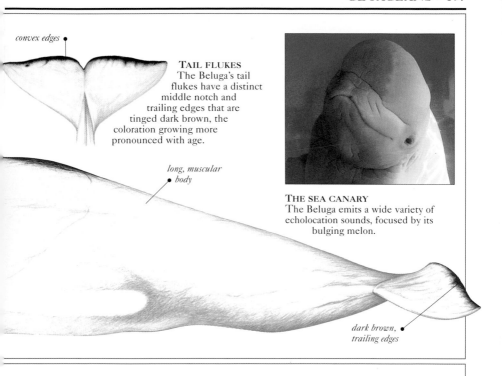

convex edges

TAIL FLUKES
The Beluga's tail
flukes have a distinct
middle notch and
trailing edges that are
tinged dark brown, the
coloration growing more
pronounced with age.

*long, muscular
body*

THE SEA CANARY
The Beluga emits a wide variety of
echolocation sounds, focused by its
bulging melon.

*dark brown,
trailing edges*

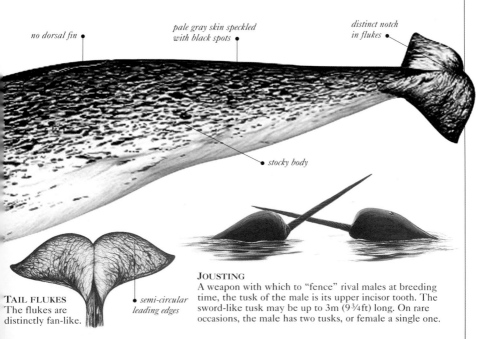

no dorsal fin

*pale gray skin speckled
with black spots*

*distinct notch
in flukes*

stocky body

TAIL FLUKES
The flukes are
distinctly fan-like.

*semi-circular
leading edges*

JOUSTING
A weapon with which to "fence" rival males at breeding
time, the tusk of the male is its upper incisor tooth. The
sword-like tusk may be up to 3m (9¾ft) long. On rare
occasions, the male has two tusks, or female a single one.

Family ZIPHIIDAE	Species *Hyperoodon ampullatus*	Status Lower risk

NORTHERN BOTTLENOSE WHALE

One of about 19 species of beaked whales, this cetacean has a steep, almost boxlike forehead with a distinct beak protruding from below. Two tusks erupt from the tip of its lower jaw, which also has a pair of throat grooves. An erect dorsal fin is found about two-thirds down its streamlined body, whose color varies from brown or orange to gray on the back. Despite their large size, these whales are capable of spectacular leaps, but they are mostly seen breathing at the surface between long dives to the seabed, where they suck up their prey.

pointed dorsal fin •

• **SIZE** Length: 20–33 ft (6–10 m). Weight: Not recorded.
• **OCCURRENCE**
N. Atlantic down to
the Spanish coast.
In open waters.
• **REMARK** This whale
is now protected,
although many are
known to choke
to death on plastic
refuse ingested
while sucking
sediment from
the seabed.

• long, slim body

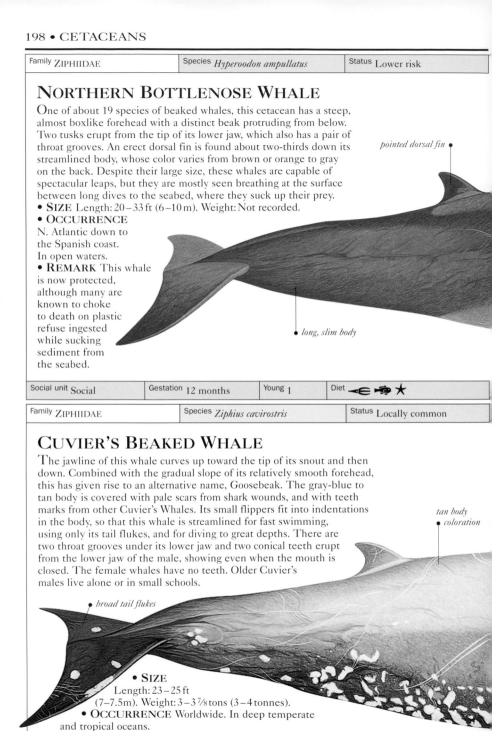

Social unit Social	Gestation 12 months	Young 1	Diet ◀€ 🐟 ★

Family ZIPHIIDAE	Species *Ziphius cavirostris*	Status Locally common

CUVIER'S BEAKED WHALE

The jawline of this whale curves up toward the tip of its snout and then down. Combined with the gradual slope of its relatively smooth forehead, this has given rise to an alternative name, Goosebeak. The gray-blue to tan body is covered with pale scars from shark wounds, and with teeth marks from other Cuvier's Whales. Its small flippers fit into indentations in the body, so that this whale is streamlined for fast swimming, using only its tail flukes, and for diving to great depths. There are two throat grooves under its lower jaw and two conical teeth erupt from the lower jaw of the male, showing even when the mouth is closed. The female whales have no teeth. Older Cuvier's males live alone or in small schools.

tan body
• coloration

• broad tail flukes

• **SIZE**
Length: 23–25 ft
(7–7.5 m). Weight: 3–3 7/8 tons (3–4 tonnes).
• **OCCURRENCE** Worldwide. In deep temperate
and tropical oceans.

Social unit Variable	Gestation Not known	Young 1	Diet ◀€ ★

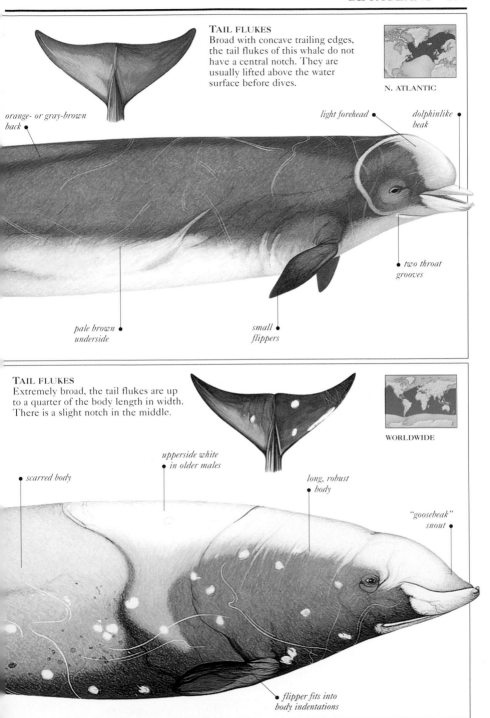

TAIL FLUKES
Broad with concave trailing edges, the tail flukes of this whale do not have a central notch. They are usually lifted above the water surface before dives.

N. ATLANTIC

orange- or gray-brown back

light forehead

dolphinlike beak

two throat grooves

pale brown underside

small flippers

TAIL FLUKES
Extremely broad, the tail flukes are up to a quarter of the body length in width. There is a slight notch in the middle.

WORLDWIDE

scarred body

upperside white in older males

long, robust body

"goosebeak" snout

flipper fits into body indentations

Family ZIPHIIDAE	Species *Mesoplodon layardii*	Status Unconfirmed

STRAP-TOOTHED WHALE

One of the largest of the beaked whales, the male Strap-toothed
Whale can be easily identified by a pair of extraordinary teeth that
grow from its lower jaw, curling upward and backward over the top
of its upper jaw – in adult whales they may grow to a length of 12 in
(30 cm). These teeth do not erupt in female whales, while in
juvenile males they are smaller and more triangular in shape. The
Strap-toothed Whale has distinct black-and-white markings, with
a black "face mask." It has a long, slender beak and slightly
bulging melon, and a relatively small dorsal fin
and flippers for its size. Rarely seen in the
wild, and difficult to approach, especially
in large vessels, this whale may
sometimes be seen basking at
the surface on calm, sunny days.

SOUTHERN
OCEAN

• scarring on body

• **SIZE** Length: 16 ½–20 ¼ ft
(5–6.2 m). Weight: 1–3 tons (1–3 tonnes).
• **OCCURRENCE** Chile, Argentina, Uruguay,
Falkland Islands, Namibia, South Africa, Australia,
Tasmania, New Zealand. In cold, temperate, offshore waters.
• **REMARK** The Strap-toothed Whale is the most
commonly reported species of *Mesoplodon* in the
Southern Hemisphere.

small, narrow •
flippers

Social unit Variable	Gestation Not known	Young 1	Diet ◄

Family ZIPHIIDAE	Species *Mesoplodon bidens*	Status Unconfirmed

SOWERBY'S BEAKED WHALE

With one of the most northerly distributions of all the beaked whales,
Sowerby's Beaked Whale is seldom sighted, in spite of being a commonly
stranded species. Males are characterized by a pair of teeth midway on the
beak, visible when the mouth is shut. The upper body of this whale is
slate-gray or bluish gray, while the underside is lighter. The beak is long
and slender, and the blowhole is situated behind the forehead bulge.

N. ATLANTIC

concave trailing
• edges

• **SIZE** Length: 13 ½–16 ½ ft (4–5 m). Weight: 1–1.3 tons (1–1.3 tonnes).
• **OCCURRENCE** E. and W. North Atlantic. In temperate and
subarctic waters.
• **REMARK** The first beaked whale to be discovered
(off the Scottish coast in 1800), it was painted by the
English artist, James Sowerby – hence its common name.

TAIL FLUKES
There is no notch between
the tail flukes, which are
dark on both sides.

teeth visible when
• mouth is shut

small, curved dorsal fin •

relatively •
long flippers

• belly may
have pale spots

Social unit Solitary	Gestation Not known	Young 1	Diet ◄ ◄

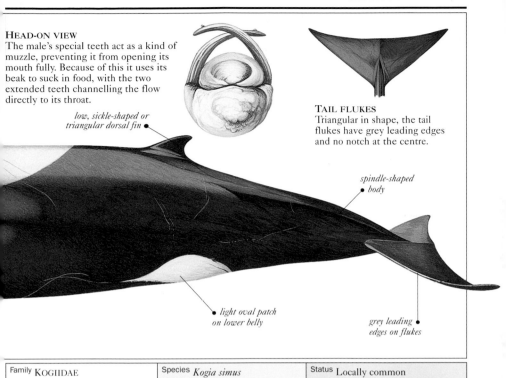

HEAD-ON VIEW
The male's special teeth act as a kind of muzzle, preventing it from opening its mouth fully. Because of this it uses its beak to suck in food, with the two extended teeth channelling the flow directly to its throat.

low, sickle-shaped or triangular dorsal fin

TAIL FLUKES
Triangular in shape, the tail flukes have grey leading edges and no notch at the centre.

spindle-shaped body

light oval patch on lower belly

grey leading edges on flukes

Family KOGIIDAE	Species *Kogia simus*	Status Locally common

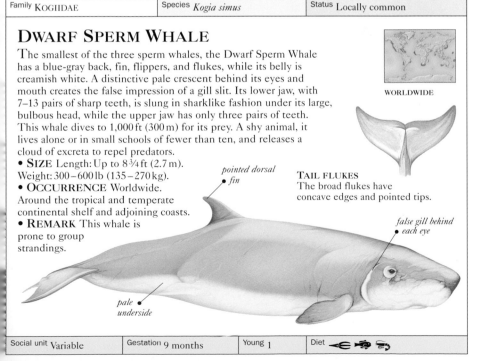

DWARF SPERM WHALE

The smallest of the three sperm whales, the Dwarf Sperm Whale has a blue-gray back, fin, flippers, and flukes, while its belly is creamish white. A distinctive pale crescent behind its eyes and mouth creates the false impression of a gill slit. Its lower jaw, with 7–13 pairs of sharp teeth, is slung in sharklike fashion under its large, bulbous head, while the upper jaw has only three pairs of teeth. This whale dives to 1,000 ft (300 m) for its prey. A shy animal, it lives alone or in small schools of fewer than ten, and releases a cloud of excreta to repel predators.
• **SIZE** Length: Up to 8¾ ft (2.7 m). Weight: 300–600 lb (135–270 kg).
• **OCCURRENCE** Worldwide. Around the tropical and temperate continental shelf and adjoining coasts.
• **REMARK** This whale is prone to group strandings.

WORLDWIDE

pointed dorsal fin

TAIL FLUKES
The broad flukes have concave edges and pointed tips.

false gill behind each eye

pale underside

Social unit Variable	Gestation 9 months	Young 1	Diet

Family PHYSETERIDAE	Species *Physeter macrocephalus*	Status Vulnerable

SPERM WHALE

This whale is known for its huge, boxlike head, a quarter to a third of its body size, in which is found the unique spermaceti organ that helps it make impressively deep dives. Between dives, it lies loglike on the surface of the water, exhaling a misty plume of air at 45° from its single blowhole. Dark gray or brown in color, it has a paler underside and a cream patch on its narrow lower jaw. This contains 50 pairs of conical teeth; there are no visible upper teeth. Male whales are twice the weight of the females and migrate further toward the poles for summer feeding. They form loose bachelor pods (groups) when young, and become solitary with age. Females stay nearer to the tropics in mixed groups containing young and juveniles. The single calf is born in summer or fall, with the next birth following in 3–15 years. Sperm Whales swim close, touching and caressing each other. They produce loud clicks and banging sounds, which may aid individual recognition.
• **SIZE** Length: 36–65 ft (11–20 m).
Weight: 19 1/2–56 tons (20–57 tonnes).
• **OCCURRENCE** Worldwide. In deep waters, at and beyond the continental shelf.
• **REMARK** The Sperm Whale is the largest carnivore in the world.

HEAD-ON VIEW
The Sperm Whale's head contains the spermaceti organ, a mass of waxy oil that works as a buoyancy aid during deep dives and changes density according to the water pressure and temperature.

• body color varies from dark grey to light brown

• head larger in male than female

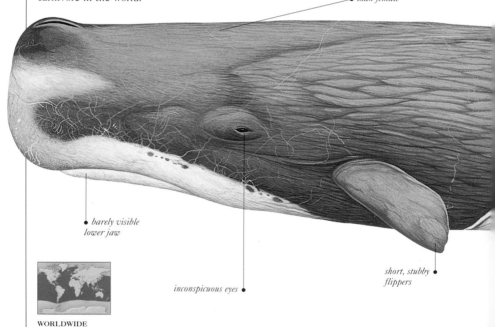

• barely visible lower jaw

• short, stubby flippers

inconspicuous eyes •

WORLDWIDE

Social unit Variable	Gestation 14–15 1/2 months	Young 1	Diet ⬗➤

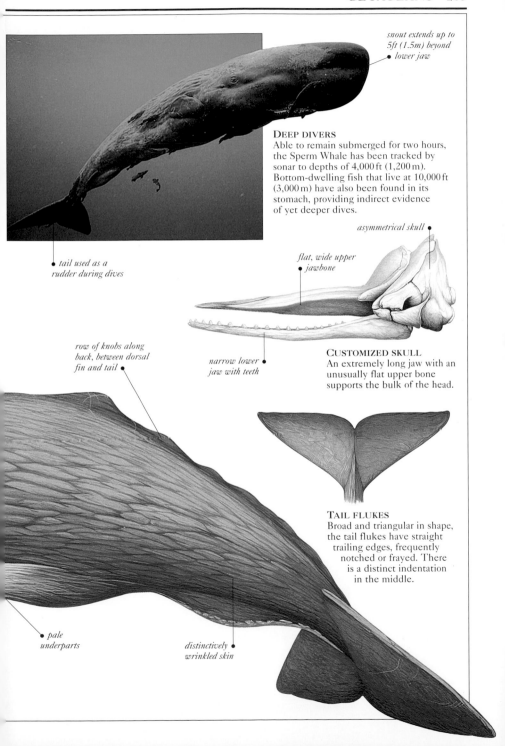

snout extends up to
5ft (1.5m) beyond
lower jaw

DEEP DIVERS
Able to remain submerged for two hours,
the Sperm Whale has been tracked by
sonar to depths of 4,000ft (1,200m).
Bottom-dwelling fish that live at 10,000ft
(3,000m) have also been found in its
stomach, providing indirect evidence
of yet deeper dives.

asymmetrical skull

tail used as a
rudder during dives

flat, wide upper
jawbone

row of knobs along
back, between dorsal
fin and tail

narrow lower
jaw with teeth

CUSTOMIZED SKULL
An extremely long jaw with an
unusually flat upper bone
supports the bulk of the head.

TAIL FLUKES
Broad and triangular in shape,
the tail flukes have straight
trailing edges, frequently
notched or frayed. There
is a distinct indentation
in the middle.

pale
underparts

distinctively
wrinkled skin

CETACEANS
BALEEN WHALES

T HE ANATOMY OF the great whales differs from that of a typical mammal perhaps more than any species. They are gigantic, almost hairless, possess front limbs modified as flippers, and have lost their rear limbs. They also lack teeth. Instead, hanging from either side of the upper jaw is a row of plates made of baleen, or whalebone, which is not true bone, but a springy material similar to cartilage. These "curtains" are used to sieve small food items from sea water.

The 12 species of baleen whales include the Gray Whale, the Right Whale and Bowhead, and the Rorquals. Members of this last family vary from the Minke, about 33 ft (10 m) in length, to the Blue Whale, the biggest living animal, at up to 98 ft (30 m) long.

Family BALAENA	Species *Balaena mysticetus*	Status Endangered

BOWHEAD

The massive head of the Bowhead accounts for about one-third of its body weight and makes up about 40 per cent of its length. The skin, unusually clear of barnacles and whale lice, is black in adults, with white around the chin and lower jaw, and at the base of the tail. The brownish or bluish black baleen plates are the longest of any whale and can be up to 15 ft (4.6 m) long. Each side of its strongly curved or "bowed" upper jaw has between 240 and 340 baleen plates. The Bowhead has two blowholes and can blow up to 20 ft (6 m). It is known to produce intense low-frequency underwater sounds, which range from simple tonal moans to elephant trumpetings and screeching, and may last up to 7 seconds or more.
• SIZE Length: 45–59 ft (14–18 m).
Weight: 49½–59 tons (50–60 tonnes).
• OCCURRENCE Northern Hemisphere, especially N. Canada, Alaska, and N. Russia. In Arctic and subarctic waters.
• REMARK Tens of thousands of Bowheads were killed by early whalers, so that populations in the N. Atlantic are now perilously small. Current threats include oil exploration.

no dorsal fin, hump, or ridge

white around lower jaw and chin

ARCTIC

Social unit Social	Gestation 12–14 months	Young 1	Diet 🦐 ★

UNDERWATER NAVIGATORS
Since it inhabits polar waters, the Bowhead spends part of the year in continuous night. Capable of navigating under ice in pitch dark, it can break through ice sheets more than 8 in (20 cm) thick. It uses echolocation to investigate the ice conditions ahead.

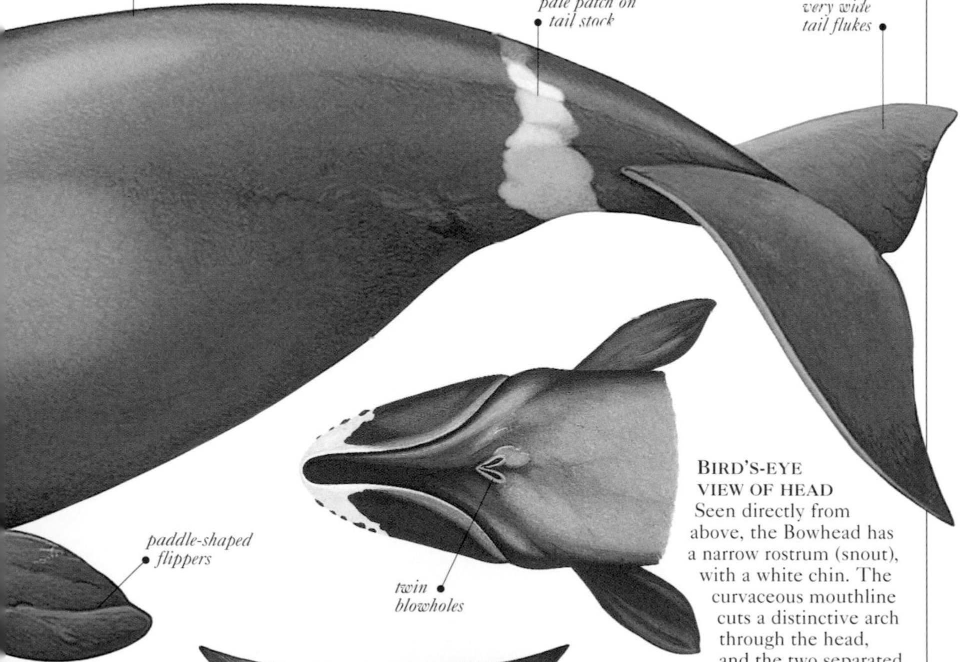

large, stocky body

pale patch on tail stock

very wide tail flukes

paddle-shaped flippers

twin blowholes

BIRD'S-EYE VIEW OF HEAD
Seen directly from above, the Bowhead has a narrow rostrum (snout), with a white chin. The curvaceous mouthline cuts a distinctive arch through the head, and the two separated blowholes are at the center.

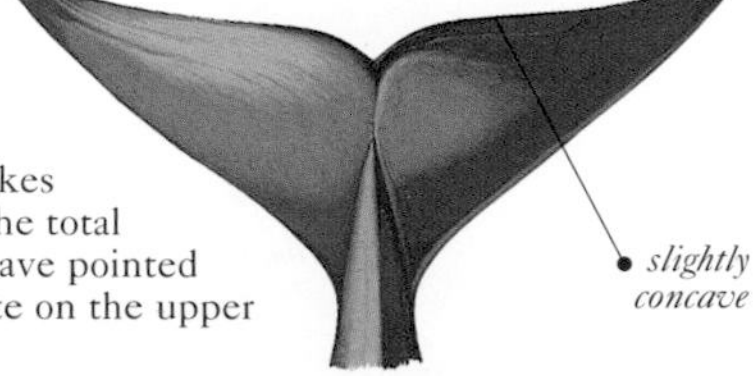

TAIL FLUKES
The width of the flukes may be almost half the total body length. They have pointed tips and may be white on the upper trailing edges.

slightly concave edges

Family BALAENIDAE	Species *Eubalaena glacialis*	Status Endangered

NORTHERN RIGHT WHALE

Perhaps the most endangered of the large whales, the Northern Right Whale was so named by whalers since it has all the "right" features to make it the ideal catch – it lives and feeds close to the shore, is easy to approach, and is a valuable source of meat, blubber, and bone. Hunted indiscriminately in the nineteenth century to near extinction, the whale has been protected since 1937, but its numbers are recovering extremely slowly. Being a slow surface swimmer that dives only for a few minutes, it is susceptible to fatalities from ship collisions or being trapped in fishing equipment. This whale's body is black with scattered white patches. Similar in shape to the Bowhead Whale (see pp. 204–205), the Northern Right Whale has a head that is up to a quarter of its body length, with a downward-curving jawline and narrow baleen plates up to 9¾ft (3 m) long. The head is encrusted with fibrous growths, or callosities, which are covered with whale lice that often add a pink, yellow, or orange tinge, and its twin blowholes create a bushy, V-shaped blow. Found singly or in small groups, it migrates to the far north or south in summer, returning to warmer mid-latitude waters in winter to breed. Despite being a sluggish swimmer, it is surprisingly acrobatic, and may be seen flipper-slapping, tail-slapping, breaching, or even doing a "headstand" by raising its tail flukes high above the surface of the water, almost at a right angle.

WORLDWIDE

JAW FACTS
The baleen plates of this whale are exceptionally long and narrow. Densely fringed with fine bristles, they number 200–270 on each side of the upper jaw. The deep, bowed lower jaw is used for closing the mouth.

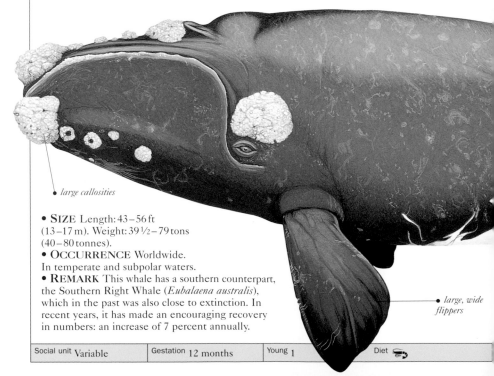

large callosities

• **SIZE** Length: 43–56 ft (13–17 m). Weight: 39½–79 tons (40–80 tonnes).
• **OCCURRENCE** Worldwide. In temperate and subpolar waters.
• **REMARK** This whale has a southern counterpart, the Southern Right Whale (*Eubalaena australis*), which in the past was also close to extinction. In recent years, it has made an encouraging recovery in numbers: an increase of 7 percent annually.

large, wide flippers

Social unit Variable	Gestation 12 months	Young 1	Diet

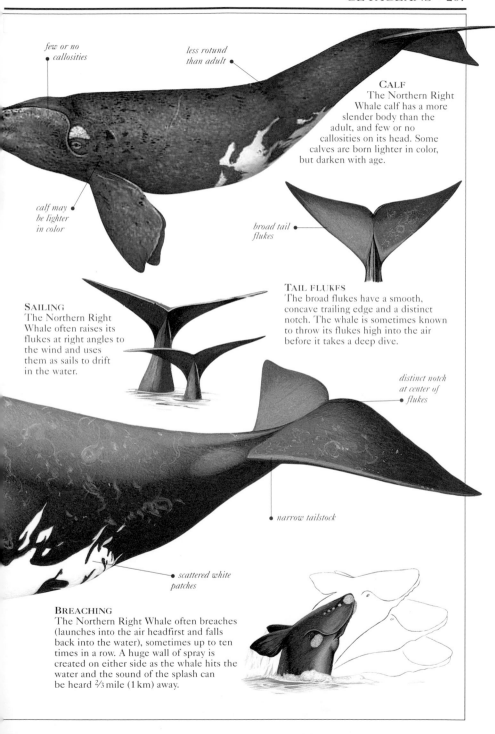

few or no
callosities

less rotund
than adult

CALF
The Northern Right
Whale calf has a more
slender body than the
adult, and few or no
callosities on its head. Some
calves are born lighter in color,
but darken with age.

calf may
be lighter
in color

broad tail
flukes

TAIL FLUKES
The broad flukes have a smooth,
concave trailing edge and a distinct
notch. The whale is sometimes known
to throw its flukes high into the air
before it takes a deep dive.

SAILING
The Northern Right
Whale often raises its
flukes at right angles to
the wind and uses
them as sails to drift
in the water.

distinct notch
at center of
flukes

narrow tailstock

scattered white
patches

BREACHING
The Northern Right Whale often breaches
(launches into the air headfirst and falls
back into the water), sometimes up to ten
times in a row. A huge wall of spray is
created on either side as the whale hits the
water and the sound of the splash can
be heard ⅔ mile (1 km) away.

Family ESCHRICHTIIDAE	Species *Eschrichtius robustus*	Status Endangered

GRAY WHALE

N. PACIFIC

Among the most active of all large whales, the Gray Whale makes one of the longest migrations of any mammal. Groups of up to ten travel to the Arctic for summer feeding, returning south to warm-water lagoons to rest and produce calves in winter. When migrating, this whale typically blows 3–6 times before diving for 3–5 minutes. It enjoys surf-riding, and is frequently found in surf (especially in Baja California) in very shallow water, sometimes lying on its side and waving a flipper in the air. Apart from filter-feeding, it also dives to the shallow seabed, scoops up huge mouthfuls of mud, and filters it for worms, starfish, shrimps, and other small creatures, making it a unique bottom-feeder among whales. Feeding near the shore, it is accessible to watchers, especially in the east Pacific. The Gray Whale swims in a coordinated fashion with other whales, staying in line or arching out of the water together. Like many other baleen whales, it spyhops, or raises its head vertically out of the water. Its mottled gray skin is encrusted with barnacles and sea lice. This whale has no dorsal fin, but a series of eight or nine bumps runs along the last third of its dorsal ridge.

• SIZE Length:43–49 ft (13–15 m). Weight:14–34 ½ tons (14–35 tonnes).
• OCCURRENCE N. Pacific Ocean. Along coastlines, within the continental shelf, up to the surf zone; breeding in sheltered lagoons in the tropics.
• REMARK Atlantic stocks were wiped out by excessive whaling before this whale was declared a protected species in 1946. The California population has since made a remarkable recovery. However, Siberian and Alaskan Inuit people are still allowed to kill a certain number every year.

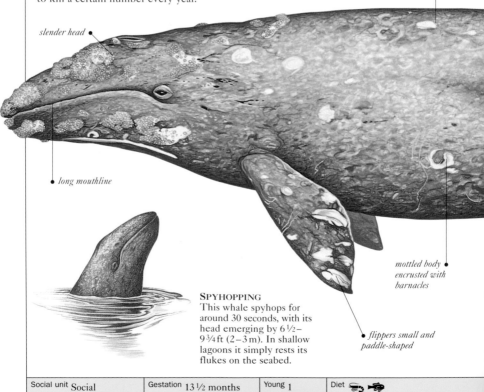

slender head

no dorsal fin

long mouthline

mottled body encrusted with barnacles

SPYHOPPING
This whale spyhops for around 30 seconds, with its head emerging by 6 ½– 9 ¾ ft (2–3 m). In shallow lagoons it simply rests its flukes on the seabed.

flippers small and paddle-shaped

Social unit Social	Gestation 13 ½ months	Young 1	Diet

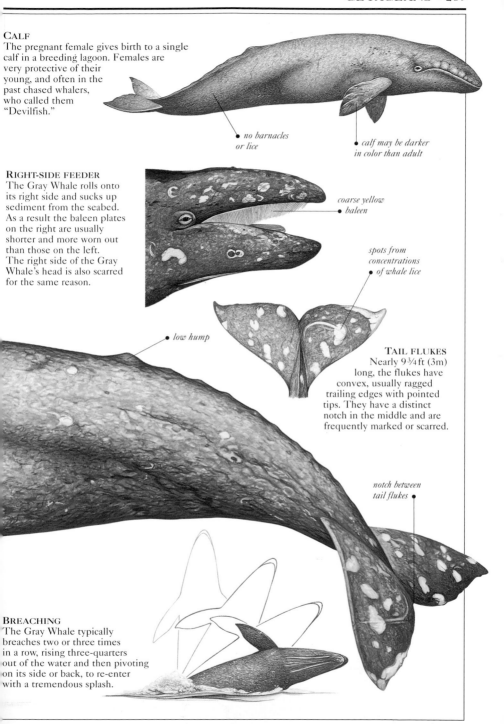

CALF
The pregnant female gives birth to a single calf in a breeding lagoon. Females are very protective of their young, and often in the past chased whalers, who called them "Devilfish."

• *no barnacles or lice*

• *calf may be darker in color than adult*

RIGHT-SIDE FEEDER
The Gray Whale rolls onto its right side and sucks up sediment from the seabed. As a result the baleen plates on the right are usually shorter and more worn out than those on the left. The right side of the Gray Whale's head is also scarred for the same reason.

coarse yellow baleen •

spots from concentrations of whale lice •

• *low hump*

TAIL FLUKES
Nearly 9¾ ft (3m) long, the flukes have convex, usually ragged trailing edges with pointed tips. They have a distinct notch in the middle and are frequently marked or scarred.

notch between tail flukes •

BREACHING
The Gray Whale typically breaches two or three times in a row, rising three-quarters out of the water and then pivoting on its side or back, to re-enter with a tremendous splash.

Family BALAENOPTERIDAE	Species *Balaenoptera physalus*	Status Endangered

FIN WHALE

The second largest whale and one of the fastest, this species can sometimes reach a speed of19 mph (30 kph). The Fin Whale has a grey back, flippers, and tail flukes, and its dorsal fin, set about two-thirds of the way along the spine, has a concave rear edge. A distinct ridge runs from its dorsal fin to the flukes, which accounts for an alternative name: Razorback. This whale is always found swimming on its right side; the left side of its mouth is black, and the right side is white. Such asymmetrical coloration is highly unusual in mammals. Like other great whales, it undertakes long migrations from high latitudes in summer toward the tropical regions for winter, when it breeds. In addition to hums and squeals, it produces an immensely deep, loud moan that can be heard hundreds of miles away.

- **SIZE** Length: 62–72 ft (19–22 m).
Weight: 44 ½–74 tons (45–75 tonnes).
- **OCCURRENCE** Worldwide, except in the Mediterranean, Baltic, and Red Seas, and Arabian Gulf. In open oceans, particularly in areas of seasonal plankton.
- **REMARK** Heavily exploited by industrial whaling, particularly in the Southern Hemisphere where around three-quarters of its population has been wiped out, the Fin Whale is currently protected. However, there is a growing concern that low-frequency sound produced by military equipment and shipping activities may disrupt the normal communication patterns of this whale, reducing its ability to navigate or find mates.

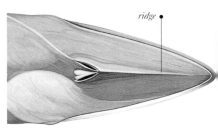

BREACHING
When breaching, the Fin Whale leaves the water at an angle, usually with its tail-end submerged. As its body begins to fall, it may twist in midair, re-entering the water with a loud splash, typically landing on its belly, and less commonly on its back.

ridge

RIDGE ON HEAD
The head of this whale is between one-fifth and one-quarter of its total body length. It usually has a single, longitudinal ridge along its rostrum, a few whales having two extra ridge

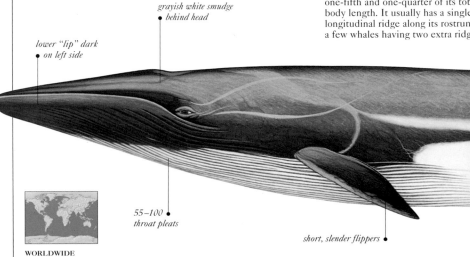

grayish white smudge behind head

lower "lip" dark on left side

55–100 throat pleats

short, slender flippers

WORLDWIDE

Social unit Variable	Gestation 11 months	Young 1	Diet

RIGHT-SIDED FEEDING

Swimming only on its right side, the Fin Whale lunges at high-speed at krill and fish such as capelin or herring. Synchronizing its attacks with those of other Fin Whales, it takes in huge volumes of water, then closes its mouth and forces out the water to trap fish in its baleen plates. The baleen plates on the right side are white in up to a quarter or third of the mouth (the left side is dark gray), and when swimming below the water's surface, the white right "lip" is often clearly visible.

broad, flat rostrum, flatter than in Blue Whale •

TAIL FLUKES

The Fin Whale rarely shows its broad, slightly triangular flukes. These have a distinct notch in the middle, and the slightly concave and trailing edges may be notched or frayed. The undersides of the flukes are white.

ASYMMETRICAL HEAD

The uneven coloration of the Fin Whale's head can be extensive, with the white patch on the right extending anywhere from the upper "lip" to the neck.

dorsal fin slopes • backwards

distinct ridge from dorsal • fin to flukes

thick tailstock •

• white underside

Family BALAENOPTERIDAE	Species *Balaenoptera musculus*	Status Endangered

BLUE WHALE

The largest animal in the world, the Blue Whale is surprisingly streamlined, with its pointed head, long body, slender flippers, and large, narrow tail flukes. It is mainly gray-blue in color, but the skin on the belly may be tinted yellow-brown by algae. Its lower jaw has 55–68 grooves running up to the navel, making the skin extremely distensible. The Blue Whale engulfs shoals of krill, its exclusive diet, with the throat swelling to four times its normal size. In a day it can consume around 5⅞ tons (6 tonnes) of food. Feeding occurs mainly in summer around the krill-rich polar waters. The Blue Whale is known to migrate south to warmer latitudes in winter, when the female gives birth. Usually found alone, or in mother–calf pairs, this whale may gather in loose groups to feed. Its grunts, hums, and moans, sometimes at volumes over 180 decibels, are the loudest of any animal sounds, and can be heard by other whales 625 miles (1,000 km) away. It blows every 10–20 seconds for a total of 2–6 minutes and then dives for 5–20 minutes (although it is able to stay underwater longer). Adult whales rarely breach clear of the water, but younger animals have been observed breaching at an angle of 45°, landing on their stomach or side.

WORLDWIDE

• **SIZE** Length: 66–98 ft (20–30 m).
Weight: 98½–157½ tons (100–160 tonnes).
• **OCCURRENCE** Worldwide, except the Mediterranean, Baltic, and Red Seas, and Arabian Gulf. In deep, open, mainly cold waters.
• **REMARK** The Blue Whale was hunted close to extinction by whalers, and some populations may never recover.

pale gray or white mottling, especially behind head

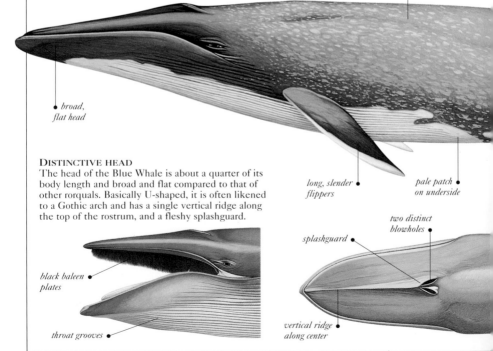

broad, flat head

long, slender flippers

pale patch on underside

DISTINCTIVE HEAD
The head of the Blue Whale is about a quarter of its body length and broad and flat compared to that of other rorquals. Basically U-shaped, it is often likened to a Gothic arch and has a single vertical ridge along the top of the rostrum, and a fleshy splashguard.

two distinct blowholes

splashguard

black baleen plates

vertical ridge along center

throat grooves

Social unit Solitary	Gestation 11 months	Young 1	Diet 

ENORMOUS WHALE
The largest of all cetaceans, and among one of the largest animals ever to have lived on earth, the Blue Whale is almost as long as a Boeing 737. A length of more than 110 ft (33 m) and weight of around 180 tons (190 tonnes) have been recorded.

tiny dorsal fin three-quarters of way along back

slender flukes

variable pale gray body

streamlined shape

thick tailstock

slightly concave edges

large, narrow flukes

TAIL FLUKES
The Blue Whale's tail flukes are up to a quarter of its body size. The trailing edges are straight or slightly concave, with a small notch in the middle.

| Family BALAENOPTERIDAE | Species *Balaenoptera acutorostrata* | Status Lower risk |

MINKE WHALE

Resembling a dolphin in shape, this species is the smallest of the baleen whales. Its back is black, and its belly, lower jaw, and throat are white, with smoky gray patterns called chevrons blurring the border between them. Its sickle-shaped dorsal fin is large compared to that of other baleen whales. The baleen plates are up to 12 in (30 cm) long, creamish in front and gray at the rear. A fast and agile swimmer, it sometimes makes spectacular leaps from the water. It is generally solitary, but is sometimes found feeding with other whales. It also hunts where other predators such as birds and fish are active, at a particularly dense supply of food. This whale is not shy and often approaches stationary boats. It communicates with grunts, clicks, ratchets, and a variety of other sounds.

relatively large dorsal fin

• SIZE Length: 26–33 ft (8–10 m).
Weight: 7 ½–13 tons (8–13 tonnes).
• OCCURRENCE Worldwide
(except E. Mediterranean).
In oceans and along
coastlines.
• REMARK A smaller form of the Minke Whale has recently been recognized as a separate species– the Antarctic Minke Whale (*Balaenoptera bonaerensis*).

white belly

| Social unit Solitary | Gestation 10 months | Young 1 | Diet |

| Family BALAENOPTERIDAE | Species *Megaptera novaeangliae* | Status Vulnerable |

HUMPBACK WHALE

This highly vocal whale is recognized by its rather dumpy shape and huge pectoral fins. These are normally used to channel prey towards its mouth, but aggressive whales can beat adversaries to death with them. The upper and lower jaws are lined with tubercles that are often encrusted with barnacles, and there is a slight ridge from the blowholes to the tip of the snout. The back is black or blue-black, with paler patches below. These color patterns vary from whale to whale and can be used to identify individuals. The dorsal fin, located on a pad of fat, may be triangular to sharply hooked. Humpback Whales migrate from warm breeding grounds in winter to fertile feeding grounds, at higher latitudes in summer. They specialize in rounding up prey by blowing underwater "bubble curtains," with sometimes a dozen or more whales hunting together.

triangular dorsal fin

ridge from dorsal fin to tail

• SIZE Length: 43–46 ft (13–14 m).
Weight: 24 ⅝–29 ½ tons (25–30 tonnes).
• OCCURRENCE Worldwide. Along coasts or in deep seas.
• REMARK This species is known to sing for over 22 hours. Each male whale has its signature tune, which it changes over the years. It may be used to attract a mate or ward off rivals.

WORLDWIDE

| Social unit Solitary | Gestation 11 months | Young 1 | Diet |

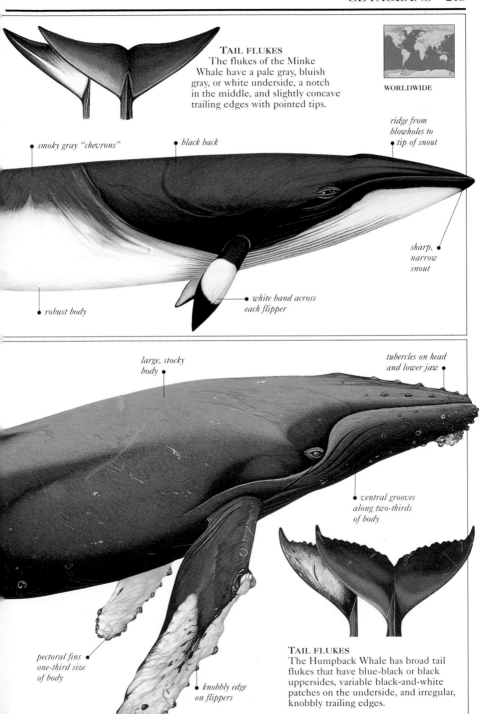

TAIL FLUKES
The flukes of the Minke Whale have a pale gray, bluish gray, or white underside, a notch in the middle, and slightly concave trailing edges with pointed tips.

WORLDWIDE

ridge from blowholes to tip of snout

smoky gray "chevrons"

black back

sharp, narrow snout

robust body

white band across each flipper

large, stocky body

tubercles on head and lower jaw

ventral grooves along two-thirds of body

pectoral fins one-third size of body

knobbly edge on flippers

TAIL FLUKES
The Humpback Whale has broad tail flukes that have blue-black or black uppersides, variable black-and-white patches on the underside, and irregular, knobbly trailing edges.

CARNIVORES
DOGS AND FOXES

T WO OF THE most familiar carnivores, the Gray Wolf (the ancestor of the domestic dog) and the Red Fox, belong to the Canid or dog family. So do another 34 species among them dingoes, coyotes, and jackals.

Canids are typified by a muscular but slender body, a long and bushy tail, powerful legs, a long muzzle and sensitive nose, large ears for keen hearing, and strong, large-toothed jaws.

Found worldwide, generally in open habitats, they have an opportunistic approach to diet. Smaller species, especially foxes, feed on insects and rodents, and live alone or in pairs. Larger species like wolves and African wild dogs live and hunt in packs.

Several canids have faced persecution over the ages, and a few, such as the Simian Jackal and Red Wolf, are now on the critical list.

Family CANIDAE	Species *Vulpes zerda*	Status Unconfirmed

FENNEC FOX

The smallest of all foxes, the Fennec is readily identified by its huge ears. It has a cream to yellowish coat with white underparts and a black-tipped tail. The soles of its feet are furry for protection when walking on hot, soft sand. Usually nocturnal, this omnivorous fox has a wide-ranging diet which includes fruits, seeds, small rodents, birds, eggs, reptiles, and insects. It is unusual in associating in groups of up to ten, but the relationships between the members are not clear. Each member digs a den several yards deep, the male marking his territory with urine and becoming aggressive during the breeding season. Mating takes place in mid- and late winter, this fox often mating again if the litter is lost. The female alone defends the nest site, and the cubs remain in the den for two months, protected by the mother. During this time the male does not enter the den.

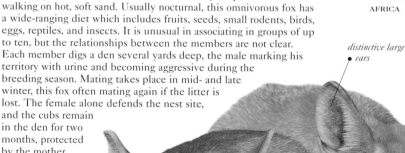

AFRICA

distinctive large ears

• **SIZE** Body length: 9½–16 in (24–41 cm). Tail:7–12 in (18–31 cm).
• **OCCURRENCE** Throughout the Sahara. In sandy desert.
• **REMARK** The Fennec Fox is trapped and sold as a pet, as well as extensively hunted for its pelt.

white underparts

Social unit Social	Gestation 50–52 days	Young 2–5	Diet 🌿 🍎 ⁞⁞ 🐁 🦎 ● 🐛 🕷

Family CANIDAE	Species *Vulpes cana*	Status Locally common

BLANFORD'S FOX

Cat-like in its appearance and movements, this small fox has a mottled coat that is black, gray, and white, dark hindlegs, and almost white underparts. This species is also characterized by its large ears and a bushy tail which often has a dark tip. Wholly nocturnal, it eats more fruits than other foxes and is often found near orchards.

• **SIZE** Body length:16 ½ in (42 cm). Tail:12 in (30 cm).
• **OCCURRENCE** W. and S. Asia. In grassland and mountains.
• **REMARK** This fox is hunted heavily for its skin.

ASIA

black, grey, and white body patches

long, bushy tail

Social unit Solitary	Gestation 50–60 days	Young 1–3	Diet

Family CANIDAE	Species *Vulpes velox*	Status Unconfirmed

SWIFT FOX

widely spaced ears

This fox is closely related to the Kit Fox (*Vulpes macrotis*) from which it can be distinguished by its widely spaced ears, rounded, doglike head, and more graceful form. Its coat is grayish on the head, back, and flanks, and its long, bushy tail has a black tip and is tinged redder in summer. Usually nocturnal, it may lie in the sun by its den during the day.

• **SIZE** Body length:12 ½–21 in (38–53 cm). Tail:7–10 in (18–26 cm).
• **OCCURRENCE** C. North America. In prairie and grassland.

grayish red coat

black-tipped tail

N. AMERICA

Social unit Pair	Gestation 50–60 days	Young 3–6	Diet

Family CANIDAE	Species *Vulpes vulpes*	Status Common

RED FOX

This fox has a coat that varies from gray and rust to flame-red, and a large, bushy, white-tipped tail. The backs of its ears are usually black and, often, so are the lower limbs and feet. However, the Red Fox has been bred extensively for its pelt and several colour morphs, including completely black or white, have been produced. This stealthy hunter is active by day and night, and feeds chiefly on rabbits and young hares in grassy or farmed areas. It stalks its prey and then makes a dash for the victim before it can reach its burrow or speed away. The fox then carries the prey by the neck to a secluded spot where it eats at its leisure. The Red Fox also feeds on a variety of other food, including carrion and refuse. It hoards food by burying it, using its keen memory to locate it afterward. It shelters in an earthen den in rabbit burrows, crevices, or in outbuildings. The primary social unit consists of a vixen (female) and a dog (male), who sometimes share their territory with nonbreeding kin. Mating takes place in late winter or early spring, when the female makes eerie shrieks (known as the "vixen's scream").
SIZE Body length: 23–35 in (58–90 cm).
Tail: 12½–19½ in (32–49 cm).
• **OCCURRENCE** Arctic, North America, Europe, W. Asia, N. Africa, and Australia. In desert, forest, mountains, tundra, and urban areas.
• **REMARK** Trapped extensively for its fur, this fox has also been killed in enormous numbers during rabies control exercises in North America and Europe.

WORLDWIDE

coat ranges fro grayish and ru to flame-red •

large, bushy tail often tipped with white hair •

• *white underside*

lower limbs • *usually black*

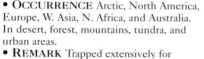

Social unit Pair	Gestation 49–55 days	Young 3–12	Diet

PINNING DOWN PREY
The Red Fox often hunts in dense vegetation for rodents and earthworms. Using its sharp hearing it first pinpoints the location of the prey. Then making a high vertical leap, the fox lands on its frontpaws, and catches its victim by pinning it.

pointed ears black on upperside

pointed muzzle

EARLY DAYS
Red Fox cubs are usually cared for by both the parents and "helper" or nonbreeding females. They remain in or near the den for the first three months, when they are vulnerable to predators.

Family CANIDAE	Species *Vulpes rueppelli*	Status Unconfirmed

RUEPPELL'S FOX

Sometimes called the Sand Fox, this species is slighter in build than the Red Fox (see pp. 218–219) and has a soft, dense, sandy or silver-gray coat to blend in with its arid habitat. It has black patches on its face, wide ears, short legs, and a conspicuously white tail-tip. In some regions (such as Oman), it appears to live in territorial pairs, but usually this gregarious fox is found in what are probably extended family groups of up to 15 individuals. During the day, Rueppell's Fox shelters in crevices and burrows, changing its den every few days.

AFRICA, ASIA

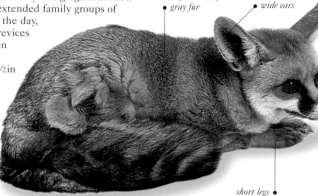

sandy or silvery gray fur

wide ears

• **SIZE** Body length:16–20½in (40–52cm).Tail:10–15½ in (25–39cm).
• **OCCURRENCE** N. Africa and W. Asia. In stony or sandy desert.
• **REMARK** Human encroachment into its habitat is a threat to this fox, which is also killed by Bedouins for food.

short legs

Social unit Social/Pair	Gestation Not known	Young 2–3	Diet 🌟 🌿 🦎 🐁

Family CANIDAE	Species *Alopex lagopus*	Status Common

ARCTIC FOX

This fox is unusual in having two color "phases" or types. Those of the "white" phase become almost completely white in winter for camouflage in snow, and gray or brown in summer to blend into plains and grassy hillocks. Foxes of the "blue" phase, found more often in coastal or shrubby habitats, are gray-brown with a blue tinge in winter, and dark brown in summer. Adapted to the freezing cold, this fox has small ears, a blunt muzzle, and short legs and tail, since these areas lose heat fastest.
• **SIZE** Body length: 21–22 in (53–55 cm). Tail:12in (30cm).
• **OCCURRENCE** Alaska, N. Canada, Greenland, N. Europe, and N. Asia. In Arctic tundra and coastal habitats.
• **REMARK** Human persecution, hunting for fur, and land development leading to habitat destruction are serious threats.

small, rounded ears

almost pure white winter coat

thickly furred body

N. AMERICA, GREENLAND, EURASIA

Social unit Social	Gestation 51–54 days	Young 6–16	Diet 🦊 🦅 ● 🐛 🦌 🥚

Family CANIDAE	Species *Urocyon cinereoargenteus*	Status Common

GRAY FOX

Also known as the Tree Fox, this species is often found in woodland, climbing branches and leaping up tree trunks like a cat. This nocturnal animal eats a variety of insects and small mammals, but may seasonally feed more on fruits and seeds. It rarely digs its own den but usually makes it in a tree hole, a crevice in rocks and logs, or on a building ledge or roof of a house. Most Gray Foxes form breeding pairs. The newborn cubs, usually four in a litter, are helpless and blind. In about 9–12 days, their eyes open, and within four weeks the cubs venture out of the den and begin to climb, accompanied by a parent. The young disperse in the first year and have been known to wander up to 50 miles (85 km).
• **SIZE** Body length: 21–32 in (53–81 cm).
Tail:10½–17½ in (27–44 cm).
• **OCCURRENCE** S. Canada to N. South America. In temperate woodland and deciduous forest, abandoned oil fields, and urban areas.

GRIZZLED GRAY
The Gray Fox's coat owes its mottled appearance to individual hairs that are banded white, gray, and black. It has a small, dark gray mane, and parts of its neck, flanks, and legs are reddish, whereas its chin and belly are white or buff.

dark band
along back

grizzled
gray coat

red-tinged neck

N., C., &
S. AMERICA

white or buff belly

Social unit Pair	Gestation 51–63 days	Young 1–10	Diet 🐜 🐀 🍎 ⋮

Family CANIDAE	Species *Chrysocyon brachyurus*	Status Lower risk

MANED WOLF

Sometimes described as a Red Fox on stilts because of its characteristic long, dark limbs, the Maned Wolf has black feet that look like they are clad in stockings. With a reddish yellow coat and a darker colored stripe running from the nape of the neck to its back, it has an erect mane and a dark muzzle. The long, bushy tail is usually dark, but may be lighter, sometimes even white. An inhabitant of open grassland or scrub, this wolf may be found peering over vegetation for prey or potential danger. It is active at twilight and night and has a varied diet that includes rabbits, birds, mice, grubs, and ants, as well as plant matter such as fruits and berries. The Maned Wolf is known to kill small livestock, especially poultry, and is hunted in some areas as a pest, although it is also kept as a pet. Female and male wolves form monogamous pairs, sharing a territory and mating every year, usually in May or June. However, they are hardly found together at other times of the year.

S. AMERICA

reddish yellow coat

• **SIZE** Body length: 4–4¼ft (1.2–1.3 m). Tail:11–18in (28–45cm).
• **OCCURRENCE** C. and E. South America. In a variety of open habitats, including grassland, scrub, and agricultural areas.
• **REMARK** The Maned Wolf probably benefits from the initial stages of forest clearance, but intensive use of land for cultivation leads to the loss of its habitat, adversely affecting this species. Disease is another major threat to its survival.

MOVING THROUGH GRASS
This wolf is not a very fast runner. Its long legs are more an adaptation to its habitat, which includes areas of tall grassland.

VOCAL WOLVES
Maned wolves make several sounds that are usually heard at night. Disputes over territory evoke typical doglike growls. Guttural barks also warn away intruders and probably help the territorial pair to keep in audible contact.

black "stockings" on lower limbs

Social unit Solitary	Gestation 62–66 days	Young 1–5	Diet 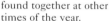

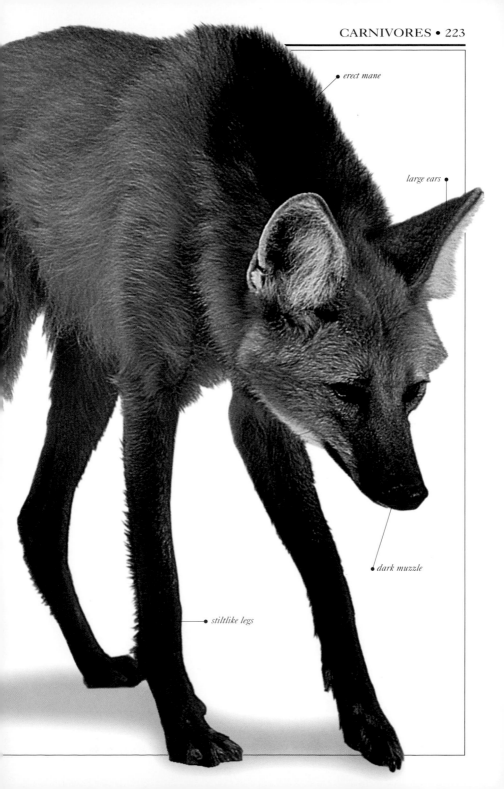

erect mane

large ears

dark muzzle

stiltlike legs

Family CANIDAE	Species *Pseudalopex culpaeus*	Status Locally common

CULPEO FOX

tawny head

A large, powerful fox with a grizzled gray coat and reddish head, neck, and ears, this species is extensively trapped and hunted for its pelt, and to prevent it preying on livestock, such as lambs and poultry. The Culpeo Fox also feeds on rodents, rabbits, birds and their eggs, as well as seasonal fruits and berries, and stores food when it is easily available, burying the excess or wedging it under logs and rocks. This fox is thought to have suffered from large-scale forest clearance, with some other species, such as the Gray Fox, benefiting at its cost.

grizzled gray on back and • shoulders

• **SIZE** Body length: 23 ½ – 47 in (60–120 cm). Tail: 12–18 in (30–45 cm).
• **OCCURRENCE** Andean and Patagonian regions of W. South America. In mountains and pampas.

fluffy tail tipped • black

S. AMERICA

Social unit Pair	Gestation 55–60 days	Young 3–8	Diet 🐸 🦫 🐦 ● 🦌

Family CANIDAE	Species *Cerdocyon thous*	Status Common

CRAB-EATING FOX

Widespread in a variety of habitats, this species shows much variation across its range, although it is usually grayish brown above and white below.
With a reddish face, ears, and legs, it is black on the tail-tip, ear-tips, and backs of the legs. Usually found in monogamous pairs, this nocturnal predator feeds on crabs – both coastal and freshwater – as well as a variety of other food. It is occasionally shot by ranchers and farmers, and is also hunted for its pelt.

gray-brown • coat

S. AMERICA

black-tipped • ears

reddish brown face

• **SIZE** Body length: 25 in (64 cm). Tail: 11½ in (29 cm).
• **OCCURRENCE** N. and E. South America. In grassland, temperate forest, and lowland tropical forest.

black backs • of legs

Social unit Social	Gestation 52–59 days	Young 3–6	Diet 🐜 🦎 🐦 🦫

Family CANIDAE	Species *Otocyon megalotis*	Status Common

BAT-EARED FOX

This fox derives its name
from its large ears, which
may be up to 4¾in (12cm)
long. It has a distinctive
small, black-masked face with
a pointed muzzle and black ear
tips. Its teeth, much smaller than
those of most canids, have eight
extra molars, and may number 48:
more than any other nonmarsupial
mammal. However, it is a typical fox
in its breeding and social habits.
• **SIZE** Body length:18–26in
(46–66cm). Tail: 9–13½in
(23–34cm).
• **OCCURRENCE** E. and S. Africa.
In open grassland, semidesert areas,
and forest margins.
• **REMARK** Probably the only canid to
have largely abandoned mammal prey, it
feeds chiefly on termites and dung beetles.

• *large, batlike ears*

gray-buff coat •

AFRICA

• *small
face with
pointed
muzzle*

• *paler beige
underside*

Social unit Variable	Gestation 60–75 days	Young 1–6	Diet 🐜 🦎 🐀

Family CANIDAE	Species *Atelocynus microtis*	Status Locally common

SHORT-EARED DOG

Rather like the Raccoon Dog (see p. 226), with
its short, rounded ears, this species has much
shorter and more velvety fur, which is dark
gray to black on top and varying
shades of tawny gray on the
underside. Also called the
Small-eared Zorro, this
chiefly nocturnal canid is
reportedly solitary,
moving stealthily in a
catlike manner across
the forest floor. It eats
mainly rodents and
some plant matter.
• **SIZE** Body length:
28–39in (72–100cm).
Tail:10–14in
(25–35cm).
• **OCCURRENCE**
Amazon Basin.
In tropical forest,
up to an altitude of
3,300ft (1,000m).

*bushy,
foxlike
• tail*

*dark gray
to black
• coat*

S. AMERICA

*short, rounded
ears* •

Social unit Solitary	Gestation Not known	Young Not known	Diet 🐀 🌿

Family CANIDAE	Species *Nyctereutes procyonoides*	Status Locally common

RACCOON DOG

EURASIA

Resembling both a raccoon and a dog, this unusual member of the canid family has a black "robber's mask" on its face, a white muzzle, sleek black legs, and a bushy tail. It has a variable yellow-tinged, brown-black coat, and the upperside of its tail is usually black. The nocturnal Raccoon Dog forages along riverbanks, lakesides, and the seashore, on a wide range of food, from birds and small mammals to fruits. Found in pairs or temporary family groups, it is abundant in Japan, but extinct in areas of China; it has spread rapidly in parts of Europe, where it has been introduced. Unlike most members of the dog family, it can climb well. It is also unique among canids in that it hibernates in winter, feasting in the fall to increase its body weight by up to 50 percent.
• SIZE Body length: 20–23 ½ in (50–60 cm). Tail: 7 in (18 cm).
• OCCURRENCE Europe, C., N., and E. Asia. In temperate woodland and forested river valleys.

BRED IN CAPTIVITY
The white coat of this Raccoon Dog indicates that it has been bred in captivity. Valued for its fur, this species has been bred in many countries. In the former Soviet Union captive animals were set free and are now living as wild populations.

brown-black fur on body

black face mask

white muzzle with black nose

black, short-furred legs

Social unit Variable	Gestation 60–65 days	Young 4–12	Diet

Family CANIDAE	Species *Canis dingo*	Status Locally common

DINGO

Variously regarded as a
subspecies of the domestic dog or of its
ancestor the Gray Wolf, or as a species in
its own right, the Dingo probably
descended from the domestic dog in the
last 10,000 years and is now able to
survive in the wild. Its coat varies from
sandy brown to a deep reddish shade,
and it has irregular white patches on its
chest, feet, and tail-tip. Breeding adults
often form settled packs, older members
teaching the young their place in the
hierarchy by nips and other rebuffs.
The dominant female may kill the
young of subordinates.
• **SIZE** Body length: 28–43 in
(72–110 cm). Tail: 8½–14 in
(21–36 cm).
• **OCCURRENCE** Australia. In desert,
grassland, tropical and temperate forest,
and forest edges.
• **REMARK** The Dingo breeds readily
with domestic dogs, and in parts of
Australia one-third of individuals are
hybrids. It is regarded as a pest since
it kills livestock and spreads rabies.

white patch on muzzle

AUSTRALIA

sandy to auburn-red coat

thickly furred, white-tipped tail

Social unit Social	Gestation 63 days	Young 1–10	Diet

Family CANIDAE	Species *Canis latrans*	Status Common

COYOTE

The grizzled buff coat of the Coyote is yellowish
on the outer ears, legs, and feet, but gray or white on
the underparts. The shoulders, back, and tail may
be tinged black. Highly adaptable in habitat and
diet, this opportunistic stalk-and-pounce predator
feeds on Pronghorns and deer, as well as
Mountain Sheep, livestock, carrion, and refuse.
It often hunts jackrabbits by rapidly sprinting
after them. The Coyote was once believed to be
solitary, but may form breeding pairs or, when
larger prey is at hand, gather as a small hunting
pack. The distinctive nighttime howl of the
Coyote usually announces the whereabouts of an
individual or its territory to its neighbors.
• **SIZE** Body length: 28–38 in
(70–97 cm). Tail: 12–15 in (30–38 cm).
• **OCCURRENCE** North America to
N. Central America. In grassland, temperate
forest, tundra, mountains, and urban areas.

black shoulder saddle

long muzzle

gray or white underparts

black tail

N. & C. AMERICA

Social unit Variable	Gestation 63 days	Young 6–18	Diet

| Family CANIDAE | Species *Canis simensis* | Status Critically endangered |

SIMIAN JACKAL

The distinctive reddish yellow fur of this wolf, also known as the Ethiopian Wolf, is lighter in females and juveniles, and has white patches on the throat, neck, and chest. Foraging alone by day, it gathers in noisy groups of 2–12 in the morning, noontime, and evening, to greet other wolves.
• **SIZE** Body length: 3 ¼ft (1 m). Tail: 13 in (33 cm).
• **OCCURRENCE** Ethiopian Highlands. In open moorland and grassland.
• **REMARK** A key species in the food chain of the Ethiopian Highlands, the three remaining populations of this species are vulnerable to disease and competition from domestic dogs and livestock. Reduction of its rodent prey, mainly due to overgrazing, is another factor leading to its rapid decline.

large ears

long, thin muzzle

reddish coat

lower half of tail black

AFRICA

| Social unit Social | Gestation 60 days | Young 2–7 | Diet |

| Family CANIDAE | Species *Canis aureus* | Status Common |

GOLDEN JACKAL

The coat of this jackal varies with season and region, but is usually a pale golden brown or brown-tipped yellow, with rufous sides, and a ginger or nearly white underside. These omnivorous foragers are usually found in territorial breeding pairs, cooperation between the two leading to highly successful hunting. Strictly nocturnal near human habitations, packs of up to 20 are found in areas where food is plentiful. The pups are cared for in a secure den, by parents, older siblings, and other young adults.
• **SIZE** Body length: 23 ½ – 43 in (60 – 110 cm). Tail: 8 – 12 in (20 – 30 cm).
• **OCCURRENCE** S.E. Europe, N. and E. Africa, W. to S.E. Asia. In grassland and desert.

reddish brown head

ginger ears

gray to black back

EURASIA, AFRICA

| Social unit Pair | Gestation 63 days | Young 1–9 | Diet |

| Family CANIDAE | Species *Canis mesomelas* | Status Common |

BLACK-BACKED JACKAL

Sometimes called the Silver-backed Jackal, this ginger-colored canid has a distinctive black saddle over its shoulders and back, and a bushy black tail. Occurring in a wide variety of habitats, from the suburbs of large cities to the Namibian Desert, male–female pairs feed during the day and at twilight, or at night near human settlements, on a variety of food. This jackal is known to attack sheep or young cattle and is viewed as a pest in parts of Africa. Cubs are reared by parents and siblings in dens, which are sometimes built in old termite mounds or abandoned Aardvark holes.
• **SIZE** Body length:18–35 in (45–90 cm). Tail:10–16 in (26–40 cm).

AFRICA

• **OCCURRENCE** E. and S. Africa. In grassland, desert, and urban areas.
• **REMARK** Female and male jackals mate for life and hunt together as a team.

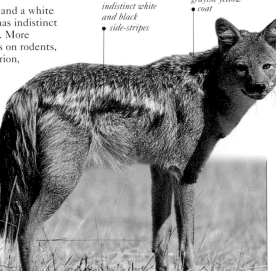

prominent ears

black saddle on back

reddish brown body

| Social unit Pair | Gestation 60 days | Young 1–8 | Diet |

| Family CANIDAE | Species *Canis adustus* | Status Unconfirmed |

SIDE-STRIPED JACKAL

Grayish yellow with paler undersides and a white tail-tip, the Side-striped Jackal often has indistinct white and black stripes down its sides. More omnivorous than other jackals, it feeds on rodents, birds, eggs, lizards, insects, refuse, carrion, and plant matter. Like the Red Fox (see pp. 218–219), it is not averse to foraging near urban areas and has been sighted near forest edges and in mixed farmland.
• **SIZE** Body length: 26–32 in (65–81 cm). Tail:12–16 in (30–41 cm).
• **OCCURRENCE** C., E., and S. Africa. In moist savanna, tropical forest, and farmland.
• **REMARK** This species died in large numbers in the early twentieth century because of distemper.

indistinct white and black side-stripes

grayish yellow coat

AFRICA

white tail tip

| Social unit Pair | Gestation 57–70 days | Young 3–6 | Diet |

Family CANIDAE	Species *Canis lupus*	Status Vulnerable

GRAY WOLF

The ancestor of the domestic dog, the Gray Wolf is the largest member of the canid family. Its great success as a hunter is due to the complex social organization into packs or family groups of 8–12 animals. The clearly defined hierarchy within a group centers around a dominant breeding pair that usually mates for life. Packs patrol large territories, marking them with scent. They announce their presence by howling, which is heard at distances of up to 6 miles (10 km), and warns rival packs to keep their distance and so avoid confrontation. A strong, stocky build and acute senses of hearing and smell also help in making this wolf a good hunter. Its thick fur is usually gray, but can vary from nearly pure white to red, brown, and black. Although a major part of the Gray Wolf's diet comprises large ungulates, such as moose, caribou, deer, and elk, it will also eat livestock, carrion, and garbage. Pups are weaned in one month and then fed on scraps of food regurgitated by adults. A well-fed pup is strong enough to travel with the pack by 3–5 months, and a juvenile may choose to leave the pack within a year.

N. AMERICA,
GREENLAND,
EURASIA

• long,
sharp teeth

• **SIZE** Body length: 3¼–5 ft (1–1.5 m).
Tail: 1–1¾ ft (30–51 cm).
• **OCCURRENCE** N. America, Greenland, Europe, and Asia: above 15°N latitude. In wilderness or remote areas, but may live close to human habitations if food is abundant.
• **REMARK** Originally one of the world's most widely distributed wild mammals, Gray Wolves have been exterminated by humans across much of their range, due to an exaggerated view of their potential ferocity.

thick fur to trap •
body heat

STRENGTH IN NUMBERS
Communal hunting allows the Gray Wolf to attack a wide range of prey, which may be ten times its own weight. After the kill, other pack members wait behind the dominant pair for access to the carcass.

• pack member
awaiting its
turn to feed

Social unit Social	Gestation 61–63 days	Young 1–11	Diet

CANIS FAMILIARIS

The modern domestic dog (*Canis familiaris*) and the Gray Wolf share a similar set of genes. The domestic dog differs from the wolf in only two significant ways – its teeth are smaller and more crowded, and its brain is about a third smaller than that of the wolf. The learning centers in the brain of the wolf used for mapping territories lost their relevance in animals that settled down in human habitations. On the other hand, the brain centers responsible for learning to adapt to other species, namely humans, increased in size and efficiency.

long, powerful
legs

gray to white,
red, brown, or
black coat

large feet
and claws

Family CANIDAE	Species *Speothos venaticus*	Status Vulnerable

BUSH DOG

Much like a weasel in appearance, the Bush Dog is found in family groups of up to ten members. This diurnal predator feeds individually on ground-dwelling birds and rodents such as the Agouti, while the pack may tackle prey as large as the Capybara, hunting them even in water. At night the Bush Dog shelters in burrows and the male brings food to the suckling female in its den.

C. & S. AMERICA

weasellike face

long, slender body

small, thick tail

short, sturdy legs

• **SIZE** Body length: 22½ – 30 in (57 – 75 cm). Tail: 5 – 6 in (12.5 – 15 cm).
• **OCCURRENCE** Central America to N. and C. South America. In tropical forest and wet savanna.
• **REMARK** The Bush Dog is the most social of small canids.

Social unit Social	Gestation 67 days	Young 1–6	Diet

Family CANIDAE	Species *Cuon alpinus*	Status Vulnerable

DHOLE

Sometimes called the Asian Wild Dog, this large carnivore is tawny or dark red with a darker, bushy tail. This territorial dog lives in extended family units of up to 25 individuals, sheltering in dens with their pups, which are fed on regurgitated food even after they leave the den.

rounded ears

ASIA

tawny to dark red coat

short legs

• **SIZE** Body length: 35 in (90 cm). Tail:16 – 18 in (40 – 45 cm).
• **OCCURRENCE** S., E., and S.E. Asia. In dense tropical, temperate, and montane forest.
• **REMARK** A widespread species, it is facing a shrinking range and declining numbers.

Social unit Social	Gestation 60 – 62 days	Young 3–9	Diet

Family CANIDAE	Species *Lycaon pictus*	Status Endangered

AFRICAN WILD DOG

Once found throughout Africa in a variety of habitats, the African Wild or Hunting Dog has now been reduced to a few fragmented populations. It is preyed upon by larger animals such as lions and hyenas, but the greatest threat comes from humans. It is trapped, shot, killed in road accidents, and suffers from habitat loss and diseases, such as rabies and distemper, carried by domestic dogs. This dog's coat of variable patches and swirls in black, white, gray, and yellow gives it the scientific name, which means "painted wolf." Probably the most social of all canids, these dogs are found in groups of 30 or more adults and young. This wild dog makes ringing "whoo"-like calls to locate lost pack members and a soft, chirring sound to indicate submission.
• **SIZE** Body length: 30–43 in (76–110 cm). Tail: 12–16 in (30–41 cm).
• **OCCURRENCE** Sub-Saharan Africa, especially in Tanzania and South Africa. In bush habitats and mountains, and along coastlines.
• **REMARK** The survival of this species depends heavily on active conservation.

AFRICA

PROTECTING THE WILD DOG
Scientists have gathered information on the African Wild Dog, such as size and weight, and blood samples for genetic analysis, in an effort to save it from extinction. This is done by anaesthetizing the dog and putting on a radio collar to track its movements.

• *pointed ears*

• *lean body*

coat of short •
hair

patches of black, white, •
gray, and yellow

Social unit Social	Gestation 69–73 days	Young 10–12	Diet 🦌

CARNIVORES
BEARS

T HE EIGHT BEAR species, known as Ursids, are similar in form and body proportions; they are strong and heavily built, with stout, powerful, large-clawed limbs, a bulky head, small ears, small eyes with poor sight, and a long muzzle with a keen sense of smell.

Although classified as carnivores, most bears are omnivorous. There are some exceptions, however: Polar Bears are almost exclusively flesh-eaters; the Spectacled Bear and Asiatic Black Bear are mainly herbivorous, and the Giant Panda is almost totally so.

Most species are solitary and, in northern regions, hibernate through winter. Their size, power, occasional attacks on livestock, and tendency to aggression, especially when raising cubs, have long made bears targets of persecution. All but two species are listed as in some way threatened.

Family URSIDAE	Species *Ursus americanus*	Status Lower risk*

AMERICAN BLACK BEAR

prehensile lips • • *large, erect ears*

medium to heavy frame •

This bear actually varies in color from black to cinnamon, brown, or blond, and even a unique gray-blue occurring on the Pacific coast. It adapts to various habitats quite easily but is usually found in heavily forested areas. An exceptional climber, the American Black Bear plucks fruits, buds, berries, and nuts with its prehensile lips. It opens up old logs and flips over stones with its powerful front limbs and curved claws to feed on insects, and may even break into outbuildings or vehicles to obtain food left by humans. This species uses a complex set of body postures to communicate. Yawning, averted eyes, or a lowered head may be used to determine social hierarchy and to minimize physical contact.

• **SIZE** Length: 4¼–6¼ft (1.3–1.9 m). Weight: 120–660 lb (55–300 kg).

• **OCCURRENCE** Canada, USA, and Mexico. In temperate and coniferous forest, and mountains.

• **REMARK** The American Black Bear has adapted to human presence successfully and is rarely known to attack humans since it prefers to avoid any confrontation.

N. AMERICA

powerful limbs •

Social unit Solitary	Gestation 6 weeks	Young 1–5	Diet

Family URSIDAE	Species *Ursus maritimus*	Status Lower risk

POLAR BEAR

One of the largest carnivores, the Polar Bear is an excellent swimmer and diver which has adapted to its aquatic life in various ways – hollow, air-filled guard hairs aid buoyancy, while its nostrils close underwater, allowing it to hold its breath before pouncing on unwary prey from beneath. This bear's diet consists chiefly of Ringed, Bearded, and Harp Seals, which it may hunt by stalking or by waiting motionlessly in front of seal breathing holes. Capable of fasting for extremely long periods when food is scarce, especially when forced ashore by melting sea ice, it can survive on morsels such as seaweeds, moss, and berries for as long as five months.

WHALE HUNTING
The Polar Bear chiefly feeds on seals, but can also effectively hunt larger aquatic mammals such as Walruses and even Narwhals. Here, it is shown attempting to catch a Beluga Whale.

• **SIZE** Length: 7–11 ft (2.1–3.4 m). Weight: 880–1,500 lb (400–680 kg).
• **OCCURRENCE** Circumpolar across the Arctic in North America, Greenland, Norway, and Russia. In polar ice, near oceans.
• **REMARK** The Polar Bear probably has the most advanced sense of smell among all bears. It can locate seal breathing holes, covered by 35 in (90 cm) of ice, from ¾ mile (1 km) away.

straight "Roman" facial profile •

black tongue •

• *relatively long neck*

partially furred paw pads retain heat and provide • *extra grip on ice*

ARCTIC

Social unit Solitary	Gestation 9 weeks	Young 1–4	Diet

Family URSIDAE	Species *Ursus arctos*	Status Lower risk*

BROWN BEAR

Large and powerfully built, the Brown Bear is the most widely
distributed of all the bear species and varies greatly in size depending
on its food and habitat. Several races have been recognized, among
them the Grizzly Bear, Kodiak Bear, Alaskan Bear, Eurasian Brown Bear,
Syrian Bear, Siberian Bear, Manchurian Bear, and Hokkaido Bear. All
share the distinctive shoulder hump of muscle, long foreclaws that help
to dig for roots and bulbs, concave facial profile, and small ears. Most
commonly dark brown in color, it can vary from blond to black. Its long
guard hairs are tipped with white, giving it a "grizzled" appearance.
Although there is not much difference in body length between the
sexes, the male Brown Bear may be twice as heavy as the female. This
bear is chiefly herbivorous, with 95 percent of its diet consisting of
grasses, roots, bulbs, tubers, berries, and nuts.
However, it also savors fish and insects. It feeds
intensively during the warmer months, putting on
weight in preparation for its long winter sleep.
• **SIZE** Length: 6½–9¾ft (2–3 m).
Weight: 220–2,200 lb (100–1,000 kg).
• **OCCURRENCE** North America, N. Europe,
and Asia. In grassland, dry desert, dense
temperate and coniferous forest, and mountains.
• **REMARK** Large tracts of wilderness are
necessary for the survival of this bear, and
habitat destruction has led to a drastic decline
in its numbers. It is also poached for its body
parts, especially the gall bladder, used in
making traditional medicines.

N. AMERICA,
EUROPE, ASIA

*dense, dark brown
coat may vary
from blond to
black* •

A FISHY DIET
Although the Brown Bear is mainly
herbivorous, some coastal populations
feed on large quantities of salmon, killing
them with a blow or sharp bite, as the fish
swim upstream to spawn.

SURVEYING THE SCENE
The Brown Bear sometimes stands upright
on its rear limbs to identify a possible
source of food or danger. Contrary to
popular belief this is not an aggressive
posture. Bears only rarely attack humans,
as the result of a sudden encounter.

short, powerful limbs •

Social unit Solitary	Gestation 9 weeks	Young 1–4	Diet 🍃 🌱 🏹 🐚 🍂 🕷 🐀 🦌 🐟

small ears

large, broad head

nonretractable front claws

Family URSIDAE	Species *Ursus thibetanus*	Status Vulnerable

ASIATIC BLACK BEAR

Resembling the American Black Bear (see p. 234) in appearance and habits, this species is often found foraging in trees. Black, with a yellow-white chest patch, it has tufted ears and a short tail. It raids crops and sometimes kills humans in sudden encounters as much of its habitat has been replaced by farmland.
• **SIZE** Length: 4¼–6¼ ft (1.3–1.9 m). Weight: 220–440 lb (100–200 kg).
• **OCCURRENCE** S. and S.E. Asia, N.E. China, far eastern Russia, and Japan. In forested hills.
• **REMARK** It is hunted for its body parts, used in local medicines.

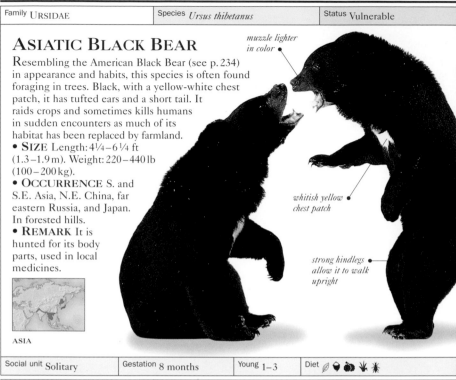

muzzle lighter in color

whitish yellow chest patch

strong hindlegs allow it to walk upright

ASIA

Social unit Solitary	Gestation 8 months	Young 1–3	Diet 🌿🍂🍎🌾🐝

Family URSIDAE	Species *Helarctos malayanus*	Status Endangered

SUN BEAR

Elusive and nocturnal, this stocky and doglike species is also known as the Dog or Honey Bear. Largely arboreal, it hauls itself up trees by hugging the trunks with its arms and gripping them with its teeth and long claws. The Sun Bear makes a rough nest out of bent branches in which to sleep. Digging into old logs and bees' nests with its claws for grubs and honey, it also pushes its 10 in (25 cm) long tongue into crevices to lick up similar food. Sometimes, it thrusts its paws alternately into termite nests, taking them out to lick off the insects. Its sleek, short fur varies from black to gray or rusty, with a U-shaped or circular creamish patch on the chest and a short, pale muzzle. If grabbed from behind by an attacker, its loose neck skin allows it to turn around and fight.
• **SIZE** Length: 3½–4½ ft (1.1–1.4 m). Weight: 110–145 lb (50–65 kg).
• **OCCURRENCE** S.E. Asia. In lowland hardwood rain forest.
• **REMARK** The Sun Bear is the smallest of the eight bear species and best-adapted to the tropics.

short, pale muzzle

U-shaped cream "sun patch"

sleek, smooth coat

very long, curved claws

ASIA

Social unit Solitary	Gestation 96 days	Young Not known	Diet 🌿🐝🍎❄️🥚🐁

Family URSIDAE	Species *Melursus ursinus*	Status Endangered

SLOTH BEAR

long hair on ears •

• *whitish muzzle*

broad white chest marking in Y, O, or U shape

One of the most distinctive looking bears, with its shaggy coat and long hair around the ears, neck, and shoulders, the Sloth Bear frequents habitats that provide its essential diet of ants, termites, and fruits. It tears open insect nests with its foreclaws, which are 3 in (8 cm) long; then, shutting its nostrils and pursing its lips, it slurps up its prey through a gap formed by missing incisors. Like other bears, it stands on its hindfeet to assess its surroundings.
• **SIZE** Length: 4½–6 ft (1.4 –1.8 m). Weight: 120 –420 lb (55 –190 kg).
• **OCCURRENCE** Indian subcontinent. In grassland, thorny scrub, and tropical forest.
• **REMARK** Threats to this species include habitat loss, hunting for body parts, and cub capture for performance.

ASIA

Social unit Variable	Gestation 6–7 months	Young 2–3	Diet 🐜 🐝 ✹ ● 🍃

Family URSIDAE	Species *Tremarctos ornatus*	Status Vulnerable

SPECTACLED BEAR

black to dark red-brown fur •

pale, circular eye-patches •

S. AMERICA

South America's only bear, the Spectacled or Andean Bear plays a prominent role in local folklore and mythology. Once found in a wide variety of habitats, this excellent climber is now increasingly restricted to cloud forest, where food is most abundant. The massive jaws of this mainly herbivorous bear enable it to chew the toughest plants. It is named after the pale, circular patches around its eyes.
• **SIZE** Length: 5 –6½ ft (1.5 –2 m). Weight: 310 –390 lb (140 –175 kg).
• **OCCURRENCE** Andes. In coastal areas and steppe, as well as forest.
• **REMARK** The largest land mammal in South America after the tapirs, the Spectacled Bear is a valuable disperser of seeds.

• *shortest muzzle among bears*

• *forelimbs longer than hindlimbs*

Social unit Solitary	Gestation 7–8 months	Young 1–4	Diet 🍃 🐝 🌿 🐜 🐸 🐦

Family URSIDAE	Species *Ailuropoda melanoleuca*	Status Critically endangered

GIANT PANDA

Immediately recognizable by its striking two-toned coloring, this stocky, barrel-shaped bear is white, except for its black ears, oval eye-patches, nose, shoulder saddle, and limbs. It has a large head, erect ears, and small, beady eyes. The Giant Panda, called "Daxiongmao" (giant bear-cat) or "Baixiong" (white bear) in Chinese, has one of the most restricted diets of all mammals, feeding almost entirely on bamboo. It eats different parts of more than 30 species of bamboo – new shoots in spring, leaves in summer, and stems in winter. The panda has the single stomach and short intestines of a carnivorous mammal and is known sometimes to eat carrion. Normally solitary, it feeds at dusk and dawn and sleeps in the bamboo thicket that constitutes its feeding area. Not strictly territorial the Giant Panda prefers to avoid conflict, and marks its home range with scent, urine, and claw scratches. The female moans, bleats, and barks (about 11 panda calls have been identified) during the breeding season; and males chase and fight each other for a receptive female. Sometimes, the male kills the newborn cubs.

• false thumb

• **SIZE** Length: 5¼–6¾ ft (1.6–1.9 m). Weight: 155–280 lb (70–125 kg).
• **OCCURRENCE** W. China (occurs in 25 separate populations in three provinces). In temperate, tropical, and mountainous bamboo forest.
• **REMARK** Unlike most bears, pandas do not hibernate.

"HAND" WITH SIX FINGERS
The padlike false thumb flexes and opposes the true thumb (first digit), helping the panda to grip bamboo stems and leaves.

coarse, oily guard • hair, up to 4 in (10 cm) long

PANDAS IN DANGER
More than 100 pandas are kept in captivity, but only 30 percent of the young born to them survive. Most wild populations are small, scattered, and genetically unfit. They are poached despite stringent laws (death sentence). Creating huge reserves may be the only answer to the panda's survival.

Social unit Solitary	Gestation 97–181 days	Young 1–2	Diet 🌾

black ears

CHINA

white face

muscular front
limbs

hindquarters
less powerful
than forelimbs

CARNIVORES
RACCOONS

WITH A "BANDIT" face mask, ringed tail, bold and busy lifestyle, opportunistic habits, and immensely adaptable diet, the Common Raccoon typifies the family of Procyonids. The 20 species also include coatis, ringtails, kinkajous, and olingos, all found in the forests of the Americas. An exception is the Lesser Panda of Asia, sometimes included with the Giant Panda in the two-member family, Ailuridae.

Members of the Procyonidae family are generally nocturnal, and remain solitary outside the breeding season. They have a long body and tail, a pointed muzzle, broad face, and smallish, rounded or pointed ears. Their legs are relatively short, and their stance is plantigrade: the soles of their feet rest on the ground (as in bears and humans). However, all procyonids have sharp claws and can climb skillfully.

Family PROCYONIDAE	Species *Ailurus fulgens*	Status Endangered

RED PANDA

Also called the Lesser Panda, this small carnivore is reddish brown to deep chestnut with whitish cheeks, muzzle, and spots above the eyes. It has a round, heavy head and large, pointed ears with white edges. The Red Panda lives mainly on the ground, but uses its partly retractable claws to climb up branches, sunning itself high up in trees in winter. It is solitary by nature, but the cub may stay with the mother for up to a year. Mainly nocturnal, it marks its territory with droppings, urine, and musklike secretions from its anal glands.
• **SIZE** Body length: 20–25 in (50–64 cm). Tail:11–20 in (28–50 cm).
• **OCCURRENCE** S. and S.E. Asia. In remote high-altitude bamboo forest.
• **REMARK** Habitat destruction and hunting are serious threats to this species.

ASIA

red-brown • to chestnut body

white spots • over eyes

hairy soles •

• white muzzle

alternating light and • dark bands on tail

Social unit Solitary	Gestation 114–145 days	Young 1–5	Diet

Family PROCYONIDAE	Species *Bassariscus astutus*	Status Unconfirmed

RINGTAIL

This slim-bodied, agile carnivore, sometimes called the Ringtailed Cat or Cacomistle, is grayish brown or buff, with a striking black-and-white ringed tail. It has black eye-rings and a white muzzle and eyebrows. An efficient nocturnal hunter, the Ringtail is known to use barks and long, high-pitched screams to communicate.
• **SIZE** Body length:12–16½in (30–42cm). Tail:12–17½in (30–44cm).
• **OCCURRENCE** C. and W. USA to S. Mexico. In desert, forest, and mountains.
• **REMARK** Extremely dextrous, this animal has hindfeet that rotate through at least 180 degrees, allowing it great flexibility.

grayish brown or buff upper coat

slim body

bold, black-and-white rings on tail

N. AMERICA

Social unit Solitary	Gestation 51–60 days	Young 1–4	Diet

Family PROCYONIDAE	Species *Procyon lotor*	Status Common

NORTHERN RACCOON

Amazingly adaptable, the Northern Raccoon or Mapache is a familiar sight in different kinds of habitat, ranging from desert to woodland and urban areas. The black "robber's mask" seems to reflect the opportunistic habits of this noisy animal. It can climb and dig, and even open doors with its forepaws to enter livestock enclosures.
• **SIZE** Body length: 16–26in (40–65cm). Tail:10–14in (25–35cm).
• **OCCURRENCE** S. Canada to Central America. In desert, tropical, temperate, and coniferous forest, near lakes and rivers, and in urban areas.
• **REMARK** Its hands are adapted to manipulate food.

gray to blackish long fur

N. & C. AMERICA

rounded, short ears

black eye-patches

Social unit Solitary	Gestation 60–73 days	Young 1–7	Diet

Family PROCYONIDAE	Species *Procyon cancrivorus*	Status Common

CRAB-EATING RACCOON

About the size of a large cat, this raccoon has short, coarse fur, and the hair on its neck is forward-pointing. This nocturnal omnivore forages near streams, marshes, lakes, and seashores, feeling for prey with its fingers. It is well-adapted to searching for prey along water edges, going in and out of water with ease. Although terrestrial, it dens in tree-holes.

C. & S. AMERICA

• **SIZE** Body length:18 – 35 in (45 – 90 cm). Tail: 8 – 22 in (20 – 56 cm).
• **OCCURRENCE** E. Costa Rica and adjacent Panama to N. Argentina and Uruguay. In areas near water.

black face mask •

grizzled brown or gray fur •

Social unit Solitary	Gestation 60 – 73 days	Young 2 – 4	Diet 🐛 🐌 🦎 🐚 🐀 🐟

Family PROCYONIDAE	Species *Nasua nasua*	Status Locally common

SOUTH AMERICAN COATI

short, rounded ears •

Also called the Coatimundi, Tejón, or Pizote, the South American Coati may range from reddish brown through yellowish to grayish brown. By day, it forages in noisy groups of 10 – 20, using its long, white-tipped snout to search for anything edible, while "sentries" around the pack's perimeter watch out for predators. Highly vocal, this procyonid uses soft calls, barks, whistles, and squeaks, as well as tail movements, to communicate.

long, tapering ringed tail

• **SIZE** Body length: 16 – 28 in (40 – 70 cm). Tail:12 ½ – 28 in (32 – 70 cm).
• **OCCURRENCE** S.W. USA, Mexico, Central and South America. In desert, forest, near water, and in mangrove swamps.

elongated snout •

N., C., & S. AMERICA

Social unit Variable	Gestation 10–11 weeks	Young 2–7	Diet 🍎 🐛 🥚 🐀

Family PROCYONIDAE	Species *Potos flavus*	Status Endangered*

KINKAJOU

Buff golden brown or tawny to dark grayish brown in color, this highly agile climber uses its strongly prehensile tail and clawed feet, with naked, padded soles, to clamber up trees. A nocturnal carnivore, it moves around the forest canopy carefully searching for food, and nests in tree hollows or thickets. The Kinkajou has a wide repertoire of calls, used variously to proclaim territory, attract a mate, or warn off predators.
• SIZE Body length:15 ½– 30 in (39–76 cm). Tail:15 ½–22 ½ in (39–57 cm).
• OCCURRENCE S. Mexico to South America. In tropical forest, near wetlands and mangrove swamps.

broad, rounded head

woolly fur

buffish gold to gray coat

prehensile tail for gripping

clawed feet with padded soles

N., C., & S. AMERICA

Social unit Solitary	Gestation 112–120 days	Young 1	Diet

Family PROCYONIDAE	Species *Bassaricyon gabbii*	Status Lower risk*

OLINGO

This slim, catlike, grayish brown to pale brown procyonid inhabits a variety of forest areas, especially cloud forest. Moving with great agility through the trees, the Olingo uses its naked-soled, clawed paws to grasp branches, and its faintly banded, non-prehensile tail for balance. Chiefly active at night, it rarely comes to the ground, foraging for food in the tree canopy, and curling up on a branch or in a tree-hole to rest. It is solitary, except in the breeding season, when males and females call out loudly and can be seen in pairs.
• SIZE Body length:14–16 ½ in (36–42 cm). Tail:14 ½ –19 ½ in (37–49 cm).
• OCCURRENCE Central to N. South America. In tropical rain forest and mountains.
• REMARK Particularly sensitive to deforestation and the disturbance of its forest habitat, the Olingo has not adapted well to cleared spaces or secondary forest.

grayish brown to pale brown coat

large brown eyes

C. & S. AMERICA

long, fluffy tail

Social unit Solitary	Gestation 73–74 days	Young 1	Diet

CARNIVORES
MUSTELIDS

A LONG, SLIM, and flexible or sinuous body, shortish legs, small ears, beady eyes, and very sharp teeth and senses typify the mustelid family.

The 67 species range in size from the Least Weasel, the smallest of all carnivores, which could curl up in a person's cupped hands, through stoats and skunks, to the Giant Otter and Wolverine, which are the size of a very large dog. The different species vary in their lifestyles, from mainly terrestrial polecats, to arboreal martens, burrowing badgers, semiaquatic minks, and almost fully aquatic otters.

Unusually for carnivores, mustelids have five clawed toes on all the feet. Glands near the tail produce musk odors, chiefly to mark territories. Mustelids are found worldwide apart from Australia, Antarctica, and some of Southeast Asia.

Family MUSTELIDAE	Species *Mustela putorious*	Status Locally common

EUROPEAN POLECAT

Considered to be the ancestor of the domestic ferret, the European Polecat was once valued for its pelt. It has long, buff to black hair, with creamish yellow underfur visible beneath, and a black mask across its eyes. Its head is small and flat, its ears rounded, and snout blunt. Long and sinuous in shape, it glides through small openings with ease, and runs, climbs, and swims agilely after a variety of prey. Since its vision is poor, this night-predator hunts by smell and hearing. Rabbits are its principal prey, which it often takes from their nests. Other prey include small rodents, birds, and amphibians. In turn, it is preyed upon by foxes and raptors, and trapped by gamekeepers as it is considered a threat to game and poultry. Male polecats are considerably larger than females and they defend exclusive territories, although these may overlap with the territories of females. If threatened, this polecat may release an unpleasant odor from its anal glands.
• **SIZE** Body length:14–20 in (35–51 cm).
Tail: 4¾–7½ in (12–19 cm).
• **OCCURRENCE** Europe.
In woodland, forest plantations, farmland, marsh, and riverbanks.

EUROPE

FRIENDLY FERRET
The domestic ferret (shown in its light winter coat), is kept as a pet, and has descended from the European Polecat.

long, sinuous body

creamish yellow underfur

small, flat head

long, buff to black fur

dark mask across eyes

Social unit Solitary	Gestation 40–43 days	Young 5–8	Diet

Family MUSTELIDAE	Species *Mustela nigripes*	Status Critically endangered

BLACK-FOOTED FERRET

One of the world's rarest mammals, the Blackfooted Ferret has
a yellow-buff coat with a distinctive black mask, and black feet
and tail tip. It nearly became extinct in the wild in the 1990s, due
to the extermination of its main prey, the prairie dog. As well as
feeding on prairie dogs, this nocturnal ferret also lives in its burrows.

N. AMERICA

• **SIZE** Body length:15–16in (38–41cm). Tail:4½–5in (11–13cm).
• **OCCURRENCE** W. North America. In open grassland, steppe,
and scrub, within the prairie dog's range.

black mask around eyes

• **REMARK** A small population of
about 190 ferrets has been bred
in captivity and released in
Wyoming, USA. Some are
breeding in the wild again.

yellow-buff coat

black tail-tip

black feet

Social unit Solitary/Pair	Gestation 42–45 days	Young 3–6	Diet

Family MUSTELIDAE	Species *Mustela erminea*	Status Locally common

ERMINE

This extremely widespread, typical mustelid has a slim body,
pointed muzzle, small eyes and ears, and short legs. A distinctive
black tip marks its tail. Active day and night, it needs only cover
and prey to thrive. In warmer climates, the Ermine's upper coat is
russet to ginger-brown with a sharply demarcated cream belly.
However, those found in the north turn almost completely white
in winter for camouflage in the snow.

N. AMERICA,
EURASIA

• **SIZE** Body length:6½–9½in (17–24cm).
Tail:3½–4¾in (9–12cm).
• **OCCURRENCE** North America and Eurasia. In tundra,
temperate and coniferous forest, and mountain areas.

black tail tip

slender body

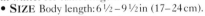

small ears

Social unit Solitary	Gestation 28 days	Young 4–9	Diet

Family MUSTELIDAE	Species *Mustela nivalis*	Status Locally common

LEAST WEASEL

One of the smallest and most widespread mustelids, the adaptable Least Weasel is found over an enormous range of habitats. Its body is long and slender, and its coat is chocolate-brown or russet on the back, limbs, and tail, and white on the underparts. Its head is small, its rounded ears are relatively large, and it has a long neck. The overall size of the Least Weasel, however, varies greatly across its range. In northern areas it is frequently larger, and turns white in the winter months. Active by day and night, in bouts of 10–45 minutes, alternating with rest periods, the Least Weasel must consume one-third of its body weight in food a day in order to survive. A specialized predator of mice and voles, and occasionally birds, it hunts chiefly by sight and smell, delivering an accurate and fatal bite on the neck of its victim. The Least Weasel hisses or screams when it is threatened, and emits a powerful, unpleasant scent from its anal glands, which is also believed to be used in communication with others of its kind.
• **SIZE** Body length: 6½–9½ in (6.5–24 cm). Tail: 1¼–3½ in (3–9 cm).
• **OCCURRENCE** North America, Europe to N., C., and E. Asia. In a variety of habitats: tundra, steppe, semidesert, open forest, farmland, and meadow.
• **REMARK** The Least Weasel survives the harsh northern winters by often hunting for prey under a thick blanket of snow. This serves as insulation in extremely low temperatures.

small, flattened head

slender, elongated neck

coat russet to chocolate-brown on back, limbs, and tail

white on underside from throat to lower belly

all four limbs short and small, with five toes on each paw

Social unit Solitary	Gestation 34–37 days	Young 1–7	Diet

slim head and body
enable it to enter
• rodent burrows

ears relatively
large in proportion
to small head

N. AMERICA,
EURASIA

SOLITARY DWELLER

The Least Weasel lives alone, making several
nests, lined with the fur or feathers of its
prey, in a crevice, tree root, or burrow
abandoned by some other animal.

small, shallow
eye sockets •

• small skull

large canine •
teeth pointed
like fangs

FLATTENED SKULL

The Least Weasel has a long, flat
head. Its front incisors are small,
and its sharp-ridged molars slice
the gristle and sinew of its prey.

tail not tipped
black as in
• stoat

tail same color
• as body

BABY WEASEL

Least Weasel young are looked
after by the mother alone for 9–12
weeks following their birth. The
female gives birth to an average
litter of 1–7 in a breeding nest
lined with soft material. Male
Least Weasels grow to be around
a quarter longer than females,
and twice as heavy.

Family MUSTELIDAE	Species *Mustela vison*	Status Locally common

AMERICAN MINK

This mink is dark brown to almost black in color, but about
one in ten is silvery gray, and a number of color variations
have also been bred on fur farms. An opportunistic predator,
it hunts at night, dusk, or dawn for a variety of small
creatures such as rats, rabbits, frogs, fish, crayfish, and
shore crabs. Although found close to water, the
American Mink is not a powerful swimmer and since
its eyesight is not well-adapted to underwater vision,
it locates its prey on the surface before pursuing it.
This mustelid has a repertoire of sounds, which
includes screams and hisses, and chuckling calls
between males and females during the breeding
season. Mating is often preceded by very
aggressive encounters between the two sexes.
Males first seek out those females whose
territories overlap their own, before searching
for others. Typical territories are 0.6–1.8 miles
(1–3 km) across for the females, and 1.2–3.1
miles (2–5 km) for the males. The female
alone takes care of the young, suckling them
for 5–6 weeks in her nesting den, built
among roots or rocks.
• SIZE Body length:12–21½in
(30–54cm).Tail:5½–8½in (14–21 cm).
• OCCURRENCE North America,
S. South America, Europe, and Asia.
In lakes and rivers, and along coastlines.
• REMARK Trapped for its luxuriant fur
over hundreds of years, the American Mink
was taken to Europe in the early part of
the 20th century for farming. Escaped
animals have established wild populations
and are regarded as pests and a threat to
native species, especially the European
Water Vole (see p.164).

small ears

N. & S. AMERICA,
EURASIA

*white patch
on chin*

*thick
underfur*

*dark
brown
coat*

*darker, coarse
guard hairs*

NEAR WATER
Semiaquatic in lifestyle, the American Mink has a
coat of dark guard hairs that waterproof its fur while
swimming. Its partially webbed feet enable it to hunt
on land as well as in water.

Social unit Solitary	Gestation 40–75 days	Young 3–6	Diet

Family MUSTELIDAE	Species *Mustela lutreola*	Status Endangered

EUROPEAN MINK

lips ringed by thin white line •

Although it is not closely related to the American Mink (see opposite), the slightly smaller European Mink resembles it in habits and appearance. Its fur is usually dark brown to almost black, and the upper and lower lips are ringed with a thin band of white fur. The males are known to be up to 85 percent larger than the females. This predominantly nocturnal predator hunts underwater and on land for water voles, fish, frogs, crayfish, and water birds. The European Mink has very few natural predators, although it is under threat from introduced species such as the American Mink. It releases a noxious secretion from its anal glands when threatened.
• **SIZE** Body length:12–16in (30–40cm). Tail:4¾–7½in (12–19cm).
• **OCCURRENCE** N. Spain, W. France, Belarus, and Russia. In lakes and slow-moving rivers, especially in or near woods.
• **REMARK** This is Europe's most endangered mammal, and is now being bred in captivity.

dark brown to blackish coat •

slightly bushy tail •

EUROPE

Social unit Solitary	Gestation 40 – 43 days	Young 4–5	Diet

Family MUSTELIDAE	Species *Poecilogale albinucha*	Status Lower risk*

AFRICAN STRIPED WEASEL

AFRICA

The long, sinuous body of this animal is black apart from a white patch running from the forehead to the neck, where it splits into two white stripes, each stripe dividing into two again along the back and sides of its body. All four stripes come together at the tail, which is bushy and white. The front claws, longer than those on the hind feet, are used for burrowing. The African Striped Weasel feeds at night, chiefly on small rodents,

white forehead •

killing those up to its own size by means of a well-directed neck bite. When faced with predators such as foxes, cats, or owls, this weasel arches its back and squirts noxious fluid from its anal glands.
• **SIZE** Body length: 10–14in (25–35cm). Tail:6–9in (15–23cm).
• **OCCURRENCE** C. to S. Africa. In grassland areas with rainfall.

Social unit Solitary	Gestation 32 days	Young 1–3	Diet

Family MUSTELIDAE	Species *Vormela peregusna*	Status Vulnerable

MARBLED POLECAT

As its name suggests, the Marbled Polecat has a black coat, mottled with white or yellow spots and stripes. A distinctive black mask over its eyes characterizes its face, while its underparts are black. It has a long, sinuous body with short legs, a small, flat head with a blunt snout, and rounded ears. When threatened, it curls its tail to display its warning coloration and emits an unpleasant odor. The Marbled Polecat enlarges rodent burrows to make its den, and hunts at night, dawn, or dusk.

bushy tail curled over body when threatened

EURASIA

• **SIZE** Body length:13–14 in (33–35 cm). Tail:4¾–9 in (12–22 cm).
• **OCCURRENCE** S.E. Europe to W. China. In dry, open steppe and semiarid regions.
• **REMARK** This species is threatened by habitat loss and depletion of steppe rodents, one of its main foods.

black mask around eyes

black underside

Social unit Solitary	Gestation 56–63 days	Young 4–8	Diet

Family MUSTELIDAE	Species *Martes foina*	Status Common

BEECH MARTEN

Adapted to human presence, this marten scavenges on refuse and hunts around farmhouses, and also eats rodents, birds, and fruits. Short in stature but long-legged, it has a dense brown coat with a "bow tie" patch of white on its throat. Also known as the Stone Marten, this typically solitary animal makes its den in a rocky crevice, tree-hole, old rodent burrow, or outhouse near human settlements. The Beech Marten is strictly nocturnal by nature.

EURASIA

• **SIZE** Body length:16¼–19 in (42–48 cm).Tail:10 in (26 cm).
• **OCCURRENCE** S. and C. Europe, and C. Asia. In deciduous woodland, rocky hillsides, and near human habitations.

long, dense fur

bushy tail

wedge-shaped head

Social unit Solitary	Gestation 30 days	Young 12	Diet

Family MUSTELIDAE	Species *Martes flavigula*	Status Endangered

YELLOW-THROATED MARTEN

An agile climber that uses its claws to grip branches and its tail for maintaining balance, the Yellow-throated Marten also bounds along the ground in long leaps. This medium-sized carnivore has orange-yellow to dark brown fur, with a creamy yellow throat "bib" and a bushy black tail. It has a wedge-shaped head and large, round ears. Hunting both on trees and on the ground at night, it also climbs trees to escape from danger, and releases a noxious smell when alarmed. It is preyed upon by eagles and other carnivores, and is occasionally hunted by humans for its pelt.

large, round ears

dark brown to orange coat

ASIA

creamy white to yellow throat patch

• **SIZE** Body length: 19–28 in (48–70 cm). Tail:14–18 in (35–45 cm).
• **OCCURRENCE** India to S.E. Asia. In temperate and coniferous forest.

long legs

Social unit Solitary	Gestation 5–6 months	Young 2–5	Diet

Family MUSTELIDAE	Species *Martes zibellina*	Status Endangered*

SABLE

Extensively hunted over centuries for its pelt, the Sable is now a protected species in many countries. It has dense brown-black fur, with an indistinct, paler brown patch on the throat, long legs with sharp, partly retractable claws, and a bushy tail. Like others of its family, it is fast and agile on the ground. However, it rarely climbs, except to escape from danger, in spite of being welladapted for this activity. Occupying old burrows for its main nest, the territory of this species is considerably larger in larch forest than in pine forest. The Sable is active both during the day and at night.

wedge-shaped head

ASIA

indistinct pale patch on throat

• **SIZE** Body length:12½–18 in (32–46 cm).Tail:5½–7 in (14–18 cm).
• **OCCURRENCE** N.E. Asia and islands of N. Japan. In temperate and coniferous forest (especially larch and pine).
• **REMARK** The Sable is almost extinct in Europe, but was reintroduced in European Russia for fur-farming and hunting.

brownish black, dense fur

Social unit Solitary	Gestation 25–45 days	Young 3–4	Diet

Family MUSTELIDAE	Species *Martes pennanti*	Status Lower risk*

FISHER

Belying its name, the Fisher hunts terrestrial prey such as rodents, porcupines, squirrels, and hares both during the day and night. This medium-sized carnivore has a wedge-shaped nose and round ears; its dark brown fur has a sheen on the head and shoulders, and its bushy tail and legs are black. An agile creature, the Fisher is welladapted to climbing and prefers to raise its young on high tree branches, although it also makes its den among rocks, roots, stumps, and bushes.
• **SIZE** Body length:18½–30 in (47–75 cm). Tail:12–16½ in (30–42 cm).
• **OCCURRENCE** Canada and N. USA. In coniferous and hardwood forest.
• **REMARK** Some 50,000–130,000 animals are trapped each year for their pelts. Habitat loss due to logging also remains a major threat.

dense, dark brown coat

N. AMERICA

black feet and tail

Social unit Solitary	Gestation 11–12 months	Young 1–5	Diet

Family MUSTELIDAE	Species *Galictis vittata*	Status Lower risk*

GREATER GRISON

Long and sinuous in shape, this mustelid has a slim, pointed head and a flexible neck, and relatively short legs and tail. The fur on its pale gray upperparts is grizzled, but its muzzle, throat, chest, and forefeet are black. The gray crown has a broad white band on the forehead above the eyes, across the ears, and down the side of its neck. Usually found living alone or in pairs, this agile runner, climber, and swimmer produces a noxious smell when threatened.
• **SIZE** Body length:18½–22 in (47–55 cm). Tail:5½–8 in (14–20 cm).
• **OCCURRENCE** S. Mexico, and Central and South America. In tropical forest and grassland.
• **REMARK** A related species, the Lesser Grison (*Galictis cuja*), occurs in southern temperate latitudes and at higher elevations. It is sometimes tamed to control rodents.

N., C., & S. AMERICA

fur grizzled pale gray

stumpy tail

short legs

• *white band across forehead to ears*

Social unit Solitary/Pair	Gestation Not known	Young 2–4	Diet

Family MUSTELIDAE	Species *Ictonyx striatus*	Status Locally common

STRIPED POLECAT

Jet black, with four white stripes fanning out across its back, the Striped Polecat (also known as the Zorilla or African Polecat) resembles a small skunk (see pp. 256–257). Its behaviour is similar too: when threatened by predators, it sprays noxious fumes from its anal glands, lifting up its tail or standing on its hindlegs, hissing and screaming. It uses its rounded muzzle to poke into leaf litter, and then uses its long front claws to dig up burrowing insect prey. A nocturnal animal, it usually shelters in tree crevices or disused animal holes, or digs its own burrow in soft earth. It is mainly terrestrial, but may occasionally climb trees.

four white stripes from head to tail

AFRICA

• SIZE Body length:11–15 in (28–38 cm). Tail: 8–12 in (20–30 cm).
• OCCURRENCE Africa, south of the Sahara Desert. In grassland, desert, and tropical forest.

jet black underparts and limbs

Social unit Solitary	Gestation 36 days	Young 2–3	Diet 🐛 🐀 🦎 🦅 🦂

Family MUSTELIDAE	Species *Gulo gulo*	Status Vulnerable

WOLVERINE

Stocky and bearlike, this large mustelid lopes across the snow, hunting prey ranging from deer and Elk to hares, birds, and mice. Also known as the Glutton, it scavenges on carcasses of reindeer, crunching the frozen meat and bones with it powerful jaws. It lives alone in a den made among roots and rocks and is active during the day and night.

N. AMERICA, EURASIA

• SIZE Body length:26–41 in (65–105 cm). Tail:6½–10 in (17–26 cm).
• OCCURRENCE Canada, N.W. USA, N. Europe, and N.E. Asia. In tundra and coniferous forest.
• REMARK The Wolverine is the largest mustelid after the Giant Otter (see p. 265).

small eyes

broad feet for walking on snow

Social unit Solitary	Gestation 30–50 days	Young 1–6	Diet 🦌 🐀 🦐 🍎

Family MUSTELIDAE	Species *Mephitis mephitis*	Status Common

STRIPED SKUNK

N. AMERICA

With a small, pointed snout, short legs, and a fluffy tail, the Striped Skunk is a typical example of its genus. Its black coat has a thin white stripe on the muzzle and two wider stripes on the back, extending from head to tail. Like all skunks, it is sluggish in its movements and relies largely on its warning coloration and spray (see right) to protect itself from predators, mostly horned owls, hawks, coyotes, bobcats, foxes, and dogs. Highly adaptable by nature, the Striped Skunk prospers in places that have been cleared for farming, where larger predators have been driven out by humans. The diet of this nocturnal animal often depends on habitat and availability of food. Generally solitary, families and individuals often gather together in communal winter dens located in abandoned burrows, buildings, or rock piles. A wide repertoire of sounds such as hisses, growls, squeals, and soft cooing notes are used to communicate. Males use their scent spray to communicate with females during the mating season. Females build nests of dried grass and weeds; the young stay with the mother for over a year.

black body fur •

• **SIZE** Body length: 22–30 in (55–75 cm).
Tail: 7–10 in (17.5–25 cm).
• **OCCURRENCE** C. Canada to N. Mexico.
In wooded or brushy temperate forest,
farmland, and urban areas.
• **REMARK** This skunk is a major carrier
of rabies in the USA, and its proximity
to humans and domestic animals
is a cause for concern.

small, pointed
• *head*

Social unit Solitary	Gestation 60–77 days	Young 5–6	Diet 🐁 🦐 🐟 🐛 🐚 🍒 🥚 🍃

ON THE PROWL
The omnivorous Striped
Skunk may be seen
ambling along in search
of food such as insects,
small mammals, fish,
crustaceans, fruits, grain,
carrion, and refuse. It will
also dig out bee and wasp
nests, and may even
rummage through
garbage cans.

white-striped
• back

UP IN THE AIR
The scientific name of the Striped
Skunk is derived from a Latin word
that means "poisonous vapor." When
threatened by predators, it stands on
its forefeet and ejects a noxious fluid
over its head, up to 9¾ft (3 m),
toward the enemy.

• fluffy tail

Family MUSTELIDAE	Species *Conepatus humboldti*	Status Vulnerable*

HUMBODT'S HOG-NOSED SKUNK

A white stripe runs along each side of this typical skunk up to the tail. Its black or reddish brown body is stocky, with a small head and bushy tail. A broad nose pad helps it root out food at night, primarily insects, but virtually anything that is edible. Like other skunks, it occupies a secure shelter under rocks, in a burrow, or among bushes, and ejects a noxious fluid from its anal scent glands when threatened. It uses a variety of sounds, from soft chittering to squeals and growls, to communicate.
- **SIZE** Body length:10–14 ½in (25–37cm). Tail:12–22½in (30–57cm).
- **OCCURRENCE** S. Chile and Argentina. In wooded, brushy areas and farmland.
- **REMARK** Like others in its family, this skunk does not spray its own kind even in the fiercest fight.

S. AMERICA

prominent nose pad

white stripe

fluffy tail

Social unit Solitary	Gestation 42 days	Young 2–4	Diet 🐜 🐁 🦎 🐛 🥚 🐌

Family MUSTELIDAE	Species *Spilogale putorius*	Status Lower risk*

EASTERN SPOTTED SKUNK

The striking black-and-white coloration of this skunk warns its predators – owls, coyotes, and foxes – of the foul-smelling fluid that it discharges, sometimes when doing a handstand. The white markings on the body differ from one individual to another, but all usually have a white forehead patch and white tail tip. This slow-moving omnivore feeds on a variety of small animals, insects, and plant matter, even rummaging in garbage heaps for food. The Eastern Spotted Skunk is more active, alert, and nocturnal by nature than the Striped Skunk (see p. 256–257). Although usually solitary, up to eight skunks may share an underground den in winter. They are also known to climb and take shelter in trees.
- **SIZE** Body length: 12–13½in (30–34cm). Tail:6½–8½in (17–21cm).
- **OCCURRENCE** E. to C. USA, and N.E. Mexico. In grassland and temperate forest.
- **REMARK** When threatened, it sometimes contorts its body in a horseshoe shape towards the aggressor in order to squirt its noxious fluid.

N. AMERICA

hair longest on tail

distinctive black-and-white pattern of stripes and spots

white patch on forehead

Social unit Solitary	Gestation 42 days	Young 3–6	Diet 🌿 ● 🐜 🐁

Family MUSTELIDAE	Species *Taxidea taxus*	Status Common

AMERICAN BADGER

white face stripe from nose to shoulder

N. AMERICA

shaggy gray upper body

Similar in appearance to the Eurasian Badger (see p. 261) but smaller, the American Badger has long, grizzled gray fur and yellowish underparts, and a prominent white crescent on either side of its blackish face. A solitary, nocturnal hunter and an expert digger, it uses its stout claws to unearth burrowing rodents such as Prairie Dogs and other ground squirrels. Although it does not hibernate, it may spend several days underground during inclement weather. The American Badger has few natural predators and displays very ferocious behavior when attacked.
- **SIZE** Body length: 42–72 cm (16½–28 in). Tail: 10–16 cm (4–6½ in).
- **OCCURRENCE** S.W. Canada and C. USA to N. Mexico. In areas with loose soil: grassland, shrub, and temperate forest.
- **REMARK** It has a transparent third inner eyelid to protect its eyes while digging.

Social unit Solitary	Gestation 42 days	Young 2–3	Diet

Family MUSTELIDAE	Species *Melogale personata*	Status Lower risk

BURMESE FERRET BADGER

With a long, flexible body rather like a ferret's, this bushy-tailed badger is much smaller than others, and is dark brown or gray in color. Its face has white or yellow cheek patches and a pale band between the eyes and from the top of the head to the shoulders. Unlike other badgers, the Burmese Ferret Badger is sometimes found in trees, the ridges on the pads of its feet providing a good grip. It feeds at night, dawn, and dusk, on insects, snails, birds, small mammals, and vegetable matter, using its massive teeth to crush mollusk shells and insects. When threatened, the Burmese Ferret Badger digs into the ground with its long claws and bites its aggressor or sprays it with a foul-smelling fluid.
- **SIZE** Body length: 13–17 in (33–43 cm). Tail: 6–9 in (15–23 cm).
- **OCCURRENCE** N.E. India, Nepal, Burma, Thailand, and S.E. Asia. In wooded hillsides, as well as open grassland.

ASIA

dark grey or brown fur

long, bushy tail

Social unit Solitary	Gestation 57–80 days	Young 1–5	Diet

Family MUSTELIDAE	Species *Mellivora capensis*	Status Lower risk*

HONEY BADGER

Also called the Ratel, this heavily built badger is characterized by silvery gray upperparts, but is black or dark brown elsewhere. The Honey Badger feeds on honey and bee larvae, as well as a wide range of prey from worms, termites, and scorpions, to hares and porcupines. It excavates large burrows, but may also live in rock crevices and holes in tree roots. It fearlessly fights off predators, sometimes producing an offensive smell in defense.

AFRICA, ASIA

• *broad head*

silvery gray upper body

• **SIZE** Body length: 23½–30 in (60–77 cm). Tail: 8–12 in (20–30 cm).
• **OCCURRENCE** Sub-Saharan and W. Africa, Middle East, and India. In grassland, desert, forest, and mountains.
• **REMARK** The Honey Badger has a unique symbiotic relationship with the Honeyguide Bird (*Indicator indicator*), which leads it to beehives and then waits for the badger to break them open, so that both can feed on grubs and honey.

Social unit Variable	Gestation 5–6 months	Young 1–4	Diet 🕸 🐜 🦫 🦎 🦔

Family MUSTELIDAE	Species *Arctonyx collaris*	Status Lower risk*

HOG-BADGER

This badger takes its name from its pig-like snout, with protruding incisors and canines on the lower jaw, with which it tends to root in the ground for grubs and plant matter. Gray to yellowish in color, the Hog-badger has a white face and ears, and a distinctive black stripe extending from the nose through the eye to the ear, on each side. It digs elaborate burrow systems, sometimes using crevices under rocks and boulders as shelters. Feeding according to seasonal availability, it uses its strong sense of smell to locate fruits, tubers, and small animals. This badger is known to fight savagely when cornered, and it sometimes escapes underground. Hunted by tigers and leopards, its black-and-white face stripe probably acts as a warning to predators.

ASIA

wedge-shaped, stocky body •

• *white ears*

• **SIZE** Body length: 55–70 cm (22–28 in). Tail: 12–17 cm (4¾–6½ in).
• **OCCURRENCE** N.E. India to China, and S.E. Asia. In lowland jungle and low, wooded hills.

gray to yellowish upperparts •

Social unit Social	Gestation 6 weeks	Young 2–4	Diet 🐾 🦎 🥔 🐀

Family MUSTELIDAE	Species *Meles meles*	Status Locally common

EURASIAN BADGER

Unusually among mustelids, the Eurasian Badger lives in clans – probably the most efficient way of hunting for irregularly distributed food. This stocky, short-limbed badger has a small, pointed head, short neck, strong limbs, and a small tail. A nocturnal omnivore, its diet varies with season and availability, but it feeds mostly on earthworms, sucking them out when they emerge from their holes on wet nights. It also eats insects, lizards, frogs, small mammals, birds and their eggs, fruits, and carrion, and sometimes digs out wasps from their nests and rabbits from their burrows with its powerful front claws. Since its vision is poor, it locates its food by means of its well-developed senses of smell and hearing. This badger vigorously defends its territory, which may range over 125–370 acres (50–150 hectares), against other clans. Badger cubs are hunted by eagles, owls, wolves, and wolverines, while adult animals also face persecution by humans.
• **SIZE** Body length: 22–35 in (56–90 cm). Tail: 4 ¾–8 in (12–20 cm).
• **OCCURRENCE** Europe to E. Asia. In woodland and steppe.
• **REMARK** The striped face of the Eurasian Badger varies slightly between individuals, perhaps allowing clan members to recognize each other, or acting as camouflage.

BADGER COLONY
A badger clan has about six individuals, with a dominant boar (male), one or more sows (females), and cubs. The extensive system of underground chambers and pathways (the "sett") is kept scrupulously clean, and enlarged over generations.

grayish brown
• *upperparts*

black •
underparts

powerful front claws •

• *elongated snout*

EURASIA

Social unit Social	Gestation 7 weeks	Young 2–6	Diet 🐜 🦎 🐸 🐀 ⚬

Family MUSTELIDAE	Species *Lutra lutra*	Status Vulnerable

EUROPEAN OTTER

Uniformly brown with a paler throat, this mustelid, sometimes called the
Eurasian River Otter, has a flat head with a broad muzzle, and small eyes and
ears. Its elongated body, waterproof coat, webbed feet, and stout, flattened tail
(used to aid propulsion and as a rudder) are adaptations to its aquatic lifestyle.
Although usually active at night, dawn, and dusk, the otters found along
coastlines are more active during the day. The holt (burrow), well hidden in
bank vegetation or under overhanging tree roots, is located within a bankside
territory, 2½–12 miles (4–20 km) long, that is marked by scent and droppings.
Mostly solitary, this species is known to form temporary pairs for two or three
months during the breeding season. The cubs are suckled for three months,
but may remain with the mother for more than a year. This otter
communicates by a variety of sounds, and
through scent emitted from its glands,
signifying identity and status.
• **SIZE** Body length: 22½–28 in
(57–70 cm). Tail: 10–16 in
(35–40 cm)
• **OCCURRENCE**
Eurasia, south of the
tundra. Near riverbanks,
lakes, and coastlines.
• **REMARK** The
European Otter is a
protected species. It has
been hunted for fur, fishery
protection, and sport. It faces
additional threats from water
pollution and from activities
such as clearance of banks,
irrigation, and water sports.

EURASIA

small eyes

*distinctive short,
rounded ears*

*long, sinuous
body*

*fairly
broad
muzzle*

*paler fur
on throat*

Social unit Solitary	Gestation 60–70 days	Young 2–3	Diet

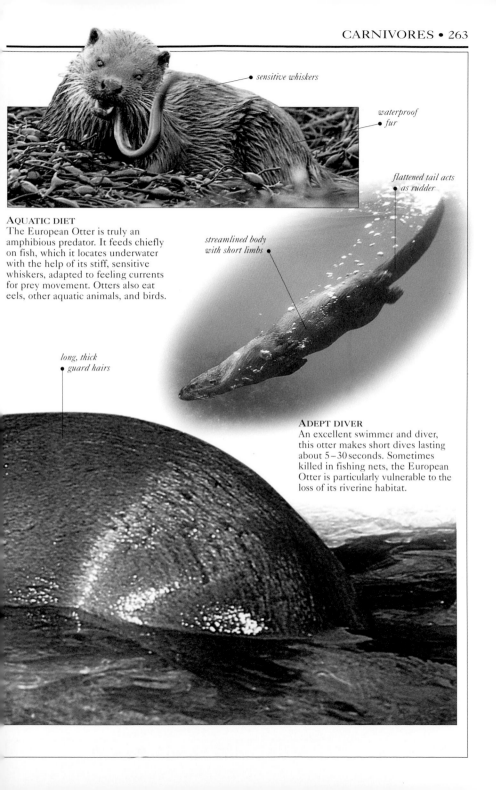

sensitive whiskers

waterproof
fur

flattened tail acts
as rudder

AQUATIC DIET
The European Otter is truly an amphibious predator. It feeds chiefly on fish, which it locates underwater with the help of its stiff, sensitive whiskers, adapted to feeling currents for prey movement. Otters also eat eels, other aquatic animals, and birds.

streamlined body
with short limbs

long, thick
guard hairs

ADEPT DIVER
An excellent swimmer and diver, this otter makes short dives lasting about 5–30 seconds. Sometimes killed in fishing nets, the European Otter is particularly vulnerable to the loss of its riverine habitat.

Family MUSTELIDAE	Species *Lontra canadensis*	Status Lower risk*

NORTHERN RIVER OTTER

This truly amphibious otter is well-adapted for swimming and diving, with eyes adapted for underwater vision, an elongated and sinuous body, webbed feet, and a flattened tail, acting as rudder. It has gray-brown or red to black, velvety fur above, while its underparts are silvery or grayish brown, and the throat and cheeks are paler.
• SIZE Body length: 26–43 in (66–110 cm). Tail: 12–18 in (32–46 cm).
• OCCURRENCE Canada and USA. In rivers, streams, lakes, and coastal marshes.
• REMARK This animal is probably one of the most numerous species of otters.

small head
light throat and cheeks
velvety fur

N. AMERICA

Social unit Solitary	Gestation 60–70 days	Young Not known	Diet 🐟🦐🐸🐦🦟

Family MUSTELIDAE	Species *Aonyx capensis*	Status Lower risk*

AFRICAN CLAWLESS OTTER

An expert swimmer, this otter has light to dark brown fur on its long, lithe body, with off-white patches on its chest. Its rear feet are webbed and have small claws on the third and fourth toes, while its forefeet have no claws and the digits are used to handle prey.
• SIZE Body length: 20–37 in (73–95 cm). Tail: 16–26 in (41–67 cm).
• OCCURRENCE Sub-Saharan Africa, excluding desert. In fresh- or seawater habitats.
• REMARK It is the largest of the two otter species in Africa.

flattened tail
dark brown fur
clawless digits resembling fingers

AFRICA

Social unit Social	Gestation Not known	Young 2	Diet 🦟🦐🐟🦑

Family MUSTELIDAE	Species *Aonyx cinereus*	Status Lower risk*

ORIENTAL SMALL-CLAWED OTTER

Unusually for an otter, this species has short claws that do not extend beyond the fleshy pads of its webbed feet. Equally unusually, fish are not an important part of its diet and its broad teeth are adapted to crushing mollusks. These playful and social otters form groups of about 12, keeping in touch through noises and scents.
• SIZE Body length: 18–24 in (45–61 cm). Tail: 10–14 in (25–35 cm).
• OCCURRENCE From India to Malaysia and S.E China. In rivers, creeks, estuaries, and along coastlines.
• REMARK This is the smallest otter.

short limbs
lithe body
flattened, webbed feet

ASIA

Social unit Variable	Gestation 60–64 days	Young 1–6	Diet 🐚🦟🦐🐟

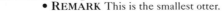

Family MUSTELIDAE	Species *Pteroneura brasiliensis*	Status Endangered

GIANT OTTER

Once widespread throughout the Amazon Basin, this otter is now very reduced in numbers. It has short legs, well-webbed toes, and a flattened, wide-based tail, which make it adept at swimming and diving. Its stout whiskers and sensitive eyes also help it to spot prey while underwater. Like other otters, this species has a sleek coat with short, dense fur. Its upperparts are rich brown, with cream spots on the chin, throat, and chest that may merge into a "bib." These noisy otters form groups of 5–9 individuals that hunt together to provide food for their young. Extremely vocal when alarmed, Giant Otters also attack in a group to defend their young against predators.
• SIZE Body length: 3 ½ – 4 ½ ft (1–1.4 m). Tail: 18–26 in (45–65 cm).
• OCCURRENCE N. and C. South America. In lowland tropical forest, rivers, and lakes.
• REMARK The largest mustelid, it faces the major threats of habitat destruction and pollution.

S. AMERICA

abundant, stout whiskers

rich brown upperparts

large, protruding eyes

base of tail very thick

short limbs with webbed digits

Social unit Social	Gestation 65–72 days	Young 2	Diet

Family MUSTELIDAE	Species *Enhydra lutris*	Status Endangered

SEA OTTER

The smallest marine mammal, this otter both lives and feeds in the ocean and has a specialized diet of abalone, sea urchins, and clams. It has excellent underwater eyesight, a rudderlike tail, and luxuriant fur (the densest of all animals) to insulate it effectively. Its lungs, twice the size of similar-sized land animals, enable it to dive up to 98 ft (30 m).
• SIZE Body length: 22–51 in (55–130 cm). Tail: 5–13 in (13–33 cm).
• OCCURRENCE N. Pacific (Kamchatka Peninsula to C. California). Along coastlines.
• REMARK The Sea Otter was once hunted for its pelt. It is now a legally protected species.

N. PACIFIC

straw-colored fur on head

long, dense coat

flipperlike hindfeet

Social unit Social	Gestation 4 months	Young 1	Diet

CARNIVORES
VIVERRIDS

T HE 76 SPECIES of civets, linsangs, genets, mongooses, meerkats, and other species in the Viverridae family resemble a combination of felid (cat) and mustelid (stoat). They are, however, more primitive, and have a longer snout and extra teeth.

The typical viverrid is long and slim, from the tapering snout to the lengthy tail. It has keen senses, moves with agile stealth, and eats a mixed diet. However, some species tend toward meat-eating, and they stalk their victims in catlike fashion. Viverrids are found from southern Europe, across Africa to southern Asia, in forest, desert, and savanna. They are generally nocturnal, and mainly terrestrial, but are good climbers. However, the Binturong is almost wholly arboreal, while the otter genets are semiaquatic.

Civets and genets tend to have spots in longitudinal rows along their bodies for camouflage, while the mongoose species are either plain or striped. Another feature that distinguishes this family is scent glands in the anal region, used to mark territories. In civets, the gland secretions are collected by people to use as a base for perfumes.

Family VIVERRIDAE	Species *Genetta genetta*	Status Common

SMALL SPOTTED GENET

Also called the Common Genet, this slender, cat-like animal has a strikingly marked, pointed face, spotted body, and a banded tail. An excellent climber, it has semi-retractable claws and a crest along its back that can be erected. This swift, omnivorous predator hunts at night, dawn, and dusk, and is considered a pest for its raids on poultry farms. The male has a larger home range than the female, and marks its territory using scent, urine, and faeces. It builds its den in a hole or tangle of roots in thick bushes.
• SIZE Body length: 40–55 cm (16–22 in).
Tail: 40–51 cm (16–20 in)
• OCCURRENCE W. Europe and W., E., and S. Africa. In woodland, savanna, and grassland.

EUROPE, AFRICA

banded tail

distinctively marked pointed face

Social unit Solitary	Gestation 70 days	Young 2–3	Diet

| Family VIVERRIDAE | Species *Prionodon pardicolor* | Status Rare |

SPOTTED LINSANG

This slender carnivore "flows" like quicksilver through the branches of trees with amazing grace and agility, using its retractable claws to grip, and its tail to balance and brake while climbing. Solitary and nocturnal, the large eyes of this viverrid are adapted for night vision, and it has dark spots on its brownish orange coat and a banded tail. It is found equally on the ground and on trees, and winds its tail around its body while sleeping. The Spotted Linsang stalks its prey and kills it with a bite on the neck.

ASIA

spotted body

large ears

orange-buff fur

- **SIZE** Body length:14½–17 in (37–43 cm). Tail:12–14 in (30–36 cm).
- **OCCURRENCE** S., E., and S.E. Asia. In hill and mountain forest, also shrub and forest at lower elevations.
- **REMARK** Male linsangs are twice the size of the females.

| Social unit Solitary | Gestation Not known | Young 2–3 | Diet 🐾🦎🐍🐀🐛 |

| Family VIVERRIDAE | Species *Viverra tangalunga* | Status Common |

MALAYAN CIVET

Like other civets, this species has many dark spots that form lines along its coat, but is distinct in having a black-and-white neck collar, white underside, black legs and feet, and about 15 bands on its tail. It has a blackish crest along its spine, which it sometimes erects, and semi-retractable claws that enable it to climb trees. Although it occasionally takes to the trees, this nocturnal animal forages on the forest floor searching for creatures including millipedes, giant centipedes, scorpions, and small mammals such as mice.

black bars and spots on torso

ASIA

banded tail

blackish legs

- **SIZE** Body length: 24–26 in (62–66 cm). Tail :11–14 in (28–35 cm).
- **OCCURRENCE** Indonesia, Philippines, Malayasia, and Borneo. In lowland tropical forest and neighbouring cultivated land.

| Social unit Solitary | Gestation Not known | Young Not known | Diet 🐛🐀🐀 |

Family VIVERRIDAE	Species *Paradoxurus hermaphroditus*	Status Common

ASIAN PALM CIVET

face mask of dark and light patches ●

This civet has a grayish brown coat with darker spots and black stripes on its back. It has a large, bushy tail, and a face mask of dark and light patches, like that of the European Polecat (see p. 246). Nocturnal by nature, this adaptable mustelid is an excellent climber, staying mainly in trees, but sometimes resting on rooftops. Fond of fruits, especially figs, it also eats buds, grasses, insects, small animals, and even poultry.

black stripes on back ●

• **SIZE** Body length:17–28in (43–71cm). Tail:16–26in (40–66cm).
• **OCCURRENCE** S. and S.E. Asia, S. China. In forested areas, as well as around human settlements.
• **REMARK** This animal is known to be particularly fond of fermented palm tree juice or toddy, hence its other name, the Toddy Cat.

ASIA

large, bushy tail ●

Social unit Solitary	Gestation Not known	Young 2–4	Diet 🐀 🥬 🐛 🐦 🦎

Family VIVERRIDAE	Species *Arctictis binturong*	Status Common

BINTURONG

Moving cautiously among branches in search of fruits, shoots, small animals, birds, and insects, the Binturong is the only carnivore with a prehensile tail, apart from the Kinkajou (see p.245). It has distinctive long-tufted ears and a shaggy black coat with lighter buffish tips. This animal has semiretractable, short, and slightly curved claws, and moves through the forest canopy on the soles of its feet, which are naked up to the heels. Often seen curled up on a secluded branch, the Binturong may even continue to feed in this position. Chiefly nocturnal, it uses scent to mark its territory.

shaggy black coat ●

ASIA

long tufts ●
on ear tips

small, pointed muzzle ●

• **SIZE** Body length: 24–38in (61–96cm). Tail: 22–35in (56–89cm).
• **OCCURRENCE** N.E. India, Bhutan, Nepal, and S.E. Asia. In dense tropical, semi-evergreen, or deciduous forest.

Social unit Solitary	Gestation 92 days	Young 1–3	Diet 🥬 🐀 🐛 🐦 🦎

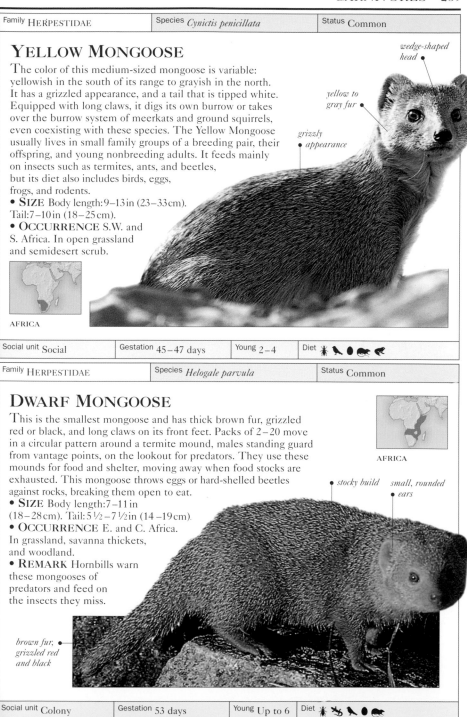

Family HERPESTIDAE	Species *Cynictis penicillata*	Status Common

YELLOW MONGOOSE

wedge-shaped head •

The color of this medium-sized mongoose is variable:
yellowish in the south of its range to grayish in the north.
It has a grizzled appearance, and a tail that is tipped white.
Equipped with long claws, it digs its own burrow or takes
over the burrow system of meerkats and ground squirrels,
even coexisting with these species. The Yellow Mongoose
usually lives in small family groups of a breeding pair, their
offspring, and young nonbreeding adults. It feeds mainly
on insects such as termites, ants, and beetles,
but its diet also includes birds, eggs,
frogs, and rodents.
• SIZE Body length: 9–13 in (23–33 cm).
Tail: 7–10 in (18–25 cm).
• OCCURRENCE S.W. and
S. Africa. In open grassland
and semidesert scrub.

yellow to gray fur •

grizzly • *appearance*

AFRICA

Social unit Social	Gestation 45–47 days	Young 2–4	Diet 🐜 🦎 ● 🐦 🐸

Family HERPESTIDAE	Species *Helogale parvula*	Status Common

DWARF MONGOOSE

This is the smallest mongoose and has thick brown fur, grizzled
red or black, and long claws on its front feet. Packs of 2–20 move
in a circular pattern around a termite mound, males standing guard
from vantage points, on the lookout for predators. They use these
mounds for food and shelter, moving away when food stocks are
exhausted. This mongoose throws eggs or hard-shelled beetles
against rocks, breaking them open to eat.
• SIZE Body length: 7–11 in
(18–28 cm). Tail: 5 ½–7 ½ in (14–19 cm).
• OCCURRENCE E. and C. Africa.
In grassland, savanna thickets,
and woodland.
• REMARK Hornbills warn
these mongooses of
predators and feed on
the insects they miss.

AFRICA

• *stocky build* *small, rounded* • *ears*

brown fur, • *grizzled red and black*

Social unit Colony	Gestation 53 days	Young Up to 6	Diet 🐜 🦗 🦎 ● 🐦

Family VIVERRIDAE	Species *Mungos mungo*	Status Common

BANDED MONGOOSE

This lively, opportunistic mongoose has a stocky, brownish gray body with a striking pattern of dark bands across its back. The populations from moist habitats are darker in color than those from drier areas. Found in packs of 15–40, they often live in enlarged cavities of termite mounds. Individuals make chirping sounds to communicate with others of the pack as they forage for food, primarily insects, during the day. This mongoose also eats eggs, breaking them open by throwing them against rocks.

about 12 bands over rump

brown-gray coat

- **SIZE** Body length:12–18 in (30–45 cm). Tail: 6–12 in (15– 30 cm).
- **OCCURRENCE** E. and C. Africa, south of Sahara. In woodland and savanna.
  - **REMARK** It is sometimes kept as a pet.

AFRICA

tapering tail covered in coarse hair

Social unit Social	Gestation 2 months	Young 1– 4	Diet 🐛 ● 🐀

Family VIVERRIDAE	Species *Cryptoprocta ferox*	Status Endangered

FOSSA

The largest carnivore found in Madagascar, the reddish to dark brown Fossa has a catlike head with prominent, forward-pointing eyes and rounded ears. Its short, sharp claws can be retracted, and its anal glands are known to produce a strong, disagreeable odor. The Fossa has the predator's typical strong jaws and teeth. Active during the day and night, this agile leaper and climber once specialized in hunting all species of lemur, but now also stalks and kills pigs, poultry, and other domesticated animals. A solitary carnivore, it occupies a large territory of more than 1½ square miles (4 square km) in area, and so population densities are low. The Fossa has been successfully bred in zoos.

short, reddish brown fur

rounded ears

- **SIZE** Body length: 23 ½–30 in (60–76 cm). Tail: 22–28 in (55–70 cm).
- **OCCURRENCE** Madagascar. In undisturbed areas of tropical forest.
- **REMARK** Confined to the tiny island of Madagascar, the Fossa is threatened by the rapid depletion of its forest habitat. It is also persecuted and hunted by humans because of its frequent attacks on livestock.

MADAGASCAR

short, sharp retractable claws

Social unit Solitary	Gestation 3 months	Young 2–3	Diet 🦌 🗡

Family VIVERRIDAE	Species *Suricata suricatta*	Status Common

MEERKAT

A silvery brown, grizzled coat with eight distinctive dark bands on the lower half of the body distinguishes the Meerkat, or Suricate as it is sometimes called. This carnivore has small, pointed ears, dark circles around its eyes, and a pointed nose. Its slender tail ends in a dark tip. Adapted to burrowing, the Meerkat can close its ears underground and has long foreclaws that it uses for digging up soil and rooting for food items. Active by day, this sociable animal is found in colonies of up to 30, which live in enlarged burrow systems of Ground Squirrels. The male marks the home range of the group, chasing off all rival pack members. At dawn, the Meerkat emerges from its burrow and warms itself by standing up on its haunches and facing the sun. While most pack members forage, mainly for insects, some act as sentries, watching out for hawks and other predatory birds. Sentries stand at vantage points, on mounds or in bushes, and cheep or cluck out warnings. Sharper barks or growls indicate more urgent threats, upon which the whole pack dives for cover. Mating is preceded by mock fights, and the young are born during the rains, when food is available in plenty.

AFRICA

pointed nose

silvery brown coat

paler belly

• **SIZE** Body length:10–14 in (25–35 cm). Tail:6½–10 in (17–25 cm).
• **OCCURRENCE** S.W. Africa. In semidesert scrub and woodland, especially stony, open country.

dark circles around eyes

hindlegs used for standing upright

Social unit Social	Gestation 11 weeks	Young 2–5	Diet 🐜 🦗

CARNIVORES
HYENAS AND AARDWOLF

T HE THREE SPECIES of hyenas and the single species of Aardwolf superficially resemble dogs. But they are in fact more closely related to other members of the carnivore family such as civets, genets, and cats.

All four species of Hyaenidae have a distinctive body profile with a back that slopes down, due to long front legs and shorter rear ones. Other common features include a large head, big ears, muscular body and limbs, and a mane that extends along the back, except in the Spotted Hyena.

Hyenas have immensely strong jaws and teeth, usually live in families, and are hunter-scavengers. The smaller Aardwolf is solitary and licks up ants and termites. All species are nocturnal and found in savanna and semiarid habitats in Africa, with the Striped Hyena's range extending to southern Asia.

Family HYAENIDAE	Species *Hyaena hyaena*	Status Lower risk

STRIPED HYENA

This medium-sized, doglike carnivore is gray or pale brown with a dark brown or black patch on its throat and five or six vertical stripes down its flanks. The mane on its neck merges with its bushy, black-and-white tail and is erected when this hyena is threatened by predators. It has well-developed forequarters and its body slopes down towards its back. The Striped Hyena essentially scavenges on kills of other predators. It crushes bones by using its massive molars and powerful jaws. It also hunts dogs, sheep, goats, and poultry, and eats invertebrates, vegetables, and fruits.
• SIZE Body length: 3¼ ft (1.1 m).
Tail: 8 in (20 cm).
• OCCURRENCE W., N., and E. Africa and W. to S. Asia. In open habitat or sparse woodland savanna – avoids extreme desert, high altitudes, and forest.

AFRICA, ASIA

erectile neck mane

dark brown or black throat patch

horizontal black stripes on forelegs

well-developed, powerful hindlegs

Social unit Solitary	Gestation 84 days	Young 1–5	Diet

Family HYAENIDAE	Species *Parahyaena brunnea*	Status Lower risk*

BROWN HYENA

Ranging further into desert than other hyenas, this shaggy,
dark brown to black species can smell carrion from a distance of
8½ miles (14 km). A typical hyena with its powerful jaws and
shearing teeth, it feeds on almost any carcass, from those of seal
pups along the Namib Desert coast to those
of Springhares in the Kalahari
Desert. It forms loose
territorial colonies, and
the size of territories
varies according to
the availability of food.
• SIZE Body length:
4¼ ft (1.3 m).
Tail: 8½ in (21 cm).
• OCCURRENCE
S. Africa – chiefly below
the Kunene–Zambezi
river system. In remote
habitats: arid grassland,
desert, and mountains.

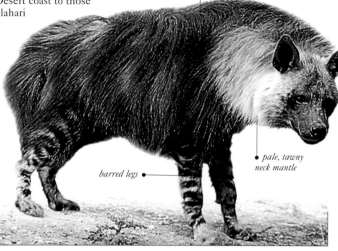

dark brown to black coat

AFRICA

pale, tawny neck mantle

barred legs

Social unit Variable	Gestation 97 days	Young 1–5	Diet 🦌

Family HYAENIDAE	Species *Proteles cristatus*	Status Lower risk*

AARDWOLF

Smaller than hyenas, the Aardwolf is unique
within its family in having a diet consisting
almost wholly of termites, particularly the
surface-foraging Nasute (snouted)
Harvester Termites. It has a pale buff to
yellowish white, down-sloping body with a
shoulder mane, which it erects under stress in order
to appear larger. Three stripes run down each side,
while diagonal stripes mark the fore- and hindquarters.
The front teeth resemble those of a hyena, but
the molars are small pegs, the food being
ground into smaller particles in the stomach.
• SIZE Body length: 26 in (67 cm).
Tail: 9½ in (24 cm).
• OCCURRENCE E. and S.
Africa. In woodland savanna
and desert.
• REMARK Aardwolf meat is
regarded as a delicacy by humans
in some areas.

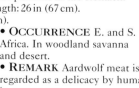

erect ears

three vertical black stripes on body

buff to yellowish white body

AFRICA

Social unit Solitary	Gestation 90 days	Young 2–4	Diet

Family HYAENIDAE	Species *Crocuta crocuta*	Status Lower risk

SPOTTED HYENA

AFRICA

The largest species of hyena, the Spotted Hyena, is like a large dog in appearance, with a sandy to grayish brown, spotted coat. The initially black spots turn brown, and finally fade out with age. A large head with powerful jaws, a downward-sloping back, with shorter hindlegs than forelegs, and a short tail that ends in a bushy, black tip, further characterize this carnivore. Its fur is coarse and bristly, and it has a mane with hair that slopes forward and is raised when the hyena is excited. The Spotted Hyena lives in clans dominated by females which vary from five or fewer animals in desert to 50 or more in the fertile savanna. The female hyena is about 10 percent larger than the male, and its large external genitals look deceptively like male organs. The clan occupies a communal den and uses communal latrines, jointly defending its territory of about 15–390 square miles (40–1,000 square km) by calls, as well as scent-markings and border patrolling. A powerful hunter, the Spotted Hyena may form a pack to kill large prey. When alone, it preys on hares, ground birds, and fish from swamps. Gorging its food, it can consume up to one-third of its total body weight in a single meal.

rounded, short ears

powerful jaws

doglike black muzzle

sandy to grayish, spotted brown coat

- **SIZE** Body length: 4½ ft (1.3 m). Tail: 10 in (25 cm).
- **OCCURRENCE** W. to E., and S. Africa. In semidesert, savanna, and woodland.
- **REMARK** The notorious "hyena laugh" signifies submission to a senior member of the clan.

large head

long front legs

MOTHER AND CUB

The female Spotted Hyena is solely responsible for rearing her young. The cubs are born black and change color after a few months. The average litter is 2 (range 1–3); the dominant cub controls access to the mother's milk and even kills its siblings to survive in times of milk shortage.

blunt claws that are nonretractable

Social unit Social	Gestation 110 days	Young 1–3	Diet

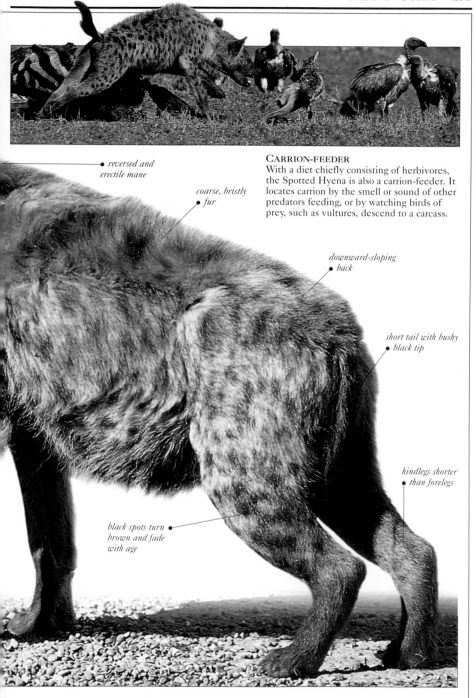

reversed and erectile mane

coarse, bristly fur

CARRION-FEEDER
With a diet chiefly consisting of herbivores, the Spotted Hyena is also a carrion-feeder. It locates carrion by the smell or sound of other predators feeding, or by watching birds of prey, such as vultures, descend to a carcass.

downward-sloping back

short tail with bushy black tip

hindlegs shorter than forelegs

black spots turn brown and fade with age

CARNIVORES
CATS

F EW MAMMAL FAMILIES display as much similarity among their members as shown by the 38 species of cats (Felidae). All are generally solitary, stealthy, and nocturnal, and are model hunters with lightning reflexes.

A typical cat has a round face, short muzzle, wide gape, large eyes, pointed ears, sharp teeth, and a lithe body, with powerful limbs and acute senses.

Cats are found all over Eurasia, Africa, and the Americas, from mountains to deserts and swamps. The seven "big" cats are the Tiger, Lion (a rare social species), Cheetah, Jaguar, Leopard, Snow Leopard, and Clouded Leopard. Traditionally all "small" cats have been grouped in one genus, *Felis*, although some authorities divide them into several different genera.

Family FELIDAE	Species *Felis silvestris*	Status Lower risk*

WILD CAT

longitudinal stripes on forehead •

long, dense fur •

Resembling a slightly larger, longer-furred (especially in winter) version of the domestic tabby cat, the Wild Cat varies from sandy to gray-brown. Active at night, and dawn, and dusk, it has several dens in tree hollows, thickets, or rock crevices, where it rests by day.

- **SIZE** Length: 20–30 in (50–75 cm). Weight: 6½–18 lb (3–8 kg).
- **OCCURRENCE** Europe, W. and C. Asia, and Africa. In mixed forest.
- **REMARK** The African subspecies, *Felis silvestris libyca*, is presumed to be the ancestor of the domestic cat.

EUROPE, ASIA, AFRICA

Social unit Solitary	Gestation 63–68 days	Young 1–8	Diet

Family FELIDAE	Species *Felis chaus*	Status Lower risk*

JUNGLE CAT

This species is more aptly called the Swamp or Reed Cat, since it hunts around marshes, riverbanks, and ponds – often near human habitations. Slender and long-legged, it has an unpatterned coat varying from yellow- or brownish gray to tawny red, and its tail has black rings and a black tip. This cat rests in thick vegetation or abandoned burrows, and is active by day and night.

plain • coat

AFRICA, ASIA

- **SIZE** Length: 20–37 in (50–94 cm). Weight: 8¾–35 lb (4–16 kg).
- **OCCURRENCE** N.E. Africa, W. to S.E. Asia. In dense woodland, near water.

tail with black • rings and tip

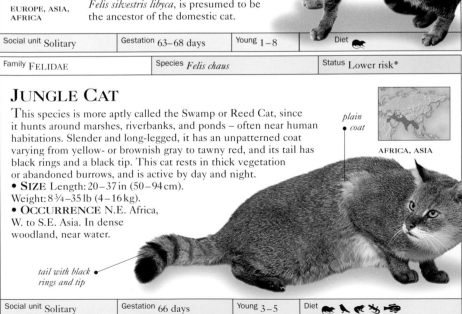

Social unit Solitary	Gestation 66 days	Young 3–5	Diet

Family FELIDAE	Species *Felis margarita*	Status Endangered*

SAND CAT

Adapted to extremely arid terrain, the Sand Cat survives on very little water, relying mostly on the moisture in its food, and has short-clawed, hairy paws for padding over sand dunes. Its fur is sandy to gray with a reddish streak from the corner of each eye, across the cheeks. The Sand Cat digs a burrow in the sand to shelter in by day, and hunts at night, dawn, and dusk, for gerbils, gerboas, other rodents, lizards, and snakes.
• **SIZE** Length:18–22½in (45–57cm). Weight:3¼–7¾lb (1.5–3.5kg).
• **OCCURRENCE** N. Africa, W., C., and S. Asia. In arid and sandy terrain.

ears set low on head

AFRICA, ASIA

sandy coat

stripes on legs

black tip on tail

broad paws

Social unit Solitary	Gestation 59–67 days	Young 2–4	Diet

Family FELIDAE	Species *Felis jacobita*	Status Endangered*

ANDEAN CAT

Small and sturdy, with a long, bushy tail, the Andean or Mountain Cat has thick, silvery gray fur, marked with brown or orange-yellow vertical stripes along its back, spots along its flanks, and dark bands on its legs and tail. This little-known species lives above the treeline.
• **SIZE** Length:23–25in (58–64cm). Weight:8¾lb (4kg).
• **OCCURRENCE** W. South America (Andes). In rocky, arid zones above 9,900–13,200ft (3,000–4,000m).
• **REMARK** This cat is not directly threatened by hunting and habitat loss like many other cats, but by the rapid decline of its main rodent prey – the Chinchilla and the Viscacha.

S. AMERICA

long and bushy tail

black bands around tail

soft, dense fur

Social unit Solitary	Gestation Not known	Young Not known	Diet

Family FELIDAE	Species *Felis serval*	Status Lower risk*

SERVAL

Resembling a small Cheetah, with its slim body and long limbs, the Serval has a yellow coat with dark spots that tend to merge into longitudinal stripes on the back and head. Its large ears are rounded, and its tail has several dark rings and a black tip. The male cats are generally larger than females. Preferring to live among reeds fringing wetlands, this cat hunts rats, birds, fish, frogs, and large insects such as locusts. It usually hunts at dusk, its long neck and legs raising its head above the tall grass, allowing it to spot its prey. Once the prey is located, the Serval can leap up to 13 ft (4 m) horizontally, and 3 1/4 ft (1m) vertically, to strike its victim with its forepaws. It uses a shrill cry to communicate, and also growls and purrs.
• **SIZE** Length: 23 1/2 – 39 in (60–100 cm). Weight: 20–40 lb (9–18 kg).
• **OCCURRENCE** W., C., and E. Africa. Along vegetated riverbanks and streams.
• **REMARK** Servals help farmers, since they prey on locusts and rats and rarely hunt livestock. Due to their concentration along riverbanks, they are exposed to the dangers of being hunted, and habitat loss.

HUNTED
Mercilessly hunted in farming areas of South Africa, the Serval is today considered to be rare in that country. It no longer occurs in populated areas.

longitudinal stripes on head

paler fur near mouth

dark spots on yellow coat

banded tail with black tip

long, thin legs

dark horizontal bars on legs

AFRICA

Social unit Solitary	Gestation 73 days	Young 2	Diet

Family FELIDAE	Species *Felis viverrinus*	Status Lower risk

FISHING CAT

Like a civet in proportions, with a long, stocky body and relatively short legs, the Fishing Cat is a semiaquatic hunter of fish, frogs, snakes, water insects, crabs, crayfish, and shellfish. However, its adaptations to water are largely behavioral, as its toes are only slightly webbed, and its teeth are not suitable for grasping slippery prey. It scoops prey from the water with its paws, often diving, and sometimes it suddenly surfaces under a waterbird. The Fishing Cat's coat is grizzled olive-gray with dark brown spots running along its body.
• SIZE Length: 30–34 in (75–86 cm). Weight: 18–31 lb (8–14 kg).
• OCCURRENCE India to S.E. Asia. Along lakes, riverbanks, and creeks; in mangrove swamps and marshes.
• REMARK Drainage of wetlands for agriculture is adversely affecting this species, which is dependent on water-edge habitats.

ASIA

dark stripes from forehead to neck
short legs
dark brown spots on fur

Social unit Solitary	Gestation 63 days	Young 1–4	Diet

Family FELIDAE	Species *Felis planiceps*	Status Vulnerable

FLAT-HEADED CAT

Slightly smaller than a domestic cat, the Flat-headed Cat lives around rivers, lakes, swamps, and canals. A semiaquatic predator of fish, it also takes shrimp, frogs, rodents, and small birds. Its toes are partially webbed and the claws cannot be retracted fully, and its upper premolars are large and sharp, helping it to grip slippery prey. The most outstanding feature of this cat, however, is its long and narrow skull with a flattened forehead and small, low-set ears. Its coat is dark brown, tinged silver.
• SIZE Length: 16–20 in (41–50 cm). Weight: 3¼–4½ lb (1½–2 kg).
• OCCURRENCE S.E. Asia. In riverine forest, swamps, and around irrigation canals.

small ears
eyes set close together

ASIA
brown fur, tinged silver

Social unit Solitary	Gestation 56 days	Young Not known	Diet

Family FELIDAE	Species *Felis marmorata*	Status Vulnerable*

MARBLED CAT

• *dark blotches on sides* • *short ears*

This cat resembles a small Clouded Leopard (see p. 288) in appearance. Varying from brownish gray to bright yellow or reddish brown, it has large dark blotches, outlined in black, along its sides. Its limbs and underparts have solid black dots, and its long, bushy tail is spotted and tipped with black. Little is known about the lifestyle of this cat, but it is thought to be nocturnal and partly arboreal. It preys mainly on birds, squirrels, and rats, and, probably, lizards and frogs.

limbs spotted with black •

• **SIZE** Length:18–21in (45–53cm). Weight:4½–11lb (2–5kg).
• **OCCURRENCE** N.E. India to S.E. Asia. In tropical forest.

• **REMARK** This cat is affected by human disturbance and habitat loss.

ASIA   *long, bushy tail* •

Social unit Solitary	Gestation 81 days	Young 1–4	Diet 🐦🐀🐁🦎

Family FELIDAE	Species *Felis wiedi*	Status Vulnerable*

MARGAY

An arboreal acrobat, the Margay is the only felid whose hindfeet can rotate through 180°, allowing it to hang upside down while descending head-first like a squirrel. Its coat is yellowish brown above and white below, with longitudinal rows of dark spots that are lighter in the middle. Resembling the Ocelot (see opposite), it is, however, more slender, with a longer tail. Its tree-dwelling prey include rats, squirrels, young sloths, birds, grubs, and spiders.

spots with light • *centres*

N., C., & S. AMERICA

large • *ears*

• **SIZE** Length:18–31in (46–79cm). Weight:5½–8¾lb (2.5–4kg).
• **OCCURRENCE** S. North America to Central and South America. In tropical rain forest.
• **REMARK** With the declining availability of Ocelot pelts, the Margay has become a highly sought-after small cat in the fur trade.

slender build •

long tail •

Social unit Solitary	Gestation 76–85 days	Young 1	Diet 🐸🐦🕷️🐚

Family FELIDAE	Species *Felis pardalis*	Status Lower risk*

OCELOT

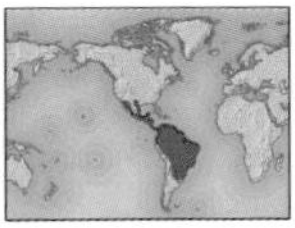

Typically catlike in its lifestyle, the Ocelot is extremely adaptable by nature. It inhabits a wide range of habitats from humid forests to dry scrubland – as long as there is dense cover provided by vegetation. Mainly terrestrial, it also climbs, jumps, and swims well, and rests by day in a tree hollow or on a branch. A nocturnal hunter, the Ocelot has a variety of prey such as rodents, birds, lizards, fish, bats, young deer, monkeys, armadillos, anteaters, and turtles.

N., C., &
S. AMERICA

- **SIZE** Length: 20–39 in (50–100 cm). Weight: 25–35 lb (11.5–16 kg).
- **OCCURRENCE** S. US to Central and South America. In tropical rain forest, grassland, and swamp.
- **REMARK** In the 1960s and 1970s, around 200,000 Ocelots were lost to the fur trade each year. Protected in much of its range, the Ocelot's numbers have risen – although it is now threatened by deforestation.

chainlike pattern of "rosettes"

BEAUTIFUL COAT
The Ocelot has a distinctive pattern of dark "rosettes" over its tawny yellow to reddish gray coat. Two black stripes mark its cheeks, and its tail is ringed.

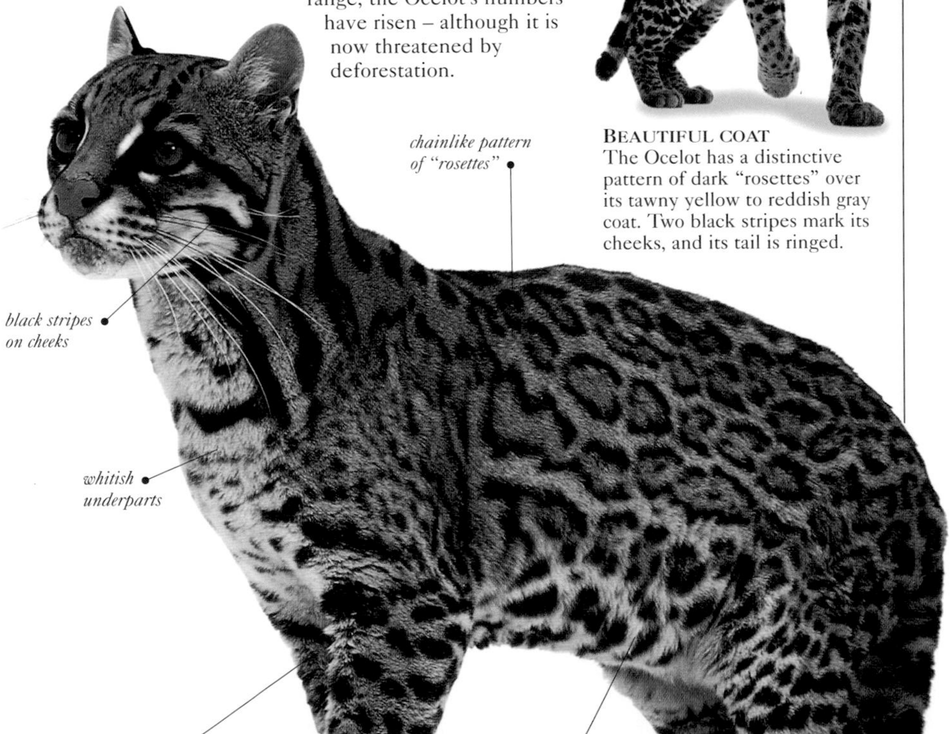

black stripes on cheeks

whitish underparts

tranverse bars on insides of legs

short, dense, velvety fur

Social unit Solitary	Gestation 79–85 days	Young 1–3	Diet

Family FELIDAE	Species *Felis rufus*	Status Lower risk*

BOBCAT

A short, "bobbed" tail gives this cat its name.
Mainly varying between shades of buff and brown,
its coat is spotted and lined with dark brown
and black. The Bobcat resembles the Eurasian
Lynx (see opposite), but is smaller, has more
slender legs, and its ears (distinctly marked with
black on the back) are less conspicuously tufted, or
not at all. As with the Lynx, it has a ruff of fur extending
from its ears to the jowls. The Bobcat is seen in a greater
variety of habitats than the Lynx. It is mainly nocturnal
and terrestrial, although it can climb with ease, and shelters
by day in a thicket, hollow tree, or crevice. It usually stalks
its prey with great stealth and seizes it after a swift leap.
Its diet consists mainly of rabbits and birds, although it
may hunt larger mammals such as deer in winter.
• **SIZE** Length: 26–43 in (65–110 cm).
Weight: 8¾–34 lb (4–15.5 kg).
• **OCCURRENCE** S. Canada, US, and Mexico.
In desert, brush, mixed woodland, and coniferous forest.
• **REMARK** Occasionally trapped and hunted by
humans, it has been exterminated over much of the
Ohio Valley, upper Mississippi Valley, and the southern
Great Lakes region.

N. AMERICA

MIXED SPOTS
The spots on the
coat vary in
density; they
are either
prominent all
over, or only
on the
underside.

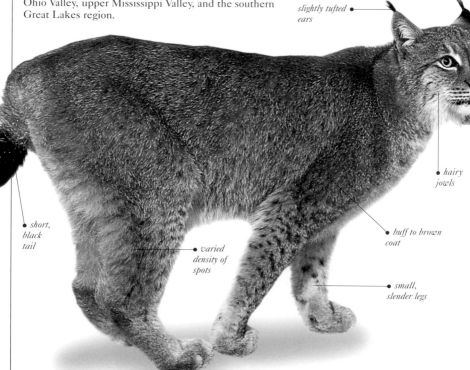

slightly tufted ears

hairy jowls

short, black tail

varied density of spots

buff to brown coat

small, slender legs

Social unit Solitary	Gestation 60–70 days	Young 2–3	Diet

Family FELIDAE	Species *Felis lynx*	Status Lower risk*

EURASIAN LYNX

Primarily an inhabitant of mixed forest, the Eurasian Lynx
has now been driven to open woods and rocky mountains due
to human presence and persecution. Its exceedingly dense coat
is more variable than that of any other cat. There are three
predominant patterns: mainly striped, mostly spotted
(as shown below), and plain. The background color
ranges from reddish brown or yellowish gray,
to almost white. Its underparts are usually white,
its ears have prominent black tufts, and its tail
is tipped black. Large feet like "snowshoes,"
which are thickly haired in winter, enable it
to walk on snow. In summer, the Eurasian Lynx's
coat is short with prominent markings, while in
winter it grows longer. The Eurasian Lynx is
able to kill prey three or four times its own size
and hunts mainly ungulates such as deer, goats,
and sheep. However, if these are scarce, it also
preys on pikas, hares, rodents, and birds.
• **SIZE** Length: 2 ½–4 ¼ ft (0.8–1.3 m).
Weight: 18–84 lb (8–38 kg).
• **OCCURRENCE** N. Europe to E. Asia.
In mixed forest and steppe.
• **REMARK** The Eurasian Lynx remains
rare in W. Europe despite conservation
efforts, since it is hunted by farmers and
frequently killed in road accidents.
It has also been observed that male
cubs have a low survival rate, likely
due to genetic reasons.

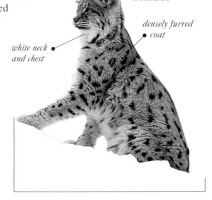

EURASIA

densely furred
coat

white neck
and chest

IBERIAN LYNX
Around half the size of the Eurasian Lynx,
and an endangered species, the Iberian Lynx
(Felis pardina) is found in S.W. Europe.

yellow-gray coat

variable pattern of
spots on coat

prominent black
tufts on ears

large eyes

large paws

whitish
underparts

relatively long
legs

Social unit Solitary	Gestation 67–74 days	Young 1–4	Diet

Family FELIDAE	Species *Felis caracal*	Status Lower risk*

CARACAL

Sometimes called the Desert Lynx because of the arid, scrubby areas that it inhabits, the Caracal is usually reddish brown, with a white chin, throat, and belly, and a narrow black band from the eye to the nose. Its distinctive pointed ears are black on the outside, and have long black tufts. The Caracal is well known for its ability to spring vertically and "bat" flying birds with its paws, often leaping as high as 10 ft (3 m). Largely nocturnal, this cat climbs and jumps well and is also believed to be the fastest feline of its size. It stalks and kills its prey after a quick dash or leap. The Caracal is territorial and marks its home range with urine. Usually solitary, it sometimes forms small groups comprising adults and young. It makes its dens in porcupine burrows, rocky crevices, or dense vegetation.

AFRICA, ASIA

• **SIZE** Length: 23½–36 in (60–91 cm).
Weight: 13–42 lb (6–19 kg).
• **OCCURRENCE** Africa, W., C., and S. Asia. In woodland, savanna, and scrubland.

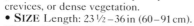

long ears with • black tufts

HUNTER'S FRIEND
Despite its ferocious appearance, the Caracal is easily tamed and is sometimes used to assist hunters in India and Iran.

• *long, slender body*

white chin •

Social unit Solitary	Gestation 69–81 days	Young 1–6	Diet 🐦 🌿

Family FELIDAE	Species *Felis aurata*	Status Lower risk*

AFRICAN GOLDEN CAT

This little-known, medium-sized inhabitant of tropical rain forest varies from gray to reddish brown, and may be faintly spotted or uniformly colored. Its cheeks, chin, and underparts are white, and it has long legs, a small head, and large paws. The male is usually larger than the female. Active during the day and night, it is mainly terrestrial but prefers areas near water. It feeds on prey such as rodents, hyraxes, small antelopes, and birds, which it usually stalks and kills with a sudden rush.

• **SIZE** Length: 24–39 in (61–100 cm). Weight:12–35 lb (5.5–16 kg).
• **OCCURRENCE** W. and C. Africa. In forest as well as mountains.

prominent ears

small head

reddish brown coat

AFRICA

Social unit Solitary	Gestation Not known	Young Not known	Diet

Family FELIDAE	Species *Felis yagouaroundi*	Status Lower risk

JAGUARUNDI

More mustelid than felid in appearance, with its pointed snout, long body, and short legs, the Jaguarundi varies from black in forested areas to pale gray-brown or red in dry shrubland. Much less nocturnal than most cats, it hunts in the morning and evening and forages mainly on the ground.
• **SIZE** Length: 22–30 in (55–77 cm). Weight:10–20 lb (4.5–9 kg).
• **OCCURRENCE** S. US to South America. In lowland forest and thickets.
• **REMARK** It is hunted and subject to habitat destruction.

small, flat head

very long, thick tail

N., C., & S. AMERICA

Social unit Solitary	Gestation 70–75 days	Young 1–4	Diet

Family FELIDAE	Species *Puma concolor*	Status Lower risk

PUMA

Also known as the Panther, Cougar, or Mountain Lion, this species is larger than some "big" cats (it is about the same size as the Leopard), but is thought to be closer to the "small" cats in classification. The Puma has an elongated body, small head, short face, and uniformly buff-colored fur. It has powerful and muscular limbs, and its hindlegs are longer than its forelegs. Throughout its range, the Puma's most important food is deer – especially Mule Deer and Elk. It stealthily stalks its prey, leaping upon the victim's back or seizing it after a rapid dash. It drags the carcass to a sheltered spot and eats its fill, then covers the remains with leaves and debris, for later consumption. This agile cat can leap to a height of 18 ft (5.5 m) from the ground and is also a good swimmer, although it prefers not to enter water. Usually solitary, individuals deliberately avoid each other except for a brief period of courtship. There is no fixed den, except when females are rearing their young. However, temporary shelter is taken in dense vegetation, rocky crevices, and caves. The Puma cannot roar like other big cats. Instead, it communicates by growls, hisses, and birdlike calls, and emits an eerily humanlike scream during courtship.
• **SIZE** Length: 3 ½ – 6 ½ ft (1.1– 2m).
Weight: 150 – 230 lb (67 – 105 kg).
• **OCCURRENCE** W. and S. North America, Central America, and South America. In montane coniferous forest, lowland tropical forest, swamps, grassland, dry brush country, or any other area with adequate cover and prey.
• **REMARK** Amazingly adaptable, the Puma has the greatest natural distribution of any indigenous mammal in the Western Hemisphere, with the exception of humans.

N., C., &
S. AMERICA

*coat uniformly
• buff-colored*

*prominent, large
• ears*

*spots on kitten's
• body*

SPOTTED KITTENS
Puma kittens have spots on their body until they are about 6 months old. They begin to feed on meat at six weeks and, if born in spring, are able to go hunting with the mother by fall, making their own kills by winter. However, they remain with their mother for several more months.

*muscular hindlegs •
for leaping*

Social unit Solitary	Gestation 90 – 96 days	Young 1– 6	Diet 🦌 🐀

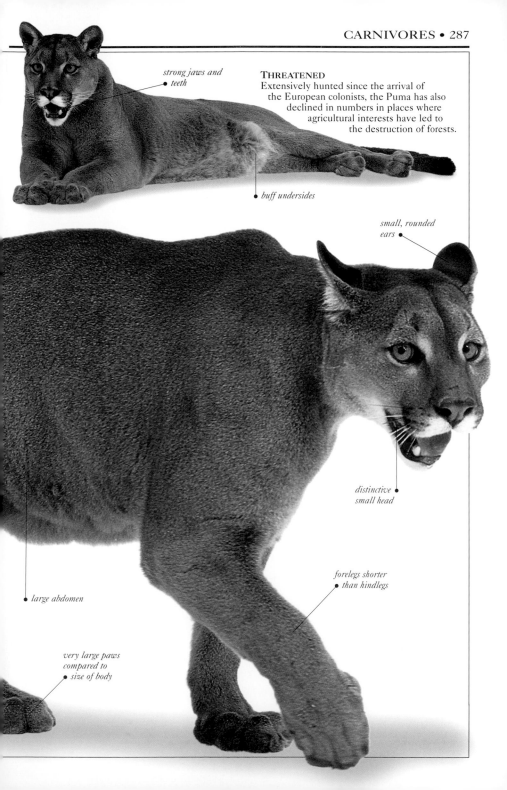

strong jaws and
teeth

THREATENED
Extensively hunted since the arrival of
the European colonists, the Puma has also
declined in numbers in places where
agricultural interests have led to
the destruction of forests.

buff undersides

small, rounded
ears

distinctive
small head

forelegs shorter
than hindlegs

large abdomen

very large paws
compared to
size of body

Family FELIDAE	Species *Neofelis nebulosa*	Status Vulnerable

CLOUDED LEOPARD

The smallest of the big cats, this species derives its name from the "cloudy," black-bordered, dark patches on its tawny, gray, or silver coat. Its forehead and legs are spotted, and the tail banded. Little is known about this elusive cat, but it is believed to be mainly arboreal, avoiding danger, resting, and stalking prey, from overhead branches. Its climbing skill rivals that of many small cats: it runs down trees head first or moves about among horizontal branches with its back to the ground.

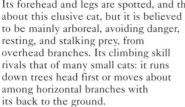

ASIA

dark "clouds"

• **SIZE** Length: 23½–43 in (60–110 cm). Weight: 35–51 lb (16–23 kg).
• **OCCURRENCE** S., S.E., and E. Asia. In tropical and temperate forest, mountains, and grassland.
• **REMARK** It is threatened by habitat loss and hunted excessively.

banded tail with spotted base

Social unit Solitary	Gestation 93 days	Young 1–5	Diet 🦌 🐾 🐀 🐟

Family FELIDAE	Species *Uncia uncia*	Status Endangered

SNOW LEOPARD

Large dark rosettes on a background of pale gray or creamy smoke-gray characterize this woolly cat. Like the Leopard (see pp. 290–291), it feeds on a wide range of prey. Often active by day, especially in the early morning and late afternoon, the Snow Leopard dens in a cavern or crevice.

solid spots on neck

• **SIZE** Length: 3¼–4¼ ft (1–1.3 m). Weight: 55–165 lb (25–75 kg).
• **OCCURRENCE** C., S., and E. Asia. In mountains and alpine meadows.
• **REMARK** Hunted for its fur, it is also threatened by the scarcity of its natural prey, and the encroachment of livestock on pastures.

small head

large rosettes on body

rings on tail

whitish below

ASIA

Social unit Solitary	Gestation 90–103 days	Young 1–5	Diet 🦌 🐀

Family FELIDAE	Species *Panthera onca*	Status Lower risk

JAGUAR

The only "big" cat found in the Americas, the Jaguar looks like the Leopard (see pp. 290–291), but its coat is patterned with dark-centered rosettes, and it is more squat and powerfully built, with a large, broad head, and heavily muscled quarters. Along the midline of its back is a row of elongated spots that may merge to form a solid line. Melanistic individuals are common; the spots of such animals may still be seen in bright light. Living in watery habitats – permanent swamps and seasonally flooded forest – the Jaguar is an excellent swimmer, even feeding on aquatic prey such as crocodilians. However, it hunts mostly on the ground, stalking or ambushing its prey and dragging it away to a sheltered spot to eat. Solitary and territorial, the Jaguar marks its range with urine and tree scrapes, communicating with others of its kind through a variety of sounds, including roars, grunts, and mews.

C. & S. AMERICA

• **SIZE** Length: 3½–6¼ ft (1.1–1.9 m). Weight: 79–350 lb (36–160 kg).
• **OCCURRENCE** Central to N. South America. In tropical forest, savanna, scrub, and wetland.
• **REMARK** Despite legal protection and reduced hunting for fur, the Jaguar is increasingly at risk from habitat loss and persecution as a predator, especially on cattle ranches.

elongated spots along midline of body

ROSETTES AND SPOTS
Varying from pale yellow through reddish yellow to reddish brown, the Jaguar has black rings or rosettes on its shoulders, back, and flanks. The head, neck, limbs, and underparts have black spots.

large, broad, head with smaller spots

compact, powerful body

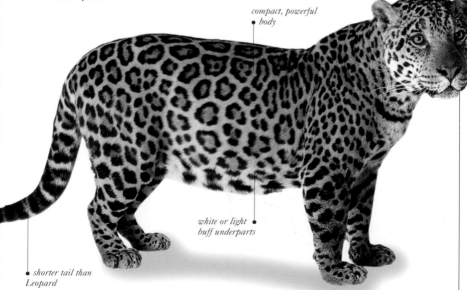

white or light buff underparts

shorter tail than Leopard

Social unit Solitary	Gestation 93–105 days	Young 1–4	Diet 🦌 🐾 🐟

Family FELIDAE	Species *Panthera pardus*	Status Lower risk

LEOPARD

AFRICA, ASIA

Widely distributed over different habitats, the Leopard is extremely varied both in appearance and in prey preference. Varying in color with habitat, these large cats may be pale yellow in deserts and deeper yellow in grassland. The Leopard's diet ranges from tiny creatures such as dung beetles to animals much larger than itself, such as antelopes. A large victim may provide enough food for two weeks, although such kills are usually made every three days, and twice as often by a female with cubs. The leopard's large head has powerful jaws that enable it to kill and dismember prey. An adept climber with immensely strong shoulders and forelimbs, the Leopard often drags its prey up into trees, for immediate consumption as well as for caching (hiding for future use). Up in the branches, it can eat undisturbed, the meat remaining safe from scavengers such as hyenas and jackals. Individual Leopards usually keep to a specific area, defending it against others, although the range of a male may include that of one or more females. The Leopard is a solitary animal, but there are reports of males remaining with females after mating and helping to rear the cubs. More adaptable than the Tiger to the presence of humans, the Leopard often hunts for prey within a few miles of large towns. It has survived well, despite numerous threats to its existence.

straw or grayish buff, to ocher and • chestnut coat

- **SIZE** Length: 3–6¼ ft (0.9–1.9 m). Weight: 82–200 lb (37–90 kg).
- **OCCURRENCE** W., C., S., E., and S.E. Asia, and Africa. In lowland forest, mountains, grassland, brush country, and semiarid desert.
- **REMARK** Persecuted as a predator, and for its beautiful spotted fur, the Leopard is also threatened by the loss of habitat and prey.

dark spots • arranged as rosettes on flanks

• ringed tail

Social unit Solitary	Gestation 90–105 days	Young 1–6	Diet 🦌 🐗 🐦 🦗

LIFE IN TREES
Usually nocturnal, the Leopard rests by day on the branches of a tree or remains hidden in dense vegetation. Large trees are important for a female with cubs, both to escape from danger and as a place to hide food for her young.

indistinct spots visible

BLACK PANTHER
The Leopard sometimes exhibits melanism, or an excessive amount of dark pigment in its skin and fur, but its spots are usually still visible.

small black spots on head

pale-centered rosettes on body

powerful jaw muscles

heavily muscled forelimbs

white underparts

Family FELIDAE	Species *Panthera tigris*	Status Endangered

TIGER

ASIA

The largest member of the cat family, the Tiger is instantly recognizable by its orange coat, vividly patterned with black stripes and white markings. Although eight subspecies of tiger have been recognized, three have become extinct since the 1950s. The remaining five subspecies are all endangered, some critically so. The Tiger's size, coat, color, and markings vary according to the subspecies. Once found as far west as eastern Turkey, the Tiger now exists in small, scattered populations from India to Vietnam, and in Siberia, China, and Sumatra. It lives in a variety of habitats, ranging from tropical forest to the freezing steppe, but its basic requirements are the same: dense cover, access to water, and sufficient prey. Tigers may require as much as 88 lb (40 kg) of meat at a time and return to a large kill for 3–6 days. Animals taken are mainly deer and pigs, cattle in certain regions, as well as monkeys, birds, reptiles, and fish. Although solitary, tigers also travel in groups, with a male occasionally resting and feeding with a female and her cubs. The Bengal Tiger (*Panthera tigris tigris* – shown here) is the most common subspecies and exhibits the classic tiger coat: deep orange with white undersides, cheeks, and eye areas, and distinctive black markings that help camouflage it in the tall jungle grass. The other existing subspecies are the Indo-Chinese Tiger *(P. t. corbetti)*, the Chinese Tiger *(P. t. amoyensis)*, the Sumatran Tiger *(P. t. sumatrae)*, and the Siberian Tiger *(P. t. altaica)*.

distinctive bla
stripes •

• SIZE Length: 4½–9¼ ft (1.4–2.8 m). Weight: 220–660 lb (100–300 kg).
• OCCURRENCE S. and E. Asia. In tropical and evergreen forest, mangrove swamps, grassland, savanna, and rocky country.
• REMARK Protected in most areas, the Tiger continues to be hunted illegally for its skin and its body parts. Several conservation projects now exist to monitor and safeguard Tiger populations.

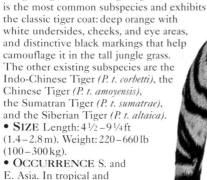

long, ringed tail •

Social unit Solitary	Gestation 93–111 days	Young 1–6	Diet 🦌 🐗 🐒 🐟

SIBERIAN TIGER
Found in Siberia and Manchuria, the Siberian Tiger (*Panthera tigris altaica*) is the biggest living cat. Its coat is the lightest among all tigers, and its fur is long and dense to protect it against the cold. Critically endangered, its numbers may be as low as 150–200.

large, rounded ears

relatively large head

white area around eyes

long, sensitive whiskers

creamy or white neck

SUMATRAN TIGER
The Sumatran Tiger *(Panthera tigris sumatrae)* is classified as critically endangered. Its numbers have decreased from 1,000 in the 1970s to about 400 in the wild, and around 194 in captivity.

sharp, retractable claws

Family FELIDAE	Species *Panthera leo*	Status Vulnerable

LION

This "big" cat is unique among the usually solitary felids in forming long-term social bonds, with related females and their young forming a group called a pride, and remaining together over several generations. Around two or three unrelated males or four or five related males form a loose "coalition" and defend a large area against other coalitions of males. They mate with the pride occupying this territory for a period of two or three years, until they are driven out by a contending group of males. The Lion usually hunts by a low stalk, alternately creeping and freezing, making the best use of cover. Pride members may hunt cooperatively, fanning out to close in on large quarry such as Wildebeest, Impala, zebra, or buffalo. Males living with a pride let the females hunt, but have first access to the kill. Varying widely in color from light buff and silvery gray, to yellowish red and dark ocher-brown, the Lion is instantly recognizable by the male's magnificent mane.

• **SIZE** Length: 5 ½ – 8 ¼ ft (1.7–2.5 m).
Weight: 330–550 lb (150–250 kg).
• **OCCURRENCE** Africa and S. Asia. In grassy plains, savanna, open woodland, and scrub.
• **REMARK** Seriously threatened by the expansion of human activities and persecution, the Lion has become extinct in Asia, except in the Gir Forest in N.W. India.

relatively large head •

AFRICA, ASIA

LION CUBS
Sometimes born with their eyes open, Lion cubs follow their mother after three months, beginning to participate in kills at about 11 months. Females of the pride tend to give birth around the same time, and suckle each other's young.

female has • no mane

yellow, brown, or reddish brown mane darkens • with age

uniform tawny • coat

Social unit Social	Gestation 110–119 days	Young 1–6	Diet

Family FELIDAE	Species *Acinonyx jubatus*	Status Vulnerable

CHEETAH

AFRICA, ASIA

The fastest land animal in the world, the Cheetah can reach a speed of over 60 mph (100 kph), for a burst of 10–12 seconds, before it begins to overheat. If its prey, consisting chiefly of small and medium-sized ungulates, can stay ahead for longer than this, it invariably escapes. Once the Cheetah overtakes its prey, it knocks the animal down by the sheer speed of its charge, seizes it by the throat, and strangles it. A female with cubs may make a kill every day, while lone adults hunt every 2–5 days. More sociable than any of the other "big" cats, except Lions, siblings leave their mother at 13–20 months, but may stay together for longer; brothers sometimes live with each other for years. The Cheetah has a slim body, long legs, and a rounded head with distinctive black stripes running down its face. Its coat is yellowish, with small black spots – the cats found in the desert being paler with smaller spots. The King Cheetah from S.E. Africa has the largest spots.
• **SIZE** Length: 3 ½ – 5 ft (1.1–1.5 m). Weight: 46–160 lb (21–72 kg).
• **OCCURRENCE** Africa and W. Asia. In grassland and arid bush.
• **REMARK** The Cheetah seems to be more vulnerable than other big cats to environmental changes brought about by human activity. Originally found from the Arabian Peninsula to C. India, and throughout most of Africa, it has now virtually disappeared from Asia, except the western parts.

very distinctive black face
• *stripes*

small black spots on coat •

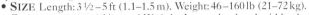

HUNTING
The Cheetah is unusual among cats in stalking rather than ambushing its prey, and then charging from about 230–330 ft (70–100 m) away.

tail with black • *rings*

• *tawny to pale buff or grayish white coat*

very long • *legs*

• *pale buff to white underside*

Social unit Solitary/Pair	Gestation 90–95 days	Young 1–8	Diet

SEALS AND SEA LIONS

T HE ORDER PINNIPEDIA (meaning "flipper-feet"), which is sometimes incorporated as a suborder of Carnivora, contains 34 species in three families: seals (Phocidae), sea lions and fur seals (Otariidae), and the single species of walrus (Odobenidae).

Nearly all have a tapering muzzle, large eyes, a short neck that merges into a smooth, torpedo-shaped body, and four flipperlike limbs. Pinnipeds are swift, graceful, underwater predators, but return to land or floating ice during the annual breeding season.

Seals have no external ear flaps, and their rear flippers point backward; they wriggle, or "hump," on land. The sea lion family has visible ear flaps, and rear flippers that can rotate, for waddling on land. The Walrus has almost no hair and possesses long tusks.

There are species of seals and sea lions in all the world's oceans, while the Walrus is found in the Arctic region.

Family OTARIIDAE	Species *Zalophus californianus*	Status Vulnerable*

CALIFORNIA SEA LION

Rarely straying away from the coast, this sea lion often enters harbors and estuaries for food and shelter. The male has a peaked head and is dark brown; females and juveniles are a uniform tan. Its main prey is shoaling fish, caught in two-minute dives of about 245 ft (75 m) deep. During the breeding season (May to July), males fight for small territories on the beach and around rock pools. However, after two weeks they swim away to feed, and, on returning, must battle again for a new territory.
• **SIZE** Length: Up to 7¾ ft (2.4 m). Weight: 610–860 lb (275–390 kg).
• **OCCURRENCE** California and Galapagos Islands. Along coastlines.
• **REMARK** The common performing seal at marine parks, it can apparently be taught to understand artificial language as with dolphins and chimpanzees.

N. AMERICA, GALAPAGOS ISLANDS

doglike muzzle with whiskers •

paddlelike flippers •

sleek, furred body •

Social unit Variable	Gestation 11 months	Young 1	Diet

Family OTARIIDAE	Species *Arctocephalus pusillus*	Status Locally common

SOUTH AFRICAN FUR SEAL

There are two subspecies of the South African or Australian Fur Seal: the one found off South Africa is darker gray-brown and dives twice as deep as its counterpart found off the Australian coast. Males fight for territory before the females come ashore, and the cows too establish their own territory for pupping. The pups play together in nursery pools, while the mothers go to sea to feed for a few days at a time.

prominent ear flaps

muzzle pointed and slightly upturned

back flippers used for waddling

- **SIZE** Length: 6–7½ft (1.8–2.3 m). Weight: 440–790 lb (200–360 kg).
- **OCCURRENCE** S. Africa, S.E. Australia, Tasmania, and islands off the Bass Straits. In open oceans and along coastlines.
- **REMARK** Namibia allows limited commercial hunting of this seal each year, while Australia has banned its hunting since 1975.

AFRICA, AUSTRALIA

smooth, sleek coat

Social unit Variable	Gestation 11¾ months	Young 1	Diet 🐟 🦐 🐛

Family OTARIIDAE	Species *Phocarctos hookeri*	Status Vulnerable

NEW ZEALAND SEA LION

Also known as Hooker's Sea Lion, this species is restricted to a few islands south of New Zealand. The male is dark brown with silvery gray hindquarters and a shoulder mane, while the females and juveniles are silvery or brownish gray above and yellowish tan beneath. Foraging up to 95 miles (150 km) out at sea, it travels ⅔ mile (1 km) inland to rest among cliffs or trees. An opportunistic feeder and expert diver, its diet includes fish, squid, crustaceans, penguins, and even seal pups. Although it forms dense breeding colonies, it is solitary at sea.

ear flaps or "pinnae"

NEW ZEALAND

broad muzzle

- **SIZE** Length: 6½–11 ft (2–3.3 m). Weight: 660–990 lb (300–450 kg).
- **OCCURRENCE** Islands south of New Zealand. In open ocean and along coastlines.
- **REMARK** Now protected all over its range, this seal has been hunted since prehistoric times for its meat, skin, and oil.

Social unit Variable	Gestation 11¾ months	Young 1	Diet 🐟 🦐 🐧 🐢 🐛 🪝

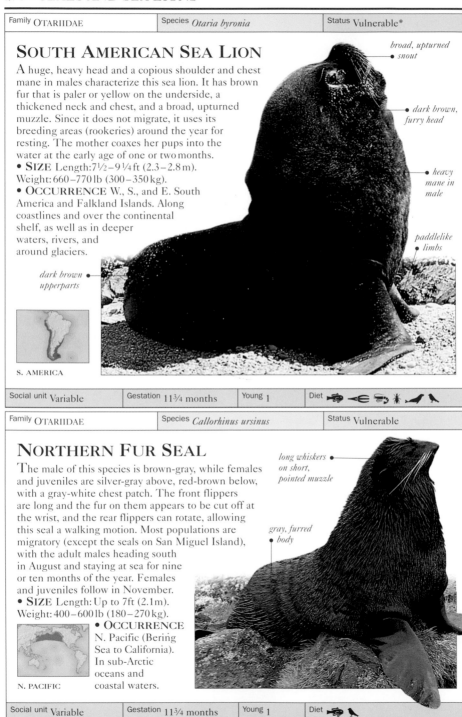

Family OTARIIDAE	Species *Otaria byronia*	Status Vulnerable*

SOUTH AMERICAN SEA LION

A huge, heavy head and a copious shoulder and chest
mane in males characterize this sea lion. It has brown
fur that is paler or yellow on the underside, a
thickened neck and chest, and a broad, upturned
muzzle. Since it does not migrate, it uses its
breeding areas (rookeries) around the year for
resting. The mother coaxes her pups into the
water at the early age of one or two months.
• **SIZE** Length:7½–9¼ft (2.3–2.8m).
Weight: 660–770lb (300–350kg).
• **OCCURRENCE** W., S., and E. South
America and Falkland Islands. Along
coastlines and over the continental
shelf, as well as in deeper
waters, rivers, and
around glaciers.

broad, upturned snout

dark brown, furry head

heavy mane in male

paddlelike limbs

dark brown upperparts

S. AMERICA

Social unit Variable	Gestation 11¾ months	Young 1	Diet

Family OTARIIDAE	Species *Callorhinus ursinus*	Status Vulnerable

NORTHERN FUR SEAL

The male of this species is brown-gray, while females
and juveniles are silver-gray above, red-brown below,
with a gray-white chest patch. The front flippers
are long and the fur on them appears to be cut off at
the wrist, and the rear flippers can rotate, allowing
this seal a walking motion. Most populations are
migratory (except the seals on San Miguel Island),
with the adult males heading south
in August and staying at sea for nine
or ten months of the year. Females
and juveniles follow in November.
• **SIZE** Length: Up to 7ft (2.1m).
Weight: 400–600lb (180–270kg).
• **OCCURRENCE**
N. Pacific (Bering
Sea to California).
In sub-Arctic
oceans and
coastal waters.

long whiskers on short, pointed muzzle

gray, furred body

N. PACIFIC

Social unit Variable	Gestation 11¾ months	Young 1	Diet

Family ODOBENIDAE	Species *Odobenus rosmarus*	Status Vulnerable*

WALRUS

Large and bulky, the Walrus has a blunt, thickly whiskered muzzle that widens rapidly to a broad body, and then tapers again at the tail, which is embedded in a web of skin. Its front flippers resemble those of sea lions, whereas the back flippers resemble those of seals; its rough, creased skin is gray to cinnamon-brown. The male Walrus is twice the size of the female, and its upper canines grow longer than the female's, to almost 3 ¼ ft (1m) in length. The Walrus dives more than 330 ft (100 m) deep, for over 25 minutes, and locates its prey with sensory nerves in its whiskers and snout. It sucks up food from the seabed, first rooting for it with its nose, aided by jets of water squirted from its mouth. Walruses remain huddled on land or ice floes in groups of 100, breaking up into smaller groups of 10 when at sea. During breeding, males establish small territories in water next to females perched on ice floes, using their tusks to defend their territories. Walruses migrate to warmer waters in April and May.

ARCTIC

COMMUNAL SUNBATHING
The skin color of Walruses basking in the sun shows through the animals' short fur and flushes rose-red, as the blood vessels dilate to absorb the maximum heat.

• **SIZE** Length: 9 ¾–12 ft (3–3.6 m). Weight: 1 ⅛–2 tons (1.2–2 tonnes).
• **OCCURRENCE** Arctic Ocean (circumpolar). In shallow, continental shelf water and along coastlines.

canines become tusks in males •

• *small head*

thick, creased skin •

tapering rump •

Social unit Social	Gestation 15 months	Young 1	Diet 🦗 🐟 🐦

Family PHOCIDAE	Species *Monachus monachus*	Status Critically endangered

MEDITERRANEAN MONK SEAL

This extremely rare species has a dark brown coat, which is said to resemble a friar's robe – hence the name Monk Seal. It has a small head and robust body. Since its hindflippers do not rotate, it cannot walk on land. One of the least social seals out of water, it is found in small, widely separated groups or mother–pup pairs. Diet comprises fish such as sardines, tuna, eels, and mullet, as well as lobster and octopus.

MEDITERRANEAN, BLACK SEA, ATLANTIC

- **SIZE** Length:7¾–9¼ft (2.4–2.8m). Weight: 550–880lb (250–400kg).
- **OCCURRENCE** Mediterranean, Black Sea, and Atlantic (N.W. Africa). Along coastlines.
- **REMARK** Disturbed by tourist activity, this seal shelters in sea caves. However, cave collapses, overfishing, pollution, and exposure to viral infection pose serious threats to its existence.

robust body with
• short flippers

compressed muzzle •

rear flippers have several branches •

Social unit Variable	Gestation 11 months	Young 1	Diet 🐟 ◀🦑 🦐

Family PHOCIDAE	Species *Lobodon carcinophagus*	Status Common

CRABEATER SEAL

Long and lithe, with a silver-gray to yellow-brown coat dotted with irregular darker spots and rings, the Crabeater Seal is oddly named, since it eats mainly krill. Its small head tapers to a thin muzzle that has short, inconspicuous whiskers. A typical seal, it has no external ears, and cannot walk on land. To feed, it dives down to a depth of 130ft (40m) for around five minutes.

slim,
streamlined
• body

ANTARCTIC, SUB-ANTARCTIC

- **SIZE** Length:7¼–8½ft (2.2–2.6m). Weight: 490lb (220kg).
- **OCCURRENCE** Antarctica. In open ocean and along coastlines.
- **REMARK** This seal is one of the most abundant and fastest-swimming seal species.

moderately small •
head with long,
pointed muzzle

Social unit Variable	Gestation 11 months	Young 1	Diet 🦐 🦐 🐟

Family PHOCIDAE	Species *Hydrurga leptonyx*	Status Locally common

LEOPARD SEAL

This seal is silver to dark gray with variable spots. It has a sinuous body and massive, reptilelike head that lacks a forehead, and a wide, deep lower jaw. It is widest around the shoulders, and its entire body, including the flippers, is furred. Unusually for a seal, it swims with its front flippers, which are tipped with claws. Its large canine teeth enable it to feed on smaller seals, penguins, and other birds.
- **SIZE** Length: 8¼–10 ft (2.5–3.2 m). Weight: 440–1,000 lb (200–455 kg).
- **OCCURRENCE** Antarctica, especially high southern latitudes. In polar and subpolar waters, and on pack ice and islands.
- **REMARK** The Leopard Seal is the largest of the four Antarctic seal species.

ANTARCTIC, SUB-ANTARCTIC

silver-gray coat with
• *variable spots*

massive
head •

• *paddlelike*
back flippers not
used in swimming

pale •
underside

wide and •
deep lower jaw

Social unit Solitary	Gestation 11 months	Young 1	Diet

Family PHOCIDAE	Species *Leptonychotes weddelli*	Status Locally common

WEDDELL SEAL

Bulky, with a small head and flippers, the Weddell Seal has a blunt muzzle with a few short whiskers, close-set eyes, and an upturned mouthline. Its coat is dark silvery gray above and off-white below, with variable dark and light patches. An expert diver, it reaches depths of 1,600 ft (500 m), staying underwater for over an hour. Its modified upper incisors are used to cut breathing holes in ice. This seal does not migrate, but moves with the ice front.
- **SIZE** Length: 8¼–9½ ft (2.5–2.9 m). Weight: 880–1,320 lb (400–600 kg).
- **OCCURRENCE** Antarctica (circumpolar). In open ocean and along coastlines.
- **REMARK** Named after the sealer, Captain James Weddell, who wrote about an encounter with this seal in 1820, today the Weddell Seal is protected from commercial hunting.

• small
flippers

proportionately
• small head

ANTARCTIC

variable •
patches
on coat

Social unit Variable	Gestation 10¼ months	Young 1	Diet

Family PHOCIDAE	Species *Mirounga leonina*	Status Locally common

SOUTHERN ELEPHANT-SEAL

The male Elephant-seal has an inflatable trunklike nose from which it earns its name. Both sexes have a uniform light to dark silver-gray coat, with a broad head, muzzle, jaw, and neck. Males are four or five times heavier than the females. They fight rivals during the two-month mating season by rearing up on their hindquarters and roaring loudly, inflating their noses in display. This is followed by a butting and slapping fight that may last from a few seconds to half an hour, leaving most animals battle-scarred. The victorious male or "beachmaster" has a harem of 20–40 cows, although even larger ones of 100 are known to occur. A creature of the open seas, this seal spends ten months (apart from breeding and molting time) foraging over wide areas. Diving continuously day and night, each dive lasting an average of 20–22 minutes, it spends 90 percent of its time underwater.
• SIZE Length:14–20 ft (4.2 –6 m).
Weight: 2 ⅛–4 ⅞ tons (2.2 –5 tonnes).
• OCCURRENCE Antarctica. North of seasonally shifting ice and around sub-Antarctic islands.
• REMARK The male Elephant Seal is the largest member of its order (Pinnipedia).

FEMALE FEATURES
The female seal has a fleshy, blunt nose instead of a proboscis. She nurses her pup for 19–23 days, during which time she does not leave the beach and loses 35 percent of her weight.

proboscislike nose in male, inflated during • courtship displays

uniformly gray • body

broad head • and neck

ANTARCTIC

Social unit Variable	Gestation 11 ¼ months	Young 1	Diet

| Family PHOCIDAE | Species *Ommatophoca rossii* | Status Vulnerable |

ROSS SEAL

With the shortest fur of any seal, the Ross Seal is dark gray to chestnut-brown, with broad, dark bands along its body. It has a distinctively blunt muzzle, wide head, and long rear flippers. Less social than other seals, on ice it is found alone or in mother–pup pairs. The smallest of Antarctic seals, it is also one of the rarest, and little is known about its lifestyle.
• SIZE Length:
5½–9¾ ft (1.7–3 m).
Weight: 290–470 lb (130–215 kg).
• OCCURRENCE Antarctica, especially Ross Sea. In open waters and along coastlines.

short, sleek hair

dark gray to chestnut coat

ANTARCTIC

| Social unit Solitary | Gestation 11 months | Young 1 | Diet |

| Family PHOCIDAE | Species *Cystophora cristata* | Status Locally common |

HOODED SEAL

This seal has a fleshy muzzle that droops over its mouth. The male intimidates rivals by inflating its nasal cavity to double the size of its head and by extruding a membrane from the left nostril that also blows up like a red balloon.
• SIZE Length: 2.5–2.7 m (8¼–8¾ ft).
Weight: 300–410 kg (660–900 lb).
• OCCURRENCE N. Atlantic to the Arctic Ocean. In open waters and on pack ice.
• REMARK The pup is weaned earliest of any mammal (four or five days).

uneven blotches on coat

N. ATLANTIC, ARCTIC

short, angular flippers

| Social unit Variable | Gestation 11½ months | Young 1 | Diet |

| Family PHOCIDAE | Species *Halichoerus grypus* | Status Common |

GRAY SEAL

There are three populations of Gray Seals: those found in the N.W. Atlantic are heavier and breed from December to February; those in the N.E. Atlantic breed from July to December; whereas those from the Baltic Sea breed from February to April. The male is brownish gray, and the female is pale gray.
• SIZE Length: 6½–8¼ ft (2–2.5 m). Weight: 370–680 lb (170–310 kg).
• OCCURRENCE N. Atlantic and Baltic Sea. In open waters and along coasts.

patchy, brown-gray coat in males

N. ATLANTIC, BALTIC SEA

furred flippers

wide front flippers

| Social unit Variable | Gestation 11¼ months | Young 1 | Diet |

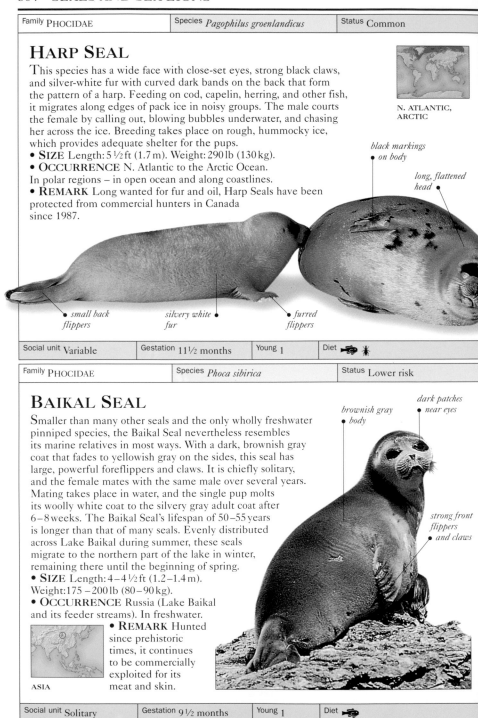

Family PHOCIDAE	Species *Pagophilus groenlandicus*	Status Common

HARP SEAL

This species has a wide face with close-set eyes, strong black claws, and silver-white fur with curved dark bands on the back that form the pattern of a harp. Feeding on cod, capelin, herring, and other fish, it migrates along edges of pack ice in noisy groups. The male courts the female by calling out, blowing bubbles underwater, and chasing her across the ice. Breeding takes place on rough, hummocky ice, which provides adequate shelter for the pups.
• SIZE Length: 5½ft (1.7 m). Weight: 290 lb (130 kg).
• OCCURRENCE N. Atlantic to the Arctic Ocean.
In polar regions – in open ocean and along coastlines.
• REMARK Long wanted for fur and oil, Harp Seals have been protected from commercial hunters in Canada since 1987.

N. ATLANTIC, ARCTIC

black markings on body

long, flattened head

small back flippers

silvery white fur

furred flippers

Social unit Variable	Gestation 11½ months	Young 1	Diet

Family PHOCIDAE	Species *Phoca sibirica*	Status Lower risk

BAIKAL SEAL

Smaller than many other seals and the only wholly freshwater pinniped species, the Baikal Seal nevertheless resembles its marine relatives in most ways. With a dark, brownish gray coat that fades to yellowish gray on the sides, this seal has large, powerful foreflippers and claws. It is chiefly solitary, and the female mates with the same male over several years. Mating takes place in water, and the single pup molts its woolly white coat to the silvery gray adult coat after 6–8 weeks. The Baikal Seal's lifespan of 50–55 years is longer than that of many seals. Evenly distributed across Lake Baikal during summer, these seals migrate to the northern part of the lake in winter, remaining there until the beginning of spring.
• SIZE Length: 4–4½ft (1.2–1.4 m).
Weight: 175–200 lb (80–90 kg).
• OCCURRENCE Russia (Lake Baikal and its feeder streams). In freshwater.
• REMARK Hunted since prehistoric times, it continues to be commercially exploited for its meat and skin.

dark patches near eyes

brownish gray body

strong front flippers and claws

ASIA

Social unit Solitary	Gestation 9½ months	Young 1	Diet

Family PHOCIDAE	Species *Phoca vitulina*	Status Common

COMMON SEAL

The most widespread pinniped, the Common or Harbor Seal has a plump body and a small, catlike head with a slight forehead and nostrils that form a V-shaped pattern. Its coat ranges from light to dark gray or brown, and has spots, rings, and blotches all over. The breeding season varies regionally, and the pups are able to crawl and swim almost within an hour of birth. There are at least five subspecies of Common Seal. One of them, the Ungava Seal, lives in freshwater in N. Quebec, Canada.
• **SIZE** Length: 4½–6¼ ft (1.4–1.9 m). Weight: 120–370 lb (55–170 kg).
• **OCCURRENCE** N. Atlantic and N. Pacific, from the polar to temperate region. In lakes and rivers, along coastlines and the continental shelf.
• **REMARK** The Common Seal feeds on many fish that are exploited commercially, leading to seal deaths in fishing nets. In several countries, it is legal to shoot these seals to protect fish farms.

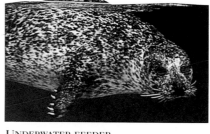

UNDERWATER FEEDER
The Common Seal feeds near the shore, diving to depths of less than 330 ft (100 m) for about 3–5 minutes. It is an opportunistic forager, feeding on herring, sandeels, sandgobies, hake, whiting, and crustaceans.

large eyes set back on head •

• short flippers

• prominent whiskers

distinctive spots, ring • markings, and blotches on body

• light to dark gray, or brown coat

N. PACIFIC, N. ATLANTIC

thin, hooked claws • on flippers

Social unit Variable	Gestation 11¾ months	Young 1	Diet 🐟 🦐 🦑

ELEPHANTS

FOR MANY YEARS, the single order Proboscidea was considered to contain one living family, Elephantidae, which had two herbivorous species, the African and Asiatic (Indian) Elephants. However, the African Forest Elephant, found deep in thickly wooded areas of West-Central Africa, has now been differentiated as a separate species from the African Elephant, which frequents bush, savanna, and scattered forest from the east to the south.

All elephants are instantly recognized by their great size, thick and almost hairless skin, huge head and ear flaps, a very long, mobile trunk (the elongated nose and upper lip), bulky body, and four pillarlike legs.

The upper incisors gradually grow into tusks in all species, but in adult Asiatic females they rarely protrude from the mouth. Elephants live in family-based groups dominated by a senior female, the matriarch.

Family ELEPHANTIDAE	Species *Elephas maximus*	Status Endangered

ASIATIC ELEPHANT

With smaller ears than its African counterpart (see pp. 308–309), the Asiatic Elephant has a single finger-like, gripping extremity at the tip of its trunk. Its tusks are relatively small and are absent, or do not protrude beyond the lips, in females. Some males (called "makhnas") lack tusks. Elephants locate, select, and pluck food with the trunk-tip, in conjunction with the tusks and forefoot, before placing it in the mouth. Young elephants learn the various techniques involved in food gathering by imitation and practice. Highly intelligent social herbivores, elephants are found in complex, matriarchal societies, made up of mothers with their offspring and juvenile females, all sharing close bonds. Young males roam in bachelor herds, while a dominant tusker mates with the adult females of the herd.

convex back

- **SIZE** Length: Up to 11 ft (3.5 m). Weight: 2–4⅞ tons (2–5 tonnes).
- **OCCURRENCE** S. and S.E. Asia. In forest, close to water.
- **REMARK** The elephant population is adversely affected by habitat loss and the disruption of traditional herd routes by human activity.

SEMIDOMESTICATED
Although this elephant has lived in close proximity with humans for centuries, it has never been wholly domesticated. Until very recently, each generation of working elephants has been captured from the wild.

tail with dark hair at the tip

Social unit Social	Gestation Up to 22 months	Young 1	Diet 🌱 🍃 🌿 🍎 🌾 🌼

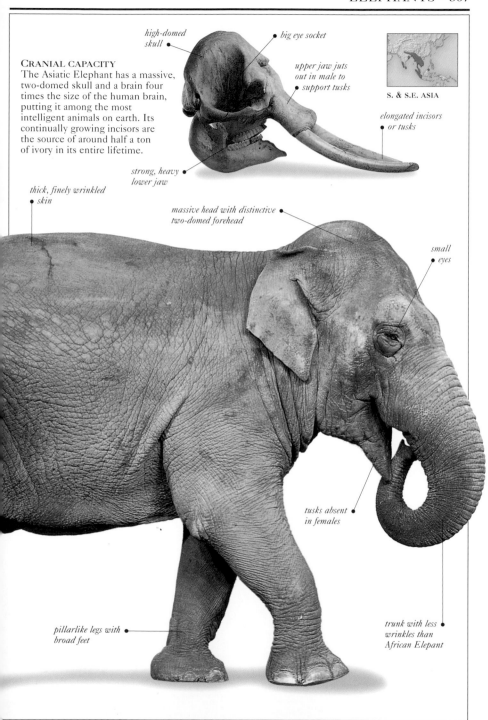

high-domed
skull

big eye socket

CRANIAL CAPACITY
The Asiatic Elephant has a massive,
two-domed skull and a brain four
times the size of the human brain,
putting it among the most
intelligent animals on earth. Its
continually growing incisors are
the source of around half a ton
of ivory in its entire lifetime.

upper jaw juts
out in male to
support tusks

S. & S.E. ASIA

elongated incisors
or tusks

strong, heavy
lower jaw

thick, finely wrinkled
skin

massive head with distinctive
two-domed forehead

small
eyes

tusks absent
in females

pillarlike legs with
broad feet

trunk with less
wrinkles than
African Elepant

Family ELEPHANTIDAE	Species *Loxodonta africana*	Status Endangered

AFRICAN ELEPHANT

The largest living land animal, the African, Bush, or Savanna Elephant, as it is variously called, lives in a range of habitats, from desert to high rain forest. Its huge, prominent ears are much larger than those of its Asian cousin, and both sexes have forward-pointing tusks, which are sometimes used to loosen the mineral-rich soil that it eats as a dietary supplement. The male may be nearly twice the weight of the female, and its tusks are thicker at the base. Feeding for 20 hours each day, this elephant consumes vegetation up to about 5 percent of its body weight. It also visits a water source each day to drink, bathe, and wallow. Foraging over large areas, a herd of elephants may cause dramatic changes to the ecosystem, especially during drought. Like the Asian Elephant (see pp. 306–307), the African Elephant lives in matriarchal societies.

AFRICA

huge ears, the biggest in all living beings

• **SIZE** Length:13–16 ft (4–5 m). Weight: 3⅞–6⅞ tons (4–7 tonnes).
• **OCCURRENCE** Sub-Saharan Africa. In grassland, desert, tropical forest, and wetlands; near lakes and rivers.
• **REMARK** The African Elephant (especially the male tusker) is widely hunted for its tusks, which are a major source of ivory.

large body with blackish, wrinkled skin

Social unit Social	Gestation Up to 22 months	Young 1	Diet 🌱 🍃 🌿 🍎 🪶 ⋮⋮

PROTECTING THE YOUNG
Vulnerable to large predators such as lions, the elephant calf may remain with its mother for the first three or four years of its life. It is also protected from danger by other females (an older sister or female cousin) in the herd.

large ears flapped constantly to reduce body heat

large, forward-curving, tusks

thick legs with flat-soled feet

trunk consists of modified nose and upper lip

AFRICAN FOREST ELEPHANT
Formerly regarded as a subspecies of the African Elephant, the smaller and lighter African Forest Elephant (*Loxodonta cyclotis*), found deep within dense rain forest vegetation, was recently accorded the status of a separate species.

HYRAXES

I N A CURIOUS twist of evolution, hyraxes resemble small-eared rabbits in size and shape, but their detailed anatomy and genetics seem to suggest that they are more closely related to primitive hoofed mammals. The eight species in the order Hyracoidea, some of which are also known as dassies or conies, are found in Africa and the Middle East.

Certain species are arboreal and tend to live singly or in small groups. Others prefer rocky outcrops and are more gregarious. All hyraxes are opportunistic herbivores, switching diet with the season and plant availability. Their climbing abilities are aided by secretions from glands under their feet, which improve grip on smooth surfaces. Another hyrax feature is their poor control of body temperature, compared to most mammals. They are often seen warming themselves in the sun or cooling down in the shade, like reptiles.

Family PROCAVIIDAE	Species *Procavia capensis*	Status Locally common

ROCK HYRAX

Also called the Rock Dassie, the Rock Hyrax has a stout body with short, dense, gray or gray-brown fur above, and a paler underside. It lives in colonies of 4–40, which consist of one dominant male, other males, females, and young. Found in a variety of habitats, it favors rocky outcrops and crags, where it makes a grass-lined nest. It is hunted for its meat and pelt by local people.

small, rounded ears •

• gray or grayish brown coat

• SIZE Body length:12–23 in (30–58 cm). Tail: 8–12 in (20–31 cm).
• OCCURRENCE S. and E. Africa and W. Asia. In grassland, desert, forest, and hills.

paler • underside

AFRICA, ASIA

Social unit Social	Gestation 7–8 months	Young 1–6	Diet 🗲 🌿 🎋

Family PROCAVIIDAE	Species *Dendrohyrax arboreus*	Status Vulnerable

TREE HYRAX

Gray-brown with buff underparts, this hyrax has a yellowish patch on its rump. Its head, legs, and tail are relatively small for its stout body. Also known as the Tree Dassie, this species lives among trees, shrubs, and creepers, nesting in tree-holes and rarely feeding on the ground.
• SIZE Body length:16–28 in (40–70 cm). Tail: 3/8–1 1/4 in (1–3 cm).
• OCCURRENCE E. and S. Africa. In tropical forest and mountains.
• REMARK It is hunted for its meat and pelt.

small, rounded ears •

gray to brownish • gray fur

AFRICA

Social unit Variable	Gestation 7–8 months	Young 1–3	Diet 🌿 🍒 🗲 ⋮⋮ ⫰

AARDVARK

THE ONLY SPECIES in its order, the African Aardvark has a specialized diet of ants and termites. Traditional anatomical studies have long suggested that, like the hyrax, its closest relatives may be hoofed mammals such as the elephant. However, newer genetic studies are challenging this viewpoint.

The Aardvark's sight is poor and it hunts mainly by smell. It has powerful limbs with long, straight, shovel-like claws for rapid digging.

There are four toes on each front foot and five on each rear foot.

The Aardvark's teeth are unique. Only 20 premolars and molars are present, and these are seldom used, since most of the prey are swallowed whole. The teeth lack the usual enamel, being covered by a bonelike substance called cementum. Inside the tooth are numerous cylindrical cavities, giving the name for the order, Tubulidentata, or "tubule-tooth."

Family ORYCTEROPODIDAE	Species *Orycteropus afer*	Status Unconfirmed

AARDVARK

One of the most powerful diggers among mammals, this nocturnal species, also known as the Ant-bear or Ant-pig, digs burrows up to 33 ft (10 m) long around its home range of ¾–2 square mile (2–5 square km). It prefers ants as food, especially in summer, when they are available in plenty. However, it also eats termites when ants are not available. The Aardvark is unusual in chewing one species of ant with its molar teeth, but swallowing other species of ants and termites whole, and grinding them in its muscular stomach. It has a distinctive curved back, and long tapering snout, ears, and tail. A dense mat of hair around its nostrils helps to filter out the dust while it is digging for food.

• **SIZE** Body length: 5¼ ft (1.6 m). Tail: 22 in (55 cm).
• **OCCURRENCE** Africa, south of the Sahara. In open woods and grassland.

AFRICA

unusual arched back

distinctive long, tapering, tubular ears

long, thick, tapering tail

Social unit Solitary	Gestation 243 days	Young 1	Diet

SIRENIANS

T HE THREE SPECIES of manatees and the Dugong make up the order Sirenia – also called "sea cows" because of their bulky bodies, slow movements, and habit of grazing on sea grasses and other aquatic plants. Despite their outward resemblance to seals, sirenians are the only purely herbivorous marine mammals (they also live in rivers and lagoons). They have very thick skin, paddlelike front limbs, a flattened tail, small eyes, and a fleshy, rounded muzzle with a mobile upper lip with which they pluck food.

The three manatee species occur in the West Indies, the Amazon region, and West Africa, whereas the Dugong lives principally in the Indian Ocean. The slow, unaggressive lifestyle of sirenians, foraging in coastal shallows, has made them vulnerable to humans. With a total population of perhaps 130,000, this is possibly the least numerous of all orders of mammals.

Family DUGONGIDAE	Species Dugong dugon	Status Vulnerable

DUGONG

With a torpedo-shaped, gray to brown-gray body, and a crescent-shaped tail, the Dugong is adapted to aquatic life in various ways: the "feet" have evolved into flippers and the tail is modified for propulsion. The thick, heavy bones provide diving weight for easier locomotion underwater. Usually diurnal, it moves daily between on- and offshore islands depending on the tide and supply of food. In certain areas, it makes longer seasonal migrations, of sometimes hundreds of miles, to follow sea grass and algae growth, and to avoid cold-water currents. Hunted by sharks, Killer Whales, and saltwater crocodiles, members of a group may congregate to intimidate and butt large predators.
• SIZE Length: 8¼–13 ft (2.5–4 m). Weight: 550–1,985 lb (250–900 kg).
• OCCURRENCE E. Africa, W., S., and S.E. Asia, Australia, and Pacific islands.
Along shallow tropical coasts.
• REMARK It is widely hunted for meat, oil, leather, teeth, and bones.

AFRICA, ASIA, AUSTRALIA

crescent-shaped
• tail

tail used •
as paddle

• gray to brown-gray,
generally hairless skin

• short, paddle-shaped
flippers

Social unit Social	Gestation 13–14 months	Young 1	Diet 🌿

Family TRICHECHIDAE	Species *Trichechus manatus*	Status Vulnerable

WEST INDIAN MANATEE

Probably the best known of the manatees (the other two are the Amazonian and the West African), the West Indian Manatee has gray-brown skin, paler below, which may harbor growths of algae. Like other sirenians, it has tiny eyes and no external ear flaps. Groups of 2–20 manatees may swell to 100 in warm waters during winter, or in areas where food is abundant. These groups are fluid and individuals come and go, ranging widely along shallow coastlines and through fresh and salt water. Most communication is tactile and includes touching, nuzzling, and rubbing. Manatees make high-pitched squeals and whistles underwater, usually during mother–calf bonding, or to warn others of danger. Auditory and tactile signals are also used during courtship when several males may compete for a single female. Only the mother cares for the calf – probably with the help of older offspring and female relatives.

N., C., &
S. AMERICA

• **SIZE** Length: 8¼–15 ft (2.5–4.5 m).
Weight: 440–1,320 lb (200–600 kg).
• **OCCURRENCE** S.E. US to N.E. South America. In shallow tropical coasts, coastal rivers and estuaries, and freshwater springs.
• **REMARK** Although protected by law, the West Indian Manatee continues to be threatened by hunting, habitat degradation, and pollution.

FEEDING
This manatee feeds from the surface down to 13 ft (4 m). It holds food with its flippers, directing it into its mouth, using flexible lips. Daily food intake is about one-quarter of its body weight.

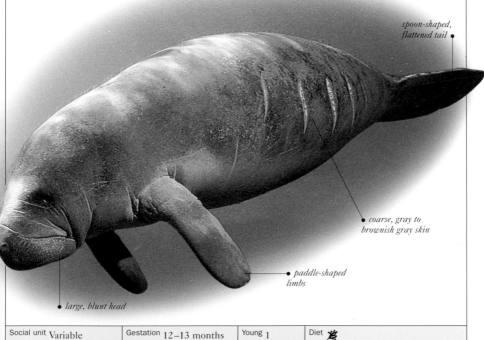

*spoon-shaped,
flattened tail* •

• *coarse, gray to
brownish gray skin*

• *paddle-shaped
limbs*

• *large, blunt head*

Social unit Variable	Gestation 12–13 months	Young 1	Diet 🌿

ODD-TOED UNGULATES
HORSES

I N ADDITION TO domesticated and wild horses, this group includes zebras and asses, such as the Onager and Kiang. There are altogether ten species of the family Equidae, which in turn forms part of the order Perissodactyla, the odd-toed ungulates.

Equids are the minimalists of the order, with just one toe on each foot, capped by a hard, horny hoof. The head is large with long jaws and batteries of cheek teeth for chewing grass and other plants. The neck and body are long and powerful, with relatively long, slim limbs for great stamina and speed, to outrun predators.

Most equids live in family groups or larger herds, in open habitats such as grassland and dry scrub, across Africa and Asia. Various species have been bred and interbred, and widely introduced around the world.

Family EQUIDAE	Species *Equus ferus przewalskii*	Status Extinct in wild

PRZEWALSKI'S WILD HORSE

Also known as the Mongolian Wild Horse, this member of the horse family is heavily built, with a thick neck, large head, and short legs. Its dun-colored coat, short in summer, becomes longer and paler in winter. Like other feral horses, it lives in herds that wander across large distances. A typical group was led by a senior mare, with 2–4 other mares, their young, and a single stallion that remains on the fringes.
• SIZE Length:7¼–8½ ft (2.2–2.6 m).
Weight:440–660 lb
(200–300 kg).
• OCCURRENCE
Unknown in the wild
since 1968. Was
native to C. Asia
and Mongolia. In
steppe grassland.
• REMARK This
horse exists in
zoos, parks,
and field stations.
Several attempts
have been made
to reintroduce it
in Mongolia.

ASIA

dark brown mane on neck

white muzzle with dark lips and nostril margins

dun-colored coat with lighter underparts

distinctive dark brown lower legs

long-haired tail

Social unit Social	Gestation 333–345 days	Young 1	Diet 🌾 ⚘ 🍃

Family EQUIDAE	Species *Equus africanus*	Status Critically endangered

AFRICAN WILD ASS

*short, sparse mane
• permanently erect*

Gray with variable stripes across its legs, this wild ass has a coat that changes from buff-gray in summer to iron-gray in winter. It survives in rocky deserts where the ground temperature exceeds 122°F (50°C), and is adapted to its habitat in various ways. Its narrow hooves give it surefootedness rather than speed and help in climbing over rocks. It feeds on almost any plant food, from grasses to thorny acacia, and can survive without water for several days.

• **SIZE** Length: 6½–7½ ft (2–2.3 m). Weight: 440–510 lb (200–230 kg).

AFRICA

• **OCCURRENCE** E. Africa. In desert.

• white underparts

variable • transverse leg stripes

Social unit Social	Gestation 360–370 days	Young 1	Diet 🌱

Family EQUIDAE	Species *Equus hemionus*	Status Vulnerable

ONAGER

• tawny to gray coat

The Onager or Asian Wild Ass, has a tawny, yellowish, or gray coat that has a dark stripe with a white border down its back. The elongated lower portion of its limbs enables it to run swiftly across long distances. Females and young form loose nomadic herds, whereas immature males gather in bachelor groups. Mature males may kick and bite rivals to occupy breeding territory.

• slender head with dark mane

long legs •

• **SIZE** Length: 6½–8¼ ft (2–2.5 m). Weight: 440–570 lb (200–260 kg).

ASIA

• **OCCURRENCE** W., C., and S. Asia. In stony desert.

Social unit Social	Gestation 11–12 months	Young 1	Diet 🌱

Family EQUIDAE	Species *Equus burchelli*	Status Lower risk*

BURCHELL'S ZEBRA

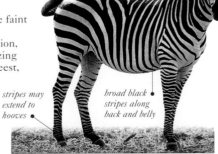

Also called the Common Zebra, this equid is characterized by a striped pattern which may have faint "shadow" bands between its larger flank stripes. It forms long-term social units consisting of a stallion, his harem, and several offspring, and is found grazing with other species such as Grevy's Zebra, Wildebeest, Roan Antelope, and Hartebeest.

• **SIZE** Length: 7¼–8¼ ft (2.2–2.5 m). Weight: 390–850 lb (175–385 kg).

AFRICA

• **OCCURRENCE** E. and S. Africa. In savanna, light woodland, and grassland.

stripes may extend to hooves •

broad black • stripes along back and belly

Social unit Social	Gestation 360–396 days	Young 1	Diet 🌱

Family EQUIDAE	Species *Equus grevyi*	Status Endangered

GREVY'S ZEBRA

The largest species of zebra, Grevy's Zebra is also the biggest wild equid. It has a black-and-white erect mane and a characteristic pattern of very narrow, densely distributed black-and-white stripes, which remain distinct all the way down to the hooves; the belly and base of the tail are white. Unlike most members of the equid family (horses and asses), which are uniformly colored, the zebra's strikingly patterned coat is believed to serve some special function: it may allow recognition of herd members, regulate temperature, or create a "dazzle" effect to confuse predators. Grevy's Zebra also has characteristic large, furry ears, and a tuft of long hair at the tip of its tail. The male is slightly larger than the female and has larger canine teeth. The female alone cares for the young, often roaming freely, accompanied by a foal and older offspring. Sometimes, she may have to leave the foal alone while she searches for water, making it particularly vulnerable to predators. Grevy's Zebra forms small, loose groups to graze, often along with Burchell's Zebra. It communicates by a range of sounds, including a series of deep grunts, punctuated by a whistlelike squeal, and through various body postures. Hunted by large carnivores such as lions and hyenas, Grevy's Zebra flees swiftly from predators, kicking and biting if cornered.
• **SIZE** Body length: 8¼–9¾ft (2.5–3 m). Tail:15–23½in (38–60cm).
• **OCCURRENCE** S. Ethiopia, Somalia, S. Sudan, and N. Kenya. In dry desert and open grassland.

AFRICA

blackish nose •

• distinct pattern of black-and-white stripes on body

tuft of longer hair
• at tail-tip

• white belly, unlike Burchell's Zebra

AUSTERE DIET
With a diet consisting of tough, fibrous grasses and other plants, Grevy's Zebra uses its upper and lower canines to crop grass. Poor quality food and this animal's small stomach means that it spends a lot of time eating. Grevy's Zebra may make seasonal migrations from arid localities where conditions are harsh, to areas where food and water are more easily available.

Social unit Social	Gestation 390 days	Young 1	Diet 🌱 🍂

SOCIAL GROUPS
Grevy's Zebras live in fluid social groups without any fixed hierarchy. Breeding stallions defend territories, which may be as large as 6 square miles (15 square km), one of the largest among herbivores. They mate with mares that range through their territory.

• *black-and-white stripes on long, erect mane*

narrow white • *zone on back*

stripes extend down • *to hooves*

ODD-TOED UNGULATES
RHINOCEROSES

ALL FIVE RHINOCEROS species are endangered, with three of these regarded as critically so. With little variation across the family, all rhinoceros are massive-bodied, with mostly bare, extremely thick skin with folds. They have short limbs, tubular ears, tiny eyes (sight is poor), and nasal horns.

The horns are not made of true horn or bone, but of matted keratin (which also forms hair and hooves). The African rhinoceros species have two horns; of the three Asian species, only the Sumatran grows two horns.

The Indian and White Rhinoceroses are grazers of swampy grassland and savanna, while the other three species live in forest and browse. Rhinoceroses tend to be solitary and mainly nocturnal, and most males are territorial.

Family RHINOCEROTIDAE	Species *Ceratotherium simum*	Status Lower risk

WHITE RHINOCEROS

The most numerous rhinoceros, this once widespread inhabitant of the African savanna saw a rapid decline in numbers over the last century, but has made a spectacular recovery since, due to conservation efforts. It is also the largest rhinoceros; its thick gray hide has few wrinkles, apart from at the foreleg joint with the body and on the flank. Almost exclusively a grazer, it has a wide, straight, and hard upper lip pad, allowing it to graze very close to the ground, and giving it the other name of Square-lipped Rhinoceros. Males weigh up to 1,100 lb (500 kg) more than females, have a more pronounced nuchal crest or hump at the shoulders, and a larger front horn that may reach 4 1/4 ft (1.3 m) in length. Placid and sociable by nature, these rhinoceroses are found in small herds of mother-calf pairs and up to seven juveniles. Mature males tend to be solitary and defend their territory of about 1 sq km (1/2 sq mile) by ritualized displays, fighting with the horn if necessary. Only the dominant male mates within his territory, and is successful only after several attempts.
- **SIZE** Length:12–13 ft (3.7–4 m). Weight: Up to 2 1/4 tons (2.3 tonnes).
- **OCCURRENCE** N.E. and S. Africa. In wooded savanna in N.E. Africa and in dry savanna in S. Africa.
- **REMARK** Although dependent on conservation, there are several secure populations of the Southern White Rhinoceros *(Ceratherium simum simum)*, totalling over 8,500, and the most numerous of all rhinos. The Northern White Rhinoceros *(C. simum cottoni)*, on the other hand, probably numbers fewer than 30 and is on the critical list.

larger front horn

hard, square lip pad

elongated head

AFRICA

Social unit Social	Gestation 16 months	Young 1	Diet 🌱

MARKING BY URINE
The male rhinoceros sprays urine between his hindlegs to mark a territory that may be about ½ sq mile (1 sq km) in area.

MOTHER AND CALF
The female White Rhinoceros gives birth to her single young, which remains with the mother for 3 years until the next birth. The mother and young use squeaks to communicate with each other.

prominent nuchal crest in male

few creases on hide

prominent fold on front leg joint

Family RHINOCEROTIDAE	Species *Diceros bicornis*	Status Critically endangered

BLACK RHINOCEROS

This rhinoceros has two horns, the front one being larger than the back. Unlike the White Rhinoceros (see pp.318 – 319), it does not have a nuchal crest (shoulder hump). Its relatively smooth, gray skin is largely hairless except for the eyelashes, eartips, and tailtip. In common with all rhinoceroses, it has a sharp sense of smell and good hearing, but poor eyesight. Feeding on a wide variety of bushes and low trees, especially at night and in the early morning, this grazer spends the day dozing in shade or wallowing in mud. Usually solitary, the Black Rhinoceros marks its home range plentifully with urine and piles of dung. It sometimes tolerates intruders – of its own species or humans – but is known suddenly to charge or jab with its horns when provoked. Mating couples remain together only for a while, but the calf stays with the mother until she gives birth to another young.

AFRICA

- **SIZE** Length: 9½ –10 ft (2.9–3.1 m). Weight: 1–1¼ tons (0.9–1.3 tonnes).
- **OCCURRENCE** Sub-Saharan Africa, except the Congo Basin. In a wide range of habitats, from desert to mountain, but primarily in woodland savanna.
- **REMARK** Trade in rhinoceros horns, used in local medicines and for dagger handles, has caused a massive decline in Black Rhinoceros numbers, which fell from 65,000 in 1970 to just 2,500 in the 1990s.

CURLED UPPER LIP
Sometimes called the Hook-lipped Rhinoceros, this species uses its pointed, prehensile upper lip to draw twigs and shoots into its mouth, then bites them off with its strong molar teeth.

front horn up to 4½ ft (1.4 m) long

hooked upper lip

no skin-crease at shoulder

large gray body

Social unit Solitary	Gestation 15 months	Young 1	Diet 🌿 🔻 🪴

Family RHINOCEROTIDAE	Species *Rhinoceros unicornis*	Status Endangered

INDIAN RHINOCEROS

deeply folded skin •

The hairless skin of this one-horned rhinoceros has tubercles on the sides and rear that resemble rivets. The pink skin within the folds attracts parasites, which are often removed by egrets and tick birds. It feeds at night, dawn, and dusk.

• **SIZE** Length: Up to 12 ft (3.8 m). Weight: Up to 2⅛ tons (2.2 tonnes).
• **OCCURRENCE** India (Brahmaputra Valley). In grassland.

ASIA

Social unit Solitary	Gestation 16 months	Young 1	Diet ⚭ ⬭

Family RHINOCEROTIDAE	Species *Rhinoceros sondaicus*	Status Critically endangered

JAVAN RHINOCEROS

thick, dark gray hide •

folded skin forms "saddle" over neck

Largely hairless except for its ears and tailtip, the Javan Rhinoceros is probably the rarest large mammal in the world. It feeds on leaves and bamboo, uprooting saplings or using its weight to push over vegetation.
• **SIZE** Length: 9¾–11 ft (3–3.5 m).
Weight: Up to 1½ tons (1.4 tonnes).

• **OCCURRENCE** S.E. Asia. In tropical forest, mangrove swamps, and bamboo groves.
• **REMARK** Habitat loss and poaching have led to a massive decline in numbers.

S.E. ASIA

Social unit Solitary	Gestation 16 months	Young 1	Diet ⬭

Family RHINOCEROTIDAE	Species *Dicerorhinus sumatrensis*	Status Critically endangered

SUMATRAN RHINOCEROS

larger front horn •

prominent shoulder fold •

skin has few wrinkles •

Also known as the Asiatic Two-horned Rhinoceros, this species is the smallest and hairiest of all rhinoceros species. It browses actively at night and during the day it keeps cool by wallowing in mud, which also coats its skin, protecting it from flies and other insects.
• **SIZE** Length: 8¼–10 ft (2.5–3.2 m).

Weight: Up to 1,760 lb (800 kg).
• **OCCURRENCE** S.E. Asia. In montane rainforest, especially primary forest on slopes.
• **REMARK** The high-altitude habitat of this rhinoceros is now subject to logging; horn poachers are also a major threat.

ASIA

long toes •

Social unit Solitary	Gestation 7–8 months	Young 1	Diet ⬭ ⬤

ODD-TOED UNGULATES
TAPIRS

T HE FOUR SPECIES of tapirs (family Tapiridae), from Central and South America and Southeast Asia, can be viewed as "living fossils," since their basic anatomy has hardly changed for close to 30 million years.

The piglike body is supported by relatively slender legs, the ears are large and erect, and the eyes small and deep-set. The flexible, trunklike snout is used for rooting up various plant foods.

All species are found in forest, close to water, and the tapir's streamlined, compact shape allows it to push through the undergrowth. It can remain almost submerged in water for hours, to stay cool or to avoid predators, using its "trunk" as a snorkel for breathing.

Although tapirs are perissodactyls (odd-toed ungulates), with three toes on each rear foot, the front foot has an extra toe.

Family TAPIRIDAE	Species *Tapirus pinchaque*	Status Endangered

MOUNTAIN TAPIR

The smallest of all tapirs, the Mountain Tapir is also the furriest. Covered with thick, woolly, dark brown to coal-black fur, it has furry white fringes around the lips and on the tips of its rounded ears. Sheltering in forest or thickets by day, it feeds at night, dawn, and dusk, on a variety of dwarf trees and shrubs. The Mountain Tapir is an important disperser of seeds for cloud forest trees and plants, which it ejects whole in its droppings.
• SIZE Length: 6 ft (1.8 m). Weight: 330 lb (150 kg).
• OCCURRENCE N.W. South America. In mountains and grassland.
• REMARK This tapir is hunted for meat and its body parts are used in traditional medicine.

S. AMERICA

woolly, dark brown to coal-black coat

highly mobile snout for selective browsing

barrel-shaped body

short, stocky legs

Social unit Solitary	Gestation 393 days	Young 1	Diet 🌿 🍒

| Family TAPIRIDAE | Species *Tapirus bairdii* | Status Vulnerable |

BAIRD'S TAPIR

The largest American tapir, this dark brown mammal has pale gray-yellow cheeks and throat, and white-fringed ears. It whistles to communicate with its young or warn other adults away from its territory.

gray-yellow throat

brown body

• SIZE Length: 6 ½ ft (2 m). Weight: 530–880 lb (240–400 kg).
• OCCURRENCE S. Mexico to N. South America. In forest, marshes, and swamps.

N., C., & S. AMERICA

| Social unit Solitary | Gestation 390–400 days | Young 1 | Diet 🍃 🍎 |

| Family TAPIRIDAE | Species *Tapirus terrestris* | Status Lower risk |

SOUTH AMERICAN TAPIR

short, stiff mane on neck

This tapir has a bristly gray coat and a short, stiff, narrow mane. Its throat and chest may be paler. A good swimmer, it often dives into water to escape predators such as Pumas or Jaguars. The young, as in all tapirs, are born with spots and stripes for camouflage in vegetation.

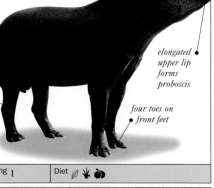

elongated upper lip forms proboscis

short legs

four toes on front feet

• SIZE Length: 5 ½ –6 ½ ft (1.7–2 m). Weight: 500–550 lb (225–250 kg).
• OCCURRENCE N. and C. South America. In tropical rain forest, gallery forest, and, occasionally, open grassy habitat.

S. AMERICA

| Social unit Solitary | Gestation 13 months | Young 1 | Diet 🍃 🌿 🍎 |

| Family TAPIRIDAE | Species *Tapirus indicus* | Status Vulnerable |

MALAYAN TAPIR

broken coloration

The largest and only Old World tapir, this species has a striking black-and-white coat, which helps to break up its body outline in shady forest for effective camouflage. The Malayan Tapir feeds on soft vegetation and fallen fruits.

• SIZE Length: 6– 8 ¼ ft (1.8–2.5 m) Weight: 550–1,190 lb (250–540 kg).
• OCCURRENCE S.E. Asia. In humid, tropical forest, swampy areas, and meadows.

long, mobile snout

white "saddle"

ASIA

| Social unit Solitary | Gestation 390– 407 days | Young 1 | Diet 🍃 🍎 |

EVEN-TOED UNGULATES
WILD PIGS

P IGS, HOGS, WARTHOGS, and boars tend to be omnivores, rooting for food in soil and leaves with elongated, blunt-ended snouts that are tough yet sensitive. The typical pig has a large head, prominent ears, small eyes, canine teeth forming tusks, and a heavy, barrelshaped body with thin legs.

About 14 species make up the family Suidae, including domesticated pigs, which are descended from the Wild

Boar. Being even-toed ungulates, each foot, or trotter, has two main hooves, with a smaller lateral hoof on each side. Various species of pigs occur naturally in forest, swamp, and grassland across Africa and Eurasia. Some have been introduced to the Americas, Australia, and New Zealand.

Most species live in sounders, which consist of a sow and her offspring; boars (males) join during the mating season.

Family SUIDAE	Species *Sus scrofa*	Status Locally common

WILD BOAR

One of the most widely distributed terrestrial mammals, the Wild Boar or Eurasian Wild Pig is the ancestor of the domestic pig. It has bristly dark gray to black or brown hair, and a mane of longer hair along its spine. The male is larger than the female and has larger tusks. The piglets are pale brown with paler stripes along the back and sides, providing camouflage when in their nest of grass, moss, and leaves in dense thicket. Females, which usually band together in groups of 20, are very protective of their young. Occupying a wide range of habitats, this pig eats almost anything, runs swiftly, and is a good swimmer.
• SIZE Body length: 3–6 ft (0.9–1.8 m). Tail: 12 in (30 cm).
• OCCURRENCE Europe, Asia, and N. Africa. In tropical and temperate forest, as well as wetland.

EURASIA, AFRICA

• bristlelike hair

long, tufted tail •

no warts • on face

Social unit Variable	Gestation 100–120 days	Young 4–6	Diet 🐾 🌿 ✿ ❁ ❀ 🐛

| Family SUIDAE | Species *Sus salvanius* | Status Critically endangered |

PYGMY HOG

dark brown body

This stocky, short-tailed species is the smallest member of the pig family, and has a sharply tapering head and snout to push through undergrowth. Dark brown in color, it has paler undersides. The male's upper canines protrude slightly from the sides of its mouth. Both sexes make nests out of hollows lined with grass. Males are solitary, while females live in groups of 4–6. The Pygmy Hog is the carrier of a unique parasite, the Pygmy Hog Louse.
• **SIZE** Body length: 20–28 in (50–71 cm). Tail: 1¼ in (3 cm).
• **OCCURRENCE** S. Asia. In riverine grassland.
• **REMARK** A legally protected species, it is still under threat from poaching and the loss of habitat.

short legs

ASIA

| Social unit Social | Gestation 100 days | Young 2–6 | Diet 🐛 ✳ 🐌 ● |

| Family SUIDAE | Species *Hylochoerus meinertzhageni* | Status Endangered* |

GIANT FOREST HOG

The largest of the African pigs, this hog has a massive head with two large, wartlike skin growths below and behind each eye, and tusks that grow out horizontally from each jaw. The blackish gray skin is covered with coarse black hair, which becomes sparser with age. The lighter colored piglets darken to brown or black as they mature. Unlike other pigs, this species does not root, but grazes and browses on grasses, sedges, shrubs, or cultivated crops.
• **SIZE** Body length: 4¼–7 ft (1.3–2.1 m). Tail: 12–18 in (30–45 cm).
• **OCCURRENCE** W., C., and E. Africa. In subalpine areas, bamboo groves, swamp forest, and savanna.

rump higher than downward-sloping shoulder

tusks relatively small

AFRICA

long, coarse black hair

short legs

| Social unit Social | Gestation 151 days | Young 2–11 | Diet 🌱 🍃 🍎 |

Family SUIDAE	Species *Potamochoerus porcus*	Status Locally common

BUSH PIG

Sometimes called the Red River Hog, this swift runner and agile swimmer is bright reddish in color and has a distinctive white stripe on its back. Its long, pointed ears have prominent tufts, and there are white stripes on its face. Highly social, the male lives with his harem and their young, defending them from intruders. Aggressive in combat, Bush Pigs erect the crest along their backs and circle each other in ritualized displays of strength. The female digs a shallow burrow and lines it with grass for her dark brown, spotted piglets.
• **SIZE** Body length: 3½–5 ft (1–1.5 m).
Tail: 12–17 in (30–43 cm).
• **OCCURRENCE** W. and C. Africa. In tropical forest.
• **REMARK** An agricultural pest, it has benefited from the reduction of predators and increase in crop area.

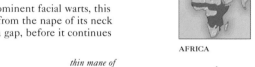

rounded back

reddish coat varies with age and locality

white stripes on face

AFRICA

Social unit Social	Gestation 4 months	Young 1–8	Diet ➤ 🐦 ❀ ❀ ➤

Family SUIDAE	Species *Phacochoerus africanus*	Status Locally common

WARTHOG

A long-legged, large-headed pig, with prominent facial warts, this species has a long, dark mane extending from the nape of its neck to the middle of its back, where there is a gap, before it continues to the rump. Its tufted tail is held straight and upright when running. The Warthog usually kneels down on its padded "wrists" to feed on newly growing grass tips, using its lips or long incisor teeth. In the dry season, it roots around for underground stems or rhizomes. Burrows, natural or excavated by Aardvarks, are used for shelter, to rear young, or to sleep.
• **SIZE** Body length: 3–5 ft (0.9–1.5 m).
Tail: 10–20 in (23–50 cm).
• **OCCURRENCE** Sub-Saharan Africa. In grassland and light mountain forest.
• **REMARK** This is the only pig adapted to grazing in savanna and grassland.

AFRICA

thin mane of coarse hair

tufted tail held upright

facial wart

Social unit Social	Gestation 150–175 days	Young 1–8	Diet ❀ ➤ 🐦 ✦

Family SUIDAE	Species *Babyrousa babyrussa*	Status Vulnerable

BABIRUSA

With a gray to brown, almost hairless body supported by long, thin legs, the Babirusa is unusual in that the male has distinctive upper tusks that grow through the muzzle and then curve back toward the face. Up to 12 in (30 cm) long, they are brittle and loose in their sockets. The lower daggerlike tusks are used by males for fighting and are kept sharp by shearing against the upper tusks and trunks of trees. Females and their young form roving groups of up to eight individuals, whereas males are usually solitary. A good swimmer, the Babirusa sometimes crosses narrow stretches of ocean to reach offshore islands.

- **SIZE** Body length: 6 1/4 ft (0.9–1.1 m). Tail: 10 1/2 –12 1/2 in (27– 32 cm).
- **OCCURRENCE** Sulawesi, Togian, and Mangole islands. In rain forest, and on the shores of rivers and lakes.

rounded body

ASIA

large folds near belly

protruding upper tusks in male

Social unit Variable	Gestation 155–158 days	Young 1–2	Diet 🌿 🍎 🐛 🐀

Family SUIDAE	Species *Pecari tajacu*	Status Locally common

COLLARED PECCARY

The smallest of the three peccary species, this pig is often referred to as the Javelina. With a barrel-shaped body and slim legs, it is usually dark gray with a whitish neck collar, and has small, downward-curving tusks. The young are reddish and have a narrow black band along the back. Extremely sociable, peccaries form groups of up to 15, of mixed age and sex, which cooperate to repel predators, usually Coyotes, Pumas, or Jaguars. Social bonding is important, and members of a group may be found grooming each other.

- **SIZE** Body length: 30–39 in (75 –100 cm). Tail: 1/2 –2 1/4 in (1.5– 5.5 cm).
- **OCCURRENCE** S.W. US to S. South America. In desert and tropical forest.
- **REMARK** The Collared Peccary is threatened by hunting, and the destruction and fragmentation of its habitat.

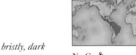

bristly, dark gray coat

N., C., & S. AMERICA

barrel-like body

whitish collar

Social unit Social	Gestation 145 days	Young 1–4	Diet 🍎 🌱 🦎 🐍 🐀

EVEN-TOED UNGULATES
HIPPOPOTAMUSES

T HE FAMILY Hippopotamidae is made up of only two species: the Common Hippopotamus and the Pygmy Hippopotamus. The former eats mainly grass and is widespread, or even abundant in places, along African rivers and lakes. The latter has a more mixed diet, and is rare, restricted only to the forests and swamps of west Africa, where it is threatened by habitat destruction and hunting.

The hippopotamus has a huge head, an enormous mouth that gapes wide to reveal its tusklike canine teeth, and very thick, fatty, almost hairless skin. The bulky body is supported by short, slim legs, each ending in four toes. Adaptations for life in water include webbed toes, and eyes, ears, and nostrils sited high on the head, so that the hippopotamus can remain almost totally submerged for long periods.

Family HIPPOPOTAMIDAE	Species *Hexaprotodon liberiensis*	Status Vulnerable

PYGMY HIPPOPOTAMUS

Merely one-fifth the weight of its huge cousin, the Hippopotamus (at right), the Pygmy Hippopotamus has a relatively small head, sloping forequarters, and narrower feet with reduced webbing on the toes, all adaptations to a more terrestrial lifestyle. It also feeds on a wider range of plant material including shrubs, ferns, and fruits. A night forager, it follows well-worn trails, spending the day hidden in swamps or in a riverside den, often enlarged from the burrow of some other animal.
• SIZE Length: 4½–5 ft (1.4–1.6 m). Weight: 540–610 lb (245–275 kg).
• OCCURRENCE W. Africa. In tropical forest and wetland.
• REMARK Evidence suggests the Pygmy Hippopotamus has always been rare. Although protected, it is hunted widely for bushmeat.

AFRICA

small, narrow head adapted to push through vegetation •

• *squat form with narrow front*

Social unit Solitary	Gestation 196–201 days	Young 1	Diet 🌱 🍂 🍑

Family HIPPOPOTAMIDAE	Species *Hippopotamus amphibius*	Status Common

HIPPOPOTAMUS

AFRICA

Despite its massive bulk, the Common Hippopotamus is a truly amphibious creature, equally agile on land and in water. The density of its body is slightly greater than that of water and it sinks slowly, walking lightly across the bottom. However, it can stay afloat by inflating its lungs when breathing at the surface, the extra air reducing its body density. The thin, outer layer of its skin dries easily and, despite mucus-producing glands, the hide soon cracks unless regularly moistened in water or mud. During summer, Hippopotamuses are often found wallowing in pools of water in large, temporary groups. Nocturnal by nature, the Hippopotamus chiefly feeds on grass, but has also been observed eating small ungulates or scavenging. The dominant male mates with females in his territory, and the single calf is born underwater. Fiercely protected by its mother, it remains with her until almost mature.

- **SIZE** Length: 9 ft (2.7 m).
Weight: 1 ⅜–1 ½ tons (1.4–1.5 tonnes).
- **OCCURRENCE** E. and S. sub-Saharan Africa. In grassland and wetland; in water by day.
- **REMARK** DNA analyses reveal that Hippopotamuses are probably more closely related to whales than to other even-toed ungulates.

YAWNING
The Hippopotamus' yawn is actually a threat display. It uses its canine and incisor teeth to defend itself, and may make unprovoked charges on land and in water.

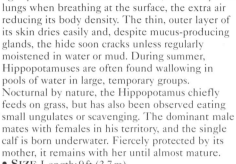

massive, grayish body

thin outer skin that dries fast

ears on top of head allow hearing in water

Social unit Solitary	Gestation 240 days	Young 1	Diet 🌱

EVEN-TOED UNGULATES
CAMELS AND RELATIVES

T HE DROMEDARY (one-humped camel), originally from Africa and West Asia, and the Bactrian Camel (two-humped) of Central Asia, give this family its name, Camelidae. Almost all camels today are either domesticated, or have descended from domestic stock and now roam free.

The other group of camelids is from South America and comprises the wild Guanaco and Vicuña, and their domestic descendants, Llamas and Alpacas.

All camelids have a small head, a split upper lip, long neck, and long legs. They have a "pacing" gait, in which the front and back legs on one side move together, producing a rocking motion. Unlike other even-toed ungulates, the weight is carried not on the hooves, but on fatty pads under the toes.

Family CAMELIDAE	Species *Vicugna vicugna*	Status Endangered

VICUÑA

A selective grazer of perennial grasses, the Vicuña has a prehensile, cleft upper lip and permanently growing incisors to facilitate feeding. It has a uniform light to dark cinnamon coat, with a variable white "bib" and white undersides. Its long legs are placed midway on its body and its hindquarters are contracted. Unlike the camels (see pp. 332–333), it must drink water every day. Groups of one male, 5–10 females, and their young occupy territories marked by dung and urine.
• SIZE Length: 5 ft (1.5 m). Weight: 88–120 lb (40–55 kg).
• OCCURRENCE W. South America, in the Andes. In alpine tundra.
• REMARK In the 1950s it was discovered that fewer than 10,000 Vicuñas survived in Peru, probably less than 1 percent of the total population that existed 500 years ago, when the Spanish colonizers first arrived in South America.

S. AMERICA

long, pointed, and erect ears

small head

long, and thin neck

ALPACA
Domesticated in the high Andes 4,000 years ago, for its fine wool, the Alpaca was once thought to be a descendant of the Guanaco. DNA tests have now traced its ancestry to the Vicuña.

Social unit Social	Gestation 342–345 days	Young 1	Diet ⭹

Family CAMELIDAE	Species *Lama guanicoe*	Status Vulnerable

GUANACO

Typically pale to dark brown in color, with a whitish chest, underside, and inner legs, the Guanaco has a gray to black head with white-fringed eyes, lips, and ears, and a long neck. Preferring cold habitats, it is found from sea level up to 13,000 ft (4,000 m). The Guanaco browses and grazes on a variety of grasses and shubs, as well as on lichens and fungi. Family groups consist of one male and around 4–7 females with their young. In the extreme south of the Guanaco's range, where there is significant winter snow accumulation, females and young migrate to more favourable areas in search of food. However, the male remains behind to guard his territory.

S. AMERICA

- **SIZE** Length: 3–7 ft (0.9–2.1 m). Weight: 210–290 lb (96–130 kg).
- **OCCURRENCE** W. to S. South America. In grassland, desert, temperate forest, and mountains.
- **REMARK** Hunted by humans, and threatened by overgrazing of their natural habitat, the four subspecies of Guanaco have been classified as vulnerable. The northernmost subspecies, regarded as the ancestor

small head

distinctive, long, pointed ears

prehensile, cleft upper lip

pale to dark brown body

neck set low on torso

thick, woolly coat

long legs

fleshy pads on feet, with nails on upper surface

LLAMA
The Llama is a domestic species, first bred from the Guanaco by the Inca civilization, around 6,000 years ago. It is the traditional pack animal of the Andes, and is farmed for its wool and meat (in countries outside South America as well).

Social unit Social	Gestation 345–360 days	Young 1	Diet 🌱 🍂 🍄

Family CAMELIDAE	Species *Camelus dromedarius*	Status Common

DROMEDARY

The domesticated one-humped camel, now extinct in the wild, is adapted to desert life in various ways. Using the fat reserves in its hump, it loses up to 40 percent of its body weight when food and water are scarce, and can survive without drinking water longer than any other domestic animal (six or seven months in colder weather). Its body temperature rises in hot weather and sweating is reduced to conserve moisture. It feeds on a huge variety of plants, including salty and thorny species, using its prehensile, split upper lip to browse; it also scavenges on dried out carcasses. Found in small herds of one male and several females and young, the male defends its group by jumping and biting, and pushing away intruders. The Dromedary ranges in color from cream through almost every shade of brown to black.
• SIZE Length: 7 ¼ –11 ft (2.2 – 3.4 m).
Weight: 990 – 1,210 lb (450 – 550 kg).
• OCCURRENCE N. and E. Africa, W. and S. Asia. In desert.
• REMARK The Dromedary has been wholly domesticated, with no record of any individuals existing in the wild since prehistoric times (3000 BC).

well-developed cleft extending into upper lip •

AFRICA, ASIA

FACING THE HEAT
The Dromedary has nostrils that moisten and cool the air it breathes. The heavy eyebrows and double row of curly lashes protect its eyes from desert sand.

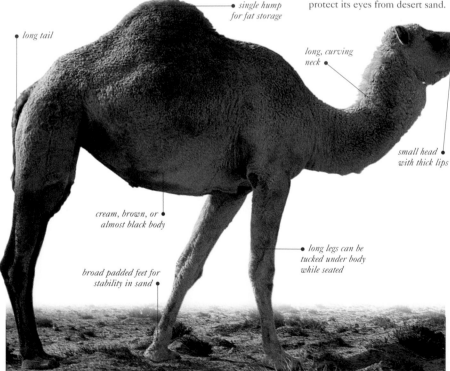

• *single hump for fat storage*

• *long tail*

long, curving neck •

small head with thick lips •

cream, brown, or almost black body •

• *long legs can be tucked under body while seated*

broad padded feet for stability in sand •

Social unit Social	Gestation 370 days	Young 1	Diet

Family CAMELIDAE	Species *Camelus bactrianus*	Status Endangered

BACTRIAN CAMEL

The two-humped Bactrian Camel is the only Old World camelid found in the wild. It can withstand temperatures from -20°F (-29°C) to 100°F (38°C). After a drought, it can drink up to 24 gallons (110 litres) of water in about 10 minutes. Uniformly light beige to dark brown in color, it has a shaggy coat in winter that it sheds in summer. The humps, composed of fat, are erect when the animal is well fed, but become flaccid as resources are used up. During the rut, the male puffs out his cheeks, extrudes a red, balloonlike sac from his mouth, grinds his teeth, and paces alongside his competitor in a dramatic, ritualistic display. The dominant male acquires a harem of 6–30 females and their offspring. This family group is not territorial and travels long distances in search of food and water.
• **SIZE** Length: 8 ½ – 9 ¾ ft (2.5 – 3 m).
Weight: 990 – 1,520 lb (450 – 690 kg).
• **OCCURRENCE** Wild populations in the Gobi Desert; domestic populations in C. Asia. In cold steppe and desert.
• **REMARK** First domesticated 3,500 years ago, this camel is an important beast of burden. Its milk and flesh are also consumed.

ASIA

FLAT-TOED
The two-toed, broad feet of this camel provide stability in sand and snow.

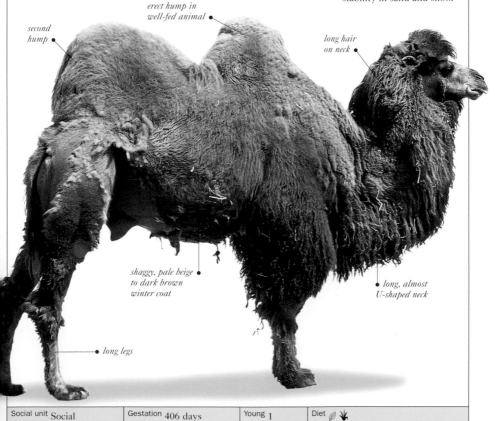

erect hump in well-fed animal

second hump

long hair on neck

shaggy, pale beige to dark brown winter coat

long, almost U-shaped neck

long legs

Social unit Social	Gestation 406 days	Young 1	Diet 🌿 🌾

EVEN-TOED UNGULATES
DEER

SOME 45 SPECIES of deer make up the family Cervidae. They are artiodactyls (even-toed ungulates), with four visible toes on each foot. The first toe is practically lost, and the second and fifth toes are small, leaving the third and fourth toes to bear the body weight. The deer's large eyes, ears, and muzzle provide it with excellent senses to detect the presence of predators.

Deer resemble antelopes, but their antlers are branched and regrow each year. Only male deer have antlers, except reindeer, where females also grow them.

Most species are browsers, at home in woodland and forest, but some also graze in grassland, swamp, or semidesert. Various cervids are found naturally on all continents, except Australia and Africa (barring the Mediterranean fringe). Many have been introduced to new regions over the centuries.

Family TRAGULIDAE	Species *Tragulus meminna*	Status Unconfirmed

INDIAN SPOTTED CHEVROTAIN

In common with other species of chevrotain (mouse deer), the Indian Spotted Chevrotain, or Spotted Mouse Deer, has four fully developed toes on each foot, unlike "true" deer, which have just two. It has a spotted back and white stripes on its throat and flanks. Males use their tusklike upper canine teeth to fight off opponents.
• **SIZE** Body length: 20–23 in (50–58 cm).
Tail: 1 ¼ in (3 cm).
• **OCCURRENCE** S. India and Sri Lanka. In tropical rain forest, especially rocky terrain up to 2,300 ft (700 m).

ASIA

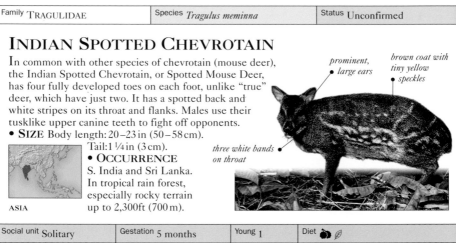

prominent, large ears
brown coat with tiny yellow speckles
three white bands on throat

Social unit Solitary	Gestation 5 months	Young 1	Diet 🐚 🌿

Family MOSCHIDAE	Species *Moschus chrysogaster*	Status Lower risk

ALPINE MUSK DEER

Found on rocky, forested mountain slopes, this stocky species has well-developed side toes, enabling it to climb rocks, and to move through snow. It has a dark brown coat, mottled light gray, and a whitish chin and ear fringes.
• **SIZE** Body length: 28–39 in (70–100 cm).
Tail: ¾–2 ¼ in (2–6 cm).
• **OCCURRENCE** Afghanistan to C. China.
In temperate and coniferous forest, as well as mountains.
• **REMARK** This deer is widely hunted for its musk, a secretion from the navel region, which is highly prized in the perfume industry.

ASIA

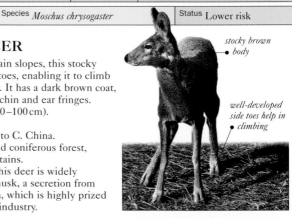

stocky brown body
well-developed side toes help in climbing

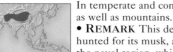

Social unit Solitary	Gestation 185–195 days	Young 1	Diet 🌿 🌾 🍄

Family CERVIDAE	Species *Dama dama*	Status Locally common

FALLOW DEER

Usually brown with white spots, this deer may also be blackish
or white. Domesticated for its graceful looks and meat, it has been
introduced to the Americas and Africa, as well as Australia. During rut,
bucks establish a small patch of territory, where they mate. The Fallow
Deer feeds at twilight on a variety of vegetation. The subspecies,
Mesopotamian Fallow Deer,
is endangered.
• **SIZE** Body length:
4½–6¼ft (1.4–1.9m).
Tail: 5½–10in (14–25cm).
• **OCCURRENCE** Europe
and W. Asia. In grassland
and forest.

EUROPE, ASIA

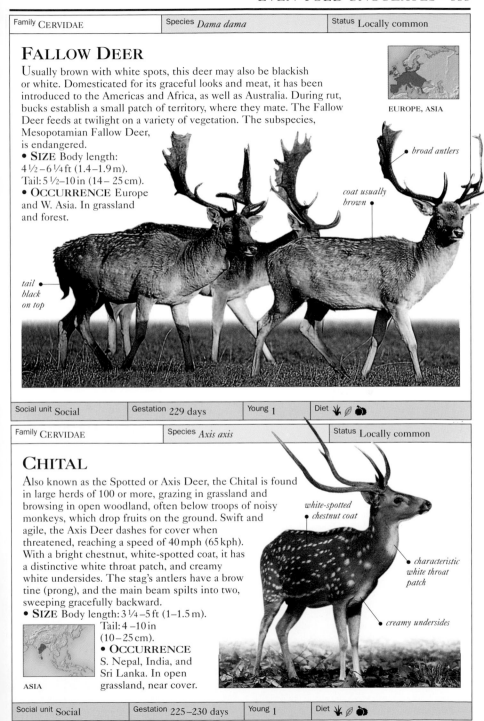

broad antlers

coat usually brown

tail black on top

Social unit Social	Gestation 229 days	Young 1	Diet 🌱 🍃 🍂

Family CERVIDAE	Species *Axis axis*	Status Locally common

CHITAL

Also known as the Spotted or Axis Deer, the Chital is found
in large herds of 100 or more, grazing in grassland and
browsing in open woodland, often below troops of noisy
monkeys, which drop fruits on the ground. Swift and
agile, the Axis Deer dashes for cover when
threatened, reaching a speed of 40mph (65kph).
With a bright chestnut, white-spotted coat, it has
a distinctive white throat patch, and creamy
white undersides. The stag's antlers have a brow
tine (prong), and the main beam spilts into two,
sweeping gracefully backward.
• **SIZE** Body length: 3¼–5ft (1–1.5m).
Tail: 4–10in
(10–25cm).
• **OCCURRENCE**
S. Nepal, India, and
Sri Lanka. In open
grassland, near cover.

ASIA

white-spotted chestnut coat

characteristic white throat patch

creamy undersides

Social unit Social	Gestation 225–230 days	Young 1	Diet 🌱 🍃 🍂

Family CERVIDAE	Species *Cervus elaphus*	Status Locally common

RED DEER

Reddish brown in summer, sometimes with a dark line along its back and neck, and indistinct flank spots, the Red Deer turns a dull brown in winter. Its tail and rump patch are straw-colored. There is great variation in appearance among the 28 or so subspecies of this deer, which include the Wapitis of China and North America. Only the stag has antlers, and the larger they are, the more females it attracts. Typically a fork or cup of points, the number of points on the antlers keep increasing with age, until the male passes its prime. Females (hinds) form herds led by a dominant hind, whereas males form separate groups except during the fall rut. At this time, stags battle each other and serious fights may take place between evenly matched animals. Using part display and part physical contest, the stags walk parallel to each other as they assess whether to fight. Once the contest begins, they interlock antlers, pushing, twisting, and shoving each other; the victor finally wins a harem. The diet of this day-and-night grazer varies with the seasons and consists of grasses, sedge, rushes, heather, and a variety of other plants which it sometimes accesses by standing up on its hindfeet.
• **SIZE** Body length: 5–6½ ft (1.5–2 m). Tail: 4¾ in (12 cm).
• **OCCURRENCE** Europe to E. Asia. Introduced in Australia and New Zealand, USA, and South America. In grassland, temperate and coniferous forest.
• **REMARK** The most widespread deer in the world, several subspecies are found across the different continents. Nine subspecies are endangered, and they face the threat of poaching as well as habitat loss and fragmentation.

• *fully grown antlers*

red-brown summer coat turns dull brown in winter •

• *white spots on coat*

"LYING UP"
The newly born fawn, reddish brown with white spots, "lies up" hidden in vegetation for the first two weeks, as with all deer young. The mother moos loudly to locate her fawn, taking care of it alone.

Social unit Social	Gestation 225–245 days	Young 1	Diet

multiple points on antlers that increase with age

cup of points at top of antler

EURASIA

female Red Deer has no antlers

buff-colored tail

paler coloration on face, cheeks, and neck

BRED IN CAPTIVITY
The Red Deer is adapted to a wide range of climates. It is now widely farmed for its meat, hide, and antler velvet, which is used in Asian medicines. Herds of Red Deer are also kept in urban parks.

male larger and heavier than female

shaggy mane

MATING SIGNALS
The male Red Deer develops a mane as it enters rut in the fall. During this time it roars, thrashes bushes, and wallows in the mud. It stops feeding and loses a lot of weight.

Family CERVIDAE	Species *Cervus nippon*	Status Critically endangered

SIKA

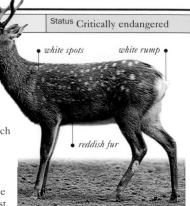

white spots   *white rump*

Kept in parks and farmed for centuries, the Sika has also been introduced in many countries. Its appearance varies among the 14 subspecies. However, it is generally rich red-brown with white spots in summer, and turns almost black in winter. Males have a dark chevron, or wavy pattern, on their forehead, and each antler has a maximum of four points.

reddish fur

• **SIZE** Body length: 5–6 ½ ft (1.5– 2 m). Tail: 4¾–8 in (12–20 cm).
• **OCCURRENCE** Vietnam, Taiwan, China, and Japan. Introduced in Europe and New Zealand. In grassland and forest.

ASIA

Social unit Social	Gestation 220 days	Young 1	Diet 🌿

Family CERVIDAE	Species *Cervus unicolor*	Status Locally common

SAMBAR

three-pronged antlers in male

thick mane on neck

Uniformly dark brown, except for rusty hues on its chin, inner legs, and underside of its black-tipped tail, the Sambar has a thick mane that is more prominent in rutting males. During this season, the male develops a hairless sore spot on the sides of the neck, and stamps on the ground, wallows in mud, and strips bark off trees. This nocturnal browser eats a variety of vegetation

uniformly dark brown coat

and is usually solitary, except for female–fawn pairs.
• **SIZE** Body length: 6½–8¼ ft (2–2.5 m). Tail: 6–8 in (15–20 cm).
• **OCCURRENCE** S. and S.E. Asia. In light woodland.

ASIA

Social unit Solitary	Gestation 240 days	Young 1	Diet 🌱 🌿

Family CERVIDAE	Species *Elaphurus davidianus*	Status Critically endangered

PÉRE DAVID'S DEER

long tail

Quite unlike a deer in form, this species (of which a female is shown here) has a horselike face, wide hooves, and a long tail. The stag's "back to front" antlers are another unusual feature. This deer's coat is grayish fawn in winter, and red-brown in summer.
• **SIZE** Body length: 7¼ ft (2.2 m). Tail: 26 in (66 cm).
• **OCCURRENCE** Reintroduced in China (in the 1980s). In open grassland.

horse-like face

• **REMARK** Once widespread in China, it became extinct in the wild, but was saved by captive breeding in the UK.

large hooves

ASIA

Social unit Social	Gestation 283 days	Young 1	Diet 🌿 🌱

Family CERVIDAE	Species *Capreolus capreolus*	Status Locally common

ROE DEER

A black muzzle band and variable white chin and throat patches characterize this deer. Red-brown in summer, it molts to a densely furred, gray coat in winter. Both sexes have a white rump patch with a tiny hidden tail. However, in females the patch is an inverted heart shape, while in males it is kidney-shaped. The fur on this patch is fluffed up in times of danger, as is the Sika's (shown left). The male has rough-surfaced, three-point antlers that it sheds and regrows each winter. Most active at dawn and dusk, the Roe Deer feeds on a variety of vegetation such as grasses, herbs, shrubs, ivy, and fruits.
• SIZE Body length: 3¼–4¼ft (1–1.3m). Tail: 2in (5cm).

three-point antlers

black muzzle

fluffy white rump

red-brown coat

• OCCURRENCE Europe to Asia Minor. In forest near glades, or woodland surrounded by pasture.
• REMARK A close relative of the Roe Deer is the Siberian Roe (*Capreolus pygargus*).

EURASIA

Social unit Variable	Gestation 300 days	Young 1–3	Diet

Family CERVIDAE	Species *Odocoileus hemionus*	Status Lower risk

MULE DEER

Widely distributed in many habitats, the Mule Deer is recorded as eating hundreds of plant species. Rusty brown in summer, and gray-brown in winter, it has variable white patches on its face and throat, and black bands on its forehead. The tail is black on the upper surface, and white below, giving this species the alternative name of Black-tailed Deer. As with many other deer, the rutting season is from September to November, and the young are usually born in June.
• SIZE Body length: 2¾–7ft (0.85–2.1m). Tail: 4–14in (10–35cm).
• OCCURRENCE W. North America. In grassland and cultivated land to woodland edges, and sometimes urban areas.

many-branched antlers in male

black stripes on forehead

variable white patches on face

rusty brown coat in summer

N. AMERICA

Social unit Social	Gestation 203 days	Young 1–2	Diet

Family CERVIDAE	Species *Blastocerus dichotomus*	Status Vulnerable

MARSH DEER

The largest South American deer, this species is reddish brown in summer and darker in winter, and has a pale face, black lips and nose, and black lower limbs. Long legs with large hooves enable it to walk over marshy or water-logged ground. The Marsh Deer feeds on grasses, reeds, water plants, and shrubs, and lives alone or in groups of 2–3, moving seasonally between marshes and raised land according to the water level.

• SIZE Length: Up to 6½ft (2 m). Weight: 220–310 lb (100–140 kg).

• OCCURRENCE S. South America. In marshes, flood plains, and forest edges.

• REMARK The Marsh Deer faces a serious threat from habitat loss caused by irrigation, agriculture, and water pollution.

no antlers in female

reddish brown coat turns darker in winter

S. AMERICA

distinctive long legs, black below, with large hooves

Social unit Variable	Gestation 9 months	Young 1	Diet ↓ 🌿 🌾

Family CERVIDAE	Species *Pudu pudu*	Status Vulnerable

SOUTHERN PUDU

One of the two species of small, stocky, and low-slung pudu, the Southern Pudu has a long-haired, coarse coat of buff to reddish brown, and hardly any tail. Its antlers are simple spikes, about 3¼in (8 cm) long. A solitary species, active both by day and by night, it takes cover in thickets and undergrowth when threatened.

• SIZE Length: 34 in (85 cm). Weight: Up to 33 lb (15 kg).

• OCCURRENCE S.W. South America. In humid forest from sea level to a height of 5,600 ft (1,700 m).

buff to reddish brown coat

reddish brown in the middle of back

rounded ears

face is buff or brown

thick, short legs

S. AMERICA

characteristic slender hooves

Social unit Solitary	Gestation 202 days	Young 1	Diet 🍂 🫐 🌿

Family CERVIDAE	Species *Rangifer tarandus*	Status Endangered*

REINDEER

Called Caribou in North America, the Reindeer is the only species of deer in which both sexes have long antlers, with a unique shovel-like brow tine on one side. American forms have chiefly brown coats with darker legs, whereas Eurasian forms are grayer. Adapted to its cold habitat in various ways, the Reindeer's coat effectively insulates it from freezing water or icy winds, while its large antlers and hooves are used to scrape the snow for lichen. Bulls lose their antlers in spring or early winter, unlike females which retain their antlers until the calves are born in May. Pregnant females use their antlers to fight males in winter when food is scarce. Reindeer feed on grasses, sedge, and herbs in summer, and lichen and fungi in winter.

N.AMERICA, GREENLAND, EURASIA

- **SIZE** Length: 4–7 1/4 ft (1.2–2.2 m). Weight: 260–660 lb (120–300 kg).
- **OCCURRENCE** N. North America, Greenland, N. Europe to E. Asia. In mountains and coniferous forest.
- **REMARK** The economy of some peoples in the Arctic depends on this deer for meat, skin, and milk; around 2 million are semi-domesticated.

MIGRATORY PATTERNS
Some Reindeer travel 9–40 miles (15–65 km) daily in the same area, while others migrate 750 miles (1,200 km) twice a year in large herds.

grayish coat of the Eurasian Reindeer •

• large, palmate antlers of males

furry coat protects it from the • cold

Social unit Social	Gestation 210–240 days	Young 1	Diet 🌾 🌿 🍃

Family CERVIDAE	Species *Alces alces*	Status Unconfirmed

MOOSE

The largest member of the deer family, the Moose has several subspecies. In the Moose found in North America, the male (shown here), usually has a much larger dewlap than that of the Moose found in Europe. All Moose have large, blunt muzzles, and wide, palm-shaped antlers in the male, spanning 6½ft (2 m), each with around 20 points. Brownish gray in summer, its grayish winter coat has longer guard-hairs with woollier underfur to withstand severe cold. Its long legs are lighter in color, and have wide hooves for wading in water and mud, and walking on snow. The Moose inhabits woodland close to swamps and lakes. In summer, it may stand submerged with only its eyes and nostrils above the surface, feeding on the roots of water-lily and other aquatic plants. It also feeds on sedges, horsetails, and other leafy vegetation, although in winter its diet mainly comprises twigs of willow and poplar. The Moose's broad muzzle and flexible lips help it to grasp water plants and strip leaves from twigs. It is usually solitary or found in small family groups, but males may form bachelor groups in winter. Rutting takes place in the fall when the usually silent male grunts and conducts head-to-head battles with other males to establish its dominance.

ALASKA, CANADA, EURASIA

wide, splayed antlers

• **SIZE** Length: 8¼–11 ft (2.5–3.5 m). Weight: 1,100–1,540 lb (500–700 kg).
• **OCCURRENCE** Alaska, Canada, and N. Europe to N. Asia. In marshy forest and taiga, close to water.
• **REMARK** The Moose is hunted for its meat and skin, and as a sporting trophy.

large, blunt muzzle

large dewlap in male

FEMALE GRAZING WITH CALF
The calf is born in May or June, and follows its mother within one or two days of its birth. It grows rapidly, fed on the mother's very rich milk; and she protects her calf from predators, using her hooves.

Social unit Variable	Gestation 242–250 days	Young 1–2	Diet 🌿

MARSHY HABITAT
Usually found in areas close to water,
the Moose is most active at dawn and
dusk. In the cold taiga, it may be
active in daylight, because of the long
hours of darkness in winter and the
reverse in summer.

*humped
• shoulders*

*brownish gray
• body*

*legs light
• in color*

*• bull larger and
heavier than cow*

EVEN-TOED UNGULATES
PRONGHORN

NAMED AFTER the forward-facing "prong" on each of its horns, this deerlike mammal is the only species in its family, Antilocapridae.

It has several features intermediate between those of deer and antelopes. Its horns consist of a horny sheath over a bony core, as in antelopes; yet they are forked, and are shed and regrown annually, like deer antlers. All males have horns; some females do, too, but these are smaller than the male's and usually do not have prongs. Each foot has two hoof-capped toes.

Pronghorns are restricted to the plains and deserts of North America. They are known to feed on a wide variety of grasses, leaves, and shrubs, as well as cacti and thornbushes. In arid places they can go for days without drinking any water, surviving on the moisture derived from their food.

Family ANTILOCAPRIDAE	Species *Antilopcapra americana*	Status Locally common

PRONGHORN

Locally known as the Prairie Ghost, the Pronghorn can run at a speed of more than 40 mph (65 kph) and vanish from sight within a few seconds. Reddish brown to tan, it has a black mane and underparts, a white rump, and two white stripes across its neck. The female has horns that seldom exceed the length of its ears, whereas in the male the horns grow up to 10 in (25 cm) long, curving backward at the tip, and with a forward-pointing "prong" arising from the upper half. The white rump hair is raised as a visual warning in times of danger and can be seen from a long distance. In winter, the Pronghorn may form herds of around 1,000 of mixed age and sex, which split into smaller groups in summer.

• **SIZE** Length: 3 ¼–5 ft (1–1.5 m). Weight: 79–155 lb (36–70 kg).
• **OCCURRENCE** S. Canada to W. and C. US. In grassland and desert.

forward-pointing prong from upper half of horn

two white stripes on neck

white rump hair raised as visual warning in danger

N. AMERICA

Social unit Variable	Gestation 252 days	Young 1–2	Diet 🌱

EVEN-TOED UNGULATES
GIRAFFE AND OKAPI

ONLY TWO SPECIES–the Giraffe and the Okapi–make up the family Giraffidae. They are both from Africa and are similar in many respects. Almost all parts of their anatomy are slim and elongated–head, tongue, neck, body, legs, and tail; this tendency is most exaggerated in the Giraffe. Both species have hornlike, cartilage-based ossicones, or short conical protrusions, on the head (although these are present only in male Okapis), and both browse with their prehensile tongues, using their peculiar, lobed canine teeth as leaf rakes.

However, in ecology and habits, the species are different. Giraffes frequent open savanna, and although they have individual home ranges, often gather in loose herds. The Okapi prefers thick forest, is solitary or found in pairs, and only males maintain territories.

Family GIRAFFIDAE	Species *Okapia johnstoni*	Status Lower risk

OKAPI

Shy and secretive, the Okapi feeds in dense forest, relying more on sound than sight to move around, and emitting a characteristic "chuff" sound on meeting another of its kind. Its sleek coat appears deep red, purple, brown, or black, depending on the angle of the light, and its face is white from the middle portion to the neck. Zebralike stripes on the rump and upper parts of the legs lend a distinctive stamp to its two-toned appearance. The female is taller and heavier than the male, and the male has a pair of short horns on his forehead. The Okapi curls its long, black prehensile tongue around vegetation to feed. The female also uses her tongue to groom herself and her young. The bond between mother and calf, however, is not as strong as it is in many other hoofed animals.
• **SIZE** Length: 6 ½ –7 ¼ ft (2 – 2.2 m). Weight: 440–770 lb (200–350 kg).
• **OCCURRENCE** N. and E.C. Zaire. In dense, damp equatorial forest.
• **REMARK** Once called the "forest zebra," the Okapi was not identified as a separate species until 1900.

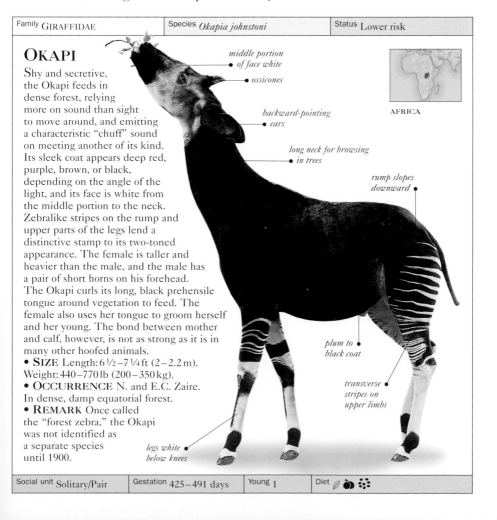

middle portion
• of face white
• ossicones

backward-pointing
• ears

AFRICA

long neck for browsing
• in trees

rump slopes
downward •

plum to •
black coat

transverse •
stripes on
upper limbs

legs white •
below knees

Social unit Solitary/Pair	Gestation 425–491 days	Young 1	Diet

Family GIRAFFIDAE	Species *Giraffa camelopardalis*	Status Lower risk

GIRAFFE

The tallest terrestrial animal, known to grow as tall as 18 ft (5.5 m), the Giraffe is adapted in several ways to browse high among trees. The combined height of its front legs, shoulders and neck, together with its elongated tongue and skull, provide it with great reach. Among the Giraffe's other distinctive features are large eyes and ears, 2–4 horns in both sexes, a back that slopes sharply from shoulders to rump, stiltlike legs with heavy feet, and a thin, tufted tail for whisking away flies. The Giraffe feeds and drinks in the morning and evening, chews cud during the hottest part of the day, and rests (on its feet) at night. Male hierarchy is established by "necking," where two males stand parallel, swinging their necks at each other and striking with the side of the head, in a slow ritualized display. Cows mate with the local dominant bulls. The newborn Giraffe calf stands 6½ ft (2 m) tall and is up on its feet within about 20 minutes of birth. It is weaned at 13 months and stays 2–5 months longer with the mother.
• **SIZE** Length: 9¾–15 ft (3.8–4.7 m). Weight: ½–2 tons (0.6–1.9 tonnes).
• **OCCURRENCE** Africa, south of the Sahara. In dry savanna and open woodland – associated with scattered acacia.

AFRICA

massive pectoral girdle to support neck •

long and flexible neck •

splayed front legs •

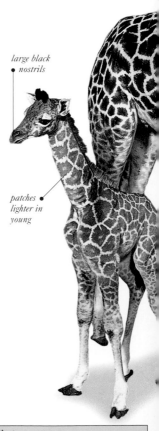

large black nostrils •

patches lighter in young •

HOW A GIRAFFE DRINKS
The Giraffe splays out its front legs and bends its neck in order to drink water. Normally its heart pumps blood all the way up to its brain at enormous pressure. When it bends, several one-way valves control the force of blood to prevent brain damage.

Social unit Variable	Gestation 457 days	Young 1	Diet 🌿

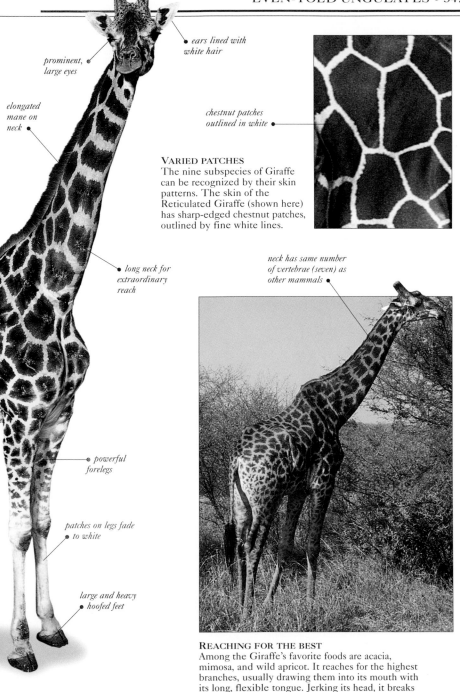

prominent,
large eyes

ears lined with
white hair

elongated
mane on
neck

chestnut patches
outlined in white

VARIED PATCHES
The nine subspecies of Giraffe
can be recognized by their skin
patterns. The skin of the
Reticulated Giraffe (shown here)
has sharp-edged chestnut patches,
outlined by fine white lines.

long neck for
extraordinary
reach

neck has same number
of vertebrae (seven) as
other mammals

powerful
forelegs

patches on legs fade
to white

large and heavy
hoofed feet

REACHING FOR THE BEST
Among the Giraffe's favorite foods are acacia,
mimosa, and wild apricot. It reaches for the highest
branches, usually drawing them into its mouth with
its long, flexible tongue. Jerking its head, it breaks
off the leaves between its lobe-edged teeth.

EVEN-TOED UNGULATES
CATTLE, ANTELOPE AND RELATIVES

T HE FAMILY Bovidae, with 140 species, is extremely diverse. Members range from the huge Bison to the small Duiker, and include antelopes such as Wildebeest and Impala, as well as sheep and goats.

However, bovids share many features. They have two large, hoof-capped toes on each foot, forming the characteristic cloven hoof of artiodactyls (even-toed ungulates); there are also usually two smaller toes, one on each side. Most bovids grow bone-cored horns, which are unbranched and often present in both sexes. The horns may be long or short, straight or curled, ridged or smooth.

Many species occur in Africa, with others in Eurasia and North America. Several domesticated bovids, including familiar farmyard cows, sheep, and goats, have been introduced worldwide and are of vast economic importance.

Family BOVIDAE	Species *Tragelaphus spekei*	Status Lower risk

SITATUNGA

Amphibious by nature, the Sitatunga has flexible foot joints and pointed, widely splayed hooves, allowing it to walk in swamps and marshes. Adult males are gray- to chocolate-brown in colour, whereas females are bright chestnut. Both sexes have white patches around the eyes, cheeks, and on the body, but only the male has ridged, spiraling horns. The Sitatunga browses on vegetation that is in flower. When faced by a predator, the Sitatunga readily takes refuge in water. The female may be found alone or in groups of around three. The solitary adult male barks avoidance calls (usually at night) to other males. On meeting, males display aggressive posturing and rub their horns on the ground.

• **SIZE** Length: 4–5½ ft (1.2–1.7m). Weight: 110–280 lb (50–125 kg).
• **OCCURRENCE** W. and C. Africa. In rain forest and wetter regions of the savanna.

ridged and spiraled horns

horns only in male

wavy pattern between eyes

gray-brown color in males

brown to bright chestnut coat of female

AFRICA

IMMERSED IN WATER
The Sitatunga browses at morning, evening, and sometimes at night, but rests in swamps by day. It may feed submerged in water, and even rears up on its hindfeet to reach tall sedges and weeds.

Social unit Variable	Gestation 247 days	Young 1	Diet 🌿

Family BOVIDAE	Species *Tragelaphus eurycerus*	Status Lower risk*

BONGO

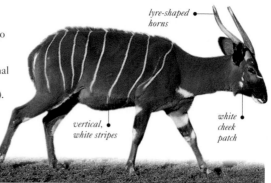

lyre-shaped horns

The most colorful antelope, the Bongo has white vertical stripes on its bright chestnut body, and white cheek and chest patches. It is a selective, nocturnal browser of high-protein vegetation.
• **SIZE** Length:5½–8¼ft (1.7–2.5m). Weight:460–890lb (210–405kg).

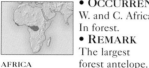

• **OCCURRENCE** W. and C. Africa. In forest.
• **REMARK** The largest forest antelope.

AFRICA

vertical, white stripes

white cheek patch

Social unit Variable	Gestation 282–287 days	Young 1	Diet 🌿

Family BOVIDAE	Species *Tragelaphus angasi*	Status Lower risk

NYALA

spiral horns

bushy tail

The male Nyala, larger than the female, is charcoal-gray with indistinct stripes, and has short horns. Females have no horns, and like juveniles are red-brown with white vertical body stripes and a white "V" between the eyes. Active in the morning and evening, both graze and browse, rearing up to reach higher branches. Females and young form small herds, while adult males are solitary.
• **SIZE** Length:4½–5¼ft (1.4–1.6m). Weight:120–280lb (55–125kg).
• **OCCURRENCE** S. Africa. In dense bush, close to water.

lower legs light brown

AFRICA

Social unit Social	Gestation 220 days	Young 1	Diet 🌿 🐚 🌾

Family BOVIDAE	Species *Tragelaphus scriptus*	Status Locally common

BUSHBUCK

only the males have horns

This antelope is primarily a browser on herbs and legumes. The male is uniformly dark brown to black, with white marks on the neck and body, varying according to the subspecies. Females inhabiting the bush are pale tawny, while those in forests are redder. The Bushbuck resembles a small Sitatunga (see left) with less twisted horns.
• **SIZE** Length:3½–5ft (1.1–1.5m). Weight:55–175lb (25–80kg).
• **OCCURRENCE** Sub-Saharan Africa, except S.W. region. In forest, near water sources.
• **REMARK** One of the most common antelopes.

powerful hindquarters

whitish lower limbs

AFRICA

Social unit Solitary	Gestation 6 months	Young 1	Diet 🌿 🌾

Family BOVIDAE	Species *Tragelaphus strepsiceros*	Status Lower risk*

GREATER KUDU

One of the tallest antelopes, the Greater Kudu has a predominantly gray, white-striped coat, with a prominent white chevron (wavy pattern) on its nose, and small spots on either side of its face. It has funnel-shaped ears and a long throat fringe. Only the male has horns– at 5½ft (1.7m), they are the longest of any species of antelope. Active during the day and night, this antelope browses on leaves, herbs, tubers, flowers, and fruits. Females form nonhierarchical groups of five or six; males associate in bachelor groups of 2–10. During the rutting season, rival males link horns, shoving and twisting in an effort to overthrow each other. This antelope's acute sense of hearing enables it to locate predators. At times of danger, it stands completely still, or moves away quietly, easily jumping over obstacles of 6½ft (2m) or more.

AFRICA

- **SIZE** Length: 6½–8¼ft (2–2.5m). Weight: 260–690lb (120–315kg).
- **OCCURRENCE** E. to S. Africa. In light forest or fairly thick bush, often in rocky or mountainous country.
- **REMARK** Threatened by habitat loss, the Greater Kudu is also hunted as a sporting trophy and for its meat.

WATER-DEPENDENT
Usually found in forest or hilly bush country, the Greater Kudu prefers to remain close to water, resting during the afternoon to avoid the heat.

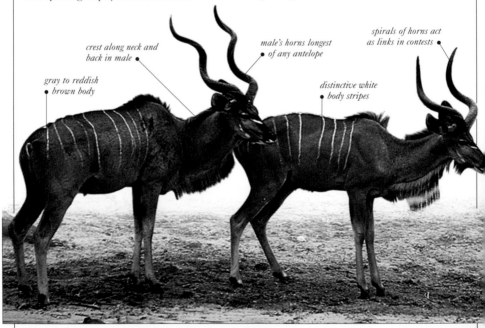

crest along neck and back in male

gray to reddish brown body

male's horns longest of any antelope

spirals of horns act as links in contests

distinctive white body stripes

Social unit Social	Gestation 9 months	Young 1	Diet 🌿🥕🍎🐛

| Family BOVIDAE | Species *Taurotragus oryx* | Status Lower risk |

COMMON ELAND

horns with tight spirals

Tight spiraling horns are a distinctive feature of both sexes of the Common Eland–the largest antelope. It has 2–15 cream vertical stripes on its upper body and the male has a brownish black "topknot" of matted hair on its head. Females band together to protect their young in the manner of cattle. Like the camel, this antelope allows its body temperature to rise by up to 13°F (7°C) during drought to avoid losing water as sweat.

shoulder hump

AFRICA

black-tipped tail

brownish fawn body

• **SIZE** Length:7–11ft (2.1–3.5 m). Weight:660–2,210 lb (300–1,000 kg).
• **OCCURRENCE** C., E., and S. Africa. In open plains, dry savanna, montane grassland, heath, and highland forest.
• **REMARK** These docile antelopes are ranched for meat, milk, and hides in Africa. They have been exported to Asia.

| Social unit Variable | Gestation 254–277 days | Young 1 | Diet 🌿 🥕 |

| Family BOVIDAE | Species *Boselaphus tragocamelus* | Status Lower risk |

NILGAI

dark mane in both sexes

Neither cow nor antelope, the Nilgai along with the Chousingha (see p.352) is a member of the subfamily Boselaphinae. Although the Nilgai is called the Bluebuck or Blue Bull, only the male is gray or bluish gray, while the female is tawny.
• **SIZE** Length:6–7 ft (1.8–2.1 m). Weight: Up to 660 lb (300 kg).
• **OCCURRENCE** S. Asia. In thinly wooded country, low jungle, and open plains.

throat tuft in male

forelegs longer than hindlegs

dark lower limbs

ASIA

| Social unit Social | Gestation 243–247 days | Young 1–2 | Diet 🌿 🌰 🌾 |

Family BOVIDAE	Species *Tetracerus quadricornus*	Status Vulnerable

CHOUSINGHA

Also called the Four-horned Antelope, this species is unique among bovids in that the male has two pairs of horns. It has a black muzzle and outer ears, and its brownish coat has a dark stripe on the front of each leg. This small, reclusive, and fast-moving antelope usually grazes near water; it uses a low whistle for identification, barking for an alarm call.
• **SIZE** Length: 32–39 in (80–100 cm). Weight: 37–46 lb (17–21 kg).
• **OCCURRENCE** India and Nepal. In wooded hillsides, near water.

large, rounded ears

brownish coat

ASIA

distinctive black muzzle

Social unit Solitary	Gestation 7–8 months	Young 1–2	Diet

Family BOVIDAE	Species *Bubalus depressicornis*	Status Endangered

ANOA

This small bovid is dark brown to black, with a pale throat "bib," and facial and leg patches. Its short horns sweep diagonally backward, enabling it to push through dense, swampy forest. It feeds in the morning on fruits, leaves, ferns, and twigs.
• **SIZE** Length: 5¼–5½ ft (1.6–1.7 m). Weight: 330–660 lb (150–300 kg).

ASIA

• **OCCURRENCE** Sulawesi. In lowland and swampy forest.
• **REMARK** This bovid is one of the smallest wild cattle.

plump, stocky body   *flattened horns*

short legs

Social unit Solitary	Gestation 9–10 months	Young 1	Diet

Family BOVIDAE	Species *Bubalus arnee*	Status Endangered

WATER BUFFALO

Domesticated for centuries and spread around the world, the Water Buffalo is found wild only in small, scattered populations. Also known as the Arni, this massive animal lives in stable clans of females, ruled by a matriarch. Dominant males move into the clan area in the wet season to mate. This buffalo feeds on lush vegetation, and wallows during midday.

ASIA

• **SIZE** Length: 7¾–9¾ ft (2.4–3 m). Weight: Up to 1 ton (1.2 tonnes).
• **OCCURRENCE** India, Nepal, and possibly Thailand. In wetland.
• **REMARK** It has the largest horns of any bovid: over 6½ ft (2 m) long.

narrow face   *wrinkled horns*

body is slate-black

Social unit Social	Gestation 300–340 days	Young 1	Diet

Family BOVIDAE	Species *Syncerus caffer*	Status Locally common*

AFRICAN BUFFALO

Africa's only cattle-like animal, this buffalo is found in a variety of habitats, but never farther than 9 miles (15 km) from water. The male is much larger than the female and has heavier horns that meet at a boss or protuberance on the forehead. It also has a thicker neck, a hump, and small fringe on its dewlap. Extremely gregarious, the nocturnal African Buffalo gathers in herds of 2,000 when food is plentiful. In the dry season, herds split into smaller groups of females and young, bachelor bands of males, and solitary older males.

• SIZE Length: 7–11 ft (2.1–3.4 m). Weight: Up to 1,510 lb (685 kg).
• OCCURRENCE W., C., E., and S. Africa. In primary and secondary forest, savanna, swamps, and grassy plains to mountains.

AFRICA

heavy boss on forehead where horns meet in male

naked muzzle

large feet with rounded hooves

Social unit Social	Gestation 340 days	Young 1	Diet 🌾 🌿

Family BOVIDAE	Species *Bos javanicus*	Status Endangered

BANTENG

This bovid resembles the domestic cow in appearance. The male is blackish brown to dark chestnut, whereas the female and juvenile are reddish brown; all have white undersides, legs, and rump patches. The male's horns are angled out and then inward, whereas the female has smaller, crescent-shaped horns. Feeding on grass in the dry season, the Banteng moves to the hills in the monsoon, to eat bamboo and herbs. Females and young live in herds of 2–40 with a single male, while bachelors form their own herds.

• SIZE Length: 6–7½ ft (1.8–2.3 m). Weight: 880–1,990 lb (400–900 kg).
• OCCURRENCE Burma, Java, and Borneo. In forest and thicket with open glades.
• REMARK The wild population of Banteng is scarce and its habitat is fast diminishing.

ASIA

proportions resemble large domestic cow

horns smaller in female

coat reddish brown in female

white "stockings"

Social unit Social	Gestation 9½ months	Young 1–2	Diet 🌾 🌿

Family BOVIDAE	Species *Bos grunniens*	Status Vulnerable

YAK

Brownish black with long, shaggy hair on either side that almost reaches the ground, the Yak has long been domesticated by the people of Asia for wool, meat, milk, leather, and as a means of transportation. The wild Yak, larger and extremely rare, is confined to desolate, bitterly cold steppe. The dense, soft undercoat of closely matted hair protects it from the extreme cold. Grazing on grasses, herbs, and even lichen, the Yak crunches up frozen ice or snow as a source of water. Females and young gather in large herds, whereas adult males are usually solitary or rove in bachelor herds. During the mating season, which begins in September and lasts several weeks, males battle each other for access to females. A single calf is born every other year and reared by the mother, becoming independent only after it is about a year old. Hunted by Tibetan wolves, Yaks flee speedily when threatened, galloping across large distances with their tails held erect.

ASIA

DIFFERENT HUES
Domestic Yak can be mottled, black, brown or red. In spring, Yak molt into a shorter summer coat that is more variable in coloration.

• **SIZE** Length: Up to 11 ft (3.3 m). Weight: Up to 1,160 lb (525 kg).
• **OCCURRENCE** Kashmir (India) east to Tibet and Qinghai (China). In desolate steppe at elevations up to 19,800 ft (6,000 m).

horns in both male and female •

high, humped • *shoulders*

dark, brownish black coat •

• *fringe around lower shoulders*

extremely long • *outer hair*

Social unit Variable	Gestation 258 days	Young 1	Diet

Family BOVIDAE	Species *Bos gaurus*	Status Vulnerable*

GAUR

The largest of the wild cattle, the Gaur, also called the Seladang or Indian Bison, has a massive, humped body in shades of red, brown, and black, and white "stockings" on its lower limbs. Both sexes have upward-curving horns up to 3 ½ ft (1.1 m) long. Males in rut "sing" with a series of low bellows that carry over long distances.
• **SIZE** Length: 8 ¼ –11 ft (2.5–3.3 m). Weight: 1,430–2,210 lb (650–1,000 kg).
• **OCCURRENCE** S. to S.E. Asia. In evergreen and deciduous, forested hills.

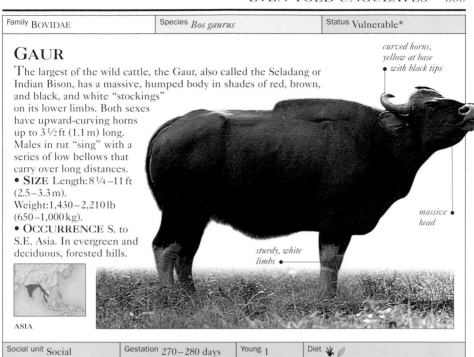

curved horns, yellow at base with black tips

massive head

sturdy, white limbs

ASIA

Social unit Social	Gestation 270–280 days	Young 1	Diet 🌾 🌿

Family BOVIDAE	Species *Bison bonasus*	Status Endangered

EUROPEAN BISON

Formerly extinct in the wild, the European Bison or Wisent has been bred in parks and reintroduced in the Bialowieza Forest (on the border of Poland and Belarus). Latest genetic research reveals that it is probably the same species as the American Bison (see pp. 356–357). It has a lighter and shorter coat, but resembles its American cousin in habits and social behavior. Both sexes have sharp, upturned horns. Mainly a browser, this bison also grazes.
• **SIZE** Length: 7–11 ft (2.1–3.4 m). Weight: 660–2,030 lb (300–920 kg).
• **OCCURRENCE** E. Europe. In woodland, grassland, and coniferous forest.

well-developed shoulder hump

EUROPE

brownish black coat

hindlegs of lighter color than forelegs

Social unit Social	Gestation 260–270 days	Young 1	Diet 🌿 🌾

Family BOVIDAE	Species *Bison bison*	Status Lower risk

AMERICAN BISON

Sometimes called Buffalo in North America, this massively built bison looks deceptively tall because its shoulder hump reaches 6 ½ ft (2 m). It has long, shaggy brownish black hair on its head, neck, shoulders, and forelegs, but the rest of its body is covered in shorter, paler hair. The large, heavy head has a broad forehead with short, upturned horns and a straggly beard. The male is significantly larger than the female. The American Bison is a swift runner despite its huge bulk, and can reach a speed of up to 37 mph (60 kph). Its sense of smell and hearing are excellent and essential for detecting danger. Found in loose herds, adult females and their young form hierarchical groups, whereas males form bachelor herds and join the females only during the mating season. Not territorial, the American Bison migrates south in winter in search of food. Mostly found within the boundaries of national parks today, herds of bison would once make annual migrations of hundreds of miles along traditional routes, when they roamed freely in the wild.

pronounced shoulder hump characterizes the male

short, upturned black horns

- **SIZE** Length:7–11 ft (2.1–3.5 m). Weight:770–2,200 lb (350–1,000 kg).
- **OCCURRENCE** Yellowstone National Park (US) and Wood Buffalo National Park (Canada). In grassland, mountainous regions, and open forest.
- **REMARK** Recent genetic evidence indicates that the European Bison (see pp. 354–355), is more similar to its American counterpart than was previously believed.

large, heavily built head with broad forehead

straggly, dark beard

CONSERVATION-DEPENDENT
Once numbering around 50 million, the American Bison was widely hunted and is now virtually extinct in the wild. Although subsequent efforts have led to an increase in numbers, most bison are either captive or come from captive stock.

Social unit Social	Gestation 285 days	Young 1	Diet 🌱

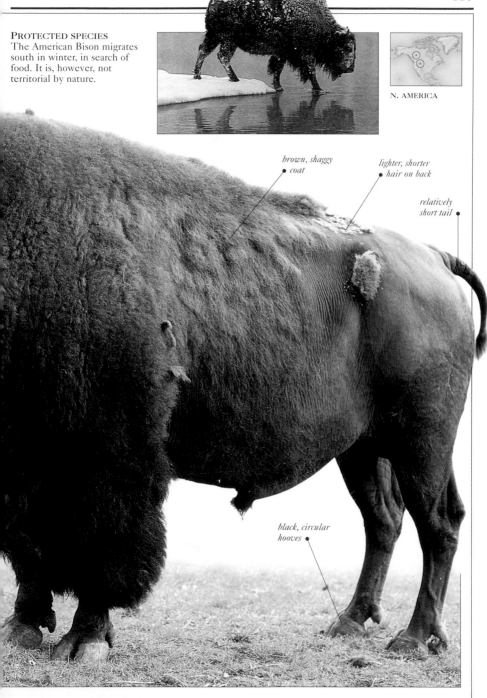

PROTECTED SPECIES
The American Bison migrates south in winter, in search of food. It is, however, not territorial by nature.

N. AMERICA

brown, shaggy coat

lighter, shorter hair on back

relatively short tail

black, circular hooves

Family BOVIDAE	Species *Cephalophus natalensis*	Status Lower risk

NATAL DUIKER

One of 18 or so duiker species, the Natal Duiker is a small, arch-backed antelope with longer hindlegs than forelegs. Red-orange to dark brown in color, it has a tail that is reddish at the base, with a tufted tip that is black-and-white. Both sexes usually have short, backward-pointing horns with a crest of long hair in between, and large scent glands beneath each eye. Duikers freeze midstride or sink into the undergrowth when they spot a predator, and dart away at great speed if discovered. They stamp their hindfeet as an alarm call, instead of the forefeet as in other savanna antelope.
• **SIZE** Length: 28–39 in (70–100 cm). Weight: 29 lb (13 kg).

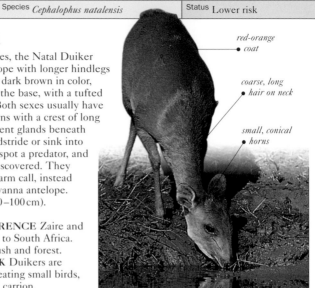
red-orange coat

coarse, long hair on neck

small, conical horns

• **OCCURRENCE** Zaire and S. Tanzania to South Africa. In dense bush and forest.
• **REMARK** Duikers are unusual in eating small birds, insects, and carrion.

AFRICA

Social unit Pair	Gestation 120 days	Young 1	Diet ↯ 🍂 🍎 🐦 🦎 ※

Family BOVIDAE	Species *Sylvicapra grimmia*	Status Locally common

BUSH DUIKER

A tufted forehead, dark nose stripe, and large, pointed ears characterize the Bush Duiker. Gray to red-yellow above, it has whitish underparts, and the male has sharp horns, around 4¼ in (11 cm) long. Female duikers are usually bigger and heavier than males. A nocturnal browser, the Bush Duiker eats leaves, fruits, flowers, tubers, insects, frogs, birds, small mammals, and even carrion. It can go without water for long periods and does not drink in the rainy season, obtaining fluids from fruits, which it often scavenges from beneath trees where monkeys are feeding. Sometimes it reaches for food standing on its hindlegs. The success of this antelope stems from its ability to adapt to a wide spectrum of habitats and food.

rear may be darker color

long tuft of reddish hair on forehead

brown to black nasal stripe

fetlocks brown to black

• **SIZE** Length: 2¼–4 ft (0.7–1.2 m). Weight: 26–55 lb (12–25 kg).
• **OCCURRENCE** Senegal to Ethiopia and S. Africa. In savanna and hilly areas.

AFRICA

Social unit Solitary/Pair	Gestation 191 days	Young 1	Diet 🍂 🐦 🦎 ※ 🐦 🦎 🐸

Family BOVIDAE	Species *Kobus ellipsiprymnus*	Status Lower risk

WATERBUCK

One of the heaviest antelopes, the Waterbuck has a long neck and body, and short legs. Ranging from gray to red-brown, its coat darkens with age. White patches mark its eyebrows, throat, muzzle, underparts, rump, and top of the hooves. Special skin glands secrete an oil that emits a musky odor and waterproofs its fur. Only the males have horns, which are ringed and grow up to 3 ½ ft (1m) long. When threatened, the Waterbuck either fights with its horns and hooves, or takes refuge underwater, exposing only its nostrils.

• **SIZE** Length: 4 ¼ – 7 ¾ ft (1.3 – 2.4 m). Weight: 110 – 660 lb (50 – 300 kg).

• **OCCURRENCE** W., C., and E. Africa. In savanna with patches of woodland and standing water.

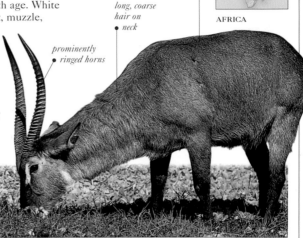

gray to red-brown • coat

long, coarse hair on • neck

AFRICA

prominently • ringed horns

Social unit Variable	Gestation 9 months	Young 1	Diet 🌱 🍃

Family BOVIDAE	Species *Kobus leche*	Status Lower risk

LECHWE

Also known as the Marsh Antelope, the Lechwe lives on floodplains and in swamps, feeding on grass and water plants that are exposed with the seasonal change in water levels. Adapted to wading and swimming, with strong hindquarters and elongated hooves, it moves over shallow water in a series of leaps, and only rests and calves on dry land. The chestnut to black coat contrasts with the white underparts and black leg stripes. Only males have thin, lyre-shaped horns. The Lechwe forms large, loose herds, and where numbers are high follows the "lek" breeding system, like the Kob (see p. 360).

• **SIZE** Length: 4 ½ – 7 ¾ ft (1.3 – 2.4 m). Weight: 175 – 230 lb (79 – 103 kg).

AFRICA

• **OCCURRENCE** C. to S. Africa. In wetland.

• **REMARK** The Lechwe is known to be the fastest moving antelope in water.

hindquarters higher • than front

faint white • stripes over eyes

elongated, wide hooves •

black marks • on legs

Social unit Social	Gestation 7–8 months	Young 1	Diet 🌱 🍃 🌾

Family BOVIDAE	Species *Kobus kob*	Status Lower risk

KOB

Strong, but gracefully built, this antelope is pale cinnamon to brown-black, with white patches on its face and throat, and black leg stripes and feet. The male has distinctive ringed, lyre-shaped horns. Where kobs are found in very dense populations, males gather on an elevated patch of ground (known as a lek), which may be only 50 ft (15 m) across. Usually the heaviest male on the lek gains mating rights over several females through a ritualized display that rarely involves fighting. However, where the density of Kobs is low, males maintain a standard territory and stop females from leaving it by herding them. Active during the morning and evening, the Kob needs to drink water daily. It makes a high bleating sound in times of danger and leaps toward the nearest reedbed to escape.
• SIZE Length: 4¼–7¾ft (1.3–2.4 m). Weight:110–660 lb (50–300 kg).
• OCCURRENCE W. to E. Africa. In moist savanna, floodplains, and margins of woodland with permanent water.
• REMARK The Kob makes up the largest antelope population in Africa after the Wildebeeste.

lyre-shaped, ringed horns in male

white around eyes

short, glossy coat

AFRICA

black markings on front of legs

Social unit Social	Gestation 261–271 days	Young 1	Diet 🌱 🍃

Family BOVIDAE	Species *Kobus vardonii*	Status Lower risk

PUKU

A uniform golden yellow in color, the Puku has a whitish area around its eyes, and on its muzzle and throat, and its legs are reddish brown. The male is usually larger than the female, with curved horns about 20 in (50 cm) long. Mostly found in small herds of 3–15, the Puku uses body postures to communicate. It resembles the Kob (see above) in its breeding system, having leks at high poulation densities and territories at lower ones. It feeds on grasses, and occasionally acacia, and like all plains antelopes, flees rapidly when in danger.
• SIZE Length: 4¼–6 ft (1.3–1.8 m). Weight:145–170 lb (66–77 kg).
• OCCURRENCE W. to E. Africa. In savanna, near marshes or riverbanks.
• REMARK The Puku could be regarded as a southern savanna version of the Kob. However, there is no interbreeding between the two species of antelope.

short horns

whitish hue on muzzle

AFRICA

uniformly reddish legs

Social unit Variable	Gestation 8 months	Young 1	Diet 🌱 🍃

Family BOVIDAE	Species *Redunca redunca*	Status Lower risk

BOHOR REEDBUCK

This small, lightly built antelope has a fawn coat and white underparts, throat, and eye-rings. A conspicuous gray patch below the ear indicates a scent gland. Larger than the female, the male has a thicker neck and more clearly defined markings. Its horns curve sharply, almost forming hooks at the tips. The Bohor Reedbuck feeds in the morning, evening, and sometimes at night, on grasses and tender reed shoots. When threatened, it gallops away, exposing the white underside of its tail. The female lives alone with her fawn, bachelors live in groups of two or three, and adult males are solitary. However, loose herds of a few hundred form in the dry season.

- **SIZE** Length: 3 ½–5 ¼ ft (1.1–1.6 m). Weight: 42–210 lb (19–95 kg).
- **OCCURRENCE** W. to E. Africa. In savanna, most commonly on wide, open floodplains.

hooked horns in male

yellowish to reddish fawn coat

long, narrow hooves

AFRICA

Social unit Variable	Gestation 7–7 ½ months	Young 1	Diet 🌾 🍃

Family BOVIDAE	Species *Hippotragus equinus*	Status Lower risk

ROAN ANTELOPE

Red to brown above with white underparts, the Roan Antelope has black-and-white markings on its face. It is the fourth largest antelope and both sexes have stout, heavily ringed horns, and an upright, black-edged mane. It can survive on very little grass, drinking water two or three times daily. Herds consist of 12–15 females and young with one dominant male, or younger bachelor males. Rival males fight on their knees with violent backward sweeps of their curved horns.

- **SIZE** Length: 6 ¼–8 ¾ ft (1.9–2.7 m). Weight: 330–660 lb (150–300 kg).
- **OCCURRENCE** W., C., and E. Africa. In savanna.

erect mane

pale reddish brown body

black blaze on face

black-and-white markings on face

AFRICA

Social unit Variable	Gestation 268–280 days	Young 1	Diet 🌾 🍃

Family BOVIDAE	Species *Hippotragus niger*	Status Lower risk

SABLE ANTELOPE

AFRICA

Distinctive facial markings, white with a central black blaze and cheek stripes, characterize this large antelope, which is similar to the Roan Antelope in many respects (see p. 361). Mature males are black, whereas females and juveniles are yellowish brown to rich chestnut, with the same facial pattern as males. Both sexes have stout and heavily ringed horns and a well-developed, erect mane from the top of the neck to the withers, with shorter hair on the throat. This antelope gathers in herds of around 100 during the dry season, splitting into smaller groups in the rainy season, both sexes following a hierarchy. Young males form bachelor groups of 2–12; dominant males vigorously defend their own territories and mate with the females residing there. This antelope is usually active in the early mornings and afternoons, although some herds may be nocturnal.

• SIZE Length: 6¼–8¾ ft (1.9–2.7m). Weight: 330–660 lb (150–300 kg).
• OCCURRENCE E. to S.E. Africa. In lightly wooded grassland.
• REMARK Once hunted for trophy heads, political unrest in Africa has also affected this animal and a subspecies, the Giant Sable of Angola, is critically endangered.

well-developed, upright mane •

long, pointed ears •

black cheek stripes •

FINDING FOOD
Primarily a grazer, the Sable Antelope also browses extensively during the dry season. It always lives within 1¼–2½ miles (2–4km) of water.

Social unit Social	Gestation 261–281 days	Young 1	Diet ↯

Family BOVIDAE	Species *Oryx gazella*	Status Lower risk

GEMSBOK

With a body in contrasting shades of gray, black, and white, the Gemsbok, or Southern Oryx as it is also known, has a fawn-tinged, gray body with a black longitudinal stripe along its belly, black upper legs and tail, and a distinctive black-and-white facial pattern. The Gemsbok is well-adapted to life in arid regions: it does not pant or sweat until its body temperature reaches 113° F (45° C), and produces concentrated urine and dry feces. Feeding at night, in the early morning, as well as late afternoon, this antelope supplements its main diet of grass and shrubs with melons and cucumbers for water.

- **SIZE** Length: 5¼–7¾ft (1.6–2.4m). Weight: 220–460lb (100–210kg).
- **OCCURRENCE** Namibia and W. South Africa. In arid scrub and desert.
- **REMARK** Almost perfectly adapted to desert life, it lives in dry conditions where few other ungulates would survive.

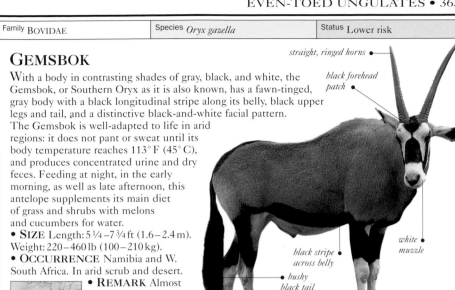

straight, ringed horns

black forehead patch

white muzzle

black stripe across belly

bushy black tail

AFRICA

Social unit Social	Gestation 260–300 days	Young 1	Diet 🌿

Family BOVIDAE	Species *Oryx dammah*	Status Critically endangered

SCIMITAR-HORNED ORYX

Pale tan in color, the Scimitar-horned Oryx has a brownish patch on its forehead, face, and across its eyes, and a russet neck and chest; both sexes have long horns that curve back in a wide arc. The Oryx shares many features with the Gemsbok (see above) to survive in arid regions; it also has enlarged hooves to bear the weight of its stocky body on the sand. Feeding on grasses, legumes, acacia pods, succulents, and fruits, in the early morning, evening, and on moonlit nights, this oryx rests in the shade by day. Mixed herds wander over great distances in search of grazing. Males fight fiercely over a mate, displaying, tussling, and stabbing with horns.

- **SIZE** Length: 5¼–7¾ft (1.5–2.4m). Weight: 220–460lb (100–210kg).
- **OCCURRENCE** Chad. On arid, rocky plains.
- **REMARK** Hunted almost to extinction, this oryx is found in a reserve in N.C. Chad. It was reintroduced in Tunisia in 1991, and further releases have been planned.

horns longer and more slender in female

ruddy chest

body washed with russet

tufted brown tail

large, broad hooves

AFRICA

Social unit Social	Gestation 222–253 days	Young 1	Diet 🌿🍎

Family BOVIDAE	Species *Addax nasomaculatus*	Status Critically endangered

ADDAX

Found in remote desert areas, this rare, little-known antelope is adapted to its arid habitat in various ways: its short legs and widely splayed hooves enable it to move easily across sand, and it rarely drinks water, getting it instead from the succulent plants it eats. Active early in the morning, evening, and first half of the night, this nomadic animal travels great distances in search of almost any desert vegetation, following rainfall. Formerly living in herds of 5–20, led by an older male, these antelopes are today found alone or in isolated groups of 2–4. The Addax has a white face patch and a chestnut forehead tuft; its sandy to white summer coat turns grayish brown in winter. Its spiral horns have up to three turns.
• **SIZE** Length:5–5½ft (1.5–1.7 m). Weight:130–280lb (60–125 kg).
• **OCCURRENCE** N.W. Africa. In desert as well as in semidesert.

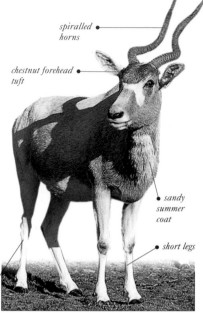

spiralled horns

chestnut forehead tuft

sandy summer coat

short legs

AFRICA

• **REMARK** Not capable of great speed, the Addax is an easy prey for humans. In recent years, it has faced the additional threat of severe drought.

white from hip to hoof

Social unit Variable	Gestation 257–264 days	Young 1	Diet 🌿

Family BOVIDAE	Species *Damaliscus pygargus*	Status Vulnerable

BONTEBOK

Rich purplish brown with a broad white blaze on its long muzzle, the Bontebok, or Blesbok as it is also called, has well-developed, lyre-shaped, ringed horns. Adult males use their horns to posture and spar – rarely engaging in actual physical fighting – to gain a territory. The herd of females and young is led by a dominant male, who keeps them together and initiates their travels. The female gives birth to its single offspring at traditional calving grounds, without isolating or concealing its young, unlike other similar antelopes. The newborn can walk within about 5 minutes, and soon follows its mother. It is weaned at about 6 months.
• **SIZE** Length:4–7 ft (1.2–2.1 m). Weight:150–340lb (68–155 kg).
• **OCCURRENCE** S. Africa. In grassland and sparsely wooded regions; now also in macchia scrub reserves.

horns have rings for most of length

brown coat with purplish sheen

AFRICA

• **REMARK** Almost extinct in the wild by the 1830s (only 17 were left), several herds of Bontebok were preserved in parks and reserves. It remains Africa's rarest antelope.

contrasting white lower legs

Social unit Social	Gestation 8 months	Young 1	Diet 🌱🌿

Family BOVIDAE	Species *Damaliscus lunatus*	Status Lower risk

TOPI

Also called the Tsessebe, this antelope has
an attractive, glossy reddish brown coat with
darker purple patches on the upperparts
of its legs, hips, and thighs. It has a long
head, a shoulder hump, and a back that
slopes downward. Both sexes have ringed,
L-shaped horns which curve inward
at the tips; the female may have a paler coat
and smaller horns. Often found in association with
Wildebeest, zebras, and Ostriches, the Topi lives in
seasonally flooded grassland and uses its long, narrow
muzzle and mobile lips to feed on grasses and
other vegetation. It has two breeding systems
according to habitat and ecology – mature males
hold territories and harems among resident
populations, but form smaller territories or
"leks"among populations that are nomadic.
Sentinels standing on termite mounds or higher
ground warn others of danger, sending them
galloping off with a rocking motion.
• **SIZE** Length: 4–7 ft (1.2–2.1 m).
Weight: 150–340 lb (68–155 kg).
• **OCCURRENCE** W., E., and S. Africa.
In open country and sparsely wooded areas,
preferring knee-high grassland.

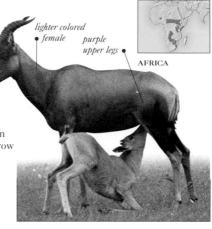

*lighter colored
female* *purple
upper legs*

AFRICA

MOTHER AND CALF
The female Topi may mate
with one or more males
in the breeding season.
The single offspring may be
kept hidden or follow
its mother around.

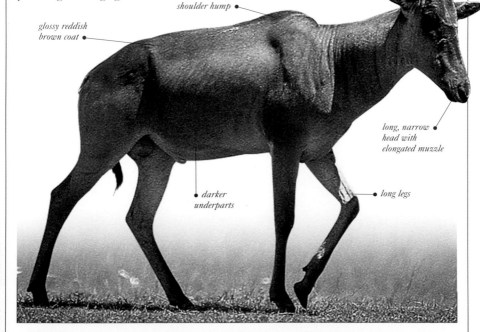

shoulder hump

*glossy reddish
brown coat*

*long, narrow
head with
elongated muzzle*

*darker
underparts*

long legs

Social unit Social	Gestation 7 1/2–8 months	Young 1	Diet 🌱 🍃

Family BOVIDAE	Species *Connochaetes taurinus*	Status Lower risk

WILDEBEEST

This large antelope, with its unmistakable clumsy appearance, is also known as the Brindled Gnu or Blue Wildebeest. With high shoulders and a large head and muzzle, it has cowlike horns and a copious black mane that spills over its forehead, neck, and shoulders. It is grayish silver with brownish bands on its neck, shoulders, and foreparts, and its beard is either black or white, depending on the subspecies. Both sexes have black, unridged horns that are horizontal at the base, and then curve upward and inward. Feeding mainly on grass, as well as succulents, the Wildebeest grazes in the early mornings and late afternoons, and rests during the heat of the day. Females and young form separate herds of 10–1,000, whereas males form bachelor groups and at 3–4 years try to form their individual territory with ritual posturing, pushing, and a typical "ge-nuu" call. Only adult males with territories can mate. Hunted by Leopards, Cheetahs, Lions, hyenas, and Hunting Dogs, the Wildebeest prances about and paws the ground when startled, galloping off with its head held low and tail waving. If cornered, the Wildebeest is known to fight viciously against its opponents.
• SIZE Length: 5–7¾ ft (1.5–2.4 m). Weight: 260–610 lb (120–275 kg).
• OCCURRENCE S. Kenya and S. Angola to N. South Africa. In open grassy plains and acacia savanna, usually near water.

long, black mane over neck and shoulders

greyish silver body colour

migratory group of Wildebeest

distinctive long, bushy tail

MIGRATING HERDS
Large groups of Wildebeest gather in the dry season, most traveling hundreds of miles in search of seasonal grazing. When crossing rivers, they are especially vulnerable to crocodile attacks.

Social unit Social	Gestation 8–9 months	Young 1	Diet 🌾 🌿

AFRICA

short, black, unridged
horns in both sexes

relatively
large ears

mane spills
over forehead

brownish bands
on neck fade
out behind

head has
conspicuous
long muzzle

horns up to
32 in (80 cm)
in male

black beard

extremely
thin limbs

FOOD AND DRINK
Wildebeest inhabit grassland close to a water
source. Although most migrate in search of fresh
pastures, they become sedentary once food
and water become available.

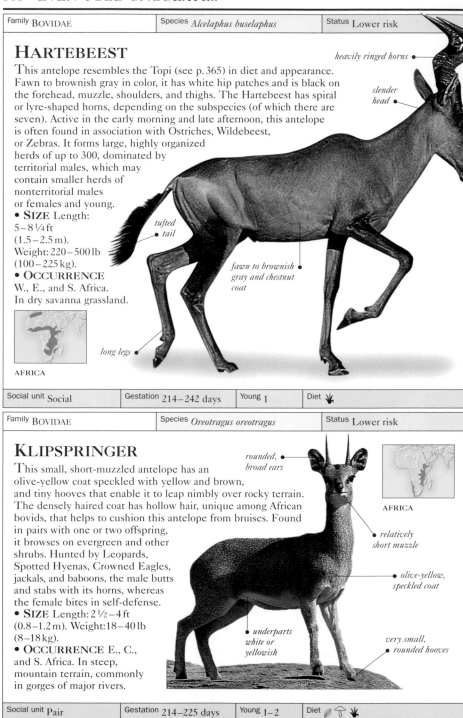

Family BOVIDAE	Species *Alcelaphus buselaphus*	Status Lower risk

HARTEBEEST

heavily ringed horns

This antelope resembles the Topi (see p.365) in diet and appearance. Fawn to brownish gray in color, it has white hip patches and is black on the forehead, muzzle, shoulders, and thighs. The Hartebeest has spiral or lyre-shaped horns, depending on the subspecies (of which there are seven). Active in the early morning and late afternoon, this antelope is often found in association with Ostriches, Wildebeest, or Zebras. It forms large, highly organized herds of up to 300, dominated by territorial males, which may contain smaller herds of nonterritorial males or females and young.

slender head

• **SIZE** Length: 5–8¼ft (1.5–2.5m). Weight: 220–500lb (100–225kg).
• **OCCURRENCE** W., E., and S. Africa. In dry savanna grassland.

tufted tail

fawn to brownish gray and chestnut coat

long legs

AFRICA

Social unit Social	Gestation 214–242 days	Young 1	Diet 🌱

Family BOVIDAE	Species *Oreotragus oreotragus*	Status Lower risk

KLIPSPRINGER

rounded, broad ears

This small, short-muzzled antelope has an olive-yellow coat speckled with yellow and brown, and tiny hooves that enable it to leap nimbly over rocky terrain. The densely haired coat has hollow hair, unique among African bovids, that helps to cushion this antelope from bruises. Found in pairs with one or two offspring, it browses on evergreen and other shrubs. Hunted by Leopards, Spotted Hyenas, Crowned Eagles, jackals, and baboons, the male butts and stabs with its horns, whereas the female bites in self-defense.

AFRICA

relatively short muzzle

olive-yellow, speckled coat

• **SIZE** Length: 2½–4ft (0.8–1.2m). Weight: 18–40lb (8–18kg).
• **OCCURRENCE** E., C., and S. Africa. In steep, mountain terrain, commonly in gorges of major rivers.

underparts white or yellowish

very small, rounded hooves

Social unit Pair	Gestation 214–225 days	Young 1–2	Diet 🌿 🐾 🌱

Family BOVIDAE	Species *Ourebia ourebi*	Status Lower risk

ORIBI

A small, slender, long-necked antelope, the Oribi has a silky coat, sandy to rufous above, white below and on the chin and rump, with longer hair on its knees. The male has spiky, ringed horns; the female is usually larger with a dark crown patch. Hunted by Leopards, Caracals, and pythons, this antelope hides in tall grass, "stotting," or jumping up, if alarmed, and bounding off at high speed. The Oribi is found in male–female pairs, or small groups of seven or eight, with two or three adult males, and is active by day and night. The male sometimes helps to groom and guard the offspring.

- **SIZE** Length: 3–4½ ft (0.9–1.4 m). Weight: 31–46 lb (14–21 kg).
- **OCCURRENCE** W. to E. and S. Africa. In savanna grassland as well as wooded areas near water, up to an elevation of 9,900 ft (3,000 m).

large, pointed ears

sandy to rufous upperparts

white chin

contrasting white underparts

AFRICA

Social unit Variable	Gestation 200–210 days	Young 1	Diet 🌿

Family BOVIDAE	Species *Raphicerus campestris*	Status Locally common

STEENBOK

Also called the Steinbuck, this antelope is bright rufous-fawn, sometimes tinged silver-gray, and paler below. Found alone or in pairs with largely separate lives, this species marks its territory with scent and dung. It browses and grazes, and digs up roots with its feet. The Steenbok is active at day and night.

- **SIZE** Length: 24–37 in (61–95 cm). Weight: 15–35 lb (7–16 kg).
- **OCCURRENCE** E. and S. Africa. In habitats with dense cover, mainly lightly wooded savanna.

well-developed hindquarters

ears white inside

short, conical head

AFRICA

Social unit Solitary/Pairs	Gestation 166–177 days	Young 1	Diet 🌿 🦡 🌾

| Family BOVIDAE | Species *Madoqua kirkii* | Status Locally common |

KIRK'S DIK-DIK

large ears •

This dwarf antelope has a soft, lank coat, grizzled gray to brown, and more reddish on the head, neck, and shoulders. Its hooves have rubbery pads to grip rocky surfaces, and only the male has antlers. It feeds mainly in the morning and late afternoon, and sometimes at night – its small body and its extremely narrow muzzle enabling it to reach the smallest food items. Along with leaves, buds, flowers, and fruits, salt also forms an important part of its diet. Kirk's Dik-diks live in close male–female pairs with their offspring, within territories.

grizzled
• *gray-brown coat*

• **SIZE** Length: 20½–28 in (52–72 cm).
Weight: 6½–15 lb (3–7 kg).
• **OCCURRENCE** E. and S.W. Africa.
On arid, stony slopes and in sandy bushland.
• **REMARK** The four species of dik-dik are

named after the alarm call they give as they dart away in an erratic zigzag pattern when faced with danger.

AFRICA

hooves adapted •
to walking on rocks

| Social unit Pair | Gestation 169–174 days | Young 1 | Diet 🌿 🍃 |

| Family BOVIDAE | Species *Antilope cervicapra* | Status Vulnerable |

BLACKBUCK

The male Blackbuck has a rich coffee-brown head, back, sides, and outer legs (these are black in the dominant male of the herd), whereas the female is yellowish fawn on its head and back. Both sexes have pale rings around the eyes, a sheeplike muzzle, white underparts, and short tail. Only the male has horns, which are tightly spiraled, sometimes with up to five turns. A single, dominant male lives with a harem and their offspring, in groups of 5–50. Dominance is established through a visual display with horns and threatening gestures. When alarmed, a single female bounds into the air, followed by others, until the entire herd is in motion. Grazing almost exclusively on grass, Blackbucks also eat cultivated grains.

spiraled •
horns

light rings around eyes •

• *white underparts*

inside of legs white •

• **SIZE** Length: 4 ft (1.2 m).
Weight: 71–95 lb (32–43 kg).
• **OCCURRENCE** Pakistan, India, and Nepal. In open plains and thorny forest.
• **REMARK** Hunted for its meat and as a sporting trophy, the Blackbuck is also

threatened by loss of habitat. However, it receives a certain amount of protection from the local Bishnoi community, which reveres animals.

ASIA

| Social unit Social | Gestation 6 months | Young 1 | Diet 🌾 🍃 |

Family BOVIDAE	Species *Aepyceros melampus*	Status Lower risk

IMPALA

This species is among the noisiest of antelopes: the males grunt loudly while rutting, calves bleat, and all emit loud warning snorts in times of danger, when they leap away kicking out their hindlegs horizontally and landing on their forelegs. The Impala has a sleek, glossy, fawn to reddish coat with lighter thighs and legs. The white ears are tipped black, and upper lip, chin, and underparts are also white; a vertical black streak appears on each side of the hindquarters and on the tail. This adaptable grazer and browser feeds on grass and leaves, and drinks at least twice a day. It forms large, mixed herds in the dry season. However, at other times females and young form herds of 10–100. The dominant male signals its status through scent secretions from glands on its forehead. It also flicks its tongue, a signal at which single females bunch up, and other males either flee or respond to the challenge thrown at them.

AFRICA

FIGHTING FOR POWER
Only male Impalas have horns and they fight to establish dominance. The highest ranking male takes over a territory and mates with the females.

• **SIZE** Length: 3½–5 ft (1.1–1.5 m). Weight: 88–145 lb (40–65 kg).
• **OCCURRENCE** Kenya and S. Angola to N. South Africa. In open woodland, and acacia savanna.

curved horns in males

dark streaks on hips

reddish upperparts

lighter thighs and legs

Social unit Social	Gestation 6–7 months	Young 1	Diet 🌾 🌿

Family BOVIDAE	Species *Litocranius walleri*	Status Lower risk

GERENUK

Also known as the Giraffe Gazelle, the Gerenuk has a slender, elongated neck and long legs. Reddish fawn in color, it has a broad, dark band along the back and uppersides. Its neck, head, and wedge-shaped muzzle are extremely narrow and allow it to probe into acacia and other thorny vegetation, and it uses its pointed tongue, mobile lips, and sharp incisors to pluck the smallest leaves and shoots. To reach its food it may stand upright on its hindlegs for long periods, curving its spine in a S shape. This allows it to browse higher than most similar-sized herbivores, in open woodland and bush country. Gerenuks are usually found in pairs or small family groups, but young males may form bachelor herds or wander alone, whereas mature males claim their own territories. Chiefly preyed upon by the big cats, the Gerenuk stands motionless to avoid detection.

large horns only in male

dark band along back

white underparts

• **SIZE** Length: 4½–5¼ft (1.4–1.6m). Weight: 62–115lb (28–52kg).
• **OCCURRENCE** E. Africa. In dry areas with a light covering of bush.
• **REMARK** This poorly known species is hunted by humans for its skin.

sturdy rear limbs

AFRICA

Social unit Variable	Gestation 6½–7 months	Young 1	Diet 🌿

Family BOVIDAE	Species *Gazella thomsonii*	Status Lower risk

THOMSON'S GAZELLE

This small, graceful gazelle has a black flank band separating its sandy fawn upperparts from its white underside. Its reddish brown head has a dark blaze, and white eye-rings that extend along the muzzle, above black cheek stripes. The most common gazelle in its region and the staple diet of big cats, it sometimes forms herds with other gazelles. Small herds of females and young join bachelor bands and males, to migrate between grassland (in the rains) and bush (during the dry season).

ringed horns

fingerlike, dark pattern on inside of ears

black flank bands

• **SIZE** Length: 3–4ft (0.9–1.2m). Weight: 33–66lb (15–30kg).
• **OCCURRENCE** S.E. Sudan, Kenya, and Tanzania. In open country or bushland up to 19,000ft (5,750m).
• **REMARK** Thomson's Gazelle is one of the few gazelles that breed twice yearly.

AFRICA

white underparts

Social unit Social	Gestation 160–180 days	Young 1	Diet 🌱🌿

Family BOVIDAE	Species *Antidorcas marsupialis*	Status Lower risk

SPRINGBOK

Cinnamon-fawn above with a white underside, the Springbok, or Springbuck, as it is also called, has a dark, reddish brown horizontal band extending from the top of its foreleg to the hip. It has a fold of skin from the middle of its back to the base of its tail, which, when opened, displays a white crest, perhaps helping to confuse predators or serving to warn other members of its herd. Both sexes have short, ringed, black horns. The Springbok is among several bovids that "stott" or "pronk" – leap high and energetically on stiff legs, as if bouncing – behavior that may deter predators. A highly social herbivore, the Springbok forms large, migratory herds, which split into smaller groups in the dry season. Once millions strong, a "large" migratory herd now consists of only about 1,500 individuals.

- **SIZE** Length: 4– 4½ ft (1.2–1.4 m). Weight: 66–105 lb (30–48 kg).
- **OCCURRENCE** S. Africa. In open, dry savanna as well as grassland.
- **REMARK** Previously hunted in large numbers since herds destroyed crops, the Springbok is also killed for its meat.

AFRICA

CRYPTIC COLORS
The Springbok's coloration and patterning allow it to practically disappear against a backdrop of dry scrubland.

black horns

reddish band on flank

reddish brown facial band

cinnamon-colored upperparts

long legs used to "stott" or "pronk"

white on inside of legs

Social unit Social	Gestation 24 weeks	Young 1	Diet 🌿 🍂 🌾

Family BOVIDAE	Species *Saiga tatarica*	Status Vulnerable

SAIGA

horns in males •

distinctive nose •

cinnamon-buff coat •

Characterized by its large, "Roman" nose and downward-pointing nostrils, this goat-antelope has a woolly, cinnamon-buff coat with a grizzled crown and rump. In winter this becomes whiter and grows thicker by 70 percent. Smaller breeding groups congregate in herds of almost 2,000, migrating to feeding grounds in winter. Males form separate herds, which travel ahead of females.

whitish underparts •

• **SIZE** Length: 3 ¼–4 ½ ft (1–1.4 m).
Weight: 57–150 lb (26–69 kg).
• **OCCURRENCE** Russia, west of the Caspian Sea,

Kazakhstan, and Mongolia. In grassy plains, often including arid areas.

ASIA

Social unit Social	Gestation 139–152 days	Young 1–2	Diet 🌿

Family BOVIDAE	Species *Oreamnos americanus*	Status Locally common

MOUNTAIN GOAT

long white coat •

short, black, curved horns •

Surviving in extreme cold among ice, snow, and glaciers, the woolly Mountain Goat is yellow-white, with dense underfur to conserve body heat. Its large hooves have hard rims and soft inner pads to grip slippery slopes. Feeding by day and night on grass, moss, lichens, and twigs, it seeks out, and sometimes fights over, salt licks. Groups rarely exceed four in summer, and grow larger in winter; males tend to be solitary.
• **SIZE** Length: 4–5 ¼ ft (1.2–1.6 m). Weight: 100–310 lb (46–140 kg).
• **OCCURRENCE** W. Canada, N. and W. US. In alpine tundra and arid areas.

N. AMERICA

large hooves for gripping slopes •

Social unit Variable	Gestation 186 days	Young 1	Diet 🌿

Family BOVIDAE	Species *Rupicapra rupicapra*	Status Critically endangered

CHAMOIS

An agile mountainclimber, the Chamois can jump 6½ft (2 m) high, leap 20ft (6 m) across, and run at 31 mph (50 kph), with its flexible hooves providing a sure grip on slippery terrain. Its stiff and coarse hair is tawny brown in summer, and grows much thicker and blackish brown in winter. A black stripe runs from eye to muzzle and it has white markings on its head and throat. Both sexes have slender, close-set, black horns that grow vertically and bend abruptly at the tips to form hooks. It is active in the early morning and evenings, feeding on herbs and flowers in summer, and lichen, moss, and pine shoots in winter. Females and young form groups of 15–30, and "sentinels" warn of danger by foot-stamping and high pitched calls.

EUROPE, ASIA

- **SIZE** Length: 3–4¼ft (0.9–1.3 m). Weight: 53–110lb (24–50 kg).
- **OCCURRENCE** Alps and mountains of S.C. Europe, Balkans, Asia Minor, and Caucasus. In rocky areas and alpine meadows.
- **REMARK** Numbers have been greatly reduced by excessive hunting, habitat loss, and competition with livestock.

black stripe around eye

stiff, coarse coat tawny-brown in summer

surefooted even on steep slopes

white patches on throat and chest

elastic hooves

STEEP TERRAIN
In summer, the Chamois stays in meadows above 6,500ft (1,800 m), never far from cliffs in which it can hide. Though not migratory, in winters it sometimes moves down to the steep slopes of forests, where snow cannot accumulate.

hooves adapted for sure grip on slopes

Social unit Variable	Gestation 170 days	Young 1	Diet 🌿

Family BOVIDAE	Species *Ovibos moschatus*	Status Locally common

MUSKOX

N. AMERICA,
GREENLAND

The Muskox is so called because of the strong odor emitted by rutting males, who charge at high speed and ram each other with their horns during the mating season. Both sexes have broad horns, which nearly meet at a central protuberance, and curve down and then up at the tips. This massive-bodied bovid has an outer coat of dark brown guard hair that slopes downward to shed rain and snow. The undercoat of soft, pale brown hair insulates it from the Arctic cold. During summer, the Muskox grazes in river valleys and meadows. In winter, it moves to higher areas, where strong winds keep the ground clear of snow. Adult muskoxen form a circle around the young to shield them from predators, sometimes charging at the enemy.

- **SIZE** Length: 6¼–7½ ft (1.9–2.3 m).
Weight: 440–900 lb (200–410 kg).
- **OCCURRENCE** Canada and Greenland. In Arctic tundra.
- **REMARK** Effective reintroduction programs have saved the Muskox from extinction.

coat of coarse, dark brown, sloping • guard hair

slight hump • at shoulder

short neck

broad, • curved horns

pale legs

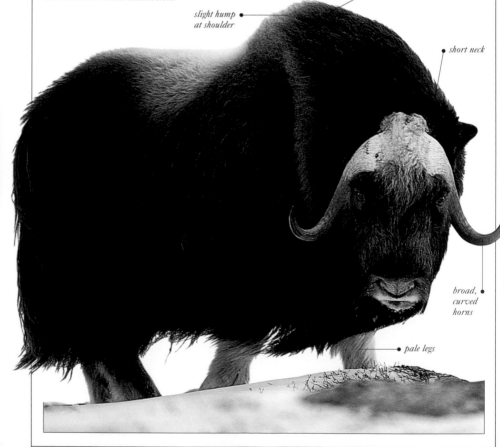

Social unit Social	Gestation 8–9 months	Young 1	Diet 🌱 🍃

Family BOVIDAE	Species *Hemitragus jemlahicus*	Status Vulnerable

HIMALAYAN TAHR

flattened horns

The sure-footed Himalayan Tahr has a shaggy mane on its neck and shoulders that reaches down to its knees; the fur on its face and head is contrastingly short. The flattened horns are twice as long in males, at 16 in (40 cm), as in females. The male Himalayan Tahr seldom grazes in open areas, except in the evenings, whereas the female is often found in clearings. During the breeding season, rutting males lock horns and try to throw each other off balance. Like many mountain mammals, the Himalayan Tahr migrates in spring, moving high into the Himalayas and returning to low temperate forest in fall. When threatened by predators, this goat clambers rapidly over the rocks, much more able to cross the difficult terrain than the pursuer.

reddish brown coat

• SIZE Length: 3–4½ft (0.9–1.4 m).

Weight: 110–220 lb (50–100 kg).
• OCCURRENCE S. Asia.
In temperate to subalpine forest up to the treeline between 8,250–16,500 ft (2,500–5,000 m).

very short tail

ASIA

Social unit Social	Gestation 5–6 months	Young 1	Diet

Family BOVIDAE	Species *Capra ibex*	Status Endangered*

IBEX

Found at or above the treeline, up to 22,000 ft (6,700 m), this large goat has a heavy body and relatively short, sturdy legs. The female sports a golden tan coat in summer, which turns gray-brown in winter, while the male has a rich brown coat with yellow-white patches on the back and rump. The enormous curved horns of the male Ibex reach up to 4½ft (1.4 m), but are a quarter the size in females.

male's horns four times as long as female's

• SIZE Length: 4–5½ft (1.2–1.7 m). Weight: 77–330 lb (35–150 kg).
• OCCURRENCE S. Europe, W. and S. Asia, and N. Africa. In mountains.
• REMARK The Ibex population has been largely wiped out by hunting.

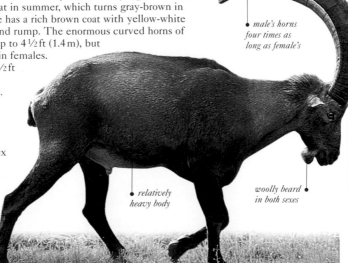

relatively heavy body

woolly beard in both sexes

EUROPE, ASIA, AFRICA

Social unit Variable	Gestation 150–180 days	Young 1	Diet

Family BOVIDAE	Species *Capra aegagrus*	Status Vulnerable

WILD GOAT

Also known as the Bezoar Goat, the female of this species is red-gray or yellow-brown, whereas the adult male has a beard (a young male is shown here), and is silver-gray with dark markings. Both sexes have horns. The Wild Goat has broad, rubbery soles on its hooves to provide a better grip on mountain slopes, and it flees to inaccessible cliffs when hunted by predators. Active during morning and late afternoon; in summer, this goat becomes a night grazer, resting during the day. Females spend most of the year in groups of 5–25; males fight, using visual displays with their horns to gain access to females.

ASIA

- **SIZE** Length: 4–5 ¼ ft (1.2–1.6 m). Weight: 55–210 lb (25–95 kg).
- **OCCURRENCE** W. Asia. In a variety of habitats, from arid scrub to alpine pasture, at elevations up to 13,800 ft (4,200 m).

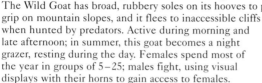

male's horns shaped like scimitar •

WILD GENES
The domestic goat is the descendant of *Capra aegagrus* and now poses a threat to the Wild Goat by competing for pasture and by interbreeding.

distinctive black shoulder stripe •

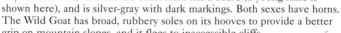

• *sooty gray face*

dark brown chest hair •

reddish buff summer coat •

hooves have broad rubbery soles •

Social unit Social	Gestation 150–170 days	Young 1–3	Diet 🌿

Family BOVIDAE	Species *Capra falconeri*	Status Endangered

MARKHOR

This reddish gray goat has a short, smooth coat in summer, which turns longer and grayer in winter. The full grown, black bearded male is almost twice as heavy as the female, and has a shaggy mane of dark hair extending downward from the neck to its feet. Its spectacular spiraled horns reach 5¼ft (1.6m), but are only 10in (25cm) long in the female. Active in the early morning and late afternoon, the Markhor rarely ventures above the snow line.
• **SIZE** Length: 4½–6ft (1.4–1.8m). Weight: 70–245lb (32–110kg).
• **OCCURRENCE** C. and S. Asia. In mountains, at a height of 2,300–13,200ft (700–4,000m).

ASIA

• **REMARK** Hunted for its horns, meat, hide, and body parts used in local medicines.

spiral horns

long winter coat

shaggy neck mane in male

Social unit Variable	Gestation 135–170 days	Young 1–2	Diet 🌿 🍂

Family BOVIDAE	Species *Pseudois nayaur*	Status Lower risk

BLUE SHEEP

Locally called the Bharal, the Blue Sheep is well-camouflaged to survive in rocky, icy mountainous areas. The male is brownish gray, tinged slate-blue, with black flanks and leg stripes. Its smooth, rounded horns splay outward. The female is smaller, with shorter horns, and lacks most of the male's black markings. This sheep freezes when alarmed, merging with the background due to its cryptic coloration, and takes refuge in the most inaccessible rocky places to escape from predators.
• **SIZE** Length: 4–5½ft (1.2–1.7m). Weight: 55–175lb (25–80kg).
• **OCCURRENCE** E. S. to E. Asia. In the alpine zone between the tree and snow line.

brownish gray body helps in camouflage

smooth, rounded horns

ASIA

Social unit Social	Gestation 160 days	Young 1–2	Diet 🌿 🌳 🍂

Family BOVIDAE	Species *Ovis canadensis*	Status Lower risk

BIGHORN SHEEP

This sheep's glossy brown coat, made up of outer brittle guard hairs and short, crimped gray underwool, fades to a lighter shade in winter. The male's horns curl almost into a circle and may weigh as much as the rest of the skeleton– up to 31lb (14kg). The female's horns, only slightly curved, are smaller. Groups of ewes and young usually consist of 8–10 individuals, whereas males form bachelor herds or remain solitary. During the rut, males walk away from each other, turn to advance with a threatening jump, and lunge to head-butt with tremendous force. This contest goes on for hours until one antagonist gives up. This sheep's thickened skull bones protect its head.

• **SIZE** Length: 5–6 ft (1.5–1.8 m). Weight: 120–280 lb (55–125 kg).

• **OCCURRENCE** S.W. Canada, W. and C. US, and N. Mexico. In mountainous areas – alpine meadows and grassy mountain slopes close to rocky cliffs.

• **REMARK** The Bighorn Sheep is threatened by human encroachment into its habitat. It is also hunted as a sporting trophy, which removes dominant males from the population.

N. AMERICA

smaller horns in female

SEASONED PATHWAYS
Young Bighorn Sheep learn about seasonal pathways from adults. They use their gripping feet and keen eyesight to pick their way over difficult rocky terrrain.

pale patch on rump

rich, glossy brown summer fleece fades in winter

male's horns curl in circle

powerful head with narrow nose

brittle guard hair

Social unit Variable	Gestation 150–180 days	Young 1–4	Diet 🌱 🍃

Family BOVIDAE	Species *Ovis orientalis*	Status Endangered

ASIATIC MOUFLON

Probably the ancestor of all domestic sheep breeds, the Asiatic Mouflon is the smallest wild sheep and is reddish brown with a dark central back stripe and paler saddle patch. Its face becomes lighter with age and it has a short dark tail and light underparts. In common with most wild sheep, ewes are found in small herds with their young, whereas males are solitary or roam in bachelor bands. There is a strict hierarchy among males based on age, strength, and size of horns; most do not begin to breed until they are six or seven years old.

curved horns, up to 25 in (65 cm) in male

reddish brown body

lighter colored underparts

- **SIZE** Length: 3 ½ – 4 ¼ ft (1.1–1.3 m). Weight: 55–120 lb (25–55 kg).
- **OCCURRENCE** W. Asia. In open woodland and on low mountain slopes.

ASIA

Social unit Variable	Gestation 5 months	Young 1–2	Diet 🌿 🌱

Family BOVIDAE	Species *Ammotragus lervia*	Status Vulnerable

BARBARY SHEEP

Also called the Aoudad, this bovid is intermediate between a sheep and a goat. It has a reddish brown, tawny coat with a short, upright mane on its neck and shoulders, and a much longer one of soft hair on the throat, chest, and upper forelegs. In the female, the manes and the horns are less developed. Grazing in the early morning or late evening, it also browses on herbaceous plants and stunted bushes.

crescent-shaped horns

rufous, tawny coat

- **SIZE** Length: 4 ¼ – 5 ½ ft (1.3–1.7 m). Weight: 88–320 lb (40–145 kg).
- **OCCURRENCE** N. Africa. In semidesert and desert highland.

typical broad hooves

AFRICA

Social unit Variable	Gestation 154–161 days	Young 1–3	Diet 🌿 🌱

GLOSSARY

• **AQUATIC**
Living exclusively or mainly in water, such as whales and dolphins. Compare Arboreal, Terrestrial.

• **ARBOREAL**
Living exclusively or mainly in trees, such as many squirrels and monkeys. Compare Aquatic, Terrestrial.

• **ARTIODACTYL**
A hoofed mammal (ungulate) with an even number of toes on all or most feet, such as camels, deer, and cattle. Compare Perissodactyl.

• **BALEEN / BALEEN PLATES**
Comblike, bristly plates or flaps of a gristly substance hanging from the upper jaw of many large whales. Used to strain small prey, such as krill, from sea water. Also known as "whalebone."

• **BLOW**
Cloud of moisture-laden air exhaled by whales, dolphins, and porpoises.

• **BLOWHOLE**
Nostril or nasal breathing opening on the top of the head in whales, dolphins, and porpoises.

• **BOSS**
A dome-shaped protuberance on the forehead of certain bovid species, where the horns meet.

• **BOVID**
An even-toed hoofed mammal that is a member of the large family Bovidae; includes wild and domesticated deer, giraffes, antelopes, gazelles, cattle, sheep, and goats.

• **BOW-RIDE**
To swim or "surf" in the wave created by the bow of a ship, or at the front of a large aquatic animal such as a whale.

• **BRACHIATION**
Hanging by the arms and swinging hand-over-hand, through the branches, like a gibbon.

• **BREACHING**
To leap clear of the water and crash back in with a large splash, as carried out by many whales, dolphins, and porpoises.

• **BROWSE**
To eat the vegation of trees, bushes, and shrubs, which is above the ground level. Compare Graze.

• **CANID**
A member of the mammalian group Canidae, all domesticated and wild dogs, wolves, foxes, and jackals.

• **CANINE**
1. A usually large, long, pointed, slightly curved tooth found near the front of the mouth, just behind the incisor teeth. Sometimes called the "eye tooth." Well developed in meat-eating mammals such as cats and dogs. 2. A member of the dog group. See Canid.

• **CANOPY FOREST**
Forest with trees of approximately the same height, with their branches intermeshing to form a rooflike canopy high above the ground.

• **CARNIVORE**
1. A mammal or other animal that eats mainly flesh or meat; a hunter or predator. Compare Herbivore, Omnivore. 2. A member of the mammalian group Carnivora, which includes cats, dogs, bears, weasels, and civets.

• **CERVID**
A member of the mammalian group Cervidae, the deer.

• **CETACEAN**
A member of the mammalian group Cetacea, the whales, dolphins, and porpoises.

• **CHANNEL COUNTRY**
Area north of the Great Artesian Basin, Australia, which is criss-crossed by rivers.

• **CHEVRON**
A V- or arrow-shape, especially as a marking on an animal, or within the shape of a horn or antler.

• **CIRCUMPOLAR**
Spread or distributed all around the polar region, at all longitudes. Applies to North or South Pole.

• **COLONY**
A group of animals living together and often sharing the tasks necessary for survival, such as foraging for food.

• **CORAL RAG SCRUB**
Scrub growing among limestone formed from coral.

• **CRUSTACEANS**
A large group of mainly sea-dwelling invertebrate animals, including lobsters, crabs, prawns, shrimps, barnacles and, on land, woodlice.

• **DEWLAP**
A fleshy, furry flap hanging from the throat and/or neck region of a mammal.

• **DIGIT**
A finger, toe, or equivalent structure, including the bones within this. The basic mammalian condition is five digits on each of the four limbs.

• **DIGITIGRADE**
Standing and moving on the toes (digits), as in horses and deer, rather than on the soles or central parts of the feet. Compare Plantigrade.

• **DIURNAL**
Active mainly during the day. Compare Nocturnal.

• **DOMESTICATED**
A mammal or other animal which has been bred to be, in various ways, easily kept and used by people, especially being less aggressive or more tame.

• **DORSAL FIN**
The fin on the back or upper surface of an aquatic mammal, such as a whale or dolphin; or a fish.

• **DREY**
The nest, den, or sheltering place of a squirrel.

• **ECHOLOCATION**
A method of sensing the location of objects in the surroundings, by sending out sounds (usually high-pitched pulses), which bounce off objects, and analyzing the returning echoes. Also known as Sonar.

• **EQUID**
A member of the mammalian group Equidae, which includes wild and domestic horses, asses, and zebras.

• **EVEN-TOED UNGULATE**
See Artiodactyl.

• **EWE**
A female sheep or similar type of mammal.

• **FALCATE**
A curved, sickle- or scythe-like shape with one convex and one concave edge, like the back-curving dorsal fin of the Bottlenose Dolphin.

• **FELID**
A member of the mammalian group Felidae, including all wild and domesticated cats.

• **FERAL**
Refers to animals originally from domesticated stock, but which subsequently take up life in the wild. Common examples include cats, dogs, horses, and deer.

• **FLIPPER**
A limb with a broad, flattened shape, effective for moving through water by swimming, rowing, or paddling.

• **FLUKES**
The tail of a whale, dolphin, or porpoise, with a broad, muscular, horizontal surface (but no limb bones inside) which is swept up and down for swimming.

• **FORAGE**
To search for food.

• **FORELIMBS**
The front or forward limbs, as opposed to the rear or back limbs (hind limbs).

• **FOSSA**
A pit or depression, usually in a bone such as the skull.

• **GESTATION**
The period of pregnancy, the time when a baby develops inside the mother's body, before birth.

• **GRAZE**
To eat the leaves, stems, or other parts of grasses and similar low-growing plants, at or just above ground level. Compare Browse.

• **GUARD HAIRS**
Longer, usually thicker hairs (fur) that form a mammal's outer coat, the guard coat. This shows over and protects the inner coat or under fur which has shorter, softer, usually more dense hairs.

• **HAREM**
A group of females that breed with one male and are defended and protected by him against rival males.

• **HERBIVORE**
An animal that eats mainly leaves, fruits, or other plant matter. Compare Carnivore, Omnivore.

• **HIBERNATION**
A period of dormancy in winter. During hibernation an animal's body processes drop to a low level.

• **HIND**
A female deer or similar mammal.

• **HINDLIMBS**
The back or rear limbs and their parts, as opposed to the front limbs.

• **HOME RANGE**
An area used regularly by an animal or group of animals, for feeding, shelter, breeding, and other needs, but not necessarily defended against others. Compare Territory.

• **INCISOR**
A usually chisel- or spade-like tooth found at the front of the mouth. Incisors are used for biting, nibbling, and gnawing, and are especially well-developed in rodents.

• **INSECTIVORE**
1. An animal that eats insects and similar smallish prey items such as worms. 2. A member of the mammalian group Insectivora, which includes, shrews, moles, and hedgehogs.

• **INTRODUCED**
A species that has been brought, usually by people, to a new area where it did not formerly occur naturally. Compare Native.

• **INVERTEBRATE**
An animal without a backbone (vertebral column).

• **KEEL**
A distinctive bulge or ridge at the base of the tail of whales and dolphins, just in front of the flukes.

• **KERATIN**
A hard, tough body protein that forms many mammalian structures, such as skin, nails, hooves, claws, and horns.

• **KRILL**
Small, shrimp-like crustaceans that form the major food of various marine mammals, including baleen whales and certain seals.

• **LAGOMORPH**
A member of the mammalian group Lagomorpha, which includes rabbits, hares, and pikas.

• **LEK**
A generally small territory held and defended by the male of a species, such as deer, during breeding to attract females.

• **LODGE**
The large, strong, stick-built nest or den for a group of beavers or similar animals.

• **MARINE**
An organism living in the sea or in salty water.

• **MARSUPIAL**
A mammal whose young are born at a very early stage of development, and which suckle and develop further in a pouch, the marsupium, on the female's front or underside.

• **MELANISM**
Extra amounts of the brown-black coloring substance melanin, which makes the skin and fur very dark.

• **MELON**
Bulbous forehead of many toothed whales, dolphins, and porpoises. It is believed to focus the outgoing and incoming sound pulses used in echolocation.

• **MOLAR**
A usually broad, flat, or ridged tooth found near the back of the mouth, often called a cheek tooth. Molars are used for crushing and chewing.

• **MOLLUSCS**
A large group of invertebrates in which the body is surrounded by a large fleshy "hood" or "cloak," and perhaps a hard, protective shell. The group includes oysters, mussels, clams, and similar "shellfish," as well as slugs, snails, octopus, cuttlefish, and squid.

• **MONOTREME**
A mammal that reproduces by laying eggs that hatch into live young. This is opposed to giving birth to formed young, as in the case of most mammals.

• **MOULTING**
Shedding fur, layers of skin, feathers, scales, or similar external structures, usually in a seasonal fashion.

• **MUSK**
A pungent-scented substance produced by various animals, especially males, such as elephants, deer, cattle, and carnivores. It usually signifies readiness to breed.

• **MUSTELID**
A member of the mammalian group Mustelidae, which includes stoats, weasels, polecats, otters, mink, sables, and badgers.

• **NATIVE**
Having been born in an area, or having naturally occurred there for a very long time. Compare Introduced.

• **NICTITATING MEMBRANE**
"Third eyelid" – a cover or flap-like lid that can be moved across the eye for reasons such as protection or to reduce illumination.

• **NOCTURNAL**
Active mainly at night or during darkness. Compare Diurnal.

• **NOSE LEAF**
A flaplike structure around the nose of certain animals, especially some bats. It helps to direct the sound pulses for echolocation.

• **ODD-TOED UNGULATE**
See Perissodactyl.

• **OMNIVORE**
An animal that eats all types of food, including flesh and plant matter.

• **OPPORTUNISTIC FEEDER**
An animal that takes advantage of many and varied foods, as and when they become available.

• **PACK**
A group of usually predatory animals, such as wolves.

• **PATAGIUM**
The thin, leathery, elastic, skinlike flight membrane of a bat or other flying or gliding mammal.

• **PERISSODACTYL**
A hoofed mammal (ungulate) with an odd number of toes on all or most feet, including horses, tapirs, and rhinos. Compare Artiodactyl.

• **PINNIPED**
A member of the mammalian group Pinnipedia ("flipper-feet"), which includes seals, sea lions, and walruses.

• **PLANKTON**
Tiny plants and animals that drift in oceans and lakes.

• **PLANTIGRADE**
Standing and moving on the soles or central part of the feet, as in bears and humans. Compare Digitigrade.

• **POD**
A coordinated group of members of the Cetacea, especially great whales. See also School.

• **PREDATOR**
A hunter; an animal that actively catches and kills other animals that form its prey.

• **PREHENSILE**
Able to grasp. Many New World Monkeys have prehensile tails.

• **PREY**
An animal which is hunted as food by another.

• **PRIMARY FOREST**
Forest that has been undisturbed (especially by human activity) for a very long time, and has reached a stable, mature end-point of development.

• **PRIMATE**
A member of the mammalian group Primates, which includes lemurs, galagos, lorises, pottos, monkeys, apes, and humans.

• **PROBOSCIS**
A flexible, elongated, or enlarged nose or snout, like the elephant's long trunk.

• **PRONK**
To move in a stiff-legged, high-leaping, bounding, or "bouncing" manner, as in the Springbok. Also called "stotting."

• **PROSIMIAN**
A member of the mammalian group Primates that is not a monkey or ape – a lemur, galago, loris, potto, or similar type.

- **RANGE**
1. To roam or travel long distances in search of food, shelter, or mates.
2. See Home range.
- **REGURGITATE**
To "cough up" or bring back swallowed food from the stomach, crop, or similar digestive storage part.
- **REINTRODUCE**
To restore or put back a type of living thing, into an area where it once occurred, but from which it has become locally extinct.
- **RETRACTABLE (RETRACTILE) CLAWS**
Claws that can be pulled back or withdrawn into fleshy pocketlike sheaths at the ends of the toes. Found especially in the cat family.
- **RODENT**
A member of the very large mammalian group Rodentia, which includes rats, mice, voles, squirrels, gerbils, beavers, and porcupines.
- **ROOST**
To rest or sleep, usually above the ground such as in a tree hole, on a tree branch, or in the roof of a cave.
- **RORQUAL**
Strictly speaking, a baleen whale of the genus Balaenoptera; however, many experts include the Humpback Whale in this group.
- **ROSTRUM**
An elongated or enlarged snout or forehead area, especially the upper jaw region of the skull, as in the "beak" of a dolphin.
- **RUTTING**
When male animals come together to display and battle each other, for breeding access to females.
- **SAVANNA**
A grassland habitat with scattered trees and bushes, and a long dry season. Often applied to the open grassland of E. and S. Africa.
- **SCATTER-HOARDER**
An animal that hides or stores (hoards) food items in many different locations, such as a squirrel burying nuts at various sites.
- **SCAVENGE**
Eating leftovers, or dying, dead, or rotting carcasses and similar remains of animals.

- **SCHOOL**
A coordinated group of members of the Cetacea, especially dolphins. See also Pod.
- **SECONDARY FOREST**
Forest which has been disturbed by human activity, wildfire, flood, etc., and is in the process of redeveloping its mature trees and animal life.
- **SEMI-RETRACTABLE CLAWS**
Claws which can be partly be drawn into sheaths. See Retractable claws.
- **SETT**
The large, complex underground home, nest site, or den of a group of badgers or similar mammals.
- **SIMIANS**
Monkeys (including marmosets and tamarins) and apes; members of the mammalian group Primates that are not Prosimians.
- **SIRENIANS**
Members of the group Sirenia, including Dugongs and manatees.
- **SONAR**
Sound Navigation And Ranging. See Echolocation.
- **SPYHOPPING**
Raising the head vertically out of the water, then sinking below the surface without much splash.
- **STAG**
A male deer or similar mammal.
- **STEPPE**
A predominantly grassland habitat, with no or few trees and bushes, and a long dry season. Often applied to the open grasslands of Asia.
- **STOTT**
See Pronk.
- **SUB-SAHARAN**
The region of Africa to the south of the Sahara Desert.
- **SUB-ANTARCTIC**
The islands and ocean to the north of the southern polar region of Antarctica, often including the southern South America and Africa.
- **SUBMONTANE**
Hilly regions, above the low plains and foothills, but below the true mountains.
- **SYMBIOTIC**
A relationship shared by two individuals or two different species, in which both gain.

- **TAIGA**
Vast region of mainly evergreen forest and woodland across northern Asia and North America.
- **TERRESTRIAL**
Living exclusively or mainly on the ground. Compare Arboreal, Aquatic.
- **TERRITORY**
An area used regularly by an animal or group of animals, for feeding, shelter, and breeding, which is usually defended against others. Compare Home range.
- **TINE**
The end or point of a branch on a deer's antler.
- **TRAGUS**
A flap or fleshy projection in front of a bat's ear.
- **TUBERCLES**
Wartlike lumps, circular bumps, or similar knobbly structures.
- **TUNDRA**
Open, treeless region of low-growing plants in the far north, covered in snow and ice for part of the year.
- **UNDER FUR**
See Guard hairs.
- **UNGULATE**
Mammal with hooves. See Artiodactyl, Perissodactyl.
- **VENTRAL**
Relating to the belly or underside of the body.
- **VERTEBRATE**
An animal with a backbone.
- **VESTIGIAL** Relating to an organ that is atrophied or nonfunctional.
- **VIVERRID**
A member of the mammalian group Viverridae, which includes civets, genets, linsangs, and mongooses.
- **WARREN**
The underground nest or den of a rabbit or similar mammal, especially those that live in colonies.
- **WEANING**
In mammals, the period when the mother gradually ceases to provide milk for her young.
- **WILD**
Not domesticated or tamed; natural and unaffected by humans.

INDEX

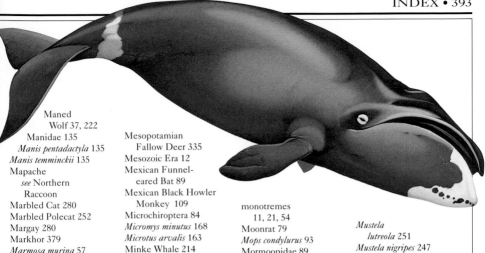